Early English
Intercourse with Burma
1587—1743

AND

The Tragedy of Negrais

Early English Intercourse with Burma

1587—1743

by

D. G. E. HALL

SECOND EDITION

with

The Tragedy of Negrais

AS A NEW APPENDIX

FRANK CASS & CO. LTD.

1968

This edition published by
FRANK CASS AND COMPANY LIMITED
67 Great Russell Street, London WC1

EARLY ENGLISH INTERCOURSE WITH BURMA

First published by Longmans, Green and Co. for
the University of Rangoon and now reprinted
with their kind permission.

First edition	1928
Second edition	1968

THE TRAGEDY OF NEGRAIS

First published in the Journal of the Burma Research Society,
Volume XXI, Part III, and now reprinted with the
kind permission of the Society.

First edition	1931
Reprinted in this volume	1968

SBN 7146 2010 6

Printed in Great Britain by A. Wheaton & Co., Exeter

PREFACE TO THE SECOND EDITION

Early English Intercourse with Burma, 1587-1743 was first published in 1928 for the University of Rangoon by Messrs. Longmans, Green and Co., and its sequel, *The Tragedy of Negrais,* three years later by the Burma Research Society as a whole number of its *Journal.* During the Japanese occupation of Burma from 1942 to 1945 the unsold copies of both were lost or destroyed. Since then the demand for works of South-East Asian history has expanded to such a degree that many long out of print and practically unobtainable are being re-issued. It is particularly gratifying to me, as the author of these two works, that they are now republished, for both are works of original research into the East India Company's records at the India Office, and since they first appeared no other scholar seems to have used the basic materials which went into their making. They tell the story of English relations with Burma from the days of Elizabeth I up to the beginning of the long break, which started in 1762 as a result of the incident in 1759 known as the 'massacre of Negrais' and only ended in 1795 when Captain Michael Symes went on his first embassy to King Bodawpaya.

In the period dealt with in this volume the East India Company was still a commercial concern *par excellence:* it had not yet acquired territorial power in India. Burma until nearly the end of the period was weak and isolationist after the decisive collapse of her empire-building efforts in the sixteenth century. Only in the seventeen-fifties, having to meet the challenge of the Mons in the south, did she revive, with dramatic suddenness, under the leadership of Alaungpaya, who began his victorious career at the moment when Josef Dupleix at Pondicherry was seeking to expand French political influence in the Indian Ocean and oust the British. He lived long enough to see the failure of the French effort. Indeed, he himself, in his successful duel with Dupleix's agent, Bruno, had some small share in the French defeat, while at the same time making sure that their British rivals were in no position to challenge his own authority.

January 22 1968   D. G. E. HALL

PREFACE TO THE FIRST EDITION

To the University of Rangoon for undertaking the publication of this work I owe a deep debt of gratitude. Though one of the youngest universities in the Indian Empire, absorbed in all the manifold problems of early development, and drawing its students from a public that is unable as yet to discriminate between the manufacture of graduates and the promotion of culture, it has from its inception generously aided and stimulated research work in the various fields afforded by the great province it serves.

I am also under great obligations to Professor H. Dodwell of the University of London, with whom I was in constant consultation during the early stages of the work leading up to this volume. He read the manuscript, when it was completed, enriching it with many valuable suggestions.

I gratefully acknowledge help on special points of Burmese history received from my colleagues: Professor Pe Maung Tin, Department of Oriental Studies, University of Rangoon; G. H. Luce, Esq., Reader in Far Eastern History, University of Rangoon, and U Kin Kyi, research student in the

Department of Oriental Studies, University College, Rangoon, and from my friend, G. E. Harvey, Esq., I.C.S., author of "History of Burma from the Earliest Times" (Longmans).

Every student who has had occasion to explore the historical sources at the India Office, has experienced the immense assistance and unfailing courtesy of the staffs of the Library and Record Department.

TAUNGGYI,
SOUTHERN SHAN STATES,
April, 1928.

CONTENTS

vii

APPENDIX

INTRODUCTION

INTRODUCTION

THE story of English intercourse with Burma is fairly well known in outline from the days of the East India Company's negotiations with Alaungpaya in 1755 onwards. The present work, however, constitutes the first attempt yet made to trace it from its origins in the sixteenth century to the middle of the eighteenth, with such degree of completeness as the existing records permit. Most of the sources drawn upon have never previously been explored for light upon this somewhat recondite subject. This statement must be qualified by the fact that Alexander Dalrymple, in writing his " Letter concerning the Negrais Expedition " (of 1753) in 1759—later published in the first volume of his " Oriental Repertory "—had access to the Fort St. George records for his preliminary sketch of Anglo-Burmese relations previous to that event. Now Dalrymple has very little to say about English enterprise in Burma before the year 1680 ; and what little he does say is almost entirely in the nature of a guess. The reason for this is to be found in the fact that the Madras records are of very little value in this connexion before 1680 : the best materials for that period lie scattered about in odd corners of the seventy-two volumes of Original Correspondence, which form, along with the Court Minutes, the main body of evidence for the history of the East India Company in the seventeenth century. These were not available at Madras.

For the period from 1680 to 1743 Dalrymple culled a few references from the Fort St. George records, with the aid of which he wrote a very cursory survey of Anglo-Burmese relations during that period. But so brief was it that he found it necessary to add the following apology for its insufficiency : " There is hardly any Information to be obtained from Public Records during this Period, so that I have scarce been able to collect any thing worthy Attention, from the

3

Records of almost a Century." As Dalrymple's object was
not so much to write an authoritative historical treatise as
to stimulate a practical interest in Burma, his search was not
a very thorough one. There are many references to Burma
in the Fort St. George records of the period 1680-1743, but
as they have never been collected together into any series,
systematic research would háve involved much more time
and industry than would have been justified in Dalrymple's
case. Later, in compiling the second volume of his monumental work, he managed to make use of the documents in
the East India House relating to the embassies of Edward
Fleetwood and Thomas Bowyear to Ava in 1695 and 1698
respectively. These documents are now to be found in the
" Factory Records : Miscellaneous," Vol. XVIII., at the India
Office.

Since Dalrymple's day nearly every writer, who has dealt
with the English connexion with Burma during the period up
to 1743, has done little more than repeat—often with em-
bellishments—what is to be found in the "Oriental Repertory."
Partial exceptions to this statement must be made in the cases
of Mr. G. E. Harvey and M. Henri Cordier. The former, in
his " History of Burma " (Longmans, 1925) makes some use
of William Methwold's valuable observations on the mission
of Forrest and Staveley to the city of Pegu in 1617, which
occur in his " Relations of the Kingdome of Golchonda,"
written for publication in " Purchas his Pilgrimes," but relegated to the supplement to the 1626 edition, and hence not
accessible in modern reprints. But beyond that Harvey
accepts Dalrymple's statements in general. Cordier, in his
short brochure, " Historique Abrégé des Relations de la
Grande-Bretagne avec la Birmanie " (Leroux, Paris, 1894),
gives brief summaries of extracts relating to Burma from the
State Papers Colonial, East Indies, covering the period 1614-
1633. He mentions the English connexion with Syriam, but
states that the date of it is unknown. From 1633 he jumps
straight to 1687, and thenceforth his sole authority appears to
have been the "Oriental Repertory."

This inadequate study of the original materials, due, as
is pointed out above, partly to the difficulties attending the
search, and partly to a too ready acceptance of Dalrymple's

statements in the " Letter concerning the Negrais Expedition,"
has given rise to many entirely erroneous ideas about the
earliest connexion of the East India Company with Burma.
These have been dealt with in Chapter II., and the Notes on
the alleged existence of English factories in Burma before the
year 1647 in Appendix II. It was the realisation of the true
cause of the conflicting details given by several writers concerning this subject, that led me, in the few spare hours that
fall to one organising a new department in a new University,
to undertake the task of collecting materials for this work.
Six months' furlough in England gave me the necessary
opportunity for raking with a fine rake the raw materials in
the India Office archives. The result was in some ways
disappointing, the amount of material discovered, relating to
the period before 1680, bearing no relation whatever to the
amount of time and energy, that had to be expended upon
the search. Less than a dozen of the many thousands of
letters included in the Original Correspondence originated
from Burma. The greater number of references to English
trade with Burma is to be found in the Masulipatam and
Fort St. George correspondence. Unlike her neighbour in
Siam, the Syriam factory never had in the Company's archives
any collected series of " factory records." The Company's
seventèenth-century records are extremely defective, and the
lacunæ naturally affect most the subject for which, in any
case, the materials are comparatively scanty. Were it not
for the excellent calendars and printed collections of documents
now available, covering the activities of the Company up to
the middle of the reign of Charles II., the task of writing the
history of its relations with Burma during that period would
be wellnigh impossible, so elusive are the scanty references
to Burma among the manuscript materials. A careful search
through the manuscript sources likely to have a bearing on
my subject revealed comparatively little more than is indicated
in Sir William Foster's invaluable " English Factories in
India," although the early volumes of Java Papers, not
utilised in that series, might have been expected to yield a
rich harvest.

For the period from 1680 to 1702 the work of the researcher
has been considerably lightened by the systematic publication

of the Fort St. George records covering that period, a task upon which the Madras Record Office has been engaged for some years with gratifying results. For the remainder of my period the " Madras Public Proceedings," with the various collections of correspondence emanating from, or directed to, Fort St. George, provided most of the material. With the exception of the printed records of Madras for the years 1741-2, these are in manuscript. Here the searcher's task is rendered needlessly difficult by the inadequacy of the Fort St. George Press Lists. With the eighteenth century the deficiencies in the East India Company's records grow fewer, and are of less importance. But the Company's loss of interest in Burma at the end of the seventeenth century—a lack of interest which continued until the beginning of the second half of the following century—has resulted in an unfortunate decrease in the number of references to Burma during that period, although the connexion between Fort St. George and Syriam was by no means unimportant. Still, for all that, the records do give us sufficient to transport us from the realm of mere guesswork to that of fact. However lacking in details the picture may be, its background and general outlines are clear ; and, moreover, what we know is of interest and value to the student of British enterprise in the East.

It has been my prime object to give to the reader, as fully as possible, such facts as are available. The previous lack of knowledge of the subject, and the intrinsic interest of much of the material itself, are, I think, sufficient justification for such a course. Copious quotations, therefore, have been made from the original in cases where the information given helps us to gain some idea of actual conditions. Having had occasion, through the invitation of various learned societies in Rangoon, to digest much of the material for the early part of this work in the form of public lectures, I have come to realise how fascinating the story is to people connected with Burma, and thus how necessary it is to present as many of the facts as are compatible with the general treatment of the subject. The pity is that the material is not more plentiful.

British enterprise in Burma during the period 1587-1743 was tentative, hesitating, fluctuating, and mainly unsuccessful. Too often the obstacles to be overcome were too great, and

the prizes to be won too uncertain, for the East India Company
to make the exploitation of trade with Burma one of its main
objects.   In the early days, when Ralph Fitch made his
adventurous peregrinations, the Portuguese were well established in Burma as mercenaries and traders.   This fact, and
the chaotic condition of the country itself, involved as it was
in its bitter struggle with Siam, prevented English merchants
from taking it into serious consideration as a field for commercial expansion.   Of course, there were other considerations
also.   Burma produced no important spices save musk.   Her
chief articles of export—wood and lac—were too bulky in
proportion to their value, to render their exploitation a sufficiently paying proposition, except as ballast for homeward-
bound ships.   During the earliest years of the East India
Company's history Burma was too far from the main stream
of English commerce with the East, especially in the days
when Japan was a serious objective, to attract English specu-
lators.   Not until the foundation of a factory at Masulipatam
did Burma begin to come within the range of English commercial activities, and at first this came about through a
purely accidental circumstance—the capture of an English
merchant, Thomas Samuel, at Chiengmai by the Burmese
king Anaukpetlun.   And it must be remembered that Samuel's
presence at Chiengmai was connected with the East India
Company's schemes for developing trade with Siam, not with
Burma.

With the planting of the Masulipatam factory, however,
the Company could not fail to be drawn—indirectly at first—
into the trade carried on from time immemorial between the
Coromandel Coast and the southern ports of Burma.   For
many years ignorance of the country, lack of capital, and
concentration upon the Persian trade played their part in
preventing the development of official trading relations
between the Masulipatam factory and Pegu, as Lower Burma
was then called by Europeans.   But the private traders
blazed the trail, and thus played their part in stimulating the
Company to take more active steps in this direction.   The
failure of de Brito's attempt to carve out a new province for
the Portugo-Spanish Empire in Lower Burma at the beginning
of the seventeenth century had opened Burma to the enterprise

of other nations, and the Dutch had speedily supplanted their old rivals at Syriam and elsewhere. The stories of their fabulous profits in Burma whetted the appetite of the East India Company. When, therefore, in the 'forties there occurred a serious slump in the Persian trade, the matter of opening a factory in Burma was taken up by the Surat authorities, and to the newly-established factory at Fort St. George was given the management of the affair, in preference to Masulipatam, where there was much opposition to the scheme. Probably the Masulipatam opposition was dictated by apprehension at the Company's intrusion upon what they regarded as their own private preserve. Until late in the century, when Fort St. George finally captured the bulk of the trade between Syriam and the Coromandel Coast, the Masulipatam factors carried on an extensive private trade with Burma. On the other hand, the private traders' experience of Burmese royal policy with regard to commercial matters may equally have convinced them that the prospects of developing organised trade in the country were extremely poor.

The Company's factory at Syriam, with the subordinate station at Ava, had a chequered existence of only a decade (1647-1657). Financial difficulties at home, complicated by losses sustained in the first Anglo-Dutch War, brought about a drastic reduction in the number of factories under the control of Fort St. George. In the general economy campaign that was started by the Directors, when the Company was almost at its last gasp, just before Cromwell's reorganisation of its affairs, orders went out for the abandonment, among others, of the " Pegu factory." Although formal possession of the buildings and land was long retained by the Company, and was confirmed by a royal grant from the Burmese Government in 1696, the Company never officially reopened its factory at Syriam. For the rest of our period the factory site was used mainly by private traders, who managed to avail themselves of the privileges granted to the Company, under cover of the fact that many of them either had been, or actually were, in its employment. While it cannot be stated in so many words that Dutch competition caused the failure of the Syriam factory, yet the strong position of the Dutch in the East at the time of the first Anglo-Dutch War, and the critical condition to which the English factories in India were reduced by that war, contributed an important share towards the ruin of the venture. It is a significant fact that the Company did not again consider the question of reopening trade with Burma until news came to Fort St. George in 1680 of the Dutch withdrawal from the country. Then it was that Streynsham Master formulated his Articles of Trade which for the next two decades provided the basis for all negotiations between Fort St. George and Ava.

The relations with the Court of Ava, renewed by Streynsham Master in 1680, resulted in hardly any development of the Company's official trade with Burma. The Directors at home, after some hesitation, refused to sanction the reopening of the Syriam factory. Although anxious to procure supplies of Burmese lac and saltpetre, they were unwilling to incur the responsibility and expense of maintaining a factory in the country. Fort St. George was, therefore, straitly charged not to make any settlement in Burma, but to give every encouragement to private traders, so that all necessary supplies of Burmese commodities might be obtained indirectly. Fort St. George, on the other hand, fearing lest the complete surrender of ancient privileges in Burma might one day be regretted, decided to assume control over the private trade between Madras and Syriam. The negotiations, therefore, were carried on with the specific purpose of securing trading rights from Ava to be enjoyed by all Madras merchants trading with the Company's licence in Burma, though not with that of reestablishing an official branch in the country. This caused some difficulties with the Government of Burma, which insisted right up to the end of the seventeenth century that any grant of trading rights was strictly conditioned by the Company's undertaking to reopen official trade.

At the same time, by wise concessions in matters of Customs duties to importers of precious stones and timber from Burma, the Fort St. George authorities managed to attract more and more Burmese trade to Madras, so that by the year 1700 it was estimated that Madras had become the chief port on the east coast of India for trade with Burma. The Burmese Government's seizure of a Madras merchant, Bartholomew Rodrigues, with his ship and crew, led to the despatch of the Fleetwood-Lesly mission to Ava in 1695, and the renewal of negotiations that had languished since 1686. On this occasion, one of the main questions at issue was the Company's request for special privileges for shipbuilding at Syriam. The Burmese refused to discuss any general terms until the Company should reopen a factory in the country. Fort St. George, therefore, compromised by sending Thomas Bowyear to assume control over the private traders at Syriam, and act as its representative in all dealings with the Burmese authorities. This arrangement, however, lasted only some three years ; terminating in 1700. Thenceforward for some years the records give us little information regarding the relations between Fort St. George and Ava. Doubtless this is on account of the fact that only private trading matters were involved. After at least one unsuccessful attempt on the part of the Fort St. George factors themselves to form a company for private trading operations in Burma, a " Pegu Joint Stock " was formed, in which Gulston Addison, the brother of the essayist, was a chief director. But this ceased operations soon after Addison's death in 1709.

Fort St. George's method of regulating the activities of the private traders during these years up to the end of the first quarter of the eighteenth century was by the appointment of a Chief of the Affairs of the English Nation at Syriam. The wielder of the authority denoted by this title was usually one of the Madras free merchants who, on his own account, made the annual trip to Burma during the sailing season, as the period from the beginning of September to the end of March was called. During his stay in Burma, he made the English factory at Syriam his headquarters, hoisted the English flag, and enjoyed a somewhat vague authority over such Madras traders as were granted the Company's licence to trade there under its protection. He was not a Company's servant, and received no emoluments. This system was given up by 1724, when the Company began to contemplate more extensive shipbuilding operations at Syriam. Thenceforward, until the end of our period, the Company's representative in Burma was called by the title of " resident." The change of title indicated little more than what the name suggests : the holder usually resided in Syriam. His functions were confined almost entirely to the supervision of shipbuilding carried on on behalf of the Company. He was not specifically in the employment of the Company, and always appears in its records classed as a free merchant.

Shipbuilding at Syriam proved unsatisfactory. Unskilled labour and crude workmanship outweighed the advantages derived from the excellence of the materials procurable in Burma. The shifty policy of the Burmese Government, in refusing to grant general permission for shipbuilding, rendered necessary the giving of expensive presents to Government officials in respect of all ships built. After ten years of experiment Fort St. George decided that the results were not such as to justify the expense of building at Syriam, and shortly before the compulsory closing of the factory through Talaing hostility, it was decided to transfer Fort St. George's shipbuilding orders from Syriam to the more efficient and less expensive Parsi yards at Bombay.

The story of these tentative, and largely unsuccessful, beginnings shows pretty clearly why what is now in natural resources perhaps the richest of all the provinces of the Indian Empire, remained in the days before the British annexation commercially a backwater, seemingly incapable of development. The light thrown by our material upon the attitude of the Burmese Government towards trade, industry, and foreign intercourse, tends not a little to explain why, in comparison with Siam, before the economic Imperialism of Europe in the nineteenth century the one lost her independence while the other maintained it. In face of the great expansion of the European demand for raw materials, the dog-in-the-manger policy was disastrous. The removal of the Burmese capital from Pegu to Ava in 1635 was, without doubt, one of the cardinal events of Burmese history. No matter what arguments there were in favour of the step, the fact remains that it signalised the triumph of the more intransigent elements in Burmese character and governmental policy—elements which contributed their full share in the first place towards the failure of early European efforts to trade with Burma, and ultimately towards the collapse of two dynasties and the political ruin of the country. At Ava, nearly a two-months' journey from the sea, the Court lost touch with the outside world. " The atmosphere of their palace," writes Mr. Harvey of the kings of Burma after the move to Ava, " was that of the Upper Burma villages among which it lay. Their ideas remained in the nineteenth century what they had been in the ninth." [1]   This is abundantly shown in their relations with the East India Company.

My subject ends with the destruction of the old Syriam factory by the Talaings in 1743, followed by the official withdrawal of the Company's " resident " early in the following year.   For several reasons this date makes a convenient stopping place.   It marks a very definite breach in the relations between the Company and Burma lasting for nearly ten years. During this time both parties underwent the most important stages of a great process of transformation which put their later relations upon an entirely new footing.   In the one case, with the destruction of the Talaing national movement and the rise of a new dynasty in Upper Burma founded by the great Alaungpaya, began the Burmese movement of Imperialistic expansion, which set all their neighbours by the ears, and finally led to British intervention in 1824.   In the other case, during the period of the War of the Austrian Succession, the Company passed through the first severe phase of its struggle with the French, which was a main factor in its transformation from a commercial to a political power. So whereas English relations with Burma before 1744 were entirely commercial, from the time of their renewal in the reign of Alaungpaya onwards they tended to become more and more political.   The period up to 1743, therefore, besides being the unknown period, has a unity all of its own.

[1] " History of Burma," p. 249.

CHAPTER I

THE EARLIEST ENGLISH CONTACT WITH BURMA

CHAPTER I

THE EARLIEST ENGLISH CONTACT WITH BURMA

BURMA, a land known to the ancient Greek geographers and touched by Roman commercial agents on their way to and from China, was entirely unknown to the peoples of Western Europe throughout the period of time from the fall of the Roman Empire of the West to the Renaissance—the Middle Ages of European history. Not until A.D. 1435 did the first European, of whom we have definite record, visit the land of peacocks and pagodas. This man, Nicolo di Conti, a Venetian merchant, landed first at the city of Tenasserim, then one of the chief ports of the East, since the small merchant craft of those days eschewed the dangerous voyage through the Straits of Malacca and travellers preferred to make the overland route between Tenasserim and Ayuthia, the ancient capital of Siam. Thence he went by sea to Arakan and across country " through mountains void of all habitation " to the Irrawaddy, " a river larger than the Ganges." After a month's voyage up stream he came to Ava upon whose throne Mohnyinthado (1427-40) was striving to maintain himself amidst the welter of internecine strife which characterised the " Shan period " of Burmese history. Conti wrote the first eye-witness account available to European readers.[1]

At the end of the fifteenth century the Portuguese discovery of the Cape Route to India brought Burma within the scope of European enterprise, and it was not long before Portuguese adventurers were importing firearms into the country and fighting as mercenaries in its armies. The sixteenth century, the greatest era of Portuguese Imperialism in the Indian Ocean, was no mean one in Burmese history.

[1] R. H. Major includes an English translation of the full text of this work in his " India in the Fifteenth Century," published by the Hakluyt Society in 1857.

It witnessed the most determined attempt at welding the peoples of Burma into a unity made between the fall of Pagan in 1287 and the rise of Alaungpaya in 1754. Two of the greatest kings of Burmese history, Tabinshwehti (1531-50) and Bayinnaung (1551-81), were the contemporaries respectively of our Henry VIII. and Elizabeth. The dynasty of the temple-builders, who between the accession of Anawrahta (1044) and the great Tartar invasions of the latter half of the thirteenth century had—to quote a recent writer—" made the sun-scorched wilderness, the solitary plain of Myingyan, to blossom forth into the architectural magnificence of Pagan," [1] failed before the twofold pressure of the Shans and the armies of Kublai Khan. The refusal of the Burmese monarch, Narathihapate, to acknowledge the supremacy of the Mongols in 1271 led to the occupation of Pagan with its sixteen square miles of temple and pagoda in 1287, and Burma relapsed into chaos. When the Tartars retired from what was in reality little more than a raid, a number of petty princelets, owing nominal allegiance to China, held independent sway over the various States into which the country split up. Their in cessant wars and, at first sight, meaningless movements and counter-movements do, indeed, revolve about one common centre of disturbance, but the confusion is so great that it is next door to impossible to view the details of Burmese history during the two centuries and a half following the fall of Pagan in their true perspective, unless we take the whole of Indo-China into our survey.

The thirteenth and fourteenth centuries in Indo-China witness the climax of the great racial movement of the Shans, the most numerous of the peoples of Indo-China at the present day. In 1229 the Shans are said to have founded the Ahom kingdom of Assam ; a century and a half later in 1350 Siam, [2] the largest of all the Shan States, had its origin. Burma, too, passed almost completely under Shan domination. The Shan invasions of Burma were not the overwhelming advance of an organised people. Like the slightly earlier Slav penetration into Europe they were a gradual infiltration of little bands of settlers swooping down upon isolated villages and slaughter

[1] G. E. Harvey, " History of Burma " (Longmans, 1925), p. 70.
[2] The word is a variant of the word " Shan."

ing or driving away the inhabitants, while Shan adventurers like Wareru the pedlar,[1] carved out small lordships for themselves from the wreck of the Pagan empire. But the Burmese of the north and centre and the Talaings of the south steadily maintained their racial identity in face of this pressure, though the Pyu peoples of the centre disappear from history. The Burmese apparently were never completely submerged politically. When most of the country was ruled by Shan chieftains, there remained in the hill stockade of Toungoo a centre of resistance that the Shans could never reduce. Little by little, as Burmese families fleeing from the Shan terror settled around its protective walls, Toungoo extended its power over the country round, until, in the fifteenth century, with the slackening of the Shan pressure, its rulers became predominant throughout Central Burma.

With the accession of Minkyinyo to the throne of Toungoo in 1486 comes the end of the period of Shan aggression. His son and successor Tabinshwehti, reunited most of the ancient territories of Pagan under Burmese rule, but failed in the much greater task of giving them a unified administration. Still, under Tabinshwehti (1531-50) and his successor Bayinnaung (1551-81), the Braginoco of contemporary European literature, Burma attained to a measure of political unity unknown since the fall of Pagan. The conquest of the Talaings of the south led these two monarchs to plant their capital at Pegu. The selection of this city for such a purpose signified on their part a more enlightened attitude towards the outside world than had hitherto characterised Burmese royal policy. Its easy access to the sea rendered Pegu the natural resort of the travellers and trading prospectors of the sixteenth century. Tabinshwehti and Bayinnaung were not only anxious to develop trade between their dominions and the outside world, but were sufficiently enlightened to realise that the sea provided the only satisfactory approach to Burma for the traders of other nations.

---

[1] Who after serving for a time in the elephant stables of a petty Siamese chief, aided a rebellious governor of Pegu—then peopled by the Talaings—to drive out the Burmese, afterwards slew his ally and became king of Lower Burma south of Prome and Toungoo, with his capital at Pegu (1287-96). Harvey, *op. cit.*, p. 110 *et seq.*; Wood, " History of Siam," pp. 54-5.

During the reign of Bayinnaung there was a large influx of foreign merchants into Pegu ; among them in 1569 came the Venetian traveller, Caesar Fredericke, who has left us the best description of Burma in the sixteenth century that we have from a European source.[1]   An English translation of it by Thomas Hickock was published in 1588.   Ten years later this was incorporated in Hakluyt's " Principal Navigations " along with the narrative of Ralph Fitch, the first recorded Englishman to visit Burma.   Unfortunately for Fitch's reputation, a comparison of the two accounts reveals the fact that he was indebted to the Venetian for by far the major part of his description of Burma.

Ralph Fitch [2] visited Burma in the years 1587 and 1588. Born probably in 1550, he had left his native land early in the year 1583 on a general prospecting journey to the East, from which he did not return until April, 1591.   Setting out with four companions from London on board a vessel named the *Tiger*, referred to in a well-known passage in Shakespeare's " Macbeth," Fitch landed at Tripoli, and made his way over-land down the Euphrates valley to Busorah on the Persian Gulf.   Thence via Ormuz they travelled by sea to Goa, " the most principall Citie which the *Portugals* haue in *India*, wherein the Viceroy remaineth with his Court." [3]   Here they were imprisoned as spies, but managing to make their escape, pursued their way across the Deccan through the kingdom of Golconda to the Court of the Emperor Akbar at either Agra or Fatehpur.

At Fatehpur in September, 1585, Fitch parted from his companions and continued alone on his journey down the Jumna to Allahabad and along the Ganges through Benares and Patna to Hugli.   On the 28th November, 1586, he embarked for Burma at the port of Serampore in a small Portuguese vessel which was so overcrowded, he relates, that " if any contrary winde had come, wee had throwne many of our things overboard : for we were so pestered with people

---

[1] I have used the edition of it given in Purchas, Vol. II. (1625 edition), pp. 1702 *et seq.*   But see also the Maclehose reprint, x., pp. 88-143.

[2] D.N.B., s.v. Ralph Fitch.

[3] Purchas, 1625 edition, II., p. 1732.   See also Maclehose edition, x, p 1 71.

and goods, that there were scant place to lie in." Sailing southwards to Negrais Point, he entered the delta of the Irrawaddy by one of its westward entrances, and landed at a town called by him " Cosmin," probably near the site of the present port of Bassein.[1] From " Cosmin " he journeyed by way of the creeks to Syriam (" Cirion "),[2] then coming into prominence as the port of Pegu, owing to the silting up of the Pegu river which closed it to seaborne vessels from the end of the sixteenth century.

After a stay of several months in Pegu, Fitch made a twenty-five days' journey across to Chiengmai (" Tamahey ") in the Lao States north of Siam, at that time hotly disputed territory between Burma and Siam. Returning to Pegu, presumably at the end of 1587, he left for Malacca on the 10th January, 1588. Here he stayed from the 8th February to the 29th March, when he began his homeward journey via Pegu to Bengal, which he reached in November, 1588.

Fitch's description of Burma owes so much to the previously published account of Caesar Fredericke that it has about it almost an air of unreality. One is tempted to wonder if he really did go there after all. Not only are his descriptions of places—particularly of the city of Pegu—and of customs, such as the Burmese method of catching elephants, obvious plagiarisms of the earlier work, but they come in exactly the same order as in the Venetian traveller's account. Thus, both writers, after describing the city of Pegu in almost identical terms, proceed to descriptions of the royal palace, the white elephants, the Burmese method of capturing wild elephants, the king's army and power, the propensity of the people of the delta region for eating serpents and other things considered by Europeans unfit for human consumption, the riches of the king, and the trade of the kingdom in the above

---

[1] Purchas, II., 1737. The writer of Fitch's life in the D.N.B. identifies this place with Bassein on the grounds that Cosmin is merely a corruption of Kau-Smin, the old Talaing name for Bassein. Some doubt, however, has been thrown by modern research upon the accuracy of this view.

[2] The Burmese name is Than Hlyin after the supposed founder of the city in 500 B.C. The Talaing name was Trawn. Furnivall and Morrison (" Burma Gazetteer: Syriam District," Volume A, p. 192) suggest that the English name has been derived from the Talaing through the Portuguese. See Hobson-Jobson, s.v. Syriam, for other suggested derivations.

order. Fitch's account of these phenomena differs from Caesar Fredericke's only in that he gives fewer details, so that his version often reads like a boiled down edition of the latter's. Only on a few points does Fitch stand with the charge of plagiarism not proven against him. The description of his journey from " Cosmin " through the creeks to Syriam has no counterpart in Caesar Fredericke's narrative, and, indeed, reads like an eye-witness account. Nor is he indebted to the Venetian writer for his interesting and faithful picture of the Buddhist monks of Burma.

Fitch's indebtedness to Caesar Fredericke can be clearly perceived by comparing a number of parallel passages from both authors. Quite apart from the question of plagiarism their interest is sufficient to justify their quotation *in extenso* here. Caesar Fredericke's description of the city of Pegu runs thus : " By the helpe of God we came safe to *Pegu*, which are two Cities, the old and the new, in the old Citie are the Merchant strangers, and Merchants of the Countrie, for there are the greatest doings and the greatest trade. This Citie is not very great, but it hath very great suburbs. Their houses be made with canes and covered with leaves, or with straw, but the merchants have all one house or Magason, which house they call *Godon*,[1] which is made of brickes, and there they put all their goods of any value, to save them from the often mischances that there happen to houses made of such stuffe. In the new Citie is the Palace of the King and his abiding place with all his Barons and Nobles and gentlemen ; . . . it is a great citie, very plaine and flat, and foure square, walled round about, and with ditches that compass the walls about with Water, in which Ditches are many Crocodiles. It hath no Draw-bridges, yet it hath twenty Gates five for every square in the Walls. . . ."

Fitch's account of this is as follows :—

" *Pegu* is a citie very great, strong, and very faire, with walls of stone, and great ditches round about it. There are two Townes, the old Towne and the new. In the old Towne are all the Merchants strangers and very many Merchants of the Countrie. All the goods are sold in the old Towne which is very great, and hath many suburbs round about it, and all

---

[1] Godown, a warehouse. See Hobson-Jobson, s.v. Godown.

the houses are made of *canes* which they call *Bambos*, and be covered with straw. In your House you have a Ware-house which they call *Godon*, which is made of bricke, to put your goods in for often-times they take fire and burne in an houre foure or five hundred houses : so that if the *Godon* were not, you should be in danger to have all burned, if any winde should rise, at a trice. In the new Towne is the King, and all his Nobilitie and Gentrie. It is a city very great and populous, and is made square and with very faire Walls, and a great Ditch round about it full of water with many Crocodiles in it : it hath twenty Gates, and they be made of stone, for every square five Gates."

Writing of the royal palace at Pegu, Caesar Fredericke says : " Within the gate there is a faire large Court, from the one side to the other, wherein there are made places for the strongest and stoutest Elephants, hee hath foure that be white, a thing so rare, that a man shall hardly finde another King that hath any such, as if this King knowe any other that hath white Elephants, he sendeth for them as for a gift. The time that I was there, there were two brought out of a farre Countrie, and that cost me something the sight of them, for that they command the Merchants to goe to see them, and then they must give somewhat to the men that bring them : the Brokers of the Merchants give for every man half a Ducket, which they call a *Tansa* which amounteth to a great summe, for the number of Merchants that are in that Citie."

Fitch deals with the same subject thus : " Within the first gate of the King's house is a great large roome, on both sides whereof are houses made for the King's Elephants, which bee marvellous great and faire, and are brought up to warres and in service of the King. And among the rest hee hath foure white Elephants, which are very strange and rare : for there is none other King which hath them but hee, if any other King hath one, hee will send unto him for it. When any of these white Elephants are brought unto the King, all the Merchants in the Citie are commanded to see them, and to give him a present of halfe a Ducat, which doth come to a great summe : for that there are many Merchants in the Citie."

Our next example is a particularly good one of the way Fitch occasionally summarises Caesar Fredericke. The latter begins his account of Burmese trade thus : " In the *Indies* there is not any merchandise that is good to bring to *Pegu*, unlesse it be at some times by chance to bring Opium of *Cambaia*, and if hee bring money hee shall lose by it.   Now the commodities that come from Saint *Tome* are the onely merchandise of that place, which is the great quantity of Cloth made there, which they use in *Pegu*, which cloth is made of Bombast wouen and painted, so that the more that kinde of Cloth is washed, the more lively they shew their colours, which is a rare thing, and there is made such account of this kinde of cloth which is of so great importance, that a small bale of it will cost a thousand or two thousand duckets. Also from Saint *Tome* they lade great store of red yarne, of Bombast died with a root which they call *Saia*, as aforesaid, which colour will never out."

Fitch's précis of this passage runs : " In India there are few commodities which serue for *Pegu*, except *Opium of Cambaia*, painted Cloth of Saint *Thome*, or of *Masulipatam*, and white Cloth of Bengala which is spent there in great quantitie.[1]   They bring thither also much Cotton, Yarne red coloured with a Root which they call *Saia*, which will never lose his colour : it is very well sold here, and very much of it cometh yearly to *Pegu*. By your money you lose much."

Fitch's last sentence would be difficult to understand were it not for Caesar Fredericke's much clearer statement on the same subject.   Our last example is an excellent illustration of the danger of plagiarising a writer without taking strict account of the context of the borrowed passage. The Venetian, much impressed by the size of the Burmese armies that were mobilised for service against Siam, was at pains to explain how it was possible to provision such large numbers of men on campaign.   " The state of his Kingdome, and maintenance of his Armie," he writes, " is a thing incredible to consider, and the victuals that should maintayne such a number of people in the warres : but he that knoweth the nature and qualitie of that people, will easily beleeue it.   I have seene with mine

---

[1] This reference to Bengal cloth may possibly have been due to Fitch's own observation, but it is significant that Caesar Fredericke, in another passage, writes : " Also there goeth another great ship from Bengala every yeere, laden with fine cloth of Bombast of all sorts."

eyes, that those people, and Souldiers have eaten of all sorts of wilde beasts that are on the earth, whether it be very filthie or otherwise all serueth for their mouths : yea, I have seen them eate Scorpions and Serpents, also they feed of all kinde of herbes and grasse. So that if such a great Armie want not Water and Salt, they will maintayne themselves a long time in a bush with rootes, flowers and leaues of trees."

Fitch's sole reference to this is contained in one sentence : " These people doe eat Roots, Herbes, Leaues, Dogs, Cats, Rats, Serpents and Snakes ; they refuse almost nothing." But, although this sentence is sandwiched in the middle of his description of the King of Burma's military power, it is in no way linked up with the sense of the passage in which it occurs. It appears as an isolated parenthetical statement without any relation to its setting, so that the reader who has not already seen the corresponding passage in Caesar Fredericke, can in no way account for the sudden intrusion of such a strange assertion. Both writers were keenly interested in State affairs and commercial matters. Their observations on these two subjects were undoubtedly of practical value to the traders of their day, and as such are of first-rate historical interest. Both emphasised the trading connexion between the Coromandel Coast and Burma as the most important source of the latter's imports : a fact made use of by the English East India Company in the following century. Both reflect the prevailing attitude of their age towards the precious metals in their awed descriptions of the king's " houses full of Gold and Silver " and " Mines of Rubies and Saphires and Spinells." The Spanish discoveries of bullion in Central America earlier in the century, coming as they did at a time when the old sources of supply of the precious metals were practically exhausted, had so spectacularly increased the military power and political prestige of Spain, that the other powers of Europe were feverishly anxious to discover further new sources which they might exploit to their own advantage. According to the Bullionist theories advanced by the economists of the sixteenth and seventeenth centuries, gold and silver constituted real wealth, and it was the duty of Governments to take all possible measures to accumulate stores of the precious metals. European trading and colonising ventures, therefore, in the sixteenth century, were either directly or indirectly in search of bullion. Small wonder, then, that the travellers of that age, with imaginations fired by dreams of undiscovered gold, exaggerated beyond all bounds of reason the riches and power of Oriental potentates. Caesar Fredericke speaks of the Burmese monarch as " exceeding the power of the great *Turke* in treasure and strength " and both writers assert that he was continually accumulating more and more treasure.[1] Both, too, were careful to note that gold and silver were articles of commerce in Pegu, bought and sold like other merchandise and subject to fluctuations of price. But Fitch adds with the scorn of such things characteristic of the Englishman of his day, that the people of the country waste vast quantities of gold in gilding their pagodas and idols. " If they did not consume their gold in these vanities," he writes, " it would bee very plentifull and good cheape in Pegu."

These two fascinating accounts of Burma became accessible to the English reading public shortly before the foundation of the East India Company in 1600. Full of excellent tips to the prospective trader, they gave him useful political information and a reasonably sound description of such things as the external trade of the country, the methods of trading with foreigners practised in Burma, the products of the country, its monetary system, its ports and the best seasons for access to and egress from them. It is at first sight, therefore, somewhat surprising to find that the East India Company did not include Burma within the scope of its early voyages, especially when we find Fitch playing a not unimportant part as adviser to the Company in its early days. Actually, however, a study of the East India Company's records reveals the fact that, with the exception of a small venture despatched by Lucas Antheunis from Masulipatam to Pegu in 1617, with no real intention of establishing permanent trading relations, the Company made no serious attempt to open up direct trade

---

[1] Caesar Fredericke : " and every day he Encreaseth it more and more, and it is never diminished."
Fitch : " and bringeth in often, but spendeth very little."

with Burma until the establishment of the Syriam factory by Thomas Breton, Richard Potter, and Richard Knipe late in the year 1647.[1]

The explanation is not far to seek. The desire to control the spice trade, or at least to secure to England a share in it free from foreign control, was the chief factor in the foundation of the East India Company, and almost the sole object of its early voyages. Burma produced neither spices nor the sort of goods that could be readily bartered for them in the markets of the East Indian Archipelago. She was obviously, therefore, outside the scope of such ventures.

But this was not the only reason for the Company's neglect of the Burmese trade. The Company was founded at a time when England was at war with Spain. In 1580 the crown of Portugal had lapsed to Spain, and the great Portuguese Empire in the Indian Ocean was officially the possession of the arch-enemy of Elizabethan England. Notwithstanding the brilliance of the exploits of the Elizabethan seamen in the Spanish Main, England was in no position to develop a frontal attack upon the Portuguese in the Eastern seas. Unlike the Dutch East Indian ventures, which were fostered and directed by the Government of the United Provinces, with the direct aim of destroying Portuguese power in the East, the English Company was a purely trading venture that could expect little or no active support from Government. It sought, therefore, to avoid contact with the Portuguese by opening up trade with only such places as were not within the actual sphere of Portuguese trade. At the time of the foundation of the Company the question of the possible scope of its operations was at Elizabeth's request referred to Fulke Greville. In his reply he stated that the Portuguese traded to Arakan, Pegu, Siam, Tenasserim, and Quedda. Thus, naturally the English merchants tended to give those places a wide berth. Notwithstanding the spectacular failure of Philip II.'s policy in the cases of England and the Dutch, the Portugo-Spanish Empire still remained intact, still appeared impervious to external attacks, and gave hardly a sign of the internal weakness that was so soon to bring about the collapse of its Eastern section. A small merchant company,

[1] *Vide* Chapter III.

without even a permanent capital upon which to float its modest and precarious ventures, could not afford to fall foul of the power which had controlled the Indian Ocean for a century, and still held all its chief strategic points. When the Company's first expedition set out for the East, the port of Syriam was in the hands of Felipe de Brito y Nicote, a Portuguese mercenary captain nominally in the service of Arakan, who took advantage of a period of disaster and anarchy in Lower Burma to seize Syriam, and hold up all foreign trade with the interior. De Brito had conceived the not altogether unstatesmanlike project of building up in Lower Burma a province of the Portuguese Empire. He seems to have been of the stuff of empire-builders. Had the Portuguese Empire not been in a moribund condition, his exploit might have had a different issue. As it was, however, the adventure was from the outset doomed to failure, though de Brito managed to maintain his hold upon Syriam for thirteen years, from 1600 to 1613, and to confine all Burma's sea-borne commerce to that port alone. It was not to be expected, therefore, that during the period of his ascendancy the East India Company would entertain any serious thought of trading to Burma.[1]

After the death of Bayinnaung in 1581 his empire had rapidly fallen into a state of disintegration. The frantic attempts of Bayinnaung and his predecessor, Tabinshwehti, to conquer Siam before they had given really effective administration to their own territories were the chief cause of the ultimate failure on the part of the Toungoo dynasty to unify Burma. When the strong hand of Bayinnaung was removed, all the various vassal lords, who were in charge of the districts into which the realm was divided up, asserted their independence of the central government and plunged the country once more into a state of chaos from which Bayinnaung's weaker successor, Nandabayin, was unable to rescue it. Instead, he frittered away his few remaining resources upon further fruit-

---

[1] *Vide* Stevens' translation of Faria y Sousa's "Asia Portuguesa," Vol. III., Part II., Chapters V., VI., VII., and Part III., Chapter II. For a more detailed account of this episode, *vide* "A Brief Account of the Kingdom of Pegu in the East Indies," a contemporary Portuguese work, of which a translation into English by A. Macgregor, Esq., I.C.S., appeared in the *Journal of the Burma Research Society*, Vol. XVI., No. II., August, 1926.

less attacks upon Siam. During this period the region of the Irrawaddy delta, one of the richest agricultural districts in the world, and to-day the most thickly populated part of Burma, became hopelessly impoverished. Depopulated by famine and by constant requisitions of man-power to main-tain the ever-dwindling numbers of Burmese armies flung away in abortive campaigns against Siam,[1] ravaged by counter-attacking Siamese armies and those of her ally, Arakan, that portion of Burma which gave her her sole access to the sea and through which the trading prospectors of the sixteenth and seventeenth centuries entered the kingdom, had become almost a desert by the end of the sixteenth century. In 1600 a combined Siamese and Arakanese raid reduced the city of Pegu to ashes, and the Arakanese carried off into captivity a daughter of Nandabayin and a royal white elephant, besides deporting some three thousand households from the Pegu district. The Jesuit missionaries who came to Burma in that year depict a scene of hopeless misery and ruin.[2] The Siamese counter-attacks had shorn Burma of her southern provinces, Martaban and Tenasserim.[3] Little more than the district immediately surrounding the city of Pegu was under royal control, the rest of the country being parcelled out among a crowd of vassal " kings " unchecked by any central authority. Small wonder that Felipe de Brito and his motley crowd of *feringi* could seize and hold Syriam for thirteen years. Pegu never recovered its position as a great trading city. Its de-struction in 1600 left Syriam the only important centre for foreign trade in Burma, but until de Brito's dominance was cut short, Syriam remained a closed port to English commerce.

[1] Fitch mentions one as being launched during his stay in Pegu : " At my being there hee went to *Odia* (i.e. Ayuthia) in the countrie of *Siam* with three hundred thousand men, and five thousand Elephants." These numbers are of course fictitious. The total population of Burma at that time has been estimated at less than three million souls. (Harvey, " History of Burma," pp. 333-5.) This expedition was Nandabayin's third invasion of Siam, which resulted in complete failure. P'ra Naret, the famous Black Prince, was then on the throne of Siam, and proved himself more than a match for the Burmese commanders. (Harvey, *op. cit.*, p. 181.)

[2] *Vide* Nicholas Pimenta in Purchas (1625 ed.), II., p. 1746 ; and Boves in *ibid.*, II., p. 1748.

[3] These remained in Siamese hands until reconquered in 1765 by Hsinbyushin, the son of Alaungpaya, the founder of the last Burmese dynasty.

In 1605 Anaukpetlun, a grandson of Bayinnaung and a man of great energy, came to the throne of Burma.   He vigorously set himself to revive the central power and restore order in the country.   Having secured the loyalty of the peoples of Upper Burma, he conquered the refractory vassal lords of the south.   Finally, in 1613, he succeeded in capturing Syriam, where he put an end to de Brito's career by impaling him.   He then began a series of heavy blows along the Siamese frontier which he temporarily pushed back beyond Chiengmai in the south-east and Tavoy in the south.   Under him Burma regained some semblance of order and trade began to revive.   Through Anaukpetlun [1] the East India Company established its first direct communications with Burma.

[1] Sometimes known by his Indianised name, Maha Dhamma Raza.

CHAPTER II

THE EPISODE OF THOMAS SAMUEL

CHAPTER II

THE EPISODE OF THOMAS SAMUEL

THE story of the East India Company's earliest contact with Burma is not lacking in romance. In 1610 the directors decided to establish trading relations with Siam. In the following year, therefore, the Company's seventh voyage was equipped and despatched. The factors in charge of it were instructed to open up trade with the Coromandel Coast, proceeding thence to Patani on the east coast of the Malay Peninsula, in the territory of Siam, and to Ayuthia, the capital of Siam.[1] The management of the venture was placed in the hands of two Dutch merchants known respectively as Peter Floris and Lucas Antheunis, who together contributed one-eighth of the total capital involved. Pieter Willemszoon van Elbingh, who assumed the name of Floris presumably as a disguise on entering the service of the East India Company, had had previous experience of the East in the employment of the Dutch East India Company. In 1608 he had visited Arakan and there had seen the daughter of Nandabayin of Pegu and his royal white elephant, part of the Arakanese booty carried off from Burma on the occasion of the great raid in 1600.[2]

It is interesting to note in passing that the establishment of factories on the Coromandel Coast and in Siam was regarded by the promoters of the voyage as not merely a desirable object in itself, but as part of a scheme for opening up trade with Japan. The leaders of the expedition were ordered to

[1] Often called Judea or Odia by the European writers of the sixteenth and seventeenth centuries. It was destroyed by the Burmese invasion of 1767, after which date Bangkok became the capital of Siam. (*Vide* Hobson-Jobson, s.v. Judea, Odia.)

[2] Purchas, Maclehose ed., III., pp. 319-42. Danvers and Foster, "Letters Received by the East India Company from its Servants in the East," III., p. 318, note.

" send one or two of our factors in such convenient shipping as you may procure to carry his Majesty's letters unto the King of Japan, together with such stock of merchandise and commodities as we have appointed our said principal merchants to provide for that purpose."[1]   The financial success of its early voyages had made the Company anxious to widen the scope of its trade, and it was beginning to put out feelers in new directions.

Floris and Antheunis with the merchants and cargo of the seventh voyage left England on board the *Globe* on the 5th February, 1611.   In the following August they arrived at Ceylon.   Thence they sailed up the Coromandel Coast, putting in at Pulicat, Pettapoli, and Masulipatam in order to buy cotton goods for sale in Bantam and Siam.   In Masulipatam they founded a factory destined to be for a time the principal station through which the East India Company's trade to Burma was conducted.   Then, leaving the coast of India, they proceeded by way of Bantam on the island of Java, to the port of Patani, whither they arrived on the 23rd June, 1612.

From Patani five of the factors were sent on ahead to Ayuthia ; they were Lucas Antheunis, Adam Denton, Thomas Samuel, Thomas Driver, and Thomas Essington.   At Ayuthia they were well received ;[2] there seemed to be an excellent prospect of opening up trade both with the interior and with Japan.   Antheunis, therefore, decided to send Thomas Samuel and Thomas Driver to Chiengmai[3] in the Lao country north of Siam " to discover the Trade of that Country."[4] With them went " a cargason of goods " which they were to endeavour to sell.[5]

They left Ayuthia probably early in 1613,[6] the year in which Anaukpetlun had captured Syriam and put to death

[1] Birdwood and Foster, " First Letter Book of the East India Company," p. 387.

[2] Anderson, " English Relations with Siam in the Seventeenth Century," p. 49.

[3] *Vide* Hobson-Jobson, s.v. Jangomay for variants of this word used by European writers of the sixteenth and seventeenth centuries.   The Burmese name for Chiengmai is Zimmè.

[4] " Cal. State Papers, Col., East Indies," Nos. 756, 771.   "Purchas his Pilgrimage " (1626 ed.), Vol. V., p. 1006.

[5] " Letters Received," V., No. 582.

[6] *Ibid.*, II., No. 113, and III., p. 322.

the Portuguese adventurer, de Brito. Immediately after this exploit the victorious King of Burma began his series of attempts to regain from Siam the ancient Burmese territories of Martaban, Tenasserim, Tavoy, and Chiengmai. In 1615, after having reduced Martaban and Tavoy, though unsuccessful in his attack upon Tenasserim, he captured Chiengmai, placed one of his vassals upon its throne, and returned to Pegu with prisoners and booty. Among these was Thomas Samuel with the unsold remainder of his goods.

The reason of Samuel's long absence at Chiengmai is unknown. From a letter dated the 27th August, 1615,[1] written by Lucas Antheunis shortly before his departure to Patani in that year, and left behind to be delivered to Samuel on his return to Ayuthia, we learn that when the latter had been pressed to return to Ayuthia because of the unwillingness of the factors to continue with the Chiengmai venture, he stayed on there sending back his companion, Thomas Driver, with the proceeds of the sale of part of his goods, " gold badly conditioned without any factory thereof, only by small bills or screets found in the bags." His answers to Antheunis's letters are complained of as having been unsatisfactory and his accounts badly kept. Antheunis accuses him of being " exceeding negligent, being your only fault (i.e. entirely your fault) to have tarried there so long, to no small hindrance and prejudice to the Company."

It is open to doubt whether Samuel's prolonged absence was due entirely to his negligence. The probability is that in the unsettled state of the country, due to the Burmese invasions, he could not get transport for his somewhat bulky goods and lingered on after Driver's departure in order to stand by the Company's merchandise that had been entrusted to him. Driver, on the other hand, would not find it so difficult to get through to Ayuthia with the gold, which, according to Antheunis, weighed only some 614 taels.[2] That the Burmese invasions had made peaceful travel almost impossible fairly soon after Samuel and Driver reached Chiengmai

[1] " Letters Received," III., pp. 152-6.
[2] The Chinese ounce, $\frac{1}{16}$ of a catty. 100 catties = $133\frac{1}{3}$ lbs. avoirdupois. So we may take the tael to be about $\frac{1}{4}$ of an ounce ; 614 taels, therefore, would be slightly less than 29 lbs. avoirdupois.

may be gathered from a letter written by John Gourney to the Company from Patani in July, 1614. " The trade," he says, " betwixt Siam and places in the land, as Langjam,[1] Jangama,[2] Pegu, etc., have their passages so stopped by the Ava king of Pegu which maketh war against the King of Siam, that we shall be fain to embark and disperse to great value to Camboja, and where we understand trade may be made." [3] When Antheunis wrote his letter to Samuel he was extremely annoyed at being unable to close the accounts of the seventh voyage because of Samuel's absence. When we bear in mind that Antheunis was one of the largest shareholders in the concern, it will be impossible to take his remarks as seriously as they read. I prefer to think that finding it impossible to move his goods from Chiengmai, Samuel chose to remain with them rather than, by escaping to Ayuthia without them, face the almost certain charge of breach of trust.

In Pegu Samuel appears to have been well treated and to have been allowed to carry on trade with the goods still remaining over from the Chiengmai venture. Not long after his arrival, however, he died. In accordance with Burmese custom, his property escheated to the Crown, but as the major portion of it belonged to the East India Company, it was held, pending an appeal from the Company for its restoration. An inventory of the goods was drawn up and steps taken to collect the dead man's debts. News of this, in due course, was brought to the Company's factory at Masulipatam by Muslim merchants engaged in the trade between the Coromandel Coast and Pegu. By a curious coincidence Lucas Antheunis, who had, in the first instance, despatched Samuel upon his ill-starred adventure, was at that time (1617) the Company's agent at Masulipatam.[4] He decided to send in a claim to the Court of Pegu for the restoration of the Company's goods. Two of his assistants, therefore, Henry Forrest and John Staveley, were despatched to Burma on board a trading vessel belonging to the King of Golconda [5] to undertake the

---

[1] Luang Praban.   [2] Chiengmai.
[3] " Letters Received," Vol. II., No. 159.
[4] Purchas (1626 ed.), Vol. V., p. 1006.
[5] " A Kinges ship of this country," O.C. No. 680.

recovery of the goods.   On the 10th September, 1617, they departed from Masulipatam, taking with them " six pees of stametts " [1] valued at 534 pagodas 13 fanams and 2¾ cash [2] to " beare the charge of the voyage and make tryall of the Trade." [3]   With them also was sent that most indispensable accompaniment to all missions in the East, a present for the king.

After slightly over three weeks in the Bay of Bengal, Forrest and Staveley arrived on the 3rd October at Syriam, the port of Pegu.[4]   The story of their sojourn in Burma, taken from their letters to Masulipatam, has been told by William Methwold [5] in his admirable " Relations of the Kingdome of Golchonda," written in 1623, and published by Purchas in the supplement to the fifth volume of his monumental work in 1626.   Before we continue with the story of Forrest and Staveley, something must be said about the too-little-known author of this paper.   A nephew of Sir William Methwold, Lord Chief Baron of the Exchequer of Ireland, who died in 1620, William Methwold entered the East India Company's service in 1615.   During his early years in the employment of the Company he travelled widely, being the first Englishman to visit the famous diamond mines of Golconda.   In the summer of 1618 he succeeded Adam Denton [6] as chief of the factory at Masulipatam, and although under sentence of recall for alleged private trading, he held that office until October, 1622, when he left for England via Batavia to answer the charges brought against him four years

---

[1] A kind of piece-goods.

[2] Letter of Thos. Jones at Masulipatam to George Ball at Bantam, dated 16th August, 1618, in Foster, " English Factories in India," 1618-21, pp. 43-4.   See also note on Coinage and Currency in Appendix I.

[3] William Methwold, " Relations of the Kingdome of Golchonda, and other neighbouring nations with the Gulfe of Bengala, Arrecan, Pegu, Tannassery, etc., and the English Trade in those parts."   In " Purchas his Pilgrimage," 1626 ed., V., p. 1006.

[4] *Ibid.*, p. 1006.

[5] *Vide* D.N.B., s.v. William Methwold.   The " Original Correspondence " and the " Factory Records : Surat," contain many references to him, most of which are accessible in Foster, " English Factories in India." In his introductions, Foster gives much supplementary information about Methwold that is not to be found in the D.N.B.

[6] Who proceeded to Patani.   For his subsequent career in Siam, *vide* Anderson, " English Relations with Siam," pp. 73-4, 77, 88-91.

earlier.[1]   He was reinstated in the Company's service, and in 1628 became a " free brother."   In 1633 he became President at Surat, and during an arduous five years of office proved himself one of the ablest and most energetic holders of that office in the first half of the seventeenth century.[2]   In 1639 he returned home on board the *Mary*.   His career culminated with his appointment as Deputy Governor of the Company in 1650, three years before his death.   It is particularly unfortunate that his valuable " Relations of the Kingdome of Golchonda " should have appeared in " Purchas his Pilgrimage," the *fifth* volume of the " Pilgrimes," since this volume, which consists of Purchas's symposium of all the original papers previously collected by him into a sort of general history with marginal references to the sources of his information, does not appear in modern reprints.   In his introduction to Methwold's paper, Purchas explains that it came into his hands too late for publication in the earlier volumes of the work.   " Now for Master Methold," [3] he writes, " I had spared some of Frederikes, Balbies and Fitches Relations, if these had comne in time, which so many times I had both by messages and in person sought, and by reason of the Authours absence or business was frustrate." [4]

Methwold illustrates his account of Forrest's and Staveley's visit to Burma by long verbatim extracts from their letters to Masulipatam, describing in graphic terms their " entertaynment " during the early months of their unduly lengthy stay in the country.   They constitute the next eye-witness account after Fitch's written by Englishmen of Burma.   Their intrinsic interest, combined with their general inaccessibility, is sufficient excuse for quoting them in full here.[5]

[1] On this part of his career, *vide* especially Foster, " English Factories " 1618-21, Introd., p. xliv, and 1622-3, Introd., p. xxxix.

[2] Foster, *op. cit.*, 1630-3, Introd., pp. xxxii-xxxiv.   In November, 1635, the Company wrote to him expressing their appreciation of his services.   He was thanked for his " well-written and digested " letters, his efforts to prevent private trade, his financial administration, and his establishment of good relations with the Portuguese.

[3] The " w " is often omitted in contemporary spelling of his name.

[4] Purchas, V. (1626 ed.), p. 972.

[5] I have been unable to discover any trace of these letters in the East India Company's Records.   They are, however, referred to in the letter written by Thomas Jones at Masulipatam to George Ball at Bantam, already referred to on p. 35, n. 2.   " Mr. Denton," he writes, " can best

" The King hearing of our comming sent foure Galliots
with Presents to the Ambassador [1] and unto us, sending
us word that he did much rejoice at our comming into
his country. These Gallies having oares of a side,[2] with
eight Noblemen in them, caused our ship to come to an
anchor before the town of Siriam,[3] the 7 of October the
King of Pegues Brother being chief Gouernour, sending
two Noblemen abord of our ship, writing our names and
our age of yeeres and the cause of our comming, wee
assuring them that wee were messengers sent from
Masulipatam by our chief Captain, having a Present and
a Letter unto the King, which when his Highness shall
be pleased to receiue, shall understand the effect of our
business, and the cause of our comming. The tenth day
of October wee were sent for on shoare by the Kings
Brother who sitting in a large house of Bamboson,[4] in
great state bedeckt with jewels in his eares with Gold
Rings, with rich stones on his fingers, being a white man
and of very good understanding demanding of us the
question the Noblemen before did, and wee answering
him as wee did before, because that our speeches should
be found always as one : wee gave him at that time a
fine (sic) for a Present, to the intent that he might speake
and write to the King his brother in our behalfe, that
wee might have accesse unto the King the sooner, that
our business might haue effect. The eight of Nouember
the King sent for us, and the King's Brother prouided
us with a boate, with six men to rowe, and also a Nobleman with us to Pegu, to be our guard, having Narsacan
and Hodges [5] Ismael with us, unto which Nobleman wee

advise you in all particulars towching this business, whoe hath their letters
received in January and March past aloung with him, which yf you please
to peruse you may perseave littell hope of recoverey either of the former
(Samuel's goods) or that caried with them more than their persons which
I wish weare heere."

[1] Probably an emissary from the " King " of Golconda.

[2] Riverine war-boats of the galley type, usually decorated with elaborate
carving and gilding, especially at the prow. Burma had no navy capable
of use at sea such as was possessed by Arakan in the seventeenth century.

[3] Punctuation requires a full-stop here, but I have retained the original
punctuation and spelling throughout.

[4] Bamboo.

[5] A corruption of Coja, a title of respect applied to rich merchants in
India.

gaue a present, for in this place heere is nothing to be done or spoken, or any business performed without Bribes, Gifts, or Presents. Arriving in Pegu the eleuenth of Nouember, hauing our Present with us, Bany Bram [1] sent his men unto us, writing our names as before time, they also bade us choose any ground where wee would for to build us a house, but at our own cost and charge as all other mens custome is.[2] Our House being finished, straightt order was given that wee must not walk anywhere out of our house to speake with any man until the King had spoken with us, and our Present deliuered. The King sent us a Present of Victuals with two Nobleman with it, which was some grace to us, though it was not of much value, and our comfort is, that all men report that the King is uery well pleased at our comming into his Country. The seuen and twentieth of December, the King sent for our Present, and sent two Horses for us, and being come to a gate of the Towne, to stay for his comming, when hee came out, hee sent for us. What speech or conference he had with us, Narsarca can certifie you, but it was to no purpose, concerning our businesse, nor could wee get none to moue the King in our businesse, more than he demands. The next our letter was sent for, and interpreted by a Portugall to the King, but one that speakes Pegu. Wee had much trouble with him about the true understanding of it, being not written in Portuguese. The next day we deliuered that present you sent to Bany Bram, who gaue us many faire speeches like to others, but wee haue found them all to no purpose. The Country is far from your worships expectation, for what men soeuer come into his Country, he holds them but as his slaues, neyther can any man goe out of his Country without his leaue, for hee hath watch both by Land and

[1] Binnya Byan, a Talaing title. Binnya=lord.
[2] *Vide* Caesar Fredericke in Purchas, II. (1625 ed.), p. 1717 : " All Merchants that meane to goe thorow the *Indies*, must carrie all manner of houshold stuffe with them which is necessary for a house, because that there is not any lodging, nor Innes, nor Hosts, nor Chamber roome in that Countrie, but the first thing a man doth when hee commeth, to any Citie is to hyre a house, either by the yeere, or by the moneth or as he meanes to stay in those parts. In *Pegu* their order is to hire their houses for sixe moneths."

Water, and he of himself is a Tyrant, and cannot eat before he hath drawne bloud from some of his people with death or otherwise. For the businesse of Thomas Samuel and the Mallayor,[1] they had a falling out some 12 monthes before he dyed, and he tooke all the Companies goods into his hands, and the Mallayor had Narsarcans [2] in his hands, and comming to Pegu he fell sicke by the way, and dyed a short time after he came to Pegu,[3] but before his death the Mallayor was called for to giue account what men were indebted to Samuel, and the Pegues [4] and Bermanes that were indebted payd it all to the King, but the Moores that were indebted said, when the English came they would pay them, we went with others to Nichesa [5] and requested him to moue the King in our behalfe for our dispatch, who returned answer : came we to demand our goods, and the English had neuer come to trade in his Country ? when our Ships came hee would giue all the goods, and what the English could demand to giue them content.

" In another Letter the first of March,[6] wee had word sent us, the King would not let us go untill some English Ships came to Pegu. For the money wee brought with us, it is all spent, and wee are here in a most miserable estate, and knowe no way to help ourselues. For the King hath neyther giuen us any of our goods, nor leaue to recover none of our debts, nor taken our Cloth, but wee are like lost sheep, and still in feare of being brought to the slaughter. Therefore we beseech you and the rest of our Countriemen and Friends to pittie our poore dis-tressed estate, and not to let us be left in a Heathen Country, slaves to a tyrannous King. Though the King gaue us nothing, yet had hee but giuen us leaue to come away, wee could haue certified your Worship of meanes to helpe to haue recouered all the mony and goods we came

---

[1] Apparently a Malay who had accompanied Samuel from Chiengmai to Pegu.

[2] i.e. Narsarca's goods. What exactly was his connexion with the episode is not clear.

[3] Samuel. [4] Talaings as distinct from Burmans.

[5] Probably the Portuguese interpreter.

[6] 1618.

for.   Lead [1] and Tinne heere is none to be sold, but if we receiue any money, wee do meane one of us to goe into the country to buy some, if any profit may be made of it. The Coast of Pegu is cleere and water enough on the Bar for any Ship : and for Pilots, there be many to be had in Musulipatam, that know the Coast very well.   Wee intreat you for God's sake to be mindfull of us, and to pitty the poore estate wee are here in, and send some Ship to release us, and wee shall be bound to pray for your Worships good health and prosperitie."

So Forrest and Staveley found themselves virtually prisoners in Pegu, able to move about with freedom so long as they made no attempt to leave the country.   Methwold goes on to relate that they " found good sale for their cloth " but soon " had consumed their Capitall, and taken up besides what their credit could supply, for which they could giue no other account, but that most was lost at play, and the rest profusely spent, whereof the Right Worshipfull East India Company are most sensible, and my selfe at that time in that place had some reason to be acquainted withall."   At the end of 1619 Methwold wrote home to the Company that in the absence of letters from the two envoys he had gleaned his information of them from passengers arriving in Masulipatam from Pegu.   They were reported, he said, in April of that year to have had their house burnt down, and were about to leave the country, when the discovery of an important plot against the king's life caused so much disturbance that they dared not ask for the necessary permission to depart.   In this way they had lost their chance of crossing the Bay of Bengal before the wet monsoon set in, and the homeward sailing season to the Coromandel Coast ended.[2]   This letter of Methwold's was dated 7th December, 1619, so that it is evident that up to the time of writing Forrest and Staveley had not put in an appearance at Masulipatam.   Yet in his " Relations of the Kingdome of Golchonda " in Purchas he states that they arrived back in April, 1619.   This must be an error, due in all probability to a slip of his memory.   In the extremely

---

[1] Probably " ganza " is here meant.
[2] Foster, " English Factories," 1618-21, p. 154.

defective records of the Company at this time there is no reference to the exact date of the two envoys' return to Masulipatam. We may, however, assume with a fair degree of probability that Methwold was exactly a year out in his computation, and should have given the date as April, 1620, in his paper in Purchas. Native trading vessels were accustomed to leave the Golconda coast for Syriam at the end of the rainy season (i.e. in September or October) and to start on their homeward voyage shortly before the commencement of the next wet monsoon (i.e. in February or March). Concerning this point Methwold gives the following interesting information in his " Relations " : " In September the Ships [1] for Achyne, Arrecan, Pegu, and Tannassery set all sayle, for it is to be understood that alongst this and all other Coasts of India, the windes blow constantly trade six moneths one way, and sixe moneths another : which they call the Monsons alternately succeeding each other, not missing to alter in Aprill and October, onely variable towards their end, so that taking the last of a monsoon, they set sayles, and with a fore-winde arriue at their desired hauen, and there negotiating their affaires, they set sayle from thence in February or March following, and with the like fauourable gale returne in Aprille unto their owne Ports." [2] This practice continued throughout the seventeenth century and well on into the eighteenth, English ships conforming to it when they began to make regular voyages between Fort St. George and Syriam towards the end of the seventeenth century.[3] As the two factors missed their chance of leaving Burma before the wet monsoon of 1619 broke, the odds are that they returned to Masulipatam with the returning Golconda boats in the following year.

In the end Anaukpetlun restored to Forrest and Staveley the property of the Company which they had come to retrieve. He would not actually hand it over, however, until the two

---

[1] i.e. of Golconda.   Purchas, V. (1626 ed.), p. 1004.

[2] *Vide* also Caesar Fredericke in Purchas, II. (1625 ed.), pp. 1716-17, where he mentions that ships from St. Thomé bound for Pegu usually departed from the former place on the 11th or 12th of September ; but he gives no information as to the time of the return journey.   The subject receives further treatment in Chapter V.

[3] Fort St. George Diary and Consultation Books, *passim*, for list of outgoing and incoming boats with dates of departures and arrivals.

factors were on the point of embarking for Masulipatam " lest
their ryot should haue consumed all," grimly remarks
Methwold.[1] From Methwold's " Relations " it would seem
that in the end the king ordered the two factors to leave the
country somewhat against their will.   They were naturally no
little perturbed at the reception they would get on their
return after such an inglorious adventure, while the king was
anxious to get into touch with the Company in order to
establish direct trading relations.   In his general letter home
to the Company dated the 15th November, 1620, Methwold
describes the close of the affair.[2]   The original letter is no
longer in existence, but the abstract of it that is to be found
in the " Factory Records : Miscellaneous "[3] is worth quoting
verbatim :—

" The factors which were sent to Pegu to recover what
was there remayning, have spent all that was sent both
first and last.   They have framed and exhib[it]ed a form-
lesse and false accompt, which he hath now sent home.
Forrest, one of these Pegu factors, makes himself indebted for the rest, for so much lost at dice.   The[y]
spent all and yet took up 100 rials per exchange, which
must be paid ; for 60 rials whereof he[4] had a pawne,
which they saie belonged to Mr. Denton.   Theis Pegu
factors were fownde to be royotous, vitious and unfaith-
full ; some of their own papeers doe evince them, which
with their persons are sent to Jaquatra.[5]   Their accompts
were forged at sea, and all their original papers they did
cast overboard, lest coming to light they might have
disclosed all their untruthes.   Forrest attempted to flee
twice but was fetcht againe ; a vearie villane, debaucht,
most audacious and dishonest.   I forbeare to send the
accompt of his expence etc., because he is more worthy
to be punished than able to satisfy.   The retourne of all
the Pegu adventure, first and last, is about 857 rials.
The first adventure[6] was made by the seventh viage,

---

[1] In Purchas, V. (1626 ed.), p. 1003.
[2] Foster, " English Factories," 1618-21, p. 209.
[3] Vol. I., p. 55.   [4] Methwold.
[5] Bantam.   [6] Samuel's.

but tourned over to the first joint stocke.   The second
adventure [1] was made by the second joint stocke.   To pay
both there is no more but 857 rials, which he will imploye
in diamondes and bring with him."

According to Methwold's account in Purchas, Anaukpetlun
followed up his remarks to the two factors regarding the
desirability of the Company sending trading ships to Syriam,
by forwarding along with them to the factors at Masulipatam
a letter " written on a Palmito Leafe, signifying his desire to
give free Trade and entertainment to the English Nation, if
they would with their shipping repaire unto his Country."
This was accompanied by a present of " a Ring set with a
Ruby, two Mats, two Betele Boxes, and two narrow pieces of
Damaske, all worth twenty Nobles or thereabouts." [2]   Methwold does not seem to have jumped at the Burman offer.
He wrote home to the Company that he thought it " not
impertinent to send a small ship to some of the King of
Pegues portes, being that King[s] speciall desire." [3]   With
the " retornes from Pegu " he bought diamonds to the value
of 534 pagodas [4] and some gum-lac, which were laden on board
the *Charles* in December, 1621, and forwarded to England.[5]

Of Forrest and Staveley I can find no further mention in
the records of the East India Company.   This is not surprising,
since many of the records of this period have been lost.   Probably they were sent home in disgrace.   It is noteworthy that
in his " Relations " Methwold gives no mention of their names,
" leaving them namelesse according to the obscurity of their
qualities, and irregularity of their proceedings," he writes.
From this fact we may possibly infer that they were alive
and in England at the time of the publication of his paper.
He would not wish to figure in a libel action.

Contrary to the view expressed by certain writers,
Anaukpetlun's invitation to the Company to send trading
ships to his country did not result in any immediate growth
of direct trading relations between the Company and Burma

---

[1] Goods sent with Forrest and Staveley.
[2] Purchas, V. (1626 ed.), p. 1007.
[3] Foster, *op. cit.*, p. 209.
[4] *Ibid.*, p. 255.   [5] *Ibid.*, p. 343.

still less in the establishment of factories at such places as Syriam, Prome, Ava, and Bhamo, although an oft-quoted passage in Dalrymple's "Oriental Repertory" has been taken to imply as much.[1] No English factory was established in Burma until the year 1647, when the Company's first settlement was made at Syriam.

For an explanation of the Company's failure to establish a factory in Burma at this date the general condition of its affairs during the years 1619-23 must be examined. After the incorporation of the Dutch East India Company in 1602 chronic hostility had developed in the East between the English and Dutch merchants. Hostile acts, committed in the first instance by the Dutch, led to reprisals and counter-reprisals, until at length an intolerable condition of affairs grew up in the Spice Islands. Officially the two nations were at peace with each other. They had behind them long traditions of past friendship and mutual aid. In order, therefore, to bring to an end this unfortunate rivalry Commissioners of the two Companies met in London at Merchant Tailors' Hall on 16th January, 1619, to discuss articles of peace and the conclusion of a Treaty of Defence.[2] In July of that year a Treaty of Defence was concluded which gave to the English a right to a share in the East Indian trade and to the shelter of Dutch fortresses. In return for these guarantees the English Company was to contribute one-third of the Dutch fort and garrison charges in the Moluccas, Bandas, and at Amboyna, one-half of those at Pulicat, and to maintain a fleet of ten ships to carry on raids upon Portuguese and Spanish trade and shipping in the East.[3]

Under the terms of the Treaty the Dutch promised to make restitution of all damage inflicted by them upon the English. When, however, they were pressed to settle the claims made against them by the Company, they delayed matters interminably by putting up counter-claims, and it was soon evident that their intention was to avoid completely the payment of any compensation whatever. This matter, in

---

[1] *Vide* note on the alleged existence of English factories in Burma before 1647 in Appendix II.

[2] "Factory Records: Java," II., Part I., 1618-25.

[3] Foster, "English Factories in India," 1622-3, Introd., p. xxxv.

fact, dragged on until the days of Cromwell and was only settled by the Treaty of Westminster at the end of the first Dutch War.

In the meantime the English factories in the Spice Islands found that the financial obligations imposed upon them by the Treaty could not be borne without help from home. But such help was not forthcoming for two reasons. In the first place, the Directors of the English Company thought that the money about to be realised by way of compensation from the Dutch would be ample for the needs of these factories. In the second place, the Company was at this time anxious to develop trade between the west coast of India and Persia, and was devoting all its available capital to promoting this enterprise. The Batavia Presidency and its subordinate agencies, therefore, were starved of capital and forced to abandon many of their trading ventures. In so precarious a state were their affairs at the beginning of 1623 that in January of that year the President and Council at Batavia resolved to abandon the factories in the Moluccas, the Bandas, and at Amboyna. The shocking " massacre of Amboyna " perpetrated by the Dutch in the following month merely served to strengthen a decision already arrived at for other reasons, and by the end of the year the factories at Patani, Pulicat, Siam, and Hirado (in Japan) were closed. Only Masulipatam, Achin, Jambi, Japara, and Macassar remained in the Batavia Presidency.[1] Under such conditions it was financially impossible for a factory to have been opened in Burma at this date.

As a result of the visit of Forrest and Staveley the Masulipatam factors apparently lost all interest in Burma. Thereafter they opposed all suggestions for reopening direct trade with a land in which the foreign merchant upon his arrival found himself hampered by all sorts of royal restrictions. The fear of Dutch hostility was also instrumental in keeping the English away from Burma. The Dutch had a trading post there from about 1627 to 1679.[2] In 1639 when the

---

[1] Methwold, op. cit. (in " Purchas his Pilgrimage," Vol. V. (1626), p. 994), refers to the disastrous effect of the Treaty of 1619 upon English trade in the Far East.

[2] Vide Harvey, " History of Burma," pp. 205, 349.

Masulipatam factors received orders from the Company to make trial of the Pegu trade by sending a ship there, they replied that such a proceeding would be equivalent to sending the ship " into the lyons clawes, we meeane with (*sic*) our competitours the Dutch."[1]   When eight years later it was decided to open a factory in Burma it is not surprising to find that this decision was strongly opposed by the Masulipatam factory.

[1] Foster, " English Factories," 1637-41, p. 144.

CHAPTER III

THE FOUNDATION OF THE SYRIAM FACTORY AND ITS EARLY PROSPERITY, 1647-52

CHAPTER III

THE FOUNDATION OF THE SYRIAM FACTORY AND ITS
EARLY PROSPERITY, 1647-52

THERE seems to have been little direct trading between the East India Company and Burma previous to the establishment of the factory at Syriam in 1647. On account of the piratical operations of the scallywag horde of *feringi* mercenaries in the pay of Arakan, voyages in the neighbourhood of that coast were attended by no little peril. In 1630, therefore, we find the Masulipatam factors recommending that the Armagon factory should be supplied with a small armed vessel of 80 to 100 tons burthen for coasting voyages to such places as Arakan and Pegu.[1] Four years later the Masulipatam factors asked for two similar vessels for their own use, and mentioned in support of their request that the Dutch favoured this type of ship because of its adaptability for either trade or fighting. " And now both their and our small vessells will be more usefull than ever," they wrote, " for theres noe thought of trade into the Bay without them, our greater ships ridinge so farre from the shoare, and the Kinge of Arrackans jelliaes (or small boats of warre) ever scoutinge betwixt them and the land, insomuch as neither goods nor provisions cann be brought of without pinnaces of some defence, such as we have nam'd, which may goe up the rivers for the same without feare and transport it to the bigger vessells." [2]

Occasionally a Company's agent on the Coromandel Coast received half-hearted instructions to inquire into the possibilities of trade with Pegu,[3] but in each case opinion appears to have been against such ventures. The few English traders who visited Burma during this period were either interlopers

---

[1] Foster, "English Factories," 1630-3, p. 86; C.S.P.C.E.I., 1630-4, p. 75.

[2] Foster, *op. cit.*, 1634-6, p. 43.

[3] *Ibid.*, 1630-3, p. 301, and 1637-41, p. 144.

or seafaring men in the employment of Indian merchants. Some of the Company's servants stationed on the western coast of the Bay of Bengal carried on clandestine trade with the land of pagodas ; notorious among these was a certain Henry Sill, who, when attached to the factory at Armagon, carried on an extensive business in exporting Coromandel cloth to Pegu, Arakan, and Tenasserim through the Company's native agents at Armagon.[1]

It has already been shown that one of the chief reasons for the East India Company's neglect to follow up its first venture to Pegu was that, on account of the development of its Persian enterprises and the financial strain imposed upon it by the terms of the Anglo-Dutch Treaty of Defence of 1619, the Batavia Presidency and its subordinate agencies were starved of capital and forced considerably to curtail their activities. In 1646 a variety of circumstances, among which local disturbances and Dutch competition were potent factors, brought the Persian trade to a somewhat abrupt standstill.[2] From Mokha, Basra, and Gombroon alike came reports of bad markets. The Surat Council, therefore, began once more to consider the possibility of opening out fresh markets on the eastern side of the Indian Ocean, and decided " to seeke out new employment for its shipping in more remote parts, as Pegou and Johore." [3]

The success of private trading voyages made to Burma by ships fitted out by individual members of the Company,[4] and the reports of the prosperous state of the Dutch trade in that quarter, whetted the appetite of those responsible for directing the Company's affairs in India for a venture to a land so famous for its rubies and lac.[5] In fact, although the Surat Council reported home in 1648 that the opening of trade with Pegu was the result of the failure of the Persian markets, we find them, as early as January, 1645, asking for more ships in order that they might send some of their smaller vessels to the Coromandel Coast for employment " to the Bay, Pegoo, Denaceree,[6] and other places, from whence, were those trades

---

[1] O.C., Nos. 1375, 1486, 1487 ; and Foster, "English Factories," 1630-3, *passim*.

[2] Foster, *op. cit.*, 1646-50, Introd., p. viii.

[3] *Ibid.*, 1646-50, p. 184. [4] *Ibid.*, 1642-5, p. 76.

[5] *Ibid.*, 1646-50, pp. 89, 98. [6] Tenasserim.

experimented, might be competant gaines."[1]   This point is all the more interesting because the historian Bruce attributed the cause of the Company's earliest trading voyages to Pegu to the war between Visiapore and Golconda in 1648-9, which wrought terrible destruction to the districts around Madras and Masulipatam.[2]

The decision on the part of Surat to extend the scope of the trading operations of the Company was remarkable in view of the pessimism prevailing at that time among the Directors at home.   For over ten years the East India Company had been fighting an uphill fight against a series of attempts made with the active connivance of Charles I.'s Government, to abolish its monopoly in the East.   The association of merchants, which under the leadership of Sir William Courten and Sir Paul Pindar had obtained licence from Charles I. in 1635 to participate in the East Indian trade, threatened the very existence of the East India Company.   To make matters worse, the Long Parliament disliked the Company because of its loyalty to the king and its creation by royal prerogative, and refused to give it any support against Courten's association until it had reincorporated itself upon a Parliamentary basis.   When, after much bribery, the Commons, in 1646, had passed a Bill which effected the necessary reincorporation and gave Courten and his associates three years in which to withdraw completely from the East Indian trade, the House of Lords rejected it in March, 1647, and the Company, unable to raise a fresh stock of capital, ordered its Presidents at Surat and Bantam to cut down their staffs and prepare to wind up its affairs in the East.   Yet, in the teeth of these instructions, we find the Surat council optimistically exploring new openings for trade, confident in the ultimate success of its undertakings.[3]

At the outset the Pegu venture was beset by great difficulties.   The Masulipatam factors were strongly opposed to it,[4] and only the loyal co-operation of Fort St. George made it possible to carry the new scheme through.   Capital to finance the undertaking was lamentably short, but the Company's

[1] Foster, op. cit., 1642-5, p. 229.
[2] Bruce, " Annals of the Honourable East India Company," p. 454.
[3] Foster, op. cit., 1646-50, p. 191.   [4] Ibid., 1646-50, p. 191.

chief creditor, Virji Vora, was persuaded to refrain from pressing for the repayment of the money (amounting to 20,000 rials) that the Surat Presidency had on loan from him.[1] This accommodating financier also went so far as to finance the Pegu undertaking to the extent of 10,000 old pagodas, carrying interest at the rate of $1\frac{1}{16}$ per cent. per month.[2]

During the winter of 1646-7, a serious famine broke out in the Madras neighbourhood, and the Fort St. George factors found themselves in such straits that they were obliged to seek help from Masulipatam. When this was not forthcoming, we find them, in January, 1647, writing to Surat for " 100 or two tunns ordinary rice to preserve the lives of those few painters, weavers and washers who remain about us ; by which meanes wee shall bee the better able to comply with yow in the Pegu investment." [3] They also complained that the civil wars by which the country was then distracted, and the famine, made it difficult to get piece-goods with which to make up the cargo for Pegu.[4]

The factors at Fort St. George hoped to despatch their first shipload of goods to Pegu before the wet monsoon of 1647 set in. But by the middle of May—when the first signs of the great change of weather were expected—no ship had turned up from Surat, and the factors were more than a little exercised in their minds at the delay, which not only hindered their plans, but made it impossible to borrow money locally for the investment.[5] Apparently the Indian brokers would not venture their money until the ship itself materialised. The non-arrival of a ship was due to the fact that the *Lanneret*, which Surat originally intended to send to Fort St. George, was sent instead to Suakin, where the Company had recently opened a factory.[6] In her place it was decided to send the *Endeavour* on her return from Gombroon.[7]

[1] Foster, "English Factories," 1646-50, p. 89.
[2] *Ibid.*, 1646-50, p. 308.   [3] *Ibid.*, 1646-50, p. 74.
[4] *Ibid.*, 1646-50, p. 71.   [5] *Ibid.*, 1646-50, p. 129.   [6] In 1646.
[7] *Ibid.*, 1646-50, pp. 89, 106. In 1644 her captain wrote of her as " the bravest Ship of her Burthen as ever came to Surratt, for shee sayleth better then any Dutch ship that ever wee mett, which doth anger them much, and workes very well." (O.C., 1876, quoted by Love, " Vestiges," I., p. 61, n. 4.) She was sunk by the Dutch in a fight off Gombroon in 1653. Foster, *op. cit.*, 1651-4, pp. 249-53.

After a short detention at Swally for repairs, the *Endeavour* set sail in April for Fort St. George.[1] On her sailed Thomas Breton, who was to take charge of the new factory in Pegu. She also carried a supply of rice and wheat for the relief of the famine-stricken garrison.[2] She arrived at Fort St. George on 22nd May.[3] In their letter to Surat dated 10th May, the factors had pointed out that owing to the monsoon no vessel could be despatched across the Bay to Pegu until August at least. This probably explains why she was not at once freighted for Pegu. In the meantime the Fort St. George factors had other more immediately profitable employment for this vessel. After landing her chief passenger and her cargo of rice and wheat, the *Endeavour* was at once sent up the coast to lade more rice for relieving the famine around Madras.[4] It was estimated by the factors that they could dispose of their surplus rice at 100 per cent. profit.[5] On her return to Fort St. George after discharging her cargo, she was partly freighted for Pegu and then despatched to Masulipatam to complete her lading. From thence she was expected to sail for Pegu in August. Actually, however, she put out from Masulipatam on 15th September with a cargo of goods valued at 20,836 rials of eight.[6]

The factors sent to Syriam on the *Endeavour* to open the first English factory in Burma were Thomas Breton, chief factor, Richard Potter and Richard Knipe. Of these, Potter alone had previously been in Burma, having made a private trading voyage thither together with Richard Cogan, a son —probably illegitimate—of Sir Andrew Cogan, one of the original founders of Fort St. George.[7] Richard Cogan, who was invited to accompany the Syriam expedition, refused to go, preferring instead to fit out a vessel on behalf of the Nawab Mir Jumla designed for the same destination. For this he was arrested and put in irons ready to be sent home to England.

[1] Foster, *op. cit.*, 1646-50, p. 126.
[2] Bruce, " Annals," I., p. 424.
[3] Foster, *op. cit.*, 1646-50, p. 134.
[4] *Ibid.*, 1646-50, pp. 134-5, 139, 164.
[5] *Ibid.*, 1646-50, pp. 74, 135.
[6] *Ibid.*, 1646-50, pp. 135, 139, 163, 165.
[7] Love, " Vestiges," I., p. 58, n. 2.

Mir Jumla, however, secured his release, and he fled to San Thomé, where he " turnd Papist rouge." [1]

In their first letter to Madras, written on 1st January, 1648, the prospecting factors reported that they sighted land on 3rd October.[2] This was probably the golden pagoda on Cape Negrais, which used to be such a landmark for sailors in the days of empirical navigation. Contrary currents, however, prevented them from making Syriam until 23rd October. The prospect in Burma on their arrival was not exactly inviting. In 1635 King Thalun had moved his capital from Pegu to Ava, which, in those days, was a two months' journey by boat from Syriam. When the East India Company's factors arrived in Syriam, they found that without royal permission they could not even relade their ship for a return voyage to the coast. To secure this, they must go in person to Ava. To make matters worse, Thalun's son Shintalok had raised what at first seemed to be a serious rebellion against his father. News of this greeted the factors on their arrival at Syriam. Shortly afterwards, however, the rebellion collapsed, and Shintalok was slain. Not until definite news of this reached Syriam did the factors deem it sufficiently safe to make the tedious journey to Ava.

" Wee found," they continued in their letter to Fort St. George, " the country standing distractedly amazed at the civill warr that then was in Ava (the metropolis of this kingdome) betweene the King and his eldest sonn, not knowing which party to take, till it pleased God to give victory to the King by the slauter of his said sonn, who had determined his death ; which was not believed in Siriam till the middle of December, when there begun to be againe corrispondence between it and Ava, reviveing these merchants in theire bussines and animating us to proceed in the sayle of our goods." [3]

They went on to say that their profits on actual sales were good, but offset by the high customs duties, " which will amount to neare $16\frac{1}{2}$ per cent., and that required in spetia, with more strictnes then wee have ever seene in any other place." Another difficulty arose out of the fact that the

---

[1] Foster, "English Factories," 1646-50, p. 198, and 1651-4, p. 260.
[2] *Ibid.*, 1646-50, p. 177.   [3] *Ibid.*, 1646-50, p. 177.

agents, through whom they had to do their selling,[1] refused to do business unless they entrusted their goods to them for not less than seven months, while a further hole would be made in their profits, they said, by " the exceeding charge which will come upon the ship by her resideing here soe long time as till wee have dispatched our bussines."

They had hoped, they continued, to send the *Endeavour* back to the coast with a cargo of rice, but even if they had not been prevented from so doing by the necessity of securing royal permission for her departure, the condition of her crew would have rendered such a proceeding too hazardous. Her captain, Robert Cherry, her chief mate, Isaac Birkdale, her surgeon and three of the best seamen had died since leaving Masulipatam, and there was much sickness among the crew, occasioned by the " very unhealthful " climate of the country. The *Endeavour* was in dry dock, " to keepe her from the wormes and repaire her sheating, and that at more charge then thought of in this reported (but not truly) cheape country." They requested, therefore, that Rickman, a former chief mate of the ship, should be sent out to take charge of her, accompanied by as many seamen as Fort St. George could spare.

The letter closed in a more optimistic mood regarding the prospects of trade. They were, they said, " not in dispaire (if the country remaine quiett) to make the voyage worth the charge of its tryall, but—they proceeded—this cannot be proved, till you see what wee shall be able to bring you in returne, neither till then can you know, whether the trade be worth the continuance, nor till our better experience of this country shall enable us to informe you, how to follow it with least expence and most advantage." [2] They themselves were about to set out for Ava, having been summoned thither by royal command. As the journey itself would not take less than two months, they estimated that they would be away from Syriam for at least a year. Richard Knipe, therefore, was to be left behind in charge of the factory to collect debts due to

[1] *Vide* Hobson-Jobson, s.v. Tarega.
[2] Foster, *op. cit.*, 1646-50, pp. 177-8, gives a few verbatim quotations from this letter. I have, however, used the original document (O.C., No. 2058) for those given here.

them on sales of goods and " keepe account of the ships expence." In view of the fact that their long stay would exhaust their provisions, they requested that such stores as were unprocurable locally, and especially butter, should be sent to them by Dutch conveyance, " and if you please to acquaint us with the tast of Sack and Beare it will be very proper for this unhealthfull place." [1]

On the journey to Ava, which was begun soon after this letter was written, a fresh disaster awaited the unfortunate factors. It shall be described in their own words. On 27th March, 1648, the Fort St. George factors received by a Dutch ship the following letter [2] from Breton and Potter dated 11th February, 1648, " 20 dayes journy short of Ava ": " When we took our leaves of you at Sirian," they wrote, " wee were sent for by the king in such hast that we have not since had opportunity againe to wright to you, and now greive at this unfortunate occasion. You have already heard how the hand of the Almighty hath been upon us in takeing from us many of our ships company before wee came to Sirian ; nor hath it there staid, but came again upon us in a most deploreable disasture which happened with us yesterday in the morning, when about four of the clock one of the Pegue boatemen, in dressing victualls for his company, sett fire on the boat where wee was, and had laden for our hon'ble Comp'ie besides what hath escaped our memory, 59 halfe bales cotton Yarne all our Salempores [3] all our white Betteelaes [4] except what sold the king which is of both but 158 pieces all our Broad Cloth all our goods rec'd for ffreight all our household stufe and provisions which by the violence of the said fire were before day consumed to little better than nothing, nor doe wee know in this confusion, what more wee have lost then this ; wee have soon utterly spoiled, nor will the hast

---

[1] In the postscript to the letter already quoted. But compare with this Hamilton's statement : " The country is fruitful and healthful, and the air so good, that when strangers come hither in a bad state of health, they seldom fail of a speedy recovery." (Pinkerton's " Voyages and Travels," VIII., p. 428.)

[2] O.C., 2069 (part only of this is given verbatim in Foster, "English Factories," 1646-50, pp. 200-201).

[3] A kind of chintz. Vide Hobson-Jobson, s.v. Salempoory.

[4] A kind of muslin. Vide Hobson-Jobson, s.v. Betheela, Beatelle.

of the boate by which this is sent to Sirian, give us leave to make further discovery in time to advise you thereof. Of what necessaries wee had of our owne wee are utterly stripped, even to our dayly weareing clothes, not haveing left us anything to lie upon in this wilderness save the bare ground ; nor have wee other remedy till wee repaire to the other boate, which conteyneth the remainder of our goods. The ruines of what wee have left, though of very little vallue, yet wee conceive them worth the carriage to Ava ; but such is the cruelty of these people that, seeing us in necessity of a boat, will not be hired to furnish us for less then 500 usest ; [1] which, though it sinck deep into the worth of our burnt goods, yet is better given then that they should be altogeather lost.

" The concideration of the premises hath almost killed our harts with greife, but in this wee finde noe remedie, and therefore must take courage to endeavour to bring what is left to better success, wherein it is impossible wee should be more carefull then wee have been already (though wee have been unfortunate) wee shall only desire your prayers for our future better fortune."

This was not the only disaster of the trip, for in a postscript to this letter they mentioned that on 23rd January Richard Manly, a sailor in charge of one of their boats, fell overboard and was drowned. Notwithstanding these disasters, however, Fort St. George was satisfied with the opening of the venture. It transpired from the list of sales which accompanied the letters from Syriam, that the proceeds were nearly three times the original cost of the goods,[2] and the Fort St. George factors were of opinion that even the loss of one boat-load of goods on the Irrawaddy by fire would not prevent a substantial profit accruing to the venture as a whole. They therefore wrote to Surat that they were glad the advice of the Masulipatam factors had not been listened to when the venture was first mooted. " The abstract of goods sold in Pegue," their letter continued, " and provided here by us in Madraspatam cannot surely chuse but give the Companie good incouragement for the prosecuteinge of the Pegue trade, and likewise

[1] A copyist's error for " viss," i.e. viss of ganza. See Foster, op. cit., 1646-50, p. 200, n.

[2] Foster, op. cit., 1646-50, p. 201.

to give the 1st actors thereof there due comendacons, notwithstanding the unhappie disaster of fire which befell our friends in carrying up of their goods. For disasters are alwaies incident unto merchants. . . . And for disasters," they piously averred later in the same passage, " wee must leave to the will of the Almighty who has the disposure of all things."

It was decided at Fort St. George to send William Curtis, chief mate of the *Farewell* to take charge of the *Endeavour* and return her to Madras, since they were in great need of shipping.[1] Curtis, with two or three English sailors and a stock of provisions, was to be sent out by a Dutch boat due to sail for Syriam in May, 1648. We have no exact information as to the date when the *Endeavour* left Syriam. As late as the end of January, 1649, President Breton of Surat, in his letter home, mentioned her as being still at Pegu.[2] In the following April he wrote that she was expected back from Pegu at the time of writing, and was to return thither with another cargo that was then being prepared for her on the coast.[3] The President and council at Bantam, however, ordered the Madras agency " by such positive comaunds as that Agent etc., pretends they durst not disobay " to send the *Endeavour* to Bantam, and much to the annoyance of Surat the Fort St. George factors complied.[4] On 6th August, therefore, she was despatched from Madras upon a long and stormy voyage to Java in the course of which she lost many of her crew.[5]

Our knowledge of the fortunes of the Company's servants in Burma at this time is sadly deficient. Very few of the letters written by the factors in Syriam and Ava have survived. After the one dated 11th February, 1648, written by Breton and Potter on their way to Ava, the records of the East India Company contain no further letters written from Burma until October, 1653. Our other source of information regarding affairs in Burma, the periodical official letters written by the Agent and Council at Fort St. George, is also

---

[1] In 1648 the Fort St. George factors wrote home to the effect that if the trade to Pegu were to be kept open, two ships of 120 tons burthen must be sent out from England. See also Bruce, " Annals," I., p. 430.

[2] Foster, " English Factories," 1646-50, p. 247.

[3] *Ibid.*, 1646-50, p. 260.

[4] O.C. Duplicates, 2147. Foster, *op. cit.*, 1646-50, p. 279.

[5] Foster, *op. cit.*, 1646-50, p. 271.

non-existent for the years 1649 and 1650.[1]   We may, however, make certain inferences.   The factors apparently were well received in Ava, since the President and Council at Surat, in their official letter to the Company, dated 25th January, 1650, mentioned that they were sending home " a ruby set in a gold ring, the present of the King of Pegue,[2] which is put into the chist of books and papers." [3]   No treaty or articles of trade were made between the Company and the Burmese monarch, but permission was granted to build a house and dock in Syriam, and certain abatements of Customs duties and other privileges were granted in favour of the English merchants.[4]

Notwithstanding the difficulties and disasters which attended it, the initial venture to Pegu was a success financially. In January, 1650, Surat reported home that making allowances for all losses, the profits of the venture would amount to " upwards of 40 per cent., if all debts stand good." [5]   It is remarkable, however, that as late as 1650, the money borrowed from Virji Vora, four years earlier, for financing the venture had not been repaid, and the large sums that had to be paid to him by way of interest caused the Surat Council no small qualms.[6]   The chief cause of the delay was that a sum of money [7] had been raised on the security of the cargo left behind in Burma by the *Endeavour*.   Richard Knipe had been sent with this money to Bengal to make purchases on behalf of the Company.   When, late in 1649, the Fort St. George Council sent the *Greyhound* to Balasore to receive the goods, Knipe and his goods were at Rajmahal, the capital of Bengal, and the boat had to return without them.[8]   Meanwhile the President and Council at Surat found the interest on its loans so heavy that in March, 1650, they wrote home begging for

[1] Foster, *op. cit.*, 1646-50, Introd., p. xxx.

[2] It is uncertain which king is here meant.   They arrived in Ava in 1648.   In that year King Thalun died and was succeeded by Pindale (1648-61).

[3] Foster, *op. cit.*, 1646-50, p. 294.   It was put up at a General Court of Sales held on 27th November, 1650, and fetched £28.

[4] Dalrymple, "Oriental Repertory," II., p. 345.

[5] Foster, *op. cit.*, 1646-50, p. 291.   [6] *Ibid.*, p. 308.

[7] " Near 30,000 ma [hmudis] " (*ibid.*, p. 291), but another account (O.C. 2200) gives it as " neere 6000 rupees."

[8] Foster, *op. cit.*, 1646-50, p. 291.

money to be sent out to enable them to clear off their lia-
bilities.[1]

The Madras factors entertained high hopes of the success
of the new trade connexion opened with Burma.   To a certain
extent their prognostications were justified.   Certainly the
reports we have of the trade to Burma previous to the opening
of the first Anglo-Dutch war in 1652 are such as would have
justified the prosecution of the enterprise.   In October, 1650,
Surat reported home that the Pegu adventure was thriving.
A second cargo of goods had been despatched to Syriam from
Fort St. George in 1640 on board the *Dove*, which had returned
to the coast in March of the following year with news of
plentiful sales and great profits.   She had brought back a
cargo of ganza, rice, and Martaban jars valued at a little over
5159 rials.   The President and Council noted, however, that
the weak spot in the trade to Burma lay in the returns (i.e.
the sales of goods exported from Burma) " which is allwayes
rather loss then gaines, or otherwise the trade would bee the
proffitablest of any you now have or (since that of Manela) [2]
have formerly prosecuted in many yeares." [3]

So optimistic were the coast factors as a result of the
second venture to Pegu, that they decided to buy and fit out
a vessel specially for voyages to Syriam.   Two circumstances
further encouraged them to take this step.   In 1650 the
political outlook in Burma was more promising than it had
previously been for some years.   Ever since the Ming dynasty
had been overthrown in 1644 China had become the prey of
freebooter armies which ravaged her outlying provinces and
made periodic incursions into Burmese territory.   Early in
the reign of Pindale, a Burmese army had been defeated by
the Chinese at Wetwin, near the modern hill-station of
Maymyo, and the invaders had laid waste the country almost
up to Ava itself.   In 1650, however, the Company's factors
at Fort St. George received news that the Burmese had defeated " their plundering neighbours and that the country
was like to be settled and in a peacefull condition." [4]

[1] Foster, "English Factories," 1646-50, p. 308.   [2] Manila.
[3] Foster, *op. cit.*, 1646-50, pp. 317-18.
[4] *Ibid.*, 1650-4, p. 19.   Actually, however, this was but an interval in
a chronic series of raids which went on for over twenty years until put a
stop to by the Manchu dynasty.

The second circumstance which rendered English trading prospects with Burma favourable was that in 1650 it was reported that " the Dutches investment was much damnified and the Nabobs utterly cast away," [1] so that markets were considered likely to prove good for the English merchants. The Masulipatam factors were therefore instructed to buy a vessel of about two hundred tons burthen and fit her out with a crew of Lascars and all necessary provisions. This was done at a cost of a little less than 1600 old pagodas. The new junk—for such she is called in the journal of Charles Wylde, purser of the *Bonito* [2]—was named the *Ruby*, after the famous product of Burma. She was armed with four guns provided by Fort St. George. In addition to her complement of Lascars, seven or eight English sailors were appointed to her, and Thomas Bland,[3] who had been twice previously to Burma as mate, became her master. On 16th September, 1650, she set sail for Syriam with a cargo valued at 3845 rials. In addition, she carried a little freight provided by native merchants trading on their own account, but the Fort factors complained that more freight of this sort would have been carried had not the Governor of Masulipatam forced all native merchants sending goods to Syriam to lade them on his own boat, that was about to sail for the same destination.[4] For three years the *Ruby* was employed in the Syriam trade. In 1653, however, she was sold to a Moorish trader for 800 old pagodas and her crew transferred to the *Bonito*.

On 3rd April, 1651, the *Ruby* returned to Fort St. George after her first voyage to Syriam, bringing with her a cargo valued at over 33,486 rials. A small portion of her cargo was landed at Madras ; about an equal amount was sent up to the Bay factories in a Moorish junk under the care of William Jearsey, who had returned from Pegu on the *Ruby* ; the ship herself was sent to Masulipatam, there to unload the major portion.[5] She brought also to Madras a present from

[1] Foster, *op. cit.*, 1650-4, p. 19. The " nabob " was Mir Jumla, who traded regularly with Burma.

[2] *Ibid.*, 1650-4, p. 6.

[3] In 1655 he was imprisoned in Fort St. George for a scandalous conspiracy with his wife against Agent Henry Greenhill. *Vide* Love, " Vestiges," I., pp. 156-60.

[4] Foster, *op. cit.*, 1651-4, p. 19.

[5] O.C. 2246. Foster, *op. cit.*, 1650-4, p. 97.

the King of Burma to the Agent of Fort St. George, which caused Henry Greenhill[1] and his Council to write home strongly hinting that in this case the Company might relax its rule forbidding its servants from taking presents from native rulers.[2] " In the Pegu invoice," they wrote, " the Kings present to the Agent stands unrated, as what is usually appropriated by the Commander of other Nations, Dutch and Portugalls to their perticuler[3] which wee (haveing noe president[4] from our predecessors) may not doe without your licence, therefore have herewith in Mr. Woods custody sent a small Ivory Box, sealed up, containing a Ruby ring valued heere about £20 sterling, the other part or peece being a small Goulden Bull with more eyes then hee should have through the thinness of the mettle, for a Betel Box[5] valued aboute £30 ; which we retaine here yet unbroaken in honour of the sender, whose Majestie adors the beast and could not in point of state have done us a greater favour."

The same letter contains information of the numbers and names of the Company's servants in Burma. Three " Pegu factors," William Jearsey, Martin Bradgate, and Thomas Howard returned to the Coast on board the *Ruby*, leaving three behind—Knipe, Francis Yardley, and Samuel Archer, who, in another document, is classed as a surgeon.[6] Of the factors who sailed to Syriam on board the *Endeavour* in 1647, Thomas Breton, after his adventurous journey to Ava, must have returned to Fort St. George on the return voyage of that ship in the summer of 1649, since he left Madras for Surat on board the *Expedition* on 3rd October of that year.[7] He had no further connexion with Burma.

It is not a little surprising to find that Richard Potter, who had accompanied Thomas Breton to Ava, was given a gratuity

[1] A full account of his career is to be found in Love, " Vestiges," Vol. I., *passim.*

[2] A précis of this letter is to be found in Foster, *op. cit.*, 1650-4, pp. 97-8. I have relied on O.C. 2246 for the verbatim extract that follows, as only a portion of it is given by Foster.

[3] i.e. perquisite.   [4] Precedent.

[5] An integral part of the regalia of most Eastern potentates. *Vide* Hobson-Jobson, s.v. Betel.

[6] O.C. 2243. I have been unable to discover any information as to the date when any of these factors, except Knipe, went to Burma.

[7] Foster, " English Factories," 1646-50, p. 290.

of £100 for his good service in Burma.[1]   In the first instance
he it was who, by " unwillingness and falce report," was
mainly responsible for the opposition of the Masulipatam
factors to the project of opening a factory in Burma ; apparently he was only with great difficulty persuaded to accompany the venture.[2]   How long he stayed in Burma we do not
know.   In January, 1651, he was reported to be in the neighbourhood of Balasore.[3]   In that year also we find him and
Richard Knipe made responsible for the bad debts to the
amount of Rs. 8000 contracted by the first venture to Syriam.[4]
These, however, were all made good by them.   The Madras
records mention a house belonging to him in that city, where
for some time he lived with his wife and daughter.   He died
in 1653.[5]

Richard Knipe, after his journey to Bengal to buy goods
with the money raised on the security of the stock left behind
by the *Endeavour* in Burma, returned to Syriam as chief
factor early in 1651.   Agent Henry Greenhill, in a letter from
Fort St. George dated 18th January, 1651, mentions him as
having gone to Pegu,[6] but his name does not appear in the
list of factors in Pegu dating from somewhere between 18th
January and 19th February of that year.[7]   As has been
shown above, however, he arrived there before the departure
of the *Ruby* in the following March.   The list referred to
gives the names of Martin Bradgate, William Jearsey, Samuel
Archer, Thomas Howard, John Lawrence, and Thomas Edwin
as factors in Pegu at the beginning of the year 1651.   Of these,
Jearsey and Howard left by the *Ruby* in March.   Lawrence
and Edwin are not mentioned in the list of factors left behind
in Pegu.   In fact, we hear nothing more of them from this
time onwards.   The conjecture may be hazarded that the
" very unhealthfull climate " was the cause of their sudden
disappearance from the East India Company's records.

Our next list, dated 10th January, 1652,[8] gives us Richard

---

[1] Foster, *op. cit.*, 1651-4, p. 16.
[2] O.C. 2072.   Letter of Tho. Ivie and William Gurney at Fort St.
George, to the President and Council at Surat, dated 28th March, 1648.
[3] Foster, *op. cit.*, 1651-4, p. 16.   [4] *Ibid.*, 1651-4, p. 47.
[5] Love, " Vestiges," I., pp. 119, n. 3, 132, 141.
[6] Foster, *op. cit.*, 1651-4, p. 21.   [7] *Ibid.*, 1651-4, pp. 43-4.
[8] *Ibid.*, 1651-4, p. 94.   Also given in Love, " Vestiges," I., p. 106, n. 9.

Knipe, Francis Yardley, and Samuel Archer as in Pegu, and Martin Bradgate[1] and William Jearsey[2] as in the *Ruby* bound for Pegu. Knipe was superseded by Bradgate on the latter's arrival at Syriam in 1652. He did not stand well with the King of Burma, who had been holding up goods the Company wished to export from Martaban, and the Fort St. George Council hoped that Bradgate, who was more popular in Burmese official circles, would manage to secure better relations with the Court of Ava.[3] Knipe's conduct on several occasions had called for severe reprimand. One of his last acts as chief factor at Syriam was to despatch a ship—presumably the *Ruby*—to Madras without a bill of lading, and one is led to suspect him of a habit of appropriating the property of deceased factors which should have been surrendered to the Company.[4] His accounts were badly kept and he caused no little trouble at Syriam after his departure in 1653 by taking with him the account books for the period from March, 1650, to August, 1653.[5] In the absence of any references to him in the Company's records after his departure from Burma we may assume that the Company had no further use for his services.

The *Ruby* left the coast on her second voyage to Syriam on 20th January, 1652. She should have started much earlier, but apparently experienced much difficulty in getting together her necessary complement of crew.[6] She left Madras with nine English seamen besides Thomas Bland, her master; Robert Smith and William Mixer, her mates; and Robert Cowper, her surgeon. She did not return to Madras until May of the following year, when she came in company with

[1] Classed as merchant. He is mentioned as a writer at Fort St. George in 1645. In 1648 he was a member of the Fort St. George Council, and as such signed a letter of that date. (Love, "Vestiges," I., pp. 63, 80, 98.)

[2] Classed as accountant. This is one of the earliest references to him in the East India Company's records. The best source of information regarding this extraordinary man is Love, *op. cit., supra.*

[3] Foster, "English Factories," 1651-4, p. 111.

[4] *Vide* O.C. 2343, for a case in Burma probably relating to the deaths of Edwin and Lawrence. See also Foster, *op. cit.*, 1651-4, p. 21, for a reference to a suspiciously similar action of his in connexion with the estate of William Hicks, a deceased factor of the Courten Association.

[5] O.C. 2343. Foster, *op. cit.*, 1646-50, pp. 32-4; 1651-4, pp. 206-7.

[6] *Ibid.*, 1651-4, p. 111.

the *Bonito*, which had been sent to Syriam in February of that year.[1] This long delay needs some explanation. Agent Henry Greenhill, writing home shortly after her departure from the coast, expressed the opinion that she would not arrive back that year.[2] Unlike the larger English-built vessels, she could not endure the stress of monsoon weather, and so by missing the return sailing season before the wet monsoon of 1652 she would have in all probability to wait for that of the following year.   In the meantime, the outbreak of the first Anglo-Dutch war in 1652, though not immediately affecting the relations between the two nations in the Eastern seas, would cause her to wait for an English ship to accompany her across the Bay.

[1] Foster, *op. cit.*, 1651-4, p. 155, and note.   [2] O.C. 2257.

CHAPTER IV

THE FAILURE OF THE SYRIAM FACTORY

CHAPTER IV

THE FAILURE OF THE SYRIAM FACTORY

THE Anglo-Dutch war of 1652-4 placed the English East India Company's agents in the East in a most uncomfortable position. The Dutch possessed a commanding naval superiority over the English in the Indian Ocean, and not only captured or destroyed several of the Company's ships, including the *Endeavour* and the *Dove*, in which the first two cargoes to Syriam had been shipped, but cooped up English shipping in port in such a way as to render trade almost impossible. Actually, the Company's Western factories around the shores of the Arabian Sea appear to have suffered worse than those on the Coromandel Coast and Bay of Bengal.

The Dutch made no attack upon the English within the limits of the Fort St. George presidency, but on account of their general predominance in the Eastern seas and on the trade routes the Fort St. George factors were literally at their wits' end as to how to get cargoes through to England during most of the year 1653 and the early part of the following one.

Of the effects of the war upon the Company's trade with Burma, we have very meagre information. In 1653 the Syriam factors reported to Fort St. George that the Dutch in Burma offered no " harme or violence " but did their best " to render us odious to the people." [1] For want of English ships they were compelled to make use of Dutch shipping to carry their correspondence. The following extract from one of their letters illustrates the methods they employed to guard against the interception of their letters by the Dutch :—

> " And for as much that at present wee are confined to our enemies shipping (which are all three bound in companie for Bengala) to bring this towards you, wee

[1] O.C. 2343.

shall say the lesse or at least noe more then that in case they should bee intercepted by them which they will narrowly search for, it shall doe them noe good, nor us any harme, but the confidence wee have of the bearer, beeing one of the Nabobs[1] servants which taketh his passage on one of their ships, with the great desire wee have to present our respective salute unto your worships etc., invits us to this single paper wherein wee shall in breefe answere some points recommended to us, and some other matters extant with us." [2]

This letter, dated 25th October, 1653, was received in Fort St. George late in December, 1653, or early in January, 1654, by way of Bengal and Masulipatam.[3] In the same letter the Syriam factors mentioned that the Dutch had intercepted and detained a letter sent from Fort St. George by a Dutch boat which had arrived in Syriam in May, 1653. They had received the letter, however, by a native boat on 8th October. It was dated 7th March. They further related that they were in great straits for want of paper and ink, having previously relied upon the Dutch factory in Syriam for their supplies of these necessaries.

We hear of only one other instance of Dutch hostility towards the English in Burma. Although it belongs to a slightly later stage of our narrative, it may be conveniently related here. The *Expedition* was due to have sailed from Syriam to Fort St. George at the beginning of the dry monsoon of 1653. Her departure was, however, delayed because three Dutch ships lay in wait for her. The Fort St. George factors managed to warn her of her danger by a message carried by a junk belonging to Mir Jumla, whose regular trading operations in Burma have already been noted. Shortly afterwards, one of the blockading ships was wrecked a little south of Narsapur on the Coromandel Coast.[4] But the *Expedition* was effectively prevented from leaving Syriam for the rest of the war. She did not, in fact, reach Madras until March or April, 1655.[5]

---

[1] i.e. Mir Jumla.   [2] O.C. No. 2343.
[3] Foster, "English Factories," 1651-4, p. 221.
[4] O.C. No. 2358. Foster, *op. cit.*, 1651-4, p. 220.
[5] *Ibid.*, 1655-60, p. 33.

The Dutch were undoubtedly in a far stronger position than the English in Burma. Consequently they secured better treatment not only from the Court of Ava, but also from the local officials, to whose palms they were in a better position than the poverty-stricken English Company to apply the requisite amount of grease. The letter written by Bradgate and his colleagues from Syriam in October, 1653, and already referred to above,[1] contains an interesting illustration of their success in dealing with the Burmese Government. " A small vessell of theirs which they formerly took from the Portuguese came hither in July last," they write, " which they say was bound for Batavia, having abord her 14 B[a] [2] of course cloth, which were taken ashore but not customed [3] and after great expence in bribes they have lycence to relade the same goods and depart with the ship and men, of all which (according to the Country Custome) it was generally thought the king would have seized on as his owne, they relateing themselves without examination that they were forced hither by fowle weather, but hee hath showed himself more generous to them then usuall (beeing incited thereto by the Grandees who were well paid for their paines)." The same letter mentions the unexpected arrival of a Dutch fly-boat, the *Overskeet*, which, to the great surprise of the English, was given permission to depart by the Burmese governor of Syriam without having to deliver up a portion of her arms and ammunition. The writers hint that the large annual presents made to the king and important officials by the Dutch were the cause of this generous treatment.

In February, 1653, Fort St. George deemed it unsafe to send the *Bonito* to Bantam ; she was therefore ordered to accompany the *Expedition* from Masulipatam to Syriam. With the two vessels went Agent Henry Greenhill. It would appear from two letters written from Bantam [4] and Surat [5] respectively, regarding this voyage, that Greenhill carried to the Syriam factors their earliest official news of the outbreak of war with the Dutch. In the absence of definite information, we are left to guess the object of Greenhill's visit to Burma.

---

[1] O.C. No. 2343.   [2] Bales.
[3] i.e. Customs duties had not been paid on them.
[4] O.C. Nos. 2283 and 2284.   [5] O.C. No. 231.

A passage in the Syriam letter of 25th October, 1653, already referred to on several occasions above, gives the impression that he went there to make enquiries into the general state of affairs in the Company's factory and into Knipe's mismanagement of the accounts. The writers thank Greenhill heartily for his pains in making up their accounts, and express the hope that in future they will be able to send them in fully made up and in proper form. They proceed to explain that most of the confusion was due to Knipe's negligence. As Greenhill returned to Fort St. George on the return voyage of the *Bonito* in April, 1653, he cannot have made the long river journey to Ava during his stay in the country. His mission, therefore, probably had nothing to do with the establishment of better relations between the Company and the Burmese Government. One is tempted to conjecture whether he went thither purely upon the business of the Company.

Martin Bradgate, who had returned to Syriam on board the *Ruby* in 1652, left shortly afterwards for Ava, which he reached on 3rd June. He was greeted by the news that the Company's warehouse there had been destroyed by fire, and with it 1655 viss 24 ticals of ganza. Having with him a consignment of goods for sale belonging to the United Joint Stock, and no place in which to store them, he was obliged to hire a warehouse for six months at a rent of 50 viss of ganza [1] per mensem. He had also to spend 1340 viss upon building a new house for the Company.[2] Very little information is to hand about this trading post at Ava. It was presumably established by Breton and Potter after their ill-starred journey to Ava in 1648. In the " Original Correspondence " there are references to an " Ava Journall and Leidger for the United Joynct Stocks accompt for the yeares 1653 and 1654," and to an "Ava and Syrian Journall and Leidger for the ffourth Joynct Stocks accompt 1650 to 1654." [3] This trading post at Ava is never referred to in the records as a separate factory. Apart from the fact that Ava was the capital of the kingdom, it was not a good trading centre, and the Company probably maintained a house there rather for the ready access it com-

---

[1] A viss of ganza was then worth about one shilling and four pence sterling (*vide* Chapter V.).

[2] Foster, " English Factories," 1651-4, p. 207.   [3] O.C. No. 2541.

manded to the royal ear and the royal godowns than for any more general commercial advantages they hoped to reap through the maintenance of a resident there.   It was, however, possible to carry on a certain amount of direct trade of a profitable nature with the king, into whose storehouses at the capital there flowed an unending stream of revenue in kind.

The city of Ava, first made a royal capital after the fall of Pagan at the end of the thirteenth century A.D., was almost continually in Shan hands until its annexation by Bayinnaung in the sixteenth century.   While the Toungoo dynasty maintained its capital at Pegu, Ava remained a provincial capital presided over by vassal rulers or viceroys. But the silting up of the Pegu river robbed the city of Pegu of its commercial advantages and paved the way for the rise of Syriam as the chief trading centre in Burma.   The cessation, too, of the successive Burmese attempts to conquer Siam caused Pegu, the scene of a fearful disaster at the close of the sixteenth century, to lose its strategic importance in Burmese eyes, while the hostility of the Talaings to the Burmese dynasty that had brought such terrible devastation upon them and their fruitful land, helped to provoke a reorientation of Burmese policy that represented a complete reaction from that inaugurated by the statesmanlike Tabinshwehti.   In 1635, King Thalun removed the capital to Ava, which thenceforward, until captured by the rebellious Talaings in 1752, remained the capital of Burma.

Mr. Harvey is rightly of opinion that a move to Syriam would have accorded better with the country's destiny.[1]   But no one who has devoted any attention to the trade policy of the Burmese kings—if, indeed, their actions in this respect may be dignified by the application of such a term—will find any cause for surprise that the commercial importance of Syriam never led Burmese kings to consider it as a possible royal capital, notwithstanding the striking lesson read to Burma by the Portuguese adventurer Felipe de Brito.   Ava's political importance lay in its ancient traditions and the fact that it was in the centre of the more strictly Burmese districts of the country.   Economically it was attractive to the Burmese Court, because it was situated at the junction of the

1 "History of Burma," p. 193.

Irrawaddy with its tributary the Myitngè, along which the rice of the Kyauksè district could be brought to supply the city. It had few, if any, real commercial advantages. Its sole importance as a trading centre was derived from the fact that as a royal city it attracted to itself a large, though mainly uncommercial, population, and contained the royal godowns, into which flowed an unending stream of tribute and taxation, mainly in kind.

Martin Bradgate, during his stay in Burma, resided chiefly in Ava, probably in order to use his influence with the Court to secure favourable trading conditions for the Company. Through him a certain amount of correspondence was carried on between Fort St. George and the Burmese Court as a result of which the Company secured a rebate of Customs duties on some of their imports into the country.[1] In October, 1653, the Syriam factors reported that he had recently arrived down from Ava, and was about to return thither in order to get the necessary permission for the Company's ships to depart the country whenever they pleased. We gather from their letter that this method of direct negotiation with his Burmese Majesty was the cheapest way of getting things done.[2] Bribery in Burma was an extremely expensive business.

The high hopes of the successful development of the Burma trade entertained by the Fort St. George Agent and Council as a result of the voyages of the *Endeavour* and the *Dove* gradually faded away. The rubies that the Company hoped to get cheaply from the land of their origin, proved so costly to procure that bills of exchange raised upon them according to their value in Burma could not be realised to their full amount in the Indian market. Consequently, in 1652, Greenhill and his Council reported that " the Pegu factors . . . durst not adventure to bring us any (rubies) thence for the account and they did well therein." [3]

On the other hand, good supplies of lac could be procured. Early in 1652 Fort St. George was able to send home 4000 lb. of this commodity in addition to a cargo despatched for sale in Persia, and Agent Henry Greenhill estimated that he could send home fifty tons annually if the Company required it.[4]

---

[1] Foster, "English Factories," 1651-4, p. 207.   [2] O.C. No. 2343.
[3] O.C. No. 2246.   [4] *Ibid.*

He further reported that mainly because of the large returns from Burma he was able to turn over stock to the value of over 37,000 rials from the Fourth Joint Stock's to the United Joint Stock's account, and was therefore encouraged to prosecute the trade to Burma " notwithstandinge the trouble and difficulties thereof."

In 1653, however, the English trade took a decided turn for the worse. " Instead of amendments of the tymes here with us, wee rather finde it to bee daily worse," wrote the Syriam factors in October of that year.[1] The prices fetched by imported goods, they continued, tended to fall, while country produce and merchandise were considerably dearer than previously. The Burmese Government had prohibited, on pain of death, the sale of tin or ivory to foreign merchants, and in order to prevent the smuggling of these articles out of the country had set " diverse new watches . . . in the way to Martavan, from whence most part of those comodities were formerly brought." [2] They would, therefore, they reported, be unable to get the goods due to them, and so would have to take money instead. Moreover, they could not hope to send much ganza because the export of this had also been stopped " and there may not be brought from Pegu more than will defray expenses in Sirian and not to exceed 200v[t] [3] at one time, for which wee must have a pass." They then proceeded to relate the following incident : " The Dutch, a while since, endeavouring by night to pass by the juncans [4] with a boate wherein was laden 3,000v[t] gance, were persued and taken, and the men brought backe bound and suffered imprisonment till such time as the factors here with costly bribes had mitigated the Princes wrath ; which after three daies obteyned their manumission. The gance is transported into the Kings godownes, where it remains dormant." It was so difficult to get commodities for export, they wrote, that had the *Expedition* not been delayed in Syriam port for other reasons, she would have had hardly any cargo with which to return to the Coromandel Coast.

---

[1] O.C. No. 2343.   [2] Foster, *op. cit.*, 1651-4, 207.
[3] i.e. viss.
[4] Customs officers (from *chungam*, a toll). Foster, *op. cit.*, 1655-60, p. 41, n.

So it happened that whereas in the early part of 1652 the Fort St. George Agent and Council had written home explaining that their large stock was due chiefly to the returns from Pegu, in November of the following year they reported that they could barely make ends meet because of the failure of the Burmese trade.[1] " Our Pegu friends," they complained, " complied not with the $\frac{1}{2}$ of what wee expected from them." On the other hand, the " Pegu friends " seem to have had some cause for complaint at the quality of the goods they were expected to vend profitably in Burma. In a letter written by Greenhill and Gurney at Fort St. George to the Company in January, 1652, occurs the following significant passage : " Lastly, be pleased to take notice that wee are advised from the Bay the Broadcloth sent thither proves soe damnified as it will not vend there, for which cause it is intended to Pegu." [2] One is led to think that this was not an isolated case of dumping inferior goods upon Burma, since we find it asserted in 1654 that the goods sent to Pegu from Masulipatam were proverbial for their badness. " If it come from Metchlapatam, wee will not medle with it," the Syriam factors are reported to have said.[3]

By the end of the first Anglo-Dutch war the East India Company's affairs were in a critical condition. The flotation of the United Stock, resulting from the Company's agreement with the Assada merchants at the end of the year 1649, had not succeeded. For this the economic condition of England at the close of the Great Civil War was responsible. Fluid capital was almost exhausted. Only one-tenth of the advertised capital of the United Stock had been actually subscribed. Many of the Assada merchants refused to join the new Joint Stock, and continued their interloping operations in the Indian Ocean. Capital was so scarce that in 1651 no ships could be sent out to the East, and the General Court actually debated whether the formality of electing officers should be discontinued. A number of London merchants was pressing for either the abandonment of the joint stock system of trade in favour of the regulated system or the opening of the trade to all comers. It was represented that the Company was able

---

[1] Foster, "English Factories," 1651-4, p. 213.   [2] O.C. No. 2246.
[3] Foster, op. cit., 1651-4, p. 305.

to carry on so little trade on its own account that its retention of its monopoly was nothing short of farcical.   Again, in 1653, when the United Joint Stock expired, the Company was unable to send ships out to the East.[1]   Added to these difficulties the Dutch war, as we have seen, had brought English commerce in the Eastern seas almost to a standstill.

Faced by such a situation, with Cromwell and the Council of State turning a deaf ear to all their entreaties for help against the interlopers, the Directors decided to reduce considerably the scope of the Company's trading operations.   In May, 1654, therefore, the Surat Presidency received instructions that its factories were to be reduced to Surat, Agra, Ispahan, and Gombroon, while those of the Madras Presidency were to be reduced to Fort St. George and Masulipatam only. The execution of these orders in the latter Presidency would involve the closing of the factories at Balasore in Orissa, Hugli in Bengal, Bantam in Java, Jambi in Sumatra, Macassar in Celebes, Camboja in Indo-China, and Syriam in Pegu.[2]

Fort St. George received news of this decision by a letter from the Company brought by the *Three Brothers* in the middle of September, 1655.   It was therein ordered that with the reduction of the factories to two in number only " noe more but three factors shall be continued in both places, namely, two at the Fort and one at Masulipatam ; which nomber wee conceive will be sufficient, wee having at present noe other occasion wherein to imploy them, except to preserve and maintain those priviledges and immunities which wee have in those parts." [3]   It was further ordained that Thomas Chamber, William Palmer, and Martin Bradgate, who had returned from Burma—presumably on the *Expedition* [4]—were to be offered the three posts.   The Fort St. George President and Council immediately set about carrying into effect the ungrateful task imposed upon them by this order.   On 16th October, 1655, President Greenhill, Thomas Chamber, and Martin Bradgate held a consultation at Viravasaram at which it was decided

---

[1] Hunter, " British India," II., p. 119.
[2] Foster, *op. cit.*, 1655-60, p. 6.   [3] *Ibid.*, 1655-60, p. 35.
[4] I can discover no actual mention of his return in the records.   He was in Fort St. George at the time of the arrival of the *Three Brothers*. (*Ibid.*, 1655-60, p. 37.)

to recall William Jearsey and Robert Cooper from Syriam, leaving behind Francis Yardley upon a salary of " 10 old pagodas or 100 veists gance at most per month . . . to gather in as many of such debts standing out as are [not] desperate and to looke after the howses and dock (which are of value and importance) ; all which upon the utter desertion of those factoryes would bee lost and seized on." [1]

A letter written home to the Company by William Curtis and John Chamber, super-cargoes of the *Three Brothers*, and dated 27th December, 1655, " ready to sayle for Bantam out of Madraspatam rode," explained the reason for this delay in closing the Syriam factory. [2] " Why wee have transgressed soe far from your Worshipps wish is for these following reasons. Those ffactors in Pegu had made soe many debts and have put you to soe much charge in bilding houses, dockes and other accomodaçon that if wee withdrawe the ffactors all your previleges debts and accomodaçon will bee lost therefore it is thought fitt that Mr. ffrancis Yardley shall remaine in Serian & hould the Companies privileges and gather in theyre debts." Greenhill and Chamber, writing home in the following February, gave further stress to this last point : [3] " For there is hopes to recover in diverse debts and by late advise[s] from thence they have gott in many thousands veists of gance that wayt but a conveyance hither," they explain with great plausibility. But the truth of the matter was that in the absence of supplies of capital from home and through their consequent inability to carry on trade on the Company's behalf, the coast and Pegu factors had very naturally employed their time in feathering their own nests. Most of them were so deeply engaged in trading on their own account in Burma that the immediate dissolution of the Syriam factory would have been a very serious matter for them. [4] " Mr. Bradgate in his voyage hath made soe many debts in Pegu," wrote Curtis and Chamber in the letter already quoted above, [5] " on his account alone you are forsed to keepe that nedles ffactory ; and at his returne to the ffort [6] his cash, his credits

---

[1] O.C. No. 2537.   [2] O.C. No. 2515.   [3] O.C. No. 2537.
[4] Foster, "English Factories," 1655-60, p. 40, quotes an interesting Dutch letter from the Hague Transcripts (Ser. I., Vol. XXI., No. 64) on this subject.
[5] O.C. No. 2515.   [6] Fort St. George.

in Pegu and all his sallary will not ballanc his accompts."
Both William Jearsey and Francis Yardley became notorious
later on for their extensive private trading, which they carried
on in defiance of the loudest thunders from London.

Jearsey and Cooper were instructed to return to Madras
bringing with them the fabulous supplies of ganza on board
a Dutch ship, on which passages had been booked for them
by arrangement with the governor of the Dutch factory at
Pulicat.[1] They were expected back at Fort St. George in
April, 1656. Cooper returned on this boat, but without the
ganza. It remained behind in Jearsey's charge, since he
refused to travel on a Dutch boat, and insisted upon waiting
to return on the *Expedition*, "for the Creditt of the Nation
(as hee said) beeing an English ship," wrote Greenhill and
Chamber somewhat incredulously home to the Directors.[2]
But it is significant that this ship, which had recently been
bought of the Fort St. George establishment for 2000 old
pagodas and her name changed to the *Prosperity* by that
indefatigable private trader, Edward Winter, then chief factor
at Masulipatam, was trading in Syriam on her owner's behalf.
She was expected to sail from Syriam three days after the
Dutch boat upon which Cooper travelled. But, by the
following November, neither Jearsey nor the ganza had
materialised, and although Fort St. George still optimistically
held out hopes that the amount of ganza to be realised was
"neere 20 candy . . . which might yeelde heere neere 800
pagodas new," they reminded the Company that Winter's
ships were usually unfortunate.[3]

What ultimately transpired is related in Greenhill's and
Chamber's next general letter to the Company from the Fort
dated 28th January, 1657.[4] "Wee formerly advised your
Wor^pps: of 7 or 800 pagodas got together of our Pegu Remaines,
and how wee had procured passage for Mr. William Jearsey
(your chiefe there) to bring it with him on a Dutch shipp which
opportunity hee neglected for a passage on the *Expedition* that

[1] O.C. No. 2537.
[2] Foster, *op. cit.*, 1655-60, p. 102.   O.C. No. 2579.
[3] *Ibid.* The book rate of the pagoda was at this time eight shillings
sterling.
[4] O.C. No. 2610.

lost her Monsoone,[1] and but lately arrived with him at Metchle-patam, who not coming hither himselfe, sent his accompts on the Dethick [2] by which wee find a great part of that summe expended in his stay there, contrary to order, besides £100 in ready money taken thereout on accompt of his small wages, which disorderly proceeding, wee noe way approve of, but will speedily endeavour to exact a reason from him (if reason can be given) for such irregular courses, and as soone as possible may bee, recall ffrancis Yardley your sole ffactor now in Pegu, being informed from thence but little more of your estate is recoverable in those parts unless bee the sale of your howses etc. which wee suppose will turne to a poore accompt."

Jearsey's departure from Burma at the end of the year 1656 really brings to a close the history of the Company's first factory in Syriam. We have no exact information as to the date of Yardley's return to the coast. In 1659 he was in Masulipatam preparing to make an interloping voyage to Burma in partnership with a certain Samuel Cropley,[3] also previously a Company's servant.[4] Probably he left Burma not later than the year 1657. At the end of Vol. XXV. of the "Original Correspondence" there is a "List of ffactory's and places where books have been kept since 1658 ; "[5] no place in Burma appears in this list. Probably, therefore, we are right in concluding that the Syriam accounts were closed before 1658.

Apparently the Company never formally surrendered its possession of the Syriam factory site. At a Court of Com-mittees for the United Joint Stock which sat on 14th October, 1656, to value the properties of the Company in the East for the purpose of selling them outright " to some Englishmen," [6] property in Pegu [7] was credited to the Company. At the end of the following year also, when as the result of the grant of a new charter by Cromwell a " New General Stock " was subscribed, and the new undertaking agreed to take over at a valuation all the property of the Company in the East, a house at Pegu is mentioned in the list of goods, privileges,

---

[1] i.e. failed to leave Syriam before the beginning of the wet monsoon.
[2] A private ship.   [3] Foster, " English Factories," 1655-60, p.271.
[4] *Ibid.*, 1655-60, p. 258.   [5] O.C. No. 2726.
[6] Court Minutes, 1655-9, p. 116. Hunter, " British India," II., p. 124.
[7] The country, not the city, is meant here.

buildings, etc. owned by the Company.[1] It almost seems as if the closing of the Syriam factory was regarded by the Company's servants at first as merely a temporary measure due mainly to the critical condition of the Company's general affairs, and partly to the fact that the trade was unprofitable. Although for over twenty years no attempt was made to reopen the factory or even to maintain possession of it, the Company continued to regard itself as the possessor of property in Burma. Thus, when, in 1680, Sir Streynsham Master began to negotiate for the reopening of direct trade between the Company and Burma, and commissioned Joao Perera de Faria Junior to proceed to Ava for the purpose of presenting certain " Articles of Commerce " to its king, the Fort St. George Council passed the following resolution : " Whereas the Company have ground and houses standing thereupon at Seriam, Pegu and Ava which are and have been made use of by strangers for some years past, It is Resolved to give Joao Perera de Faria Junior order to take possession of the said houses." [2]

From this we may infer that when the Company closed its factory in Syriam, the private traders, some of whom, such as Jearsey and Yardley, who had already been to Burma in its employment, continued to use its houses and land. These two men, like so many others who were dismissed the Company's service owing to the economy cuts of the Commonwealth period and found themselves stranded in the East without even passages home provided for them, went to Masulipatam and turned private traders. Jearsey was for some time in association with Sir Edward Winter, who carried on an extensive private trade with Arakan, Burma, and Tenasserim. It has been related above how Jearsey returned from Syriam to the Coromandel Coast late in 1656 or early in 1657 on one of Winter's ships. In the latter year Winter was freighting

---

[1] Foster, *op. cit.*, 1655-60, p. 141.

[2] " Factory Records : Fort St. George," Vol. II., p. 28 (1st March, 1679-80). The word " Pegu " is applied somewhat loosely by writers of this period to both the city of that name and the territory later known as Lower Burma. Here it reads as if the city is meant. No English factory seems ever to have existed in the city of Pegu. Probably the equivocal use of the word in earlier documents is responsible for this error on the part of the Fort St. George Council.

a vessel named the *Tiger* at Masulipatam for a trading voyage to Burma, when she capsized with all her passengers and freight, and was completely wrecked.   The loss was reckoned at not less than 50,000 pagodas.[1]   Small wonder that Winter's boats had a bad name.

After its reorganisation by Cromwell the Company began to take stronger measures against the interlopers and other private traders.   Orders were accordingly sent out for the ships and goods of all such persons to be confiscated.[2]   Complaints regarding the operations of Winter and Jearsey had already been made to Fort St. George,[3] and the Masulipatam factors were ordered to arrest these daring traders.   Their defiance of the Company's orders caused even the Surat Council to take up the matter.[4]   Little, however, was done. Probably the Company's servants themselves were too deeply involved in the business to take the necessary drastic measures. A ship of Winter's, the *Winter Frigate*, which Jearsey and Thomas Turner were freighting for a voyage to Burma, was seized, but although the Fort St. George Council threatened to go themselves to Masulipatam to " unroost " the private traders, the illicit trade to the Eastern coasts of the Bay of Bengal could not be put down.   It is unnecessary here to pursue further the fortunes of Winter,[5] Jearsey, and the other interlopers [6] who traded to the ports of Arakan and Burma during the period between the closing of the Company's factory at Syriam and the embassy of Joao Perera de Faria Junior to Ava.   Only scattered references to their connexion with Burma are to be found in the East India Company's records, and these are usually too vague to be of much value or interest.

One is tempted to wonder why, after Cromwell's reorganisa-

---

[1] Foster, " English Factories," 1655-60, p. 137 : 50,000 pagodas, about £20,000.   [2] *Ibid.*, 1655-60, p. 151.
[3] *Ibid.*, 1655-60, p. 185.   [4] *Ibid.*, 1655-60, p. 273.
[5] Winter gave up the struggle shortly afterwards and left for England with his wife, family, and estate in January, 1660, having made his peace with the Company.   He returned to Fort St. George two years after as President, and his subsequent career was romantic.
[6] Christopher Hatton, Chief at Masulipatam, 1678-80, had, previously to his appointment to the Company's service in 1670, traded in Burma for eleven years.   (*Vide* Temple, " Diaries of Streynsham Master," II., p. 135.)

tion of the East India Company, the old factory at Syriam was not reopened. Probably the restrictions imposed upon trade by the Court of Ava constituted the chief reason. The official records of a later date explain the Company's withdrawal from Burma in 1656-7 as due to unprofitable trade and the attitude of the Burmese Government. " It was the trouble we suffered under the government in Pegue which caused us to Relinquish our trade in that Country heretofore," wrote Sir Streynsham Master in his instructions to Joao Perera de Faria Junior in 1680.[1] In 1683 the Directors wrote to Fort St. George that the Company had previously withdrawn its trading posts from Burma " because y^e: Trade of such places did not maintain y^e: Charge of y^e: Factory Presents &c^a: but wee must confess Wee think y^e: fault might not altogether be in y^e: places, but in y^e: men, Management and direc̃con of them." [2] Possibly the reopening of the Ayuthia factory in Siam in 1662 after nearly forty years of disuse, partly explains the Company's neglect of Burma during this period. The policy of Siam towards foreign merchants was far more enlightened than that of Burma. In 1659, when the Cochin-Chinese plundered the English and Dutch factories at Camboja, the fugitive factors were given such courteous and kindly treatment in Siam by the king [3] that the Company cannot have failed to make mental comparisons between the two Indo-Chinese Governments. In 1663 the Court of Directors placed the Siam trade under Fort St. George on the ground that the cotton goods obtained from the Coromandel Coast were the best for the Siam market. But for some years the trade was comparatively unsuccessful, partly owing to Dutch opposition and to the effects of the second and third Dutch wars, and partly owing to the private trading ventures of Sir Edward Winter and William Jearsey.[4]

[1] " Factory Records : Fort St. George, Diary and Consultation Book," January, 1680-81, pp. 17-19.
[2] " Records of Fort St. George : Despatches from England, 1681-6," p. 38. See also Dalrymple, "Oriental Repertory," II., p. 345, where, in his instructions to Fleetwood and Lesly in 1695, Governor Nathaniel Higginson, of Fort St. George, says that the Company withdrew its previous factories from Syriam and Ava, " the trade proving unprofitable."
[3] Anderson, " English Intercourse with Siam," p. 89.
[4] *Ibid.*, pp. 90-111.

Nevertheless, the extremely friendly attitude of the Siamese king and his willingness to grant trading licences on generous terms made the Company continue to prosecute its Siamese trade, in preference to that with Burma, during the seventh and eighth decades of the seventeenth century.

CHAPTER V

CONDITIONS OF TRADE EXPERIENCED BY ENGLISH
MERCHANTS IN BURMA IN THE SEVENTEENTH
CENTURY

CHAPTER V

CONDITIONS OF TRADE EXPERIENCED BY ENGLISH MERCHANTS IN BURMA IN THE SEVENTEENTH CENTURY

ALTHOUGH the East India Company did not think it worth while to establish a factory in Burma until nearly the end of the first half of the seventeenth century, a certain amount of trade was done with the country through Muslim (" the Moors ") merchants who made the yearly excursion from the Coromandel Coast to Syriam at the end of the wet monsoon. Through these intermediaries they obtained from Burma such things as Martaban jars, small supplies of gold, copper, tin and benzoin, and particularly lac.

Burmese lac seems to have been the best procurable in the East in the seventeenth century. The great demand for this commodity in those days was occasioned mainly by its extensive use in the manufacture of sealing-wax. At the end of the sixteenth century Linschoten was much impressed by the excellence of Burmese lac, and included in his " Voyage to the East Indies " a full account of the manner of its production.[1] In his abridged version of this famous compendium of commercial information, Purchas adds the following interesting note on the use to which lac was put : " They beate the *Lac* to powder, and melt it, and so mixe all manner of colors upon it as they list, red, blacke, greene, yellow, or any other color, and make peeces thereof, such as are sold here to seale letters withall." [2] Linschoten mentions the existence of much trade in this commodity between Burma and Sumatra, where it was bartered for pepper, and whence it was carried to the Red Sea ports, Arabia and Persia. William Methwold, in his " Relations of the Kingdome of Golchonda," [3] describes

---

[1] Vol. II., pp. 88-9, Hak. Soc. edition.
[2] Purchas, *op. cit.*, II., p. 1784 ; Maclehose reprint, X., p. 315.
[3] Purchas, *op. cit.*, V. (1626 ed.), p. 1004.

the trade between that kingdom and Pegu in the following terms : " To Pegu they export much Silver in Rials of eight, Cotton yarne, and Beethyles[1] dyed red, with several sorts of paintings, and bring from thence the perfect Rubies and Sapphires which are dispersed through the World, much Gold, the best Gum Lack, with some Tin and Quicksilver." Methwold, while at Masulipatam, on several occasions sent home small quantities of Burmese lac.[2] But the large general demand for this useful article made the supply of it uncertain, and often caused its price to rise very high.   In December, 1623, President Brockedon at Batavia wrote home to the Directors that the price of lac in Masulipatam depended upon the supplies coming from Pegu and Tenasserim, which were most uncertain.[3] Methwold considered Burmese lac so superior to the Indian variety that he always kept a watchful eye on the Pegu market.[4]   " Burmese lac," he wrote, in 1636, " doth afford to our knowledg a farr deeper tincture (than Indian) and would therefore be more valued in the generall use whereunto it is now imployed."[5]   Three years later President Fremlen at Surat wrote home to the Company of it as a sort " which noe part of the world besides can aequall." " William Methwould," he continued, " remembreth to have sent you such from Mesulapatam, when the way to make use of the tincture was hardly known in England."[6]

Martaban jars—often called Pegu jars—were in great demand in those days for storage purposes on board ship, as well as for ordinary household use.   Extremely large ones could be procured.   We are told by an eighteenth-century visitor to Martaban that he saw some large enough to contain two hogsheads of liquor.[7]   Being low conductors of heat, they were used for carrying fresh water and grain on the merchant vessels of the Indian Ocean.[8]   The East India Company

---

[1] A kind of muslin (*vide* Hobson-Jobson, s.v. Betteela, Beatelle).   The name was often applied to white chintz or organdie.

[2] Foster, " English Factories," 1618-21, p. 343, and 1622-3, p. 45.

[3] Foster, *op. cit.*, 1622-3, p. 338.   [4] *Ibid.*, 1634-6, pp. 66, 146.

[5] *Ibid.*, 1634-6, p. 146.   [6] *Ibid.*, 1637-41, p. 94.

[7] Hamilton, " A New Account of the East Indies," II., p. 63.   He visited Burma in 1709.

[8] Linschoten, "Voyage to the East Indies," I., pp. 30, 268, etc. (Hak. Soc. edition).   See also Hobson-Jobson, s.v. Martaban, where many references to them are collected from works covering the period 1350-1851.

records of the seventeenth century contain many references to them showing how widespread was the demand for them. In view of the large number of references to them that are to be found collected together in that mine of information, Hobson-Jobson, one instance alone, culled from a more recondite source, must suffice. In August, 1650, the Bantam factors wrote to Fort St. George : " When it shall please God to arrive the shipp from Pegu wce desire you to fitt us with as many great Martavans as possible you can and to send us by the first conveyance fild with rice and wheate or in case you have any at present by you, pray send us them." [1]

Bullion was always a welcome commodity to the Company. Having, in the teeth of much opposition, to export bullion from England for trading purposes—in those days England produced few articles of commerce that found a ready market in the East—the Company was always on the look-out for possible supplies in the East, that would partially or wholly relieve it of this difficulty. Its early attempt to exploit the Japanese trade was inspired largely by the desire to obtain silver. In fact, a project for coining silver in Japan, for exchange purposes in Siam and Burma, was once discussed, but came to nothing, because it was found to contravene the law of the land.[2] Gold could be bought for silver at great profit in the bazaars of Pegu. Japanese silver, the factors at Batavia wrote home in 1627, could be exchanged for gold in Pegu at nearly 100 per cent. profit.[3] The great demand for silver in Pegu had its counterpart in a corresponding demand for gold on the Coromandel Coast. In the first half of the seventeenth century the main coinage used by the Company's factors for trading purposes in the Bay of Bengal consisted of the gold pagoda, the standard coin of South India since the days of the Hindu Empire of Vijayanagar, and its subsidiary coin, the fanam, also of gold, though with a very large percentage of alloy.[4] The Company found it more profitable to

---

[1] " Factory Records : Java," Serial No. 3, Part III., 16th August, 1650.
[2] *Vide* letter of William Adams in Purchas, *op. cit.*, II. (Maclehose ed.), p. 338 ; C.S.P.C.E.I., 1617-21, Nos. 86, 226 ; Anderson, " English Intercourse with Siam," pp. 68, 86, 101-2, 192.
[3] O.C. No. 1256, calendared in C.S.P.C.E.I., 1625-29, p. 373.
[4] *Vide* Appendix I., p. 245.

pay its Coromandel weavers (who produced the cotton piece-goods, the main article of commerce exported to the eastern side of the Indian Ocean) in gold than silver, the former, according to report, " being more easily concealed from their Governors." [1]

Although Burma imported silver in the seventeenth century, it was not used for monetary purposes. The Burmese had no coinage proper until 1861, when King Mindon introduced one adapted to that of British India. Payments for merchandise in Burma in the sixteenth and seventeenth centuries were made in ganza (bell-metal), a mixture of copper and lead, according to Caesar Fredericke.[2] He asserts that merchants were accustomed to specify " that their paiment shall be in so many *Ganza*, and neither Gold nor Silver : because that with *Ganza* they may buy and sell everie thing with great advantage." [3] Payments in ganza were made by the viss.[4] As, however, there was no fixed standard maintained by Government, the actual value of the metal varied much according to the amount of lead alloy in its composition. It is impossible, therefore, to give its equivalent in English money of that period with any exactness. In 1650 the East India Company's factors at Swally Marine sent home the accounts of the first venture to Syriam in " vists of gance," stating that " each vest is nearest 16*d* starling." [5] Owing to the grave risk of fraud in payments made in such unregulated bullion currency, the services of an assayer [6] were employed by

---

[1] Foster, " English Factories," 1624-9, p. 181 ; C.S.P.C.E.I., 1625-9, pp. 370-3.

[2] Sanskrit *kansa*, " bell-metal " (*vide* Hobson-Jobson, s.v. Ganza). Ralph Fitch calls it " a kind of brasse " (Purchas, *op. cit.*, II. (1625 ed.), p. 1739, Maclehose reprint, X., p. 191). Hamilton ("A New Account of the East Indies," II., p. 41) calls it simply lead, but it had greatly depreciated in value by his time (*vide* Chapter X., p. 203).

[3] Purchas, II. (1625 ed.), p. 1718, Maclehose reprint, X., p. 132.

[4] One viss = 3 lbs. 5 ozs. 50 dwts. avoirdupois. Cf. Caesar Fredericke in Purchas, Maclehose reprint, X., pp. 131-2 : " This Ganza goeth by weight of Byze (= viss), and this name of Byza goeth for the account of the weight, and commonly a Byza of a Ganza is worth (after our account) halfe a Ducket, litle more or lesse : and albeit that Gold and Silver is more or lesse in Price, yet the Byza never changeth : every Byza maketh a hundredth Ganza of weight, and so the number of the money is Byza."

[5] O.C. Duplicates, No. 2147.

[6] Burmese " pweza " (broker).

merchants in transactions involving a large sum of money.[1] These intermediates were remunerated at the rate of 1 per cent. of the amount of the sale.[2]

Foreign merchants trading to Burma in the days before the British occupation had to conduct all their purchases of commodities for export through another class of broker appointed for this purpose by Government. The tarega,[3] as this half-official, half-broker was called, is mentioned in European accounts of Burma in the sixteenth century when his remuneration seems to have been at the rate of 2 per cent. of the amount of the transaction. The writers of the end of the eighteenth century, however, give it as only ½ per cent.[4] He seems to have been employed by Government to put a check upon the export of certain commodities. The export of various kinds of bullion, particularly gance, was usually forbidden. Saltpetre also might not be exported.[5] Sometimes, too, tin and ivory might not be taken out of the kingdom.[6] These restrictions were extremely galling to the English merchants of the seventeenth century, and were a contributory cause of the rupture of direct trading relations between the East India Company and Burma after the short-lived Syriam venture (1647-57).

Foreign traders and trading prospectors who came to Burma in the sixteenth and seventeenth centuries found their journeys to and from the " land of pagodas " dominated by the North-East and South-West monsoons, which imposed upon travellers certain definite sailing seasons. It was customary for ships proceeding to Burma from the eastern coast of India to set out in September just as the South-West monsoon was on the change. With regard to the outward voyage, the Venetian traveller, Caesar Fredericke, who came to Burma in 1569, has some interesting observations : " Every year there goeth a great ship from St. Thomé to Pegu, of

[1] On this point, see R. C. Temple, " Currency and Coinage among the Burmese," Chapter IV., in " Indian Antiquary," 1897, pp. 197-204.

[2] This system remained in vogue in Upper Burma until long after the introduction of minted coins by Mindon Min in 1861.

[3] *Vide* Hobson-Jobson, s.v. Tarega.   [4] Temple, *op. cit.*, p. 199.

[5] *Vide* Hamilton, *op. cit.*, II., p. 41 : " Saltpetre they have in Abundance, but it is Death to export it."

[6] Foster, *op. cit.*, 1651-4, pp. 206-7.

great importance," he says, " and they usually depart from
Saint Thomé to Pegu the eleventh or twelfth of September, and
if she stay until the twelfth, it is a great hap if she return not
without making her voyage." [1]   This ship, he continues, used
to set out on 6th September, but because she was laden with
a particular kind of dyed cloth that required to be carefully
dried, the ship's departure was put back some days to enable
the cloth to be better dried.   In this way she ran the risk of
being unable to make the coast of Burma before the North-
East monsoon set in.   " For," says he, " in those parts the
winds blow firmly for certain times, with the which they go
to Pegu with the wind in poop, and if they arrive not there
before the wind change, and get ground to anchor, perforce
they must return back again : for that the gales of the wind
blow there for three or four months together in one place with
great force.   But if they get the coast and anchor there, then
with great labour they may save their voyage."

Voyagers from Bengal to Burma usually waited for the
dry monsoon to set in firmly before they embarked upon their
journey.   Thus Caesar Fredericke writes : " Also there goeth
another great ship from Bengala every year, laden with fine
cloth of Bombast of all sorts, which arriveth in the harbour of
Pegu, when the ship that cometh from St. Thomé departeth."
The English traveller Ralph Fitch, who went from Bengal to
the Irrawaddy delta in a Portuguese vessel at the end of the
year 1586, set out from the port of Serampore on 28th
November.

William Methwold's observations on this interesting subject have been quoted above in connexion with the problem
of the date of the return to Masulipatam of the envoys sent
by Lucas Antheunis in 1617 to apply for the restoration of
Thomas Samuel's goods to the East India Company.[2]   These
two factors, it will be remembered, left Masulipatam on board
a vessel belonging to a local rajah on 10th September, 1617.
The circumstances connected with their return to the Coromandel Coast are of especial significance to this discussion.
They attempted to return in April, 1619, but on account of
political troubles failed to obtain the necessary royal per-

[1] Purchas, *op. cit.*, Maclehose reprint, X., p. 128.
[2] In Chapter II., p. 41.

mission, sufficiently early to depart before the beginning of the wet monsoon. This caused them a year's delay.

Let us take another example of this dominance of the monsoons over sailings across the Bay of Bengal. In 1647, as has been noted above,[1] when the Surat President and Council decided to open a factory at Syriam, the *Endeavour* was sent from Surat to Fort St. George to be freighted for the voyage to Burma. Although she arrived at Madras on 22nd May of that year, she did not set sail from the coast for Burma until 15th September. There were other reasons than climatic that partly explain her delay, but they do not fully explain it, and one is left with the impression that she was detained in Indian ports—she ultimately sailed from Masulipatam— mainly in order to wait until the customary sailing season. She returned to Madras shortly before the wet monsoon of the following year broke.

But our best source of information concerning this sailing season for boats plying between the Coromandel Coast and Burma is in the Fort St. George Diaries and Consultation Books. From about 1680 onwards for many years these contain particulars of all ships arriving at and departing from Fort St. George, Madras, in each case with the master's name and the name of the port of departure or destination as the case may be. With few exceptions we find that September was the favourite time for departure from Madras to Burma, and April the usual month for their return. A few ships leave Madras in August and October, and a few return as early as January and as late as May, but the rule applies to the great majority of sailings. The Diary for 1694 shows us three ships sailing from Madras to Burma. Two of them set sail on the 4th, the other on the 8th, of September. The same Diary records the arrival of five ships from Burma, one at the end of February, one in March and three in April. The Diary of 1699 records the arrival of five ships from Burma, two of them in March and three in April. It records also the departure of four ships bound for Burma, one, an exception to the usual rule, on the 17th of April, one on the 31st August, and two early in September.

[1] In Chapter III., p. 53.

The journey between the Coromandel Coast and Syriam took roughly three weeks or a month. Forrest and Staveley left Masulipatam on the 10th of September, and arrived in Syriam on 3rd October. The *Endeavour*, which carried to Burma the factors who opened the first English factory at Syriam, left Masulipatam on 15th September and sighted the coast of Burma on 3rd October, though she did not actually reach Syriam until 23rd October, being delayed by contrary currents. Edward Fleetwood, whose embassy to Ava in 1695 is dealt with in the second volume of Dalrymple's "Oriental Repertory," sailed from Madras on board the *Loyall Captain* on 12th September,[1] and arrived at Syriam on 14th October.[2] When we bear in mind that at the present day Madras is only three days distant from Rangoon in a modern steamship, this tedious, toilsome voyage of the seventeenth century gives us some idea of the progress of applied science in matters of navigation.

But if the voyage from the Coromandel Coast to Burma was tedious, how much more so was inland travel ? Fitch records that the journey from the bar of Negrais through the creeks to the city of Pegu took ten days.[3] Caesar Fredericke writes of the journey by water from Martaban to Pegu as taking three or four days, and explains that the water route was cheaper than the overland one for merchants with merchandise.[4] Forrest and Staveley, in 1617, took three days to do the river trip from Syriam to Pegu in a Burmese boat with six rowers.[5]

The removal of the capital of Burma from Pegu to Ava in 1635 imposed a severe handicap upon traders, since in order to secure permission to trade and licence to depart the country, it was usually found necessary to interview the king in person. The first Englishmen to make the upstream journey from Syriam to Ava were Thomas Breton and Richard Potter, two of the factors sent to open the East India Company's factory at Syriam in 1647. Before starting, they wrote to Fort St. George that the journey was expected to take not less than

---

[1] " Madras Public Consultations," XXII., p. 318.
[2] Dalrymple, " Oriental Repertory," II., p. 355.
[3] Purchas, Maclehose reprint, X., p. 185.
[4] *Ibid.*, X., p. 119.   [5] *Ante*, Chapter II., pp. 37, 38.

two months. The tragic events of this journey have already been related.[1] It is, however, unfortunate that we have no record of the exact dates of the departure of these factors from Syriam and their arrival at Ava. The utter inadequacy of the information contained in the letters of the East India Company's factors in Burma at this time is extremely galling to the investigator. Not a man among them had one-tenth of the descriptive powers of men such as Caesar Fredericke, Fitch, or Methwold. Many letters of this period have undoubtedly been lost, but there is not the slightest trace of anything of the nature of a diary kept by any of the Syriam or Ava factors. A description of Burma in the middle of the seventeenth century, written by Potter, or Bradgate, or even the notorious William Jearsey, however defective, would have proved invaluable to the historian.

Not until the end of the century have we exact details of a journey from Syriam to Ava and back. These are given in the diary of Edward Fleetwood, who was sent upon an embassy to Ava in 1695.[2] Fleetwood left Syriam on 9th November, and arrived in Ava on 23rd December, after what was apparently an uneventful journey. On his return journey he left Ava on 9th February, 1696, arrived at Prome on the 22nd, and at Syriam on the 28th. So it was possible to accomplish the down-stream journey in a much shorter time than the up-stream one. In his diary he mentions that he was in a hurry to get to Syriam, and made all haste possible, so probably he did the journey in record time. His object, of course, was to get his merchandise laded and the ship clear of the coast of Burma before the wet monsoon brought the sailing season to a close. He left Syriam for Madras on 17th March, on the same boat upon which he had made the outward voyage to Burma.[3]

In the sixteenth century foreign ships coming to trade in

[1] *Ante*, Chapter III., pp. 55-58.
[2] Dalrymple, *op. cit.*, II., pp. 355-89.
[3] But the ship was forced to put into Acheen by contrary winds, and did not arrive in Madras until ten months after she left Syriam (*vide* Chapter IX., p. 183). The overhead expenses of carrying on trade between India and Burma must have been enormous, and although we hear that the merchants engaged in it often made gross profits of about 300 per cent., these must have been largely swallowed up by the cost of maintaining ships and sailors idle for so long at Syriam.

Burma put in at either Martaban, Syriam, or a port called by contemporary writers Cosmin, and identified by most modern writers with Bassein. Caesar Fredericke, coming up the coast of Tenasserim, naturally entered Burma by way of Martaban. But the journey to Pegu by the Sittang River was even then (1569) a most unpleasant one, owing to the silting up of the river. He graphically describes the way boats bound for Pegu were forced to catch the "bore" in order to get through the narrow channel to the city—a somewhat dangerous proceeding :—

"And in this voyage you shall have a Macareo, which is one of the most marvellous things in the world that Nature hath wrought, and I never saw any thing so hard to bee beleeved as this, to wit, the great encreasing and diminishing of the water there at one push or instant, and the horrible Earth-quake and great noise that the Macareo maketh where it commeth. Wee departed from Martaban in Barkes, which are like to our Pilot-Boats, with the encrease of the water, and they goe as swift as an Arrow out of a Bowe so long as the Tide runneth with them, and when the water is at the highest, then they draw themselves out of the channell towards some banke, and there they come to anchor, and when the water is diminished, then they rest on drie land : and when the Barkes rest drie, they are as high from the bottome of the channell, as any house top is high from the ground. They let their Barkes lie so high for this respect, that if there should any ship rest or ride in the channell, with such force commeth in the water, that it would overthrow ship or Barke : yet for all this, that the Barkes be so farre out of the channell, and though the water hath lost her greatest strength and furie before it come so high, yet they make fast their Prow to the streame, and often-times it maketh them very fearfull, and if the anchor did not hold her Prow up by strength, shee should be over throwne and lost with men and goods. When the water beginneth to encrease, it maketh such a noise, and so great, that you woulde thinke it an earth-quake, and presently at the first it maketh three waves. So that the first washeth over the Barke, from stemme to sterne, the second is not so furious as the first, and the third raiseth the anchor, and then for the space of sixe hours while the water encreaseth, they rowe with such swiftnesse that you would think they did flie : in these tides there must be lost no jot of time, for if you arrive not at the stagions before the Tide bee spent, you must turne back from whence you came." [1]

Ralph Fitch, coming to Burma from Bengal, landed at Cosmin. He describes it thus : " The Land is very high that we fall withall ; but after we be entered the Barre, it is very lowe and full of Rivers, for they (the inhabitants) goe all to and fro in Boats, which they call Paroes, and keepe their houses with wife and children in them." He then proceeds to relate how he journeyed from Cosmin to Pegu in one of these " Paroes " passing by Dalla and Syriam on the way. Dalla, he says, " is a very faire Towne, and hath a faire Port into the Sea, from whence go many ships to Malacca, Mecca and many other places." Syriam was " a good Towne, and hath a faire port into the sea, whither come many ships from Mecca, Malacca, and Sumatra, and from divers other places. And there the ships stay and discharge, and send up their goods in Paroes to Pegu." [2]

In earlier days, before the silting up of the river, the city of Pegu had been a seaport, but towards the end of the sixteenth century sea-borne traffic could no longer make her harbour, and ships had to unlade their goods at Syriam, and transfer those destined for Pegu into river vessels. With the beginning of the seventeenth century Cosmin, too, lost its importance as a port, partly owing to the terrible devastation of the Delta region, due to Nandabayin's disastrous foreign policy, and partly through the prominence given to Syriam by Felipe de Brito's occupation of it during the years 1599-1613. De Brito's ships blockaded the coast of Lower Burma, and forced all external commerce to pass through Syriam. Throughout the seventeenth century the importance of Syriam completely overshadowed that of either

[1] Purchas, Maclehose reprint, X., pp. 119-20.
[2] *Ibid.*, X., p. 186.

Martaban or "Cosmin." All the English trade and nearly all the Dutch trade to Burma passed through Syriam. Occasionally we hear of Martaban being used for smuggling such goods as tin and ivory out of the country; export of these commodities was sometimes forbidden by the Burmese Government, as has been previously related.

Possessing few ports, Burma could, and did, maintain a strict Customs system. Its rigour vastly impressed Caesar Fredericke. Ships from St. Thomé and Bengal, he said, usually discharged their cargoes at Cosmin, "whither the customers of Pegu come to take the note and markes of all the goods of every man, and take the charge of the goods on them, and convey them to Pegu, into the King's house, wherein they make the Custome of the merchandise, when the Customers have taken the charge of the goods, and put them into Barkes, the Rector of the Citie giveth licence to the Merchants to take barke, and goe up to Pegu with their merchandise; and so three or foure of them take a Barke and goe up to Pegu in companie. God deliver every man that he give not a wrong note, and entrie, or thinke to steale any Custome: for if they doe, for the least trifle that is, he is utterly undone, for the king doeth take it for a most great affront to bee deceived of his Custome; and therefore they make diligent searches, three times at the lading and unlading of the goods, and at the taking of them a land."[1]

The East India Company's factors who opened the first English factory at Syriam have a similar tale to tell. Their profits on sales, they said, were good, but offset by the high Customs duties, "which will amount to neare $16\frac{1}{2}$ per cent., and that required in spetia, with more strictness then wee have ever seene in any other place." Besides the severity of the Customs administration—which, however, could be mitigated by judicious, though heavy, bribes—we notice another interesting feature of Burmese policy: the names of all foreigners entering the country were carefully registered, and no man could depart the country without special permission. When Forrest and Staveley arrived at Syriam in 1617, they were met by two officials sent by the Myosa[2] to record in

---

[1] Purchas, Maclehose reprint, X., p. 129.
[2] "Eater of the town," i.e. governor.

writing their names, ages, and the cause of their coming to Burma.[1] The reason for this was somewhat disconcerting to them : " for what men soever come into his country, he holds them but as his slaves, neyther can any man go out of his Country without his leave, for hee hath watch both by Land and Water." Ships not actually bound for Burma, but forced by stress of weather or lack of provisions to put into Burmese ports, were liable to seizure by the Government. Their cargoes would be confiscated and their crews forcibly detained in the country.

These customs were ironically commented upon by Captain Alexander Hamilton, who visited Syriam in 1709. " When any foreign ships arrive at Syriam," he wrote, " the number of people on board, with their age and sex, are sent to him (i.e. the King of Burma) to let him know that so many of his slaves are arrived to partake of the Glory and Happiness of his reign and Favour. . . . If a stranger has the misfortune to be shipwrecked on their Coast, by the Laws of the Country, the Men are the King's slaves." [2] The chief object of Edward Fleetwood's mission to Ava in 1695 was to secure the release of a Madras merchant named Bartholomew Rodrigues, whose ship had been forced to put in to Martaban for want of wood and water, and had been seized with all she carried, both crew and cargo, by the Burmese royal officials.[3] Hamilton relates that the hpoongyis would often intercede for a shipwrecked mariner and secure his release. In writing of this matter, he pays such a striking tribute to the humanity and hospitality of the old-time Buddhist priesthood of Burma that the passage deserves quoting in full : " When the unfortunate strangers (i.e. shipwrecked mariners) come to their Baws, they find a great deal of hospitality, both in food and raiment, and have letters of recommendation from the Priests of one Convent to those of another on the road they design

[1] See *ante*, Chapter II., p. 37.
[2] Hamilton, " A New Account of the East Indies " (1727 ed.), II., pp. 46, 62.
[3] Dalrymple, " Oriental Repertory," II., pp. 337-9. " Factory Records : Misc.," Vol. 18, ff. 23-5. Anderson, " English Intercourse with Siam in the Seventeenth Century," pp. 271-2, quotes Davenport (" Historical Abstract ") concerning a certain Joseph Demarcora, brother of John D., a " mandarin at Pegu," and described as " the Redeemer of many poor *English* Men, and others, at his vast charge, out of Captivity in *Pegu*."

to travel, where they may expect vessels to transport them to Syrian ; and if any be sick or maim'd, the Priests, who are the Peguers chief Physicians, keep them in their Convent, till they are cured, and then furnish them with letters, as is above observed, for they never enquire which way a stranger worships God, but if he is human, he is the object of their charity." [1]

Apparently it was a long-established Burmese custom to provide with wives all foreigners who were forced to make a protracted stay in the country, either by shipwreck or for commercial reasons. The custom was commented upon by Linschoten in the sixteenth century.[2] No foreigner on leaving the country, however, might take away with him either his Burmese consort or her children. Probably many of the English traders and sailors who frequented Syriam in the seventeenth century, made alliances of this kind. The Fort St. George records of the year 1655 contain a reference to this custom.[3] It would seem that Thomas Bland, a sea-captain whose employment on voyages to Burma by the Company we have already noted,[4] had a real wife in Madras and a temporary Burmese wife in Syriam. The real wife is said to have wished to accompany her husband to Syriam, and to have been with difficulty dissuaded from so doing on the grounds that the Burmese wife would poison her if she put in an appearance at Syriam. Martin Bradgate was responsible for this imputation against the character of the Burmese lady in question, and Thomas Howard is reported in the same document to have said " that when he was at Madraspatam that if any one carried his wife to Pegue, that had kept another in Pegue, she would certainly be the death of her."

The persistence of this custom into the eighteenth century was noted by Hamilton, whose observations thereon are of sufficient interest to be quoted. " The Women," he wrote, " are very courteous and kind to strangers, and are very fond of marrying with Europeans, and most part of the strangers

---

[1] Hamilton, " A New Account of the East Indies," II., pp. 62-3.
[2] Linschoten, J. H., " Voyage to the East Indies," I., p. 98.
[3] " Factory Records : Fort St. George," Vol. I., p. 3.
[4] *Ante* Chapter III., p. 61, and n. 3.

who trade thither, marry a wife for the term they stay."[1]
Referring to the product of these mixed marriages, he continued : " the children cannot be carried out of the kingdom
without the King's Permission, but that may be purchased
for 40 or 50 L sterl. and if an irreconcilable quarrel happen
where there are children, the Father is obliged to take care
of the Boys, and the Mother of the Girls. If a Husband is
content to continue the Marriage, whilst he goes to foreign
Countries about his Affairs, he must leave some Fund to pay
her about six shillings eight pence *per* Month, otherwise at
the year's end she may marry again, but if that sum is paid
her on his Account, she is obliged to stay the Term of three
years, and she is never the worse, but rather the better lookt
on, that she has been married to several European Husbands."[2]

It must by now be obvious to the reader that the general
failure of the great European companies of commerce to
develop a permanent settled trade with Burma was mainly
due to the high cost of maintaining a factory in the country
combined with the general inaccessibility of the resources of
the country for trading purposes on a large scale. Royal
policy and the customs of the country doubtless contributed
their share in augmenting this latter difficulty to a somewhat
abnormal degree.

We are therefore forced to the conclusion that although
certain Burmese commodities strongly attracted the foreign
trader, trade with Burma on a big scale was not a paying
proposition in the seventeenth century. This will be all the
more obvious when we study the attempts made at the end
of the century to reopen an English factory in Syriam.

---

[1] Hamilton, *op. cit.*, II., p. 51.   [2] *Ibid.*, pp. 52-3.

CHAPTER VI

NEGOTIATIONS WITH BURMA, 1680-1686

CHAPTER VI

NEGOTIATIONS WITH BURMA, 1680-6

In 1676 the Dutch East India Company's Council at Batavia decided to close its trading station in Burma. The cause of this step is somewhat obscure : probably the Dutch, like their English competitors, found that the maintenance of a permanent factory in Burma was not a sufficiently paying proposition.[1] Dalrymple's wild assertion that the Dutch, and with them the English, were expelled from Burma because the former " threatened (if they did not even attempt) to bring in the Chinese," [2] cannot be accepted ; but there seems to have been some dispute between the Dutch and the Court of Ava over the question of a proposed Dutch trading station, presumably at Bhamo, for exploiting the trade between Burma and China. In this connexion two entries in the diary of Sir Streynsham Master, made in January, 1680, are illuminating.[3] In the first, he reports having seen a small Dutch ship and sloop off Narsapore which were " bringing all their Factory from Pegu." In the second, he explains that the Dutch withdrawal from Burma was " because the King would not permit them to settle a Factory upon the borders of his Kingdome next China and to be custome free."

The departure of the Dutch from Burma coincided with a revival of interest in the Burmese trade on the part of the Directors of the English East India Company greater than at any time since the closing of the old Syriam factory in 1657. A strong demand had arisen for two important Burmese commodities—sticklac (i.e. lac in its raw condition when first

---

[1] Harvey, " History of Burma," pp. 346-7, has a note on this subject.
[2] " Oriental Repertory," I., p. 98:
[3] " The Diaries of Streynsham Master, 1675-80 " (edited Temple), II., pp. 365, 391.

taken from the tree) and saltpetre.[1] The demand for Burmese lac recurs constantly in the Company's general despatches to Fort St. George in the latter half of the seventeenth century. In the seventies the usual request is for not less than one hundred tons a year ;[2] it is listed as " best Pegu Sticklack, black." Evidently the Burma variety was still considered superior to the Indian, as it had been earlier in the century, since in the General Letter from the Court of Committees to the Hugli factory dated the 24th February, 1675, the following directions are given : " And if you cannot procure the full quantity of Black Pegu Sticklack, then you are to make it up with the best and blackest of such Sticklack as is procurable in the Bay, and Lett it not be shott but sent home in Bales." [3] In 1680 the Agent-Governor and Council of Fort St. George were ordered to increase their next year's cargo of Burmese lac, if possible, by fifty tons.[4]

Saltpetre was an important item in the East India Company's trade, being not only in constant demand for the manufacture of gunpowder, but of great use as ballast in ships returning homewards from the East. Probably, however, the Company's chief anxiety to procure supplies of saltpetre from Burma was dictated by the necessity for arming and fortifying its stations on the mainland of India against the Marathas. Under their brilliant leader, Sivaji, the Marathas had, during the past decade and more, proved themselves a serious danger to the English factories in India. After a series of attacks upon the Western stations which culminated with the capture of Surat in 1677, Sivaji made a great incursion into Southern India in that year, and actually threatened Madras. In the following year Madras was barely saved from plunder by a Maratha reverse in Mysore. The Directors at home, not realising the gravity of the situation and the inability of the Mughal power to protect the English traders, were unwilling to incur the expense of fortifying the Com-

[1] " Factory Records : Fort St. George," Vol. II., " Diary and Consultation Book, 1680-81," p. 14.
[2] *Vide* " The Diaries of Streynsham Master, 1675-80," I., pp. 254, 308, 315, 317.
[3] *Ibid.*, I., p. 315.
[4] " Records of Fort St. George : Despatches from England, 1680-2," p. 14.

pany's factories. But, notwithstanding opposition at home, the work of fortification was undertaken by responsible men on the spot, and feverish attempts were made to put the threatened stations in as defensible a state as might be.

The special demand for these two commodities, coming at the time of the Dutch withdrawal from Burma, led the Fort St. George Council to debate the possibility of reopening the old Syriam factory and planting other trading stations in Burma. It happened that at this time the direction of affairs at Madras was in the energetic hands of Sir Streynsham Master, who was appointed Agent-Governor there in 1677 in succession to Sir William Langhorne. Master had had a long and distinguished career in the service of the Company. His excellent financial work at Surat between 1660 and 1671 had earned for him much praise, while his behaviour on the occasion of Sivaji's attack upon Surat in 1670 had won the thanks of the Directors and a gold medal. Such was the man who, in 1680, reopened negotiations between Fort St. George and the Court of Ava.

The form and method of the negotiations were decided upon by the Fort St. George Council at a consultation held on 23rd February, 1680.[1] It was decided to entrust a Portuguese inhabitant of Madras named Joao Perera de Faria Junior, who knew Burma well, with a commission to treat with the King of Ava concerning eighteen articles of trade that were drawn up by the Council. In the minutes of this meeting the causes of the move are stated to have been the Company's special demands for saltpetre and lac, and the hope of establishing a successful trade with Burma, in view of the recent withdrawal of the Dutch.

In return for his services in negotiating the Treaty, if it were successfully carried through, Joao Perera was to receive one-half of the difference between the Customs duties actually paid on the first full shipment of English goods to Syriam after the Treaty should come into effect, and the usual rate of duties levied at the Burmese port. It was stated that the normal Burmese Customs amounted to " 14 per cent. taken in specie and 2½ per cent. in mony for the Queene after sale of the

---

[1] " Fort St. George Diary and Consultation Book, 1679-80, 1680-1," ff. 14-16.

Remainder of the goods which together is about 16⅛ per cent."
As Master was asking for a reduction of Burmese Customs
duties on British goods to 5 per cent. it was hoped that 11⅛ per
cent. would thereby be saved. The Council therefore expressly stated that the moiety of this 11⅛ per cent. " or soe
much as shall be saved by virtue of the King's concession
upon this Treaty, upon the whole cargo only of the first ship
of the Companys that shall arrive at Sirian after the conclusion of the Treaty," should be paid to Joao Perera " in
consideration of his care and charge in negotiating the said
Treaty." He was also to be allowed the sum of thirty
pagodas towards his expenses and especially for the purpose
of having the Articles translated " into Barma language."
At a later consultation, held on 1st March of the same year,
it was decided to give Joao Perera powers to take possession
of the Company's ground and houses in Syriam and Ava.[1]

In his instructions [2] to the Portuguese envoy, Master
advised him to inform his Burmese Majesty that under the
privileges granted to the Company by the Mughal power,
the import and export of all goods duty free without examination was allowed ; that the Company was absolved from the
burden of making presents to the Mughal and of sending ambassadors to his Court. Moreover, he was to hint that the
obstacles placed in the way of trade by the Burmese Government were the chief cause of the Company's earlier abandonment of its trading stations in the country. If it were possible
to get cheap supplies of saltpetre, Master expressed the hope
that the Burmese Government would allow the Company to
employ native labour in its manufacture, and to export any
quantity of it that might be necessary as ballast for ships
homeward bound, " and for our Kings want of it by reason
of the great expence of Powder in his Sea Warrs with his
neighbours." What, above all, was required was " such a
freedom and liberty for our ffactorys and ships, as may not
discourage our people, for," continued the instructions, " we
have forsaken many profitable Trades by reason of the inconveniences that attend an over-strict and severe usage,

---

[1] "Fort St. George Diary and Consultation Book, 1679-80, 1680-1,"
f. 28.
[2] *Ibid.*, ff. 17-19.

which is altogether needless to the English, who are a friendly and true People to what they promise as they have approved themselves at all times, and upon the Acc^{tt} that they are so acceptable to all Princes in those places where they have any trade their privileges are greater than any other European Nation."

The proposed articles of commerce are of great interest, not only in throwing light upon the peculiar trading conditions experienced by foreign merchants in Burma, but also as giving us an idea of the sort of conditions deemed necessary for successful trading in the East in those days. No apology, therefore, is necessary for giving them here in full. They run thus [1] :—

Articles of Commerce to be proposed to the King of Barma and Pegu in behalfe of the English Nation for the settling of a trade in those Countreys.

1. That the English with their Ships and Merchandize may freely come into the country and Kingdome of Barma and Pegu there reside in safety, be treated with Civillity and Respect, and none of the King's Governours or Ministers or any others suffered to hinder or molest them or their servants, or any belonging unto them, but that they may voyage to and fro at their pleasure in persuance of their trade, sell, buy, and barter according to the Custome of the Country, and as shall be conceded unto these articles without any let or hindrance from the Governours or other the Kings Ministers they may tarry there as long as they think good and depart the Country again when they please.

2. That for and upon all goods and merchandize which the English sell, buy or barter to and with his Majesty the King of Barma and Pegu noe manner of Custome or other duties shall be paid either for importation or exportation of the same, and for and upon all goods and merchandize which the English shall sell, buy or barter to and with the Merchants or Natives of the Country they shall pay but 5 per cent. custome upon the goods imported only and nothing upon goods Exported, and for Silver, Gold, Rubies, Timber, Rice and Provisions of all sorts, no Custome is to be paid in or out.

[1] "Fort St. George Diary and Consultation Book, 1679-80, 1680-1," ff. 19-23.

3. That no Customes shall be paid upon goods which are not sold there, but after six months the English may freely carry the same goods away againe, or pay the five per cent. Customes, which five per cent. to be paid for Customes is to be paid in the currant money of the Country and not in spetie,[1] the goods to be valued at 5 per cent. under the Bazar rate, and in regard it is very inconvenient and prejudiciall to have every parcel of goods opened therefore the English shall give in a list of all their goods, and the officers of the Customes shall if they please only open one parcell of ten chusing which parcells they please.

4. That all the goods which are carryed in the Ships belonging to the English shall pay but halfe the Customes usually paid in the Country although the said goods doe not belong to the English but to Marchants that lade the goods upon freight.

5. That the English may settle ffactorys at Serian Pegu [2] and Ava, and have their old or new ground gratis apointed them by the King and may build them houses and warehouses of Brick or Stone to preserve their goods, and when they shall depart the Country may sell and dispose thereof to their best advantage and alsoe that they may settle a ffactory in like manner at Martavan and send their ships there if they shall think it convenient, and their houses may not at any time be forced or entered into by armed men by vyolence.

6. That the English may freely buy or make Saltpetre and Indico in any parts of the Country, paying the Natives hire for their labour, and export the same in such quantitys as they please, alsoe Lack and all other Commoditys which the Country produces they may export, they promising and obliging themselves not to sell or dispose of any Saltpetre to any other

[1] The distinction here is between ganza and specie, i.e. gold and silver. The value of ganza, in relation to other forms of money current in the Bay of Bengal, was depreciating fast; the Burmese Government throughout the century forced foreign merchants to pay customs in silver. For a discussion of this point, see Chapter X., p. 204.

[2] There seems to have been no real intention to establish a factory in the city of Pegu; on account of the confusion in the use of this word, Master probably thought there had once been an English factory in the city. The word "Pegu," however, when applied to the English factory of the period 1647-57, means no more than "in the land of Pegu," and usually refers to Syriam.

People, but to carry it bona fide to Madraspatam or some other their ffactories in India.

7. To prevent delays in the Despatch of their ships, it shall be permitted them at all times to depart from the Port when the English shall despatch them without attending of orders or license from Ava as hath been accustomed.

8. In case any Rack of Ship or Vessell belonging to the English shall happen in the Kings Dominions (which God forbid) the Kings Ministers and all his subjects shall be obliged to use all meanes possible to save the ship, goods, men and whatsoever else belonging unto them, to restore whatsoever shall be saved, and to prevent all manner of Imbezlement,[1] and to let the Persons goe free with the same.

9. In case of the Mortality of any of the English, the goods, and estate of the Deceased shall be at the dispose of the surviving English according to their manner, and the Kings Ministers shall not intermeddle therein.

10. Offences committed by any of the English shall be punished and accomodated by the Chief of the English and in case any abuse be offered to the English by any of the Kings subjects or others not in the English service, the Kings Governours or Ministers shall doe them present Justice, and the English shall not be obliged to apeale to any Court of Judicature, but only to the King himselfe for the ending of any controversy that may arise, and they shall be free from paying the Acock [2] or 10 per cent. fees or any other fees in law sutes.

11. In case any of the English or any other in their Imployment shall disert their service and fly unto the King or his Ministers or to any others for service or protection, it shall not be laufull to detaine them, but the said person or persons shall be delivered up to the Chief of the English Nation and none of the Kings Ministers may intermeddle in matters which happen between one Englishman and another, or any that serve the English, without the consent of both partys and the Chiefe of the English.

[1] Embezzlement.
[2] Given as Aka by Symes (" Embassy to the Kingdom of Ava," London, 1800), who calls the collector of customs Akawoon. Also written Akaok.

12. That the English may freely exercise the use of the Christian Religion within their ffactorys without any molestation, and if any shall deride or disturb them therein, they are to be punished for soe doing.

13. In case any marchant of the Country shall be indebted to the English or shall refuse or neglect to comply with any agreement made with the English, the Kings Ministers shall use meanes to force every such Person to performe his agreement, and in default thereof the English shall and may take and keepe such Persons as prisoners in their houses until satisfaction be made them, and if any Person be indebted to others besides the English, the Debt which he oweth to the English shall be first satisfied.

14. In case any of the English houses or warehouses shall be robed or plundered, or any their goods or monys forceably taken from them, or their Persons carryed Captive within any of the Kings Dominions by the Kings Vassalls or Subjects, the Kings Majesty is obliged to make Restitution and satisfaction to the English both for the estate and the persons so robed, or plundered or Captivated.

15. That the English shall not be obliged to give any Presents to the Governours either at the Arivall or at the Despatch of their ships, and what is usually paid to those officers of the Kings which doe use to accompany the boates between Ava and Serian, shall be settled at more moderate rates than heretofore.

16. That the English may freely have the disposure of the children which they may have by the women the Natives of the Country to carry or send the same children out of the country, at their pleasure notwithstanding the lawes of the Country.

17. If the King shall hereafter grant any more or other priviledges to any other Nation then what are comprehended in these Articles, the same priviledges are to be granted to the English.

18. Lastly that the King shall issue out his Phyrmaund [1] or Letters of Command to all his Governours, Officers and Ministers of what quality soever, strictly charging and com-

---

[1] From Persian *farmān*, an order ; a word adapted by the East India Company from Mughal governmental terminology.

manding them under severe penaltys to observe these Articles
of agreement with the English Nation upon all occasions
whatsoever.

STREYNSHAM MASTER.

The first and most striking feature of these articles of
commerce is their close application to the peculiar trading
conditions experienced by previous English merchants in
Burma : they constitute a sort of commentary upon the relations between the Company's servants and the Government
of Burma. Point by point they deal with the special dis-
abilities to which foreign merchants were subjected through
Burmese governmental practice or popular custom : the high
rate of Customs duties, the extraordinary restrictions imposed
upon foreigners in regard to departure from the country and
the disposal of their children by Burmese mothers, the harsh
treatment of shipwrecked mariners and the vexatious system
of presents to all officials from the highest to the lowest.

The special powers asked for by Master in order to enforce
the payment of debts and the performance of contracts on
the part of Burmese merchants, refer to an old Burmese
custom noted by both Caesar Fredericke and Ralph Fitch in
connexion with the Burmese system of brokerage.[1] It shall
be described in the words of the latter : " If the Broker pay
you not at his day," he writes, " you may take him home, and
keepe him in your house : which is a great shame for him.
And if he pay you not presently, you may take his wife and
children and his slaves, and binde them at your doore, and
sette them in the sunne ; for that is the Law of the Country." [2]
All foreign traders in Burma had to sell their goods through
these brokers. Article 15 should be read in the light of the
list of goods consigned to Edward Fleetwood and James Lesly
for presents to the King of Burma and the various officials,
both high and low, on the occasion of their embassy to Ava
in 1695. They [3] were valued at no less a sum than 998
pagodas, or nearly £400 sterling.[4] The reference in this

---

[1] Described in the previous chapter.
[2] Purchas, Maclehose reprint, X., p. 191.
[3] Dalrymple, "Oriental Repertory," II., pp. 352-4.
[4] The bulk of these were for the king, but the presents given to each
official will be found *ibid.*, II., pp. 362, 364, 366-7, 371-2, 382-6, 388.

article to the royal officials whose duty it was to accompany merchants travelling by water between Ava and Syriam is interesting, since it leads one to conjecture whether Burmese suspicion of the foreigner, or the semi-independent condition of the royal vassals, was the cause of this proceeding. There is ample evidence from Burmese sources to show that the Burmese Government in the seventeenth century maintained strict control over the riverine communications between Syriam and the capital.

In surveying these articles, we must not allow our knowledge of what the Company ultimately developed into at the end of the next century to affect our interpretation of their spirit. There is no sign of any aggressive or Imperialistic aim in them. How could there be ? Threatened by the Marathas, by the Mughal viceroy of Bengal, and by any petty rajah strong enough to blockade one of its stations ; assailed by bitter criticism at home on the part of rivals such as the Levant Company and the big textile manufacturers, who feared the effects of the import of Indian piece-goods upon their industry, the Company, notwithstanding its financial prosperity and the support of Charles II., was in no position to dictate unequal trading terms to any Eastern potentate. The Company doubted the possibility of conducting successful trade with Burma. These terms, therefore, were regarded by the Fort St. George Agent-Governor and Council as the only reasonable conditions upon which organised trade could be reopened. Far were they from constituting any attempt to secure either unfair commercial advantages or anything of the nature of political influence in the country. And it must be remembered that the privileges of freedom of access to, and egress from, the country, remission of a portion of the Customs duties, and exemption from the obligation of giving presents and of maintaining agents at the Court, were no more than were actually conceded to the Company by the Mughal in respect of its trade in India.

At the same time as this commission was granted to Joao Perera, the Fort St. George authorities decided to issue a cowle or " letter of promise of kind usage "[1] inviting

---

[1] " Fort St. George Diary and Consultation Book, 1679-80, 1680-1," f. 16. Cowle is the Arabic *ḳaul*, a promise. In the minutes of the consultation,

" Pegu ruby merchants " to bring their stones for sale in Madras.

The export of rubies and other precious stones from Burma to the Coromandel Coast dated from time immemorial. The earliest reference to it by a European writer was by Duarte Barbosa early in the sixteenth century.[1] According to him, the merchants of Pulicat bartered Indian coloured cotton stuffs for Burma rubies and spinells of good quality. In the middle of the seventeenth century, as we have seen, the East India Company's factors tried without success to trade in Burma rubies. Probably this was because the rubies of Ceylon were then more acceptable in the Indian market. Tavernier, writing at a slightly later date, states that these latter were " generally finer and clearer than those of Pegu." [2] Writing of Burma, he says : " This is one of the poorest countries in the world, producing nothing but rubies, and those not in so great a number as is generally believed, seeing that taking one year with another the exportation does not amount to one hundred thousand crowns. In the number of these stones you rarely meet with a fine one weighing three or four carats, by reason of the great difficulty of conveying them away till the king has seen them, who always retains all the fine ones he meets with." [3] In Streynsham Master's day

at which this was passed, it was stated that " The Marchants of Pegu having desired a Cowle. . . . It is thought fit to gratifie them therein."

[1] " Description of the East Indies and Countries on the Sea-board of the Indian Ocean (c. 1514)," Hak. Soc., Vol. XXXV., p. 177. For this reference, see Pringle, " Selections from the Diary and Consultation Books of the Agent-Governor and Council of Fort St. George, 1680-1," p. 64, n. 24.

[2] In Pinkerton's " Voyages and Travels," Vol. VIII., p. 251.

[3] Ibid., VIII., p. 250. He also gives the following interesting account of the relative weights and prices of Burma rubies : " The following is an account of the price of some rubies, that might pass for fine ones, which I have in my various travels seen for sale by merchants who came from the mine (i.e. Mogok), when I was at Masulipatam and Golconda. All rubies are sold by a weight called a ' ratis,' which is three grains and a half, or seven-eights of a carat, and the payment is made in old pagodas.

A ruby weighing 1   ratis has been sold for 20 pagodas.

,,	,,	2 and $\frac{1}{8}$	,,	,,	,,	85	,,
,,	,,	3 ,, $\frac{1}{4}$	,,	,,	,,	185	,,
,,	,,	4 ,, $\frac{5}{8}$	,,	,,	,,	450	,,
,,	,,	4	,,	,,	,,	525	,,
,,	,,	6 ,, $\frac{1}{2}$	,,	,,	,,	920	,,

When a ruby weighs more than six ratis and is perfect, it will fetch almost any price."

the Armenians were apparently strongly entrenched in this trade, and Masulipatam is said to have been its chief Indian centre. Probably Master thought that if by special concessions Madras could be made the chief emporium on the Coromandel Coast for Burma stones, its trade in other Burmese commodities would be proportionately enhanced.

In his cowle it was set forth that ruby merchants from Pegu and Ava might freely bring precious stones, gold and silver in any form to Fort St. George. They were to pay no Customs duties on arrival, but were merely to show and register their packages at the Choultry "without being obliged to open the seales." Only brokerage was to be paid on actual sales at the rate of $1\frac{1}{2}$ per cent., plus the Town Broker's fee of $\frac{1}{2}$ per cent. Unsold goods were to be freely carried away without payment of Customs.[1] In order that news of these concessions should be published as widely as possible, it was ordered that the cowle should be translated into Portuguese, " alsoe into Persian, the Gentue (Telugu) and Malabar (Tamil) Languages," and that copies should be sent to various places. It is significant that no mention is made of the necessity of translating it into Burmese. The " Pegu ruby merchants " were not Burmans. Few, if any, Burmans in those days left their country to carry on trade in foreign parts.

What was the upshot of all these preparations for re-establishing English trade with Burma ? On 24th January of the following year Joao Perera returned from Burma to Fort St. George with an answer from the king, which at a consultation held on that day, was ordered by the Agent-Governor and Council to be translated into English and sent home to the Directors.[2] I have been unable to discover any trace of this document ; [3] we are left, therefore, to guess at its contents. This can, however, be done with some degree of certainty, since in a letter from the Government of Burma received some years later at Fort St. George, which will be

---

[1] " Fort St. George Diary and Consultation Book, 1679-80, 1680-1," ff. 23-4.

[2] Pringle, "Selections from the Diary and Consultation Books, etc., 1680-1," p. 2.

[3] No copy is to be found either in the Original Correspondence or the " Factory Records of Fort St. George."

dealt with in due course, a reference was made to the answer entrusted to Perera.[1] The Burmese Government refused to bind itself to any written assurances. If the Company wished to trade with Burma, let it send its own representative to appear with presents before the golden feet, whereupon due favour and pity would be shown. Such was the substance of the reply.

Meanwhile the Directors at home, on hearing of Master's project, were thoroughly opposed to any settlement in Burma. In their despatch to Fort St. George dated 5th January, 1681, they emphasized the fact that although they were particularly anxious to secure large supplies of Burmese lac, they had " no purpose at present to settle a trade at Pegu." [2] Later on in the same letter they repeated their request for Burmese lac, and at the end of the letter, in the list of goods to be provided on the homeward shipping they included 150 tons of " Pegu Sticklack." [3] A year later, in a letter dated 8th February, 1682, they reiterated their intention not to countenance the settlement of a factory in Burma. " Pegu Sticklack," they wrote, " we like well, procure and send us all you can thereof but we do not think it worth our charge to settle a factory there. We hope that you being persons that will study our interest and having so many Portugal and other merchants living under your government and some that trade to Pegu and Acheen contrive with and so encourage them, that they may in the course of their own trades bring to our town of Madras, benjamin and the commodities of Acheen and black Sticklack from Pegu, which you may buy of them at moderate rates and which may come much cheaper to us than by settling of factories in places of such small trade." [4]

The most hopeful result of Joao Perera's visit to Burma was that he was accompanied back to Madras by a number of ruby merchants with considerable quantities of rubies, who promised to settle their trade there.[5] Orders were issued to the Customs officer that he should treat them with a special

---

[1] Pringle, *op. cit.*, Vol. IV., pp. 24, 183-4. Dalrymple, " Oriental Repertory," I., p. 103.

[2] " Records of Fort St. George : Despatches from England, 1680-2," p. 16.

[3] *Ibid.*, 1680-2, pp. 21, 29.   [4] *Ibid.*, 1680-2, p. 72.

[5] Pringle, *op. cit.*, 1680-1, p. 2.

degree of civility in order to encourage more to come. Apparently the scheme was successful. The substitution of brokerage on actual sales for Customs duties constituted treatment so much more liberal than these merchants received in other ports that large numbers of them were attracted to Madras. Sir Josiah Child in 1682 wrote to Fort St. George urging the Agent-Governor and Council to encourage and cultivate this trade, " which peradventure may cheapest be done by such of the Portuguese who you can confide in and that live under your protection," he wrote, " and by their means you may arrive at a large and constant supply of that black Pegu sticklack which we have so often designed and would be very serviceable to us." [1] The extent of the development of this trade from 1681 until the end of the century may be gauged from a despatch from the Directors to Fort St. George dated 9th March, 1703, wherein the Burma trade is called " a considerable branch of the trade of that place " and, what is still more striking, is said to have caused Madras to have become the chief seat of trade with Burma on the Coromandel Coast, a position previously held by Masulipatam [2]

In 1683 the Company's resolution not to settle a factory in Burma was temporarily shaken. Probably as a result of the increase of trade in Burmese commodities in Madras, due to the influx of the ruby merchants, supplies of Burmese musk were obtained, and the Company sent instructions that this trade should be encouraged.[3] Southern Burma had long been known to Europeans for its musk. " Here is all the musk in the world," wrote Alvaro Velho of Pegu in 1498,[4] while another Portuguese observer, in 1505, mentioned a ship from Pegu with a rich cargo of lac, benzoin and musk.[5] Previous to 1683 the East India Company had procured most of its musk from Cochin China.[6] Now the chance of obtaining supplies from a nearer source led Fort St. George once more to press the Directors at home to reconsider their decision against reopening the Syriam factory.

[1] " Records of Fort St. George : Despatches from England, 1680-2," p. 80.   [2] *Ibid.*, 1701-6, p. 46.

[3] Pringle, " Selections from the Diary and Consultation Books, etc., 1683," p. 34.

[4] *Ibid.*, 1683, p. 125. Quoted also in Hobson-Jobson, s.v. Pegu.

[5] Correa, I., p. 611. Quoted in Hobson-Jobson, s.v. Pegu.

[6] Pringle, *op. cit.*, 1683, p. 125.

But the Directors' resolution was shaken not so much by the arguments of Fort St. George as by the extraordinary yarns about the rich profits to be derived from Burmese trade, that were pitched into the ears of James, Duke of York, by a renegade Dutchman named Spar, who had once been head of the Dutch factory in Burma. Our information concerning this episode is contained in two despatches sent by the Directors to Fort St. George in July and October, respectively, of the year 1683.[1] The July one runs thus :—

" Wee see you still incourage y^e: Settlement of a Factory at Pegu and suppose our Ag^t: [2] may remember that wee had formerly a Factory there, and in many other places, w^{ch}: we were forc'd afterwards to withdraw, because y^e: trade of such places did not maintaine y^e: Charge of y^e: Factory Presents, &c^a: but wee must confess Wee think y^e: fault might not altogeather be in y^e: places, but in y^e: men, Management and direc͠con of them. Now wee are so well satisfyed y^t: you will truely weigh and consider y^e: Cost wth: y^e: conveniency for us as cordially as for yor: Selves, Wee shall permitt you to settle there in such manner and upon such termes as you shall thinke most for our advantage, and y^e: rather because a dis-oblig'd Dutchman y^t: was formerly many yeares Chiefe of y^t: place hath given us hyperbolicall comenda͠cons of it, He sayth (if he may be believ'd) he made 40 Tonn of Gold profitt there for the Dutch Comp^a: in a few yeares."

The October despatch contains a fuller account of Spar's statements :—

" There was lately here one Spar. That was formerly Chief for the Dutch at Pegu. Some of Us by his Royall Highnesses [3] Direc͠con have had discourse with him, he seems to be a knowing experienced but an ill natured boysterous, prating fellow, and therefore Wee thought not fitt to trust him. He says Pegu after the Loss of Bantam is the best place of India to build a Fort at, to

---

[1] " Records of Fort St. George : Despatches from England, 1681-6," pp. 38, 55.
[2] William Gyfford, 1681-7.   [3] James, Duke of York.

command our China Trade, and that the Proes[1] of Sumatra may easily and safely bring their pepper thither without hindrance of the Dutch, We told him there was nothing there besides Sticklack towards the Loading of a ship, though there be some Gold, Rubies, Ambergreece, and other fine Goods, accidentally, And that the King of Pegu was a great and proud Prince and would not admitt of Building a Fortificacion nor the trade of that place be worth it, But he abounded in his own sence and would be persuaded to no other. Wee have told you this Story that being nearer and better acquainted with the place you may consider of it, (tho' Wee think there is little incouragem[t]: in it being much more remote from the Pepper Trade than Atcheen) and give Us yo[r]: opinion thereof."

The reasoned wisdom of the Directors' replies to this prater is very striking. They realised clearly that the value of a trading station in Burma depended ultimately upon two factors : the commercial products of the country and the royal policy in relation to trade. Both of these were considered unfavourable to the development of a settled trade on the spot, and whatever hypothetical advantages Burma might afford in connexion with the trade of China and Sumatra were completely offset by these actual and already-experienced disadvantages.

Having been given an inch, the Fort St. George authorities proceeded to take an ell. In September, 1684, it was decided to reopen negotiations with Ava through a certain Captain Peter Dod, master of the *Providence*, a private trading vessel plying between Madras and Syriam.[2] Little information is forthcoming about Dod. In 1675 he was serving as mate of the *Recovery*, a private ship belonging to a certain Robert Fleetwood. Later on he is described as a free " mariner and inhabitant " of Masulipatam engaged in shipbuilding.[3] Dod was instructed to use Sir Streynsham Master's Articles of Trade as the basis of his negotiations, but in addition he was

---

[1] Boats. *Vide* Hobson-Jobson, s.v. Prow, Parao.
[2] Pringle, "Selections from the Diary and Consultation Books, etc., 1684," p. 25.
[3] " The Diaries of Streynsham Master," II., p. 106, n. 3.

asked especially to enquire into the possibilities of opening a station at Bhamo.[1] Evidently the Dutchman's suggestion about making Burma an entrepôt for overland trade with China was seriously considered. For many centuries the bulk of Burma's trade with China had passed along the Taping River, in earlier days through Kaungsin, until the importance of that place was overshadowed by Bhamo from the fifteenth century onwards. It is interesting that the Dutch idea of establishing a station at Bhamo, one of the chief causes of their withdrawal from Burma, should have been passed on to the English by no less a person than the late chief of the Dutch factory at Syriam. Under the particular conditions of foreign trade in Burma, however, the idea was worthless.

Dod sailed for Burma on 15th September, 1684, on board the *Prosperous*.[2] On 4th February of the following year he returned to Fort St. George, bringing with him two letters from an official styled in the Fort St. George Diary the " Chief Governour." They had neither name nor date on them, and although they are stated to have been " enter'd in the Coppy Book of Letters received,"[3] only one of them, in a seriously dilapidated condition, is now on record. In this one the title of the writer is given as " Geakeadar," the Burmese equivalent of which seems to have been " Sitkèdaw." This title was given at Ava to a General ; but it would be unlikely for such an official to negotiate trading matters on behalf of the Burmese Government. On the other hand, the head of the police administration of a provincial capital was termed a " Sitkè," so that in all probability Dod on this occasion did not go in person to Ava, but conducted his business through the Sitkè of Syriam.[4] We have no proof that he actually went to Ava, though he claimed (and received) the sum of 15 pagodas to defray the cost of sending a present to the king at Ava. It is significant that in the official entry of the sanction for this payment in the Consultation Book, the

---

[1] Pringle, *op. cit.*, 1684, p. 101. Dalrymple, " Oriental Repertory," I., pp. 102-3.

[2] *Ibid.*, 1684, p. 104.   [3] *Ibid.*, 1685, p. 25.

[4] The honorific affix " daw " was usually applied only to officials attached to the central government, but as Syriam in those days was always administered by a near relative of the king, some of its chief officials may have been allowed the use of this affix. Or the Sitkè may have assumed it to impress Fort St. George with his greatness.

word " send " is used. As this letter is the earliest direct communication now extant from a Burmese official to an East India Company's servant, it is of especial interest. It also furnishes us with our only first-hand knowledge of the reception accorded by the Burmese authorities to Streynsham Master's proposals. Its style is extremely crude, and its grammar and spelling atrocious, even for the late seventeenth century. One wonders who translated the original; possibly the official interpreter at Syriam—usually a Portuguese. The full text is as follows :—[1]

" I Geakeadar by great lucke and continuall meriting and deserving of my person I bow my head constantly and under y^e: feet of God of y^e: great ma^{ty}: and my King and Lord, I do know and understand y^e: English superior, y^t: we have doe translate into Barmas Languadge y^t: letter w^{ch}: he had sent us, out of w^{ch}: we understand his desire for y^e: establishm^t: of Factories at Syam (Syriam), Pegu and Ava, item y^t: our subaltare Governours, ought to deliver y^m: a good treatment and respect, and by case our Chapmen buy some merchandize wares from y^e: English, and after y^t: did not pay y^m:, then he may oblige y^t: man to pay w^t: he debt to him, item if their ship suffers shipprack, may y^e: saved men return back again at their country without any hinder, item all goods of the deceased Englesman, may his owne people get it in their power, without any conitradiction and contrarity, concerning this 4 or 5 articles, we doubt not his approbation, as w^n: y^e: English superior will service his ma^{ty}: the King my Lord as is his obligation, and upon all ye other articles is not possible to grand approbation, but y^e: sayd superior will come or send somebody heare y^n: we will take our councell in such manner y^t:, we may move y^e: King to piety [2] and I shall do all possible diligence in this matter.

" Since y^e: time of y^e: predecessors of his ma^{ty}: till y^e:

---

[1] Two transcriptions of this letter are available to the student—one, the better, is in Pringle, " Selections from the Diary and Consultation Books, etc., 1685," pp. 183-4 ; the other, in the printed " Records of Fort St. George : Letters to Fort St. George," Vol. III., pp. 27-8. I have used Pringle's transcription here.   [2] Pity.

time of this our King is y^e: use to pay custome of each v
(   )[1] one and therefore men cannot say it must be so or
so but as w^n: you appear before the gold feet of his ma^{ty}:
and service him, y^n: may pray y^m: if he please to do this
favour and grant leave for y^e: export of salpetter, likewise alsoe that yow may exercise yor Cristian duty in yor
Factory, item w^n: the Engles have some pleadings against
another that it may agree before themselfe or may
apresented before his ma^{ty}: y^e: king, item w^n: somebody
owed to an English man and alsoe to another man, must
pay first y^e: Englishman, item Children as well son as
daughter, w^{ch}: an Englishman may begett wth: a woman
of this country he may bring y^m: out of this place without
any molest and hinder, item as when a ship come in
heare he may depart hence again w^n: he please without
takeing leave of y^e: Gov^{er}: of this court, all this and the
rest moor hath told us y^t: cap^t: J^n: Perera de farra,
thereupon we answer its not convenient to propound all
this question, but as well Englishman as other nation,
that come hence and appear wth: their present before the
gold feet of our Royall Person and service them, and
being servant then he may pray his ma^{ty}: to doe him
some favour, and according his deserve he shall receive
it and then we shall see w^t: is just to helpe you in such
manner as shall be necessary."

It is significant that not one word is said about Bhamo.
Nor do we find any further mention in the records of the
project to establish a station there. Either Dod reported
against it, or the Burmese refused to listen to the proposal.
In any case, the Directors at home had no faith in the scheme
for establishing overland trade with China through Burma.
Fort St. George was in no way discouraged by the flat refusal
of the Burmese Government to bind itself by definite articles
of trade. It was decided to send Peter Dod once more to
Burma " to discourse againe with the great men, about our
Settlement there." [2] On this occasion he sailed to Burma on

---

[1] ? viss ; but more than one word is omitted here, so it is impossible
to make sense.

[2] Pringle, *op. cit.*, 1685, p. 51.

the *Providence* shortly before the break of the wet monsoon of 1685. His second mission was like the first, a failure. Returning to Madras in February, 1686, he brought with him another letter, this time from the Government at Ava.[1] This, like so many of the records of the seventeenth century, is no longer extant, but its contents may be inferred from a remark in Dalrymple's "Oriental Repertory."[2] Evidently the Burmese Court did not think Dod a person of sufficient standing to negotiate on behalf of the East India Company, of which he was not even a member.

Poor Dod met with a tragic end. On 25th March, 1686, when his ship, the *Providence*, was weighing anchor in Madras harbour for a return voyage to Burma, he was accidentally killed "by a Barr of the Capstern."[3] By this time, however, the Directors had finally made up their minds not to settle a factory in Burma. The prospects of developing a satisfactory trade in musk were uncertain. "The pot of Pegu musk you sent us by the London," wrote the Directors to Fort St. George in September, 1684, "proved but indifferent; some cods very dry, and some falsified; at the price you paid for it, vizt: 25 Pagodas per catty,[4] there is no profit on it. We used to pay for Tonquin cod-musk no more. However if you can't get it cheaper send us 1000 to 1500 oz. But if to be had at 20 pagodas per catty, you may send five to six thousand ounces : pray let great care be had to its goodness."[5]

On the other hand, adequate supplies of lac were forthcoming as a result of indirect trade,[6] and the Directors were of opinion that without exceptionally good trading privileges in Burma the profits of the trade might be swallowed up by the cost of maintaining a factory there, and then, they wrote, "We do but rise to fall, and make a noise for nothing."[7] So

---

[1] "Fort St. George Diary and Consultation Book, 1686," p. 20.

[2] I., p. 103. "But in 1686, All thoughts of settling were given up, as they insisted, very reasonably, that some Person of consequence should be sent."

[3] "Diaries of Streynsham Master," II., p. 106.

[4] Chinese weight, now equal to 1⅓ lbs. avoirdupois, but in those days it was liable to fluctuate ; Captain John Davis, in 1604, estimated it as equal to 21 ounces avoirdupois. *Vide* Hobson-Jobson, s.v. Catty.

[5] "Records of Fort St. George : Despatches from England, 1681-6," p. 96.

[6] *Ibid.*, 1681-6, p. 88.   [7] *Ibid.*, 1681-6, p. 154.

finally, in August, 1685, they once more sent out definite instructions that the project of establishing a factory in Burma was to be given up. " Pegu will never be a place for us, worth the charge of a factory," they wrote, " so we would have you proceed no further therein." [1]   These orders arrived in Madras some time in 1686, and there for the time being the matter ended. When next it was re-opened, it was the Court of Ava that took the initiative.

[1] " Records of Fort St. George: Despatches from England, 1681-6," p. 165.

CHAPTER VII

THE NEGRAIS EPISODE, 1686-1687

CHAPTER VII

THE NEGRAIS EPISODE, 1686-7

FOR some years after the failure of the negotiations set on foot by Streynsham Master, the project of re-establishing an English factory in Burma was in abeyance. In the meantime, however, the attention of the Fort St. George Agent-Governor and Council was directed to the advantages to be derived from making a settlement on the island of Negrais, near the cape of that name at the southern extremity of Arakan. In the seventeenth century common parlance ascribed the name of Negrais to two islands. Inside the mouth of the Bassein River lies what Alexander Hamilton called " the great island of Negrais," better known in Burma by its Burmese name of Haing-Gyi. But there is also another island directly to the south of the entrance to the Bassein River, usually called then, as now, from its rhomboid shape, Diamond Island. Hamilton called this " the other island of Negrais." [1] It was to the island of Haing-Gyi that the Fort St. George Council referred, when at a consultation on Monday, 12th July, 1686, it recorded the following minute :—

> " Having had a description of Negraes and finding by the Map, that itt is conveniently scituated, for a Harbour for Shipping and provision for men, and having no place for the R^t: Honble: Comp^{as}: Ships to ride out the Monsoon, and that we are advised by severall Pilots, they may Sayl to and from Ballasore Road and this Coast, att any time of the Year, and that the Island is so fertile, time and industry may produce all sorts of Indian goods, as Silk, Sugar, Cotton, Pepper, &c^a: and will be a great check upon Bengall, Pegu and Arrakan, and may be a Mart for the commodities of these parts, we therefore think

[1] Hamilton, " A New Account of the East Indies," II., p. 31.

129

it worth further consideration to have a Settlement there." [1]

A week later it was decided to send " a handsome Present " to the King of Arakan,[2] who had already on several occasions made friendly overtures to Fort St. George, with the request that he cede Negrais to the Company, " he having been the last possessor of itt, and now no Inhabitants there." [3]

The obvious question to ask is : What was behind this move ? There may have been advantages in using Negrais as a place of shelter for ships during the worst months of the wet monsoon. But the other reasons given for the proposed occupation of the island strike one as being somewhat unreal. It is possible, of course, that Fort St. George did seriously believe in the brilliant possibilities of Negrais from the purely trading point of view. Extraordinary and wonderful tales of the commercial value of the place were current in Madras until the tragic failure of the Company's factory there in the middle of the eighteenth century dispelled the illusion. Illusion there undoubtedly was, as the above minute bears witness. But probably for a complete explanation of the step proposed in 1686 we must look further afield and study developments in Siam, which at this time occupied much of the attention of Fort St. George.

King Narai of Siam, who succeeded to the throne in 1658, was unfavourably disposed towards the Dutch, as the latter for some years after his accession had used their naval power to wring special trading concessions out of the unwilling monarch. In order to raise up a counterpoise to them in Siam, Narai sedulously encouraged other European traders, notably the English and French, to settle in the country and extend their commercial activities. In 1661 the English East India Company reopened its factory at Ayuthia, basking

---

[1] " Fort St. George Diary and Consultation Book, 1686," p. 54.

[2] Waradhammaraza (1685-92), one of the puppet-kings set up by the followers of the murdered Mughal refugee, Shah Shuja. These, in the pay of the Court as "Archers of the Guard," dominated Arakan from 1684 to 1710. Probably Fort St. George was unaware of the turn of events in Arakan, and thought it was dealing with Sandathudamma (1652-84), whose policy towards Europeans was rather more enlightened than that pursued by the Court of Ava.

[3] " Fort St. George Diary and Consultation Book, 1686," p. 55. The present was to be of the value of from 150 to 200 pagodas.

in the sunshine of royal favour. Shortly afterwards there arrived from France a batch of Jesuit missionaries, upon whom all manner of royal favours was bestowed. So pleased were the French with their reception, that they began to dream dreams of converting Siam to the Catholic faith, and ultimately of making French political influence supreme there. At first, however, this latter object was not clearly evident, although the Jesuits' efforts to Christianise Siam received the personal encouragement of Louis XIV. Not until the French " Compagnie Royale des Indes Orientales " opened its factory at Ayuthia in 1680 was the full design of France put into operation.[1]

The pro-French policy pursued by the Siamese Government tended to bring about bad relations between Siam and the East India Company. These, in fact, were consciously and deliberately stimulated by that extraordinary adventurer, Constant Phaulkon who, after a meteoric rise, became Minister for Foreign Affairs at Ayuthia in 1683. Phaulkon, through his association with those notorious interlopers George and Samuel White, flouted the Company's claims to a monopoly of English trade in Siam. As time went on, his frequent bickerings with the Company's servants led him to throw his influence increasingly into the scale on the side of its French rivals. In 1680 an ill-fated Siamese embassy, which was shipwrecked off Madagascar, had set out for France, with the intention of offering to cede the rebellious district of Singora, on the eastern side of the Malay Peninsula, to Louis XIV. A little over three years later, in January, 1684, another Siamese embassy left for France, and in September of the following year a magnificent French embassy, headed by the Chevalier de Chaumont, and accompanied by a large body of Jesuits, arrived at Ayuthia, escorted by two French warships.

While the French embassy was being fêted, and was negotiating extensive trading and religious concessions in Siam, an English mission to Ayuthia, despatched by the Agent-General and Council of Fort St. George, arrived to find its pitch so badly queered by the French, that it had to retire

---

[1] Anderson, " English Intercourse with Siam," gives much information concerning French relations with Siam at this period, but a more concise survey will be found in Wood's " History of Siam," pp. 195-221.

with nothing achieved. At the same time, the piratical exploits of two Englishmen in the service of Siam, John Coates and Alexander Leslie, against shipping belonging to the King of Golconda, brought much undeserved blame upon the Company's head, and a state of war between Siam and Golconda. The departure of another Siamese embassy to Versailles at the end of the year 1685, for the purpose of asking Louis XIV. to send troops to garrison Siam, brought matters to a crisis. Alarmed at the francophile trend of Siamese policy, and with its patience exhausted by many " incidents " hostile to English shipping, that arose out of the war between Siam and Golconda, the Company, early in 1686, decided to adopt a policy of reprisals against Siam. For this purpose it was suggested that a settlement at Negrais would have obvious strategic advantages.

In September and October of the year 1686 the first definite steps were taken for the settlement of the island. On 16th September the Fort St. George Council recorded the following arrangements for sending an expedition to the place : " Having taken into our further consideration the Settlem[t]: of Negraes and finding itt absolutely convenient for the R[t]: Hon[ble]: Comp[a]: for many advantages more particularly att this time, we do order as followeth that the Loyal Adventure att her return from the Southern Factorys do go thither M[r]: Higginson [1] to be Chief during his Stay, and return upon her hither, M[r]: Thomas Yale [2] to be Second, to Stay or return, as he shall like of, M[r]: Moody third, to remain there, (till he requests to be removed), with a Writer, Souldiers, Slaves, handicraftmen, and all other provisions and necessarys convenient for the voyage and such a Settlem[t]: which is committed to the care of the Warehouskeeper, and Purser to provide." [3]

[1] Nathaniel Higginson, President of Fort St. George, 1692-8 ; an American by birth.

[2] He entered the Company's service in 1683, when he was sent out from England together with William Strangh to conduct an investigation into the condition of the Company's affairs in Siam. (Wood, " History of Siam," pp. 202-3 ; Love, " Vestiges of Old Madras," I., p. 484, n. 1.) Thomas Yale was brother to Elihu Yale, President of Fort St. George, 1687-92. Like Higginson, the Yales were Americans, Bostoners by birth. (Anderson, "English Intercourse with Siam " p. 267.)

[3] " Fort St. George Diary and Consultation Book, 1686," p. 76.

A few days later, however, the Council changed its plans. It was feared that the unavoidable delay caused by the provision of " Stores and necessarys " for such a large expedition would, on account of the change in the monsoons at that time, prevent it from making its destination.[1]   It was therefore decided to send only Mr. Ambrose Moody on board the sloop *Thomas*, " to make a discovery of the place, and to give us the best acc^t: he can, concerning those Islands, that when itt is a convenient Season, to prosecute the Said Settlement, we may know the better how to order our business." [2]   This decision was made on 27th September, but the *Thomas* was not ready to sail until nearly a month later.   On the morning of the 25th October she put out from Fort St. George, having aboard Ambrose Moody and his party, with a small squad of soldiers " for better defence of those, who go upon the discovery of the place." [3]   Twelve days later, however, she returned, " being drove back by contrary Winds and Currants," [4] and the project was dropped.

Meanwhile, news of the Company's intention to occupy Negrais was conveyed privately to Siam by the captain of the *Phœnix*, which arrived at Bangkok on 18th October, 1686. There he poured the story into the ears of no less a person than the notorious interloper, Samuel White, who since 1683 had held the post of Shahbandar [5] at the Siamese port of Mergui, where he was associated with another renegade servant of the Company, Richard Burneby, lately Chief of the Company's factory at Ayuthia, but in 1686 in the service of Siam as P'ra Marit, or Governor, of Mergui.   From their vantage point at Mergui these two gentlemen were in a position which gave them practical control over the rich trade of Tenasserim.   The captain of the *Phœnix* assured White that the Company's sole object in occupying Negrais was that of " annoying Tenassery." [6]   At the time when he received this

---

[1] *Vide* discussion of this point in Chapter V., pp. 91-4.

[2] "Fort St. George Diary and Consultation Book, 1686," p. 79.

[3] *Ibid.*, 1686, pp. 89, 92, 93.   [4] *Ibid.*, 1686, pp. 106-7.

[5] A Persian word meaning " King of the Haven," applied at native ports throughout the Indian Ocean to an officer vested with special authority over foreign traders and shipping, and hence often chief Customs officer. (Hobson-Jobson, s.v. Shahbunder.   Anderson, *op. cit.*, p. 201 and f. n.)

[6] *Ibid.*, p. 306.

news, White was on his way from Ayuthia to Mergui. Anderson[1] is of opinion that the captain of the *Phœnix* was referring not to the attempt to occupy Negrais that we have described above, but to a rumour that the island was to be occupied by an expedition, consisting of ten ships under the command of Captain Nicholson, that was on its way from England to the Bay of Bengal. The main objective of this expedition was the port of Chittagong, which was to be seized and used as a base of operations against the Mughal Empire, with which at the time the East India Company was engaged in a bitter quarrel.[2] Nicholson's expedition aimed also at conducting reprisals upon Siamese shipping, and for this purpose might well be expected to use Negrais. But White did also hear—from another source—of the projected expedition from Fort St. George under the leadership of Higginson and Yale.

This news evidently caused White no little alarm. He knew full well that if war were actually to break out between the Company and Siam, the former's first objective would be Mergui, the strategic importance of which, as commanding the overland routes to Ayuthia, was known to Great Britain. He himself was in extremely bad odour with Fort St. George, not only because of his interloping activities and his general hostility to the East India Company, but in particular because of his harsh treatment of a number of Madras merchants who had been captured early in 1686 on their way back from Syriam by a Siamese warship commanded by Captain Cropley, and taken to Tenasserim.[3]   In April of that same year they had returned to Madras, where they had submitted to the Governor, William Gyfford, a report of the affair, in which they asserted that they had been robbed of goods to the value of 5158 pagodas,[4] of which 2041 pagodas' worth had been taken from them at the time of their capture, and the rest at Tenasserim by Samuel White. Their account of their treatment is illuminating ; it runs thus :—

[1] Anderson, " English Intercourse with Siam," p. 311.

[2] Hunter, " British India," II., Chapter VII., gives a fairly full account of it.

[3] " Fort St. George Diary and Consultation Book, 1686," pp. 34-5.

[4] About £2063.

" Nilicand Nacoda of the Ship Traga Raja (and other Merchants Mallabars hereunder named) of which Chinnah Vencatadry is owner which sent from this Port to the Port of Sirian, and the foresaid Ship Traga Raja, going out of the Road of Sirian to come to Madras, M^r: Cropley who came first with his Ship took her, and thrust Souldiers on board Said Ship Traga Raja and began to Rob her, and afterwards this Ship which is in this Road, belonging to the King of Siam carrying them all (after robbed) to Tenasseree, and in Tenasseree put them all in prison in a Godown, where they were 8 dayes without eating or drinking undergoing many troubles, untill they could no longer endure out of pure hunger which they Suffered, they began to make a noise, Shouting, and afterwards the Shabunder sent to call them all, and told them they Should pass a paper Signed by them how the said Shabunder did nothing to them, nor take anything from them, and they being oppressed with So much hunger, and troubles which they underwent, they passed not only one but two papers, to which they all signed, not being able to undergo what they had underwent."

Then follows a detailed list of the amount taken from each merchant ; only in one case, however, are the actual items given : " From Nacoda Nilacand the Shabander took 325 Pag^o: in Gold and Silver, and that which they robbed in his Pillow Pocket,[1] Earings which he had in his Ears, and a parcell of Rubies, Musk and other things."

The Fort St. George Governor and Council immediately wrote off to White demanding restitution. The letter was entrusted for delivery to Captain Edward English, commander of the Siamese ship mentioned in the merchants' complaint as being anchored off Madras at the time,[2] having arrived there

---

[1] The words " and that " should be omitted to make sense according to modern usage.

[2] This ship is the one referred to in the letter quoted above. In April of the following year English and his ship, the *Revenge*, were captured at Balasore by Nicholson's squadron, and English was " sent prisoner to Fort St. George to answer several misdemeanours he had committed." (Letter in the *London Gazette*, 18th-22nd August, 1687, quoted by Anderson, *op. cit.*, p. 319.)

late in February, carrying business correspondence from
White at Mergui to Robert Freeman, the Company's chief
factor at Masulipatam. Apparently White never replied.
Nor did he refer to the incident in his petition to the House
of Commons in 1688, when, having escaped the clutches of
the Company in the Indian Ocean, he strove to protect himself from its vengeance on his return to England.[1] When,
therefore, in 1686 he heard of the Company's intention of
occupying Negrais, he at once decided to send an expedition
to seize the island for Siam. Captain Cropley was thereupon
placed in command of two sloops with twenty Siamese soldiers
and provisions for twelve months, and despatched to Negrais
with instructions to leave the soldiers in occupation of the
island. The expedition took with it a placard in Portuguese
claiming the island for the King of Siam.[2] This rash move,
typical of the men who engineered it, came to nothing. Early
in 1687, when Phaulkon heard of it, he issued peremptory
orders for the recall of the expedition. The rest of the story
may be briefly told. Nicholson's expedition failed miserably
in its operations against the Mughal Government in Bengal,
and hence never made any use of Negrais for reprisals against
Siam. The Directors, hearing of the despatch of a second
and much more imposing French embassy to Siam, accompanied by 1400 troops and 300 artificers under the command
of the Maréchal Des Farges, persuaded James II. to write
a personal letter to Burneby and White, asking them to desert
the service of Siam, and hand over Mergui to an English
frigate. Before the letter arrived, however, these two adventurers no longer held Mergui. Two English frigates, the
Curtana and the *James*, commanded by Captain Anthony
Weltden, had arrived off Mergui in June, 1687, bringing with
them a proclamation of James II., ordering all Englishmen
to leave the service of Siam. Weltden's subsequent high-
handed behaviour deeply offended the Siamese officials, who
opened fire on the *James*, which they sank, and stirred up
the populace to massacre all the English on shore. About

---

[1] Anderson, "English Intercourse with Siam," p. 274: the petition is
printed in full on pp. 429-38 of this work, which contains the most detailed
account available of White's romantic career.
[2] *Ibid.*, pp. 311-12.

fifty Englishmen, including Burneby, were killed. White escaped, and, as we have seen, ultimately made his way back to England. Weltden, who was on shore at the time, was felled to the ground in the general scrimmage, but his life was saved by the stoutness of his beaver hat. On regaining consciousness he made good his escape to the *Curtana*, put out to sea, and made his way to Negrais.[1] Here he destroyed the huts and inscription set up by the Siamese expedition under Cropley a few months earlier. Then, having made a survey of the island and hoisted the English colours, he " left an Inscription on Tin, of his Proceedings," and departed.[2]

No further attempt was made by the East India Company to settle the island until 1753.[3] Although Weltden took formal possession of it in the name of Great Britain, this was never made the basis of any claim to it, either by the Company or by any other responsible British authority. The Mergui massacre brought about actual war between Siam and the Company ; but the Siamese preoccupation with the nearer, and more real, danger from France, soon caused this war to die a natural death. The Company, seriously embarrassed by its struggle with Aurungzeb, had to employ all its sea power for the next few years in maintaining its position in India, and could not afford to waste any energy upon developing a naval station at Negrais.

Strictly speaking, the Negrais episode belongs rather to the Company's relations with Siam than to the subject of this book. But the story cannot be omitted, since it illustrates clearly the conditions influencing English action in Indo-China at this time. Lurking behind these activities, and indeed their main cause, lay fear of French attempts to dominate the Bay of Bengal by the exertion of overwhelming naval force. But France, under Louis XIV. and Louvois, was too much bent upon schemes of Continental aggrandisement in Europe to follow a consistent naval policy. Judged in the light of her naval exploits in the war with England and the Dutch, which began very shortly after this episode, she

---

[1] The full story is given in Anderson, *op. cit.*, pp. 308-56. *Vide* Appendix III. for Hamilton's account of the occurrence.

[2] Dalrymple, "Oriental Repertory," I., pp. 103-4.

[3] *Ibid.*, I., p. 97.

cannot be said to have yet developed any conception of the real strategic use of a fleet.   Notwithstanding a French naval expedition to the Bay of Bengal in 1690, as will be seen in the next chapter, the Company was no longer sufficiently alarmed to reconsider the now-discarded project of settling at Negrais. The real objective of the French fleet was Siam.   But French policy in Siam had badly overreached itself, and was about to receive a decisive check.   This fact, coupled with growing exhaustion at home in the struggle against the great European coalition, built up by the diplomacy of William III., rendered French antagonism in the Bay of Bengal for many years inconsiderable.   Partly for that reason—though also largely because the storm-centre of Anglo-French hostility shifted to the mainland of India—we hear no more talk of an English settlement at Negrais until after the close of the War of the Austrian Succession.[1]

[1] *Vide* Appendix IV. for note on the alleged settlement at Negrais in 1687.

CHAPTER VIII

PRIVATE TRADE AND THE AFFAIR OF BARTHOLOMEW RODRIGUES

CHAPTER VIII

PRIVATE TRADE AND THE AFFAIR OF BARTHOLOMEW RODRIGUES

NOTWITHSTANDING the failure of the negotiations with the Court of Ava opened by Streynsham Master through the medium of Joao Perera de Faria in 1680, and the similar fate of Peter Dod's efforts, a considerable private trade developed between the ports of Madras and Syriam. Private merchants and shippers of various nationalities, living under the protection of the East India Company's officers at Fort St. George, managed by personal arrangements with the Burmese authorities to obtain individual grants of privileges, and partial immunity from payment of Customs duties in Burma. The ground, house, and dock once occupied by the Company, continued to be called the " English Factory," though used only by the private traders.[1] The long stay at Syriam, imposed upon ships by the sailing seasons, was of great service to those needing repairs, since excellent materials and useful, though unskilled, labour could be procured for this purpose. The Company allowed English private traders free scope to trade in Burma, so long as they did so in its name and subject to its authority.[2] The Madras traders therefore usually departed for Burma in August or September and returned in March or April, making the English factory at Syriam their headquarters during their stay in the country.

Shortly after the Negrais episode, described in the preceding chapter, the Burmese Government changed its attitude of haughty indifference towards the Company, and began to make overtures to Fort St. George, inviting the settlement of a permanent factory at Syriam. In March, 1688, Henry Burton, master of the *James*, arrived in Madras with letters to the President and Governor from the chief minister at Ava

---

[1] Dalrymple, "Oriental Repertory," II., p. 345.   [2] *Ibid.*, II., p. 346.

and the Governor of Syriam.[1] The letters themselves are no longer extant, but their tenor may be understood from the minutes of a consultation concerning them, held by the Fort St. George Council on 8th March, wherein they are described as " inviting us to a Settlement, upon unusuall good tearms, and priviledges, and that the King would grant us anything, wee could reasonably desire in a Settlement there." [2] This invitation, however, resulted in no renewal of negotiations. In view of the repeated instructions of the Directors that no official settlement was to be made in Burma, Fort St. George dared not move in the matter.

Other reasons also compelled Fort St. George to take no notice of the Burmese offer. The war with the Mughal power, started in 1686, had gone badly. Not only had the English been forced to evacuate the factory at Hugli, but a general attack upon the English stations had resulted in the seizure of the factories at Patna, Cossimbazar, Masulipatam, and Vizagapatam, and the siege of Bombay. Captain Heath, coming out from England with reinforcements in 1688, had been unable to improve matters. Having forced Job Charnock and the Bengal factors to evacuate their post at Sutanati, he made futile attacks upon Balasore and Chittagong; then, after fruitless attempts to enter the service of the King of Arakan, he sailed via Negrais to Madras,[3] having brought the English name into very bad odour.[4]

At home, too, during this period the Company's affairs were once more in a critical condition. The great profits realised by it during the Restoration period had raised up much antagonism to its monopoly; and when, with the " Glorious Revolution " of 1688, it lost its patron, James II., its various opponents were able more effectively to use Parliament as a weapon for breaking their redoubtable antagonist. The failure of the war with the Mughal brought this opposition to a head. A new company, known at first

[1] " Fort St. George Diary and Consultation Book, 1688," p. 43.
[2] *Ibid.*, 1688, p. 46.
[3] *Ibid.*, 1689, p. 13. At Negrais, according to Hamilton, the expedition stayed " to pass the Southwest Monsoons away," and he adds : " The Country assisted them plentifully with Provisions, but they had no other Commerce " (" A New Account of the East Indies," II., p. 30).
[4] Hunter, " History of India," II., pp. 262-4.

as the Dowgate Association, came forward, backed by the Government, to whom it had lent the sum of £2,000,000, and in 1694 the Old Company's monopoly was virtually abolished by a resolution of Parliament opening the trade to the East Indies to all subjects of England equally. Thenceforward, for the next eight years the Old Company was engaged in a life and death struggle with the New Company, as the Dowgate Association came to be called, until the amalgamation of the two companies in 1702 produced the " United Company of Merchants of England trading to the East Indies " and a new era of security at home.

Throughout this period of critical struggles concerning the maintenance of the monopolistic form of trading in the East India Company's sphere of operations, the Company strove to appease its opponents by wise concessions. All English subjects below the age of forty might settle in any place in the East, where it maintained a factory, and freely engage in commerce, so long as they did not trade in prohibited commodities between the East and Europe. Its servants in the East were allowed much latitude in the matter of private trade, and on the expiry of their terms of service were permitted to continue in the East as private traders under the Company's protection. Even its captains and seamen were granted liberal privileges in carrying freight on their own account. Private traders were forced to register with the Company : annual lists of all such living within the jurisdiction of each factory were kept. If the Company were unable or unwilling officially to open up some new field of trade, the private traders would be encouraged to make the first plunge. They often acted as feelers for the Company. This, in fact, was especially their function in the development of trade between Madras and Syriam during the last two decades of the seventeenth century, when the great struggle was raging at headquarters between the supporters of the monopolistic form of trading, led by Sir Josiah Child, and its opponents under Thomas Papillon.

As has been mentioned above, the Company encouraged the private trade between Madras and Syriam : specific instructions to this effect were sent by the Directors to Fort St. George. Permits also were issued by the latter to a number of English inhabitants of Madras, allowing them to depart with their families and settle in Burma. In 1688 and 1689, when Madras was suffering from famine, a number of people, among whom were some of the Company's servants, migrated to Burma. In September, 1688, for instance, Augustine Hart, a merchant trading regularly with Syriam, and the owner of a ship named the *Pegu Merchant*, left Madras for Burma with his family, " and severall of the Inhabitants of this place with him to dwell there by reason of the Great famine here which caused their removalls hence." [1] In the following year one of the Company's sea-captains, Thomas Lacy, commander of the frigate *Sapphire*, was allowed to leave the Company's service in order to embark upon a private trading venture in Burma. [2] Another Company's servant, Thomas Makreeth, in return for permission to leave the Company's service temporarily in order to " make a voyage to Pegu," promised his best services in procuring privileges for the Company from the King of Burma, " and that he would be at the charge of repaireing the factory there, and maintaine such a post as may be to the honour of the R^t: Honble: Comp^a:." The Fort St. George Council, however, ordered that his salary and all other allowances should cease for the period of his absence from Madras. [3] Makreeth did not avail himself of the permission he had sought. Probably he was deterred from pursuing his design by what he must doubtless have heard in Madras about the failure of previous attempts of this nature. European private traders in the East, as we have already seen in the cases of Samuel White and his associates, were often of a lawless type. Those who traded between Madras and Syriam were probably no better than most of their kind. For instance, in June, 1699, upon an official complaint from Siam, Augustine Hart was tried by the Fort St. George authorities and found guilty of robbing a Siamese vessel at Negrais in October, 1697. He was fined 4000 pagodas, half to be paid to the Government of Siam, and half to the Company. Siam's share, however, was appropriated by Fort St. George on behalf of the Company in part satisfaction of a debt, owed

---

[1] " Fort St. George Diary and Consultation Book, 1688," p. 143.   He was a Dutchman.
   [2] *Ibid.*, 1689, p. 66.   [3] *Ibid.*, 1689, p. 68.

to it by the King in respect of money lent to the Siamese Ambassador in Persia.[1]

The most important result of the development of trade between Syriam and Madras, stimulated by Streynsham Master, was in connexion with the building and repair of ships. The teak of Burma had long been famous for ship-building purposes. If we may believe the anonymous author of the " Brief Account of Pegu," [2] the Portuguese Viceroy of Goa, in the sixteenth century had cultivated the friendship of the Burmese kings in order to prevent " the Soldan of Babylonia, and then the Turk, from availing themselves of that country's abundance of wood and other things required for the building of fleets." [3]   Purchas, in 1626, mentioned the existence of a large shipbuilding industry in the Delta at a place called Dian, where vessels as large as galeasses were said to have been built, " having on both sides quite through, roomes for merchandize ; and in the midst a kinde of dwelling house, where they trade." [4]   Very little, if any, European shipbuilding, however, was carried on in Burmese ports before the end of the seventeenth century. Although the East India Company's agents eagerly bought up Burmese timber (" Pegu plank "), when any was offered for sale on the Coro-mandel Coast,[5] not until 1689 have we definite record of a Company's ship being sent to Syriam for repairs. In that year a variety of factors combined to cause the Fort St. George authorities to decide upon sending the frigate *Diamond* thither for repairs, instead of to Vizagapatam. The circum-stances relating to this decision may be best related in the words of the Minute recording it passed by the Council on 23rd August, 1689 :—[6]

" The Persons we sent to survey the Dyamond friggot report that she is much out of repair and in a very leaky Condition, whereupon we had thoughts of sending her to

[1] " Fort St. George Diary and Consultation Book, 1699," pp. 51, 58, 66.
[2] " Journal of the Burma Research Society," August, 1926.
[3] *Ibid.*, pp. 113-14.   [4] 1626 ed., Vol. V., p. 499.
[5] E.g., " there being a parcell of Pegu plank and they writing for some from Bengall, it is order'd that Mr. Freeman do buy a parcell that is offer'd to sale, att the best rates procurable " (" Fort St. George Diary and Consultation Book, 1688," p. 69).
[6] *Ibid.*, 1689, p. 71.

Vizagapatam to fitt there, but late advices thence tells us, that Planks and other materialls are so scarce and dear there, that they cannot gett sufficient to repair those Shipps already sent them, and there being noe other convenient place left us for that service on this Coast, Tis agreed and orderd that she be dispatch't for Pegue with what can be procured on freight and that we send something on the R^t: Honble: Comp^a: Acc^t: for the charge of her repair, and lade her back with salt provisions, Sticklack, Timbers, Mortivans,[1] Graine etc. Commodities proper for the supply of y^s Garrison for which to send 1000 Pag^s: in Silver, broad cloth fine, and Ordinary Perpetuanoes,[2] one Chest Rose water, etc. and to be consigned to the Master and one writer we shall send upon her, and to be recomended to the care and assistance of M^r: Thom^s: Makrith and Capt: Thomas Lacy who also are designed thither upon their own Acc^{ts}: and the reason of our sending for Provisions is, there being so very scarce and dear here as also for store for this garrison against a siege, but if no occasion that way then to dispose it to the Shipping or send it to Bombay."

The commander of this boat was Captain George Heron, who had long served the Company as a Hugli pilot, and was destined in later years to have a close connexion with Burma. It is interesting to note that at this time, when it was decided to send his ship to Syriam for repairs, Heron threw up the Company's service, and was allowed to settle in Madras as a free merchant. In his place Captain Howell was appointed to the *Diamond*.[3] If it is true that, in the seventeenth century, the average length of life in the East for an Englishman was less than five years, George Heron had a phenomenally long career in India. Born in 1646, one year after the battle of Naseby in the Great Civil War, he came out to the Hugli as a pilot apprentice in 1668, the year of the Triple Alliance made by England, Sweden, and the Dutch against Louis XIV.

---

[1] Martaban jars.

[2] A cloth exported from England to the East, so named because of its durability. (*Vide* Hobson-Jobson, s.v. Perpet, Perpetuans.)

[3] "Fort St. George Diary and Consultation Book, 1689," p. 70.

He left the Hugli probably at the time of Job Charnock's withdrawal from Bengal in 1688, the year of the " Glorious Revolution." Thereafter he lived throughout the reigns of William and Mary, Anne, and George I., dying in the same year as the last-named, 1727, at the advanced age of eighty.[1] Apparently after leaving his native land in 1668 he never saw it again. He married a " Georgian " (Armenian) woman, and his daughter, who married Captain John Powney of the well-known Madras family, died a centenarian in 1780.[2] We shall hear more of Heron later.

On 9th September, 1689, the *Diamond* was ready to sail for Syriam, and the Governor and Council of Fort St. George issued their commission and instructions [3] to her captain, James Howell, and her supercargo, Nathaniel Halsey.[4] They were informed that the ship was to sail to Syriam for repairs because it was " the best & cheapest Port for that service." For fear lest the European goods laden on the *Diamond* would not easily sell in Burma, the sum of 1000 pagodas in silver was entrusted to them to cover their expenses ; but they were particularly requested to do their utmost to open a market for the sale of English broadcloth, " we haveing great quantetyes decaying by us." They were to buy rice and salt pork in Martaban jars, lac, saltpetre and elephants' teeth ; also timber and oil for use at Fort St. George. A John Berlue was sent with the expedition in order to assist in looking after the workmen and in managing the provisions, but they were warned to keep strict check upon his extravagance. Their instructions further impressed upon them the necessity of setting a good example to the other English there, both in prudence and sobriety, and advised them that they should " by noe means or provocation disoblige that arbitrary Governm[t]: nor testy people least our Nation or the Hon[ble]: Comp[a]: Suffer thereby either in purse or reputation." If

---

[1] Love, " Vestiges," II., p. 212. On his tombstone in the Powney vault at Madras he is stated to have died on " the 2nd May 1727 in the 81st year of his age, then a sojourner in India 61 years."

[2] *Ibid.*, II., p. 14, n. 4.

[3] " Letters from Fort St. George, 1689," p. 42.

[4] Previously in charge of the Customs warehouse of Fort St. George. Upon his return in 1690 he was sent on board the *Princess of Denmark*, along with a number of other factors, to reopen a factory in Bengal.

they were unable to obtain a sufficient cargo of goods on the Company's behalf for the return voyage of the ship, they were to do their utmost to procure freight and passengers to make up the deficiency.   Halsey and Berlue evidently had a reputation for thirst, since the following amusing passage occurs in the instructions : " We have provided liquors suffitient for M^r: Halsey & John Berlue till their returne soe they must put (?) the Honble: Comp^a: to noe more charge in that there's enough for their voyage & at Pegu tis extremely cheap."   So, when supplies ran short, they were to make shift with Burma toddy.

The last paragraph of these instructions is of interest in connexion with previous discussions concerning the Company's claim to the possession of the old factory site in Syriam, and the permission to use it granted to private merchants.   " You are to dwell in the Honble: Comp^a: ffactory under their fflagg," it runs, " & you may permitt such others to reside with you as you may thinck Convenient, but in all things be very just frugall & orderly avoydeing all royating & other Scandalls w^{ch}: pray have a great regard to as you are Christians & Englishmen & to Confirme you therein as well as for the due discharge of your dutyes be constant & reverend in your devotions both aboard Shipp & ashoar."

No exact details are forthcoming as to the *Diamond's* voyage to Syriam and back, save that on 22nd March she returned to Fort St. George in company with the *James*, bringing a cargo of " Ellephants Teeth, Plancks Tynn Oyle, and Mortavan Jarrs," and was sent shortly afterwards to Porto Novo with sufficient timber and oil for refitting the " Bencolen frigate " there, such commodities being too scarce and dear in that quarter.   She brought back also from Syriam some of the European goods entrusted to her for disposal in Burma.[1]   Evidently Hamilton's observation on this subject at a later date was true.   " They (i.e. the people of Burma) wear none of our European Commodities but Hats and Ribbons," he wrote, " Cotton Cloths from Bengal and Chormondel, with some striped silks, are best for their Market." [2]

The East India Company did not immediately follow up

[1] " Fort St. George Diary and Consultation Book, 1690," p. 21.
[2] " A New Account of the East Indies," II., p. 42.

this move by sending more ships to Syriam for repairs ; but it is noticeable that from this time the import of Burma timber into Madras vastly increased.   In order to encourage the trade in this useful article, it was allowed to be brought in free of Customs duties.   From this time onwards also we find many instances of the Fort St. George Council procuring large supplies of Burma timber for general building purposes. Thus—to cite one from our present period—on 7th April, 1690, the Fort St. George Council recorded the following decision :   " Pegue Timbers being now plentifull and cheap, it is judg'd a good oppertunity to make a foot draw bridge over the river nearest the fort for the conveniency of bringing in provisions in time of Seige or raines also for goeing over to y^e: Powderhouse, and many other benefitts to the Comp^a: and towne, w^ch: will in a few years recompence y^e: charge w^ch: by calculation will not exceed 200 Pag^s:." [1]   Possibly the French rivalry, which had caused the recent failure of the East India Company's trade in Siam, caused Fort St. George to be wary about establishing a repair depot for ships at Syriam at this time.   But we have no evidence of this.

French policy at this time was bent upon securing a predominant influence on the eastern shores of the Bay of Bengal. The French Compagnie des Indes is said to have planted a trading station at Syriam in 1688, just when England and France were about to meet for the first time as great naval rivals.   In this same year, however, occurred a revolution in Siam, which brought about the downfall of the great Constant Phaulkon, and the consequent failure of French policy in that country.   But the French attempt to dominate Siam did not collapse immediately.   In 1690 a French fleet of six ships appeared in the Bay bound for Siam.   Before making its real objective, where fresh negotiations were to be opened with the Court of Ayuthia, it sailed up the Coromandel Coast, inflicting some damage upon Dutch and English shipping, and making a fruitless attack upon Fort St. George.   At Balasore it turned, and after crossing the Bay, put in at Negrais to refit and take on provisions.   There one of the French men-of-war and some smaller craft surprised an English private trading vessel, the *Recovery*, on her way from

---

[1] "Fort St. George Diary and Consultation Book, 1690," p. 24.

Madras to Syriam. She put up a fight, however, and managed to make good her escape back to Madras.[1] The French fleet pursued its way to Siam without attempting further interference with English trade in Burma.

During the next three or four years following this incident the Fort St. George records contain little more than bare entries of ships setting out for, or returning from, Burma, and of purchases of " Pegue timbers." The most regular vessel to make the annual voyage was one named the *Santa Rosa*, owned by Augustine Hart. Other masters or owners of ships frequently mentioned were Captain Armiger Gosling,[2] Antonio de Silva, Francis Holt, Peter Bromsden, the stalwart master of the *Recovery*, and George Heron, who apparently began his long connexion with Burma in 1690, when he freighted a sloop, named the *George*, presumably after himself, for a voyage to Syriam. The names of their ships sound delightfully old-world and romantic. Thus, among the English boats we have the *New Morning Star*, the *Good Hope*, the *Welcome*, the *John and Mary*, the *Dolphin*, the *Friendship* and the *Loyal Captain*, and among the Portuguese, the *Senhora de Rosara* and the *Nossa Senhora de Concension*.

In 1692 an incident occurred which led to the renewal of negotiations between Fort St. George and Ava, and indirectly to the establishment of closer relations between the Company and Burma. A small sloop, the *St. Anthony and St. Nicholas*, the master and owner of which, Bartholomew Rodrigues, an Armenian, was a citizen of Madras, living under the jurisdiction of Fort St. George,[3] while proceeding from Acheen to Bengal, was forced through lack of wood and water, to put into the Burmese port of Martaban. Not being specifically bound for that port, she was seized by the Burmese authorities, her cargo transferred to the royal godowns, and her crew sent prisoners to Ava. This treatment, as we have seen above, was strictly in accordance with Burmese custom, but bearing in mind the recent attempts of the Court of Ava to persuade the East India Company to reopen official trade with Burma,

---

[1] " Fort St. George Diary and Consultation Book, 1690," p. 89.

[2] Often spelt Gostlin or Gostling.

[3] Not to be confused with another Bartholomew Rodrigues, a prominent man of affairs in Madras, who died in 1692.

one is left with the impression that this opportunity was especially taken advantage of, in order to force Fort St. George to negotiate.   Adequate bribes could usually secure freedom to depart to a ship in such a plight.   This view is further supported by the fact that somewhere about this time a Dutchman, Adrian Tilbury, long resident at Madras, and married to a woman of that city, had died intestate in Tavoy or Martaban, while on a trading voyage there, and the Burmese Government had seized his possessions in exactly the same way as in the case of Thomas Samuel many years earlier.[1]

News of the former occurrence reached the Fort St. George authorities in 1694, probably through an Armenian named Gregory, resident in Ava, who apparently wrote to another Armenian in Madras, Cojee Gregory Paron, asking him to move the Governor and Council to take action in the matter. At about the same time, the widow of Adrian Tilbury also applied for the assistance of the Council for the recovery of her deceased husband's estate.   On 8th September of that year therefore, at a consultation, it was decided to send letters " to the King of Ava and his four Principall Governours " through the Armenian Gregory at Ava, with presents provided by Cojee Gregory Paron, praying for the redemption of Bartholomew Rodrigues, his ship, crew and cargo, and of Adrian Tilbury's estate.[2]   The letters and presents were despatched on board a ship named the *Nossa Senhora de San Juan*, belonging to Antonio de Silva, which left for Syriam on the same day as the consultation took place.   They never reached their destination.   In March, 1695, an English seacaptain returning from Syriam reported that the *Nossa Senhora de San Juan* had been completely wrecked off the island of Negrais in one of those terrible October storms that so often attend the change of monsoon at that time.   The short graphic description of the loss of this boat to be found in the Fort St. George Diary and Consultation Book of the year 1695 runs thus :—[3]

---

[1] Dalrymple, " Oriental Repertory," II., p. 339.   " Fort St. George Diary and Consultation Book, 1694," p. 95.
[2] *Ibid.*   [3] *Ibid.*, 1695, p. 41.

"21 March 1695. Thomas Plumbe Master of Shipp Jelpha Merchant from Pegue arriveing this day reports that the shipp of Antonia de Silva which went from hence in September last bound for Sirian, and fetch'd Point Brago [1] where finding the north Easterly winds sett in put back for Negrais to stay there till the winds changed, and anchored between the Island and the main about the 17th: of October. The next day the monsoon came on, and the wind blew wth: that extremity for Severall days as drove the Shipp ashoare & oversett her at the same time the flood comeing in, increased to that height as covered the Shipp and forced the [men] to leave her, those that swam well escaped to the shore when the water increaseing upon, and by degrees covering the Island, they betooke themselves to the trees dureing the Tide, which was so violent that the Shipps rudder and the Capston were afterwards found on the Tops of the Bamboes, and few of the men lived to Pegue, above a dozen Pegue Merchants who had freighted goods to a considerable value were all lost."

When, later, Nathaniel Higginson, writing of the occurrence to the Government of Burma, attributed the disaster to the ignorance of the pilot, he was probably not far from the truth.[2] The word Negrais is said to be a corruption of the Burmese *Naga-rit*, meaning " Dragon's Whirlpool," [3] and the locality was notoriously dangerous by reason of the set of the tide, which was liable to carry vessels ashore and wreck them.

The wreck of the *Nossa Senhora de San Juan* caused the Fort St. George authorities to reconsider the whole question of their relations with Burma. Probably Cojee Gregory Paron was unable or unwilling to provide further presents for the King of Burma and his four chief ministers. It was left, therefore, to Fort St. George to move in the matter. This was not an easy task. Obviously Ava desired the re-establishment of official trading relations, but in face of the Directors'

---

[1] Baragua Point.
[2] Dalrymple, " Oriental Repertory," II., p. 338.
[3] *Vide* Hobson-Jobson, s.v. Negrais.

flat prohibition of any such step, Fort St. George was not in a position to accede to the Burmese wishes. There were, however, certain factors in the situation, which could not be ignored. Bartholomew Rodrigues had given out to the Burmese authorities that he was in the service of the East India Company's Governor of Fort St. George. This was not strictly true, but his ship at the time of her seizure was carrying goods belonging to Nathaniel Higginson, who naturally could not tamely submit to their loss.[1] Further, both Rodrigues and the deceased Adrian Tilbury were inhabitants of Madras, enjoying the protection of the Company, which was, therefore, expected to do something in their behalf. Failure to respond to the King of Burma's gesture might bring about the loss of such trading privileges in Burma as could still be claimed by the Company ; and as it was always within the realm of possibility that the Directors might one day change their minds, and decide to reopen the Syriam factory, this would be a very serious matter.

But the loss of the ancient privileges at Syriam would have more immediate effects. The Madras private traders undoubtedly reaped a rich harvest from the Burma trade, and in this respect benefited the Fort St. George Customs receipts. As some of the Company's servants participated in this lucrative trade, they could not afford to let the matter of the seizure of Bartholomew Rodrigues drop. Moreover, still one more possible development had to be considered : the time might soon arrive when it would be desirable to build ships at Syriam.[2] Shipbuilding in Burma with such magnificent supplies of teak to draw upon, would, it was estimated, cost no more than half what it cost at Surat, even if it were left in the hands of private builders with some experienced person placed in permanent control there by the Company.[3]

So, at a consultation extraordinary held on 11th September, 1695, Higginson and his Council decided to send Edward Fleetwood and Captain James Lesly to the Burmese capital with large presents to the king and chief ministers,

---

[1] Dalrymple, *op. cit.*, II., pp. 343-4. Higginson succeeded Elihu Yale in 1692.

[2] *Ibid.*, II., p. 347.

[3] " Fort St. George : Public Despatches to England, 1694-6," p. 15.

to negotiate the release of Bartholomew Rodrigues and his crew, and the restoration of all the goods seized by the Burmese authorities. They were also to discuss with the Government of Burma the general relations between the Company and Ava, and to seek to procure an extension of trading privileges along the lines mapped out earlier by Streynsham Master.[1] The Minutes of this consultation show clearly that Fort St. George did not send this mission to Ava with any intention of establishing an official factory in Burma. It is necessary to stress this point, because the opposite has so often been asserted by writers of Burmese history, notwithstanding the fact that the documents given in Dalrymple's second volume show definitely what were the true objects of the mission.[2] These Minutes, however, do not appear in Dalrymple, and as they sum up concisely Fort St. George's reasons for reopening negotiations with Ava, the exact words in which these are stated are of importance. The paragraph dealing with the matter runs thus :—

" The Right Hon ble: Company having long since withdrawn their factory from Pegue, & forbidden making any settlement again at their charge, but doth expressly permit and encourage the carrying on of private trade from this Port, and whereas the King of Pegue doth yet continue the use of the English factory to all English ships which goe thither for trade and repair, undr: the name and Priviledge of the Company, and it being for the Rt: Hon ble: Comps: service that the Ancient Priviledges of the factory be preserved, and the trade mannaged by due regulation as [well for] the benefitt of the Private trade at present as for their own business if hereafter they should find reason to resettle, which Priviledges probably may be impaired or lost partly by the disorderly carriage and partly by the ignorance of private Merchts: unacquainted with the customs of the place, and there being a good opportunity by a ship now goeing whereby there will be occasion to address the King of Pegue in behalf of Bartho: Rodriguez's ship lost three years past on that

---

[1] " Fort St. George Diary and Consultation Book, 1695," pp. 116-17.
[2] Dalrymple, " Oriental Repertory," II., pp. 337-95.

Coast and the Cargo secured, and an Inhabitant of this place who dyed there and his Estate secured by the Government for the claims of his widdow or heirs, wherein M^r: Edward Fleetwood and Capt: James Leslie are employed and the King's officers at Serian having often declared to the English their great desire of our resetling. The Presid^t: hath prepared Instructions to direct them in treating w^th: the King as well relating to y^e: release of Bartholomew Rodriguez and Adrian Tilbary's Estate, as the setling of the trade and procureing Privileges, which were read and approved."

Such were the objects of this mission, regarding which we possess more detailed information than in the case of any other before the second half of the eighteenth century.

CHAPTER IX

THE MISSION OF EDWARD FLEETWOOD AND JAMES LESLY TO AVA, 1695-1696

CHAPTER IX

THE MISSION OF EDWARD FLEETWOOD AND JAMES LESLY TO AVA, 1695-6

THE two envoys sent upon this interesting mission to Ava left Madras on 12th September, 1695, on board the *Loyal Captain*, of which Armiger Gosling, previously in command of the *New Morning Star*, had been appointed master.[1] Along with them went a rich present for the King of Burma, and correspondingly smaller ones for all officials, both high and low, with whom they were likely to come into contact. The total value of these presents was listed at 998 pagodas 35 fanams.[2] The real nature of the negotiations will be at once evident, when it is realised that Nathaniel Higginson stood the whole cost of the presents out of his own pocket. Fleetwood and Lesly were sent to procure the release of a private trader, the restoration of the goods of another deceased private trader, and the grant of privileges to be enjoyed primarily by private merchants, or Company's servants trading in a private capacity. Higginson took up the case partly because he was a private loser by the Burmese seizure of the cargo of Bartholomew's ship. Moreover, the present that he sent to Ava was of the nature of a private speculation, seeing that he hoped to make a substantial profit out of the present the king would send him in return. Fleetwood, as chief of the embassy, was instructed

---

[1] " Fort St. George Diary and Consultation Book, 1695," p. 118.

[2] Dalrymple, "Oriental Repertory," II., p. 354. Fleetwood's " Instructions and Diary," and the other documents relating to this embassy, published by Dalrymple, are to be found in " Factory Records : Miscellaneous," Vol. 18, ff. 23-78. For convenience of reference I have used Dalrymple. From a comparison of the two I have discovered only one discrepancy in Dalrymple's transcription : on p. 356 the date (Oct.) 22nd is omitted by the words, " I delivered to each their Present," on the third line from the bottom of the page. Bowyear's " Instructions " on proceeding to Burma in 1697 are included in the same volume of " Factory Records," together with his account of his earlier mission to Cochin-China.

to ask for rice and lac in return for the present.[1] He and Lesly were to be allowed 3 per cent. of the value of such of the goods of Rodrigues and Tilbury as should be restored by the Burmese Government, and 10 per cent., equally divided between them, of the king's return present to Higginson. " It therefore will be to your Interest to procure as much as you can," wrote the Governor, " though it cannot be expected, that he should make an equall return, if he delivers the *Cargo*, which is so considerable, and is, by the *Laws* of the *Country*, forfeited to him." [2]

" If the *King* makes a return equall to the *Present*," he continued later in the instructions, " there will be more *Lack* and *Rice* than will lade one Shipp ; you may therefore ask for half this Year, and half the next, when demanded." As much of the royal present as could not be carried away on the return voyage of the *Loyal Captain* was to be stored in the English factory at Syriam, until a convenient opportunity arose for bringing it away. " I have been told by one that made a *Present* to the *King*," wrote Higginson, in his additional instructions, " that the return being much less than the *Value*, upon his *complaint*, the *King* ordered an *Addition*. If you find occasion take advice whether it be practicable." [3]

Higginson's explanation of his action to the Fort St. George Council is amusing. He laid great stress upon his " risgoe " [4] in financing so large a present, for which there was little hope of an adequate return, and upon his generosity on behalf of the captured merchant and crew. The present that Bartholomew Rodrigues had suggested should be sent to the king, seemed to him (Higginson) to be too small. He had therefore taken upon himself to double its value, because of the big issues at stake. The King of Burma was accustomed to give in return for a present another of equal value, according to the estimation of his officials.[5] But when the donor of the present obtained special privileges or some great boon from the king, he would receive a present of correspondingly lower value. In this case, seeing that not less than the

---

[1] Dalrymple, "Oriental Repertory," II., p. 350.　　　　[2] *Ibid.*
[3] *Ibid.*, II., p. 351.　　　　[4] Risk.
[5] Who usually much over-valued presents of European origin, so the meaning of " equal value " needs qualification.

restoration of a ship and cargo was sought, the king would probably disregard a small present. " Therefore the President doeth enlarge the Present at his [owne cost] to render it the more acceptable and effectual as well for the releasement of Bartho: Rodriguez as for the procureing Priviledges of trade in the Rᵗ: Honᵇˡᵉ: Compˢ: name, for the generall good, and is content to run the risgoe of yᵉ: sea and to accept of what the King of Pegue shall give in returne of the present, thô it be less, and therefore thinkes it reasonable he should enjoy the benefit of it if it be more and he is so far from expecting great advantages by it, that he will be content to quit all pretensions to any part of the returnes, if any one will secure to him a profit upon the money expended here equal to the profit shall be made by others upon their own adventures." The Council, " after full consideration of yᵉ: hazard and all circumstances of the case," expressed its unqualified approval of the Governor's action.[1]

The extent to which Higginson bluffed the Government of Burma regarding the real nature of the embassy, and the intentions of the Company in the matter of the settlement of a factory, will be realised from a comparison of the chief items in his official letter to the king with his private instructions to Fleetwood. Much of what he wrote in his letter to the king was so far from the strict truth, that it was necessary in his instructions to explain to the chief envoy the correct " interpretation " of it, that he must bear in mind, so as not to commit himself to any indiscretions likely to place Higginson in a difficult position with either London or Ava. Thus the official letter to the king contains the following passage on the crucial question of the Company's resettlement in Burma : " I humbly pray your *Majesty's fountain* of *goodness* to continue your wonted favours to the Right Honourable English Company, and to permit our Factors to buy and sell, in such Commoditys, and under such Priviledges, as your *Royall bounty* shall be pleased to grant ; and allow us such conveniencys, as are necessary for the repair of Shipps, whereby I shall be encouraged to send my Shipps Yearly to your *Majesty's* Port, having orders from the Honourable

Company, to send Shipps and *Factors* into all Parts of *India*, when their Service requires it, and pray your *Majesty* to give me leave to send a *Factor*, next Monsoon, to reside at *Syrian*." [1]

The explanation of this passage, so contradictory to the statement recorded in the Minutes of the meeting of the Council, at which the embassy had been decided on, was given thus in Higginson's instructions to Fleetwood : " The *Letter* to the *King* begins with a *Petition* for the Company's enjoying Priviledges of *Trade*, conveniencys of repairing of Ships, and liberty of settling a *Factory* at *Syrian* next *Monsoone ;* which is first mentioned, not so much because there is occasion to petition the *King* for it, but because they are very desirous, and have many Years urged that we should settle a *Factory* at *Syrian*, and therefore I think the mentioning of it, will facilitate his granting the following requests, which are the first occasion and first intention of your proceeding to *Ava*."

The passage relating to Bartholomew Rodrigues in Higginson's letter to the king is a model of diplomatic bluff : " About 3 years agoe I ordered *Bartholomew Rodrigues*, Master of a small *Sloop*, called *St. Anthony* and *St. Nicholas* to go from *Acheen* to *Bengall*, laden with divers Commodity's ; while I was expecting to hear from my *Factors* in *Bengall* of her arrival there, the Ship that came hither last Year from *Syrian*, brought me advice that the said Sloop was fortunately arrived within your *Majesty's Kingdoms*, and calling there for *Wood* and *Water*, your Officers not knowing who she belonged to, had taken care, by your *Majesty's* Order, for the safe keeping the *Sloop* and *Cargoe*, which great favour I thought myself obliged to acknowledge, and therefore by the first opportunity, sent your *Majesty* a letter of thanks, with a small Present, by a Shipp that went last Year from hence for *Syrian* ; but unfortunately lost by the ignorance of the Pilott,[2] I have now sent this by my *Factors*,[3] *Edward Fleetwood* and *James Lesly*, and humbly pray your *Majesty* to cause *Bartholomew Rodrigues* and his *People*, and that *Sloop* and *Cargo*, to be delivered to

[1] Dalrymple, "Oriental Repertory," II., p. 338.
[2] The *Nossa Senhora de San Juan*.
[3] Neither Fleetwood nor Lesly were "factors" ; the names of both appear in the " List of Seafaring Men not Constant Inhabitants " of Fort St. George for the year 1695. Fleetwood's name appears in the same list for several years afterwards.

my said *Factors ;* who have orders to bring all to me ; and fearing the *Sloop* may be uncapable of going to Sea, I have sent a ship to bring away the Cargoe and men." [1]

Higginson's explanation of this paragraph to his envoys is interesting : " *Bartholomew Rodrigues* gave out, that he belonged to the *Governor* of *Madrass*, and it is the general opinion of all that came since from *Pegu*, that the *King* does reserve the Sloop and Cargo, in expectation of an Address from me, and that he will thereupon deliver all, and the Men from their *Captivity*. But if *Bartholomew Rodrigues* have any Enemies, or if any of the Courtiers shall oppose the delivery, upon account of the *King's Laws* or *Interest*, it is not improbable but some scruple will be raised against it ; I know not what they will be, and therefore know not how to answer them ; But if there be any, it is probable this will be one ; That *Bartholomew Rodrigues* is not an *Englishman*, nor does the *Sloop* or *Cargoe*, belong to *me*, or The *Company*. If this be objected, it will be difficult to clear it, because it is not true that the Sloop and whole Cargoe belongs to me, as a Proprietor, nor is he my Servant, in such manner as to receive his Wages from me ; but he hath been long an *Inhabitant* of *Fort St. George*, living under the protection and Government of the Right Honourable Company, and as I am Governour of the *Place*, ought to own all such as belonging to the Right Honourable Company, in which sence I own him, in my letter to the *King*, and we make no distinction between the Right Honourable Company, and those who belong to them. [2]

" Secondly, the Honourable Company doe employ *Portuguese*, and other *Nations*, as well as *English*, by Sea as well as by Land, as may be proved by the *English Ships* which goe to *Pegu*.

" Thirdly, I had goods laden upon the Sloop, for my own account, as may appear by Mr. *Delton's Original Invoice*, consigned to the *Agent* of *Bengall*, which I herewith deliver you.

" I offer these Considerations to be made use of, as occasion shall require, but since *Bartholomew Rodrigues* has, from the

---

[1] Dalrymple, *op: cit.,* II., pp. 338-9.

[2] Thus in his letter to the king he calls Adrian Tilbury " my Servant for many Years."

first, given out, that he belongs to *me*, I think you must insist upon that single point, that *he* and *I* and *all of us* and the *Trade* belong to The Honourable English Company ; and for that reason if the *King* deliver the *Sloop*, *Cargoe* and *Men*, It is necessary that they be delivered to *you*, and that *Bartholomew Rodrigues* do in all points follow your Orders."

These are the words of an astute diplomatist. But, although in one sense Higginson may have been bluffing the Burmese Government, what alternative course was open to him ? To have told the plain truth would have doomed the negotiations to failure. The Burmese Government wished the Company officially to reopen the English factory at Syriam. The Directors refused to allow such a proceeding. But Syriam was the centre of a lucrative English private trade with Burma, and might become important one day as a shipbuilding depôt. It would have been madness for Fort St. George to have jeopardised English prospects in Burma by remaining supine at this time. Yet, in view of the Directors' attitude, no negotiations aiming at the official resettlement of the factory could be entered upon, a point which had the Burmese Government realised, would probably have led them at least to refuse to grant the real objects of the mission. And, humanitarian principles apart, it was necessary for the maintenance of the Company's prestige, that the release of the captured merchant and crew should be effected. Hence the necessity for bluff. Higginson's aim in undertaking these negotiations was certainly not to involve the Company with the responsibility of reopening its factory at Syriam. But he wished to conserve ancient privileges and, if possible, secure more reasonable conditions of trade for English merchants in Burma. At the same time, he aimed at bringing the private trade at Syriam more closely under the Company's control ; and although his promise to send a factor to reside at Syriam must not be taken literally, he certainly had in view the appointment of some person, authorised by the Company to look after its interests in Burma, and assume some sort of control over the private trade. His action, therefore, in providing so lavish a present out of his own pocket, was probably more public-spirited than it at first appears to be.

In order to establish the relations of the Company with

the Government of Burma upon a more definite basis, the two envoys were instructed to use " Agent Masters " Articles of Trade as their guide. Higginson counselled them to peruse these often, " but because I do not propound the *Settling* of *Factory's* in the *Kingdom*, on the Right Honourable Company's Account, There are some Articles, which ought not to be insisted on, because they cannot be complyed with, on our parts, so long as there is only a private Trade carryed on ; and some because they seem very improbable to be granted ; and the *very asking*, may be an occasion of their denying the rest, I therefore give you a List of those which may be asked and insisted on." [1] These were Articles 1 to 6, 8, 9, 11, and 13 of those given in Chapter VI. The rest were to be dropped. " But," continued the instructions, " the 6th is very consider-able and a *maine point ;* they have not yet given leave for *Saltpetre* to be *exported*, though solicited by the Dutch ; prob-ably because they are fearfull and jealous, least it should be used against themselves, and therefore not to be urged too far ; But you may advise, and propound it, and there is one great argument for it, viz. That all the *Goods*, usually exported from *Pegu*, are grown so dear there, that the *Exporters* loose by them, so that they will be forced to leave the *Trade*, unless they have the liberty of buying some other sorts of *Goods*, cheaper, and whatever is paid for the *Saltpetre* is so much clear gain to the Country.

" There is one thing more to be added, which is necessary ; that we have *free liberty* of *repairing* and *building* of *Ships*, at *Syrian ;* and liberty of making a *Dock*, with *Timber*, so that it may be always fitt to receive Shipps, and that the *Governour* of *Syrian*, shall assist in compelling *Cooleys* to work as occasion requires. Also a liberty for all *English Ships* to export *Timber* and *Rice* for the supply of *Madrass*." Later in the instructions Higginson returned to this subject : " If you find a difficulty of obtaining the desired liberty of *building New Ships*, don't urge it too far, but be content with the free liberty of repairing." [2]

In order that the envoys might not be ignorant of the actual state of English relations with Burma previous to their embassy, Higginson explained that " in former years " the

[1] Dalrymple, "Oriental Repertory," II., p. 346.   [2] *Ibid.*, II., p. 350.

Company had had factories at Syriam and Ava, but withdrew them because the trade was not sufficiently profitable. The terms on which they had settled there were not known, because no written agreement had ever been made with the Company by the King of Burma. In 1680 " Agent Masters " had employed " John Ferrera de Faria " to negotiate his Articles of Commerce with the Court of Ava, and, although the negotiations fell through, an important private trade had developed between Fort St. George and Syriam, the king making special grants of privileges to individuals. " And there is reason to believe," wrote the Governor, " that the *King* would as readily grant the same, to the English Company, if it were asked ; for notwithstanding the *Withdrawing* of the *Factorys*, the *English* have still enjoyed the same *freedom* of *Trade*, and *repairing* their *Ships*, as they had before ; and there remains, in Syrian, a piece of *Ground*, a *House* and a Dock, which passes under the name of the *English Factory* ; and it is the opinion of all who are acquainted with the *Place* and *People*, that the *King*, and his *Officers*, are very desirous that the *English* would resettle ; and we have been invited to it ; But the Right Honourable Company have not yet thought fit to resettle there, on their own accounts, But they have given free liberty of a *private Trade*, which must be carried on, in their names for two reasons (1st.) Because all the *English* in *India* are *Subjects* to their *Authority* and *Government* ; (2dly.) The Trade will be the more durable and profitable, when managed by due regulations, and supported by the Credit and Authority of the Honourable Company." [1]

If the king granted their requests, they were to do their best to secure a royal order to that effect ; but if they themselves were required to " signe any writing," they were to be extremely cautious, and, if possible, obtain permission to bring it to Fort St. George for consideration, before pledging themselves on the Company's behalf. They were warned to act with equal caution in their dealings with the natives of the country, and to avoid offering any affront to them, " for they are excessive proud, and will not bear it. . . . One imprudent action of that nature may give you a great deal of trouble." So Higginson admonished them that on their first arrival at

---

[1] Dalrymple, "Oriental Repertory," II., pp. 345-6.

Syriam they should make themselves acquainted with the customs of the country in regard to strangers.

Fleetwood and Lesly were provided with letters to the king, to the " three Governors of Ava," styled therein " Mung Nemn Zangiah, Governor of the Dominion," " Mung Bix Rundasoo," and " Mung Xia Nundaneck " respectively, and to " Mungra Naarra, Govern^r: etc. Councill of Syrian, and his Majesty's Sea Ports." [1] The copies for presentation to these officials were translated into Portuguese, but the envoys carried with them the English originals for their own private perusal.[2] Immediately upon their arrival in the country they were to deliver Higginson's letter to the Governor of Syriam and the chief officers of the Myoyon (" Runday "), with an appropriate present to each. They were then to ask that special arrangements should be made to expedite their journey to Ava, so that they might return to Syriam in time to allow the *Loyal Captain* to cross the Bay before the break of the next wet monsoon. The journey to Ava, they were informed, was a very long and tedious one, but by judicious bribery boats could be obtained, that would convey them thither in 25 to 30 days. Arrived in Ava, their first consideration must be the best method of conveying the present to the king, so as to enhance its value as much as possible in his eyes ; " concerning which I can only recommend two things," wrote their astute adviser, " (1st.) That I am informed *Presents* are carryed to the *King*, not in *Bales*, but by *Cooleys* carrying each a *single piece*, upon their heads, in fitt *dishes*, or *Baskets*. (2nd.) That it is in the power of those who are appointed to value the *Present*, to lessen *or* increase the *Price*, very considerably, and therefore they are to be obliged." [3] They must also bear in mind that the estimation of the value of the present depended largely upon the number of coolies employed to carry it into the royal presence ; but it would be wise for them to find out " in what order things are to be carryed, whether the best first or last." [4]

The list of goods consigned to the *Loyal Captain* by way of presents to the Burmese monarch and officials is interesting, as showing us the kind of things acceptable there in this

---

[1] Dalrymple, *op. cit.*, II., p. 340.   [2] *Ibid.*, II., pp. 337-41.
[3] *Ibid.*, II., pp. 341-2.   [4] *Ibid.*, II., p. 351.

capacity in the late seventeenth century. The major portion
of it is made up of piece-goods, especially Beetelas.[1] Among
the higher-priced materials we have gold shawls and sashes,
red velvet, China silk, girdles and fine muslins. Then there
were chests of rose-water, boxes of cinnamon, cloves, nutmets
and mace, cannisters of sugar, a few guns and, specially listed,
" one China Woman Clockwork," valued at 25 pagodas. In
the expenses of the embassy provision was made for gilding
the letter to the king.[2] Thus equipped, the mission arrived
before the city of Syriam on 14th October, 1695, and three
days later was permitted to land. Time was no object in
Burma in those days.

Fleetwood, as chief of the embassy, was requested by
Governor Higginson to keep a diary of his " proceedings."
This he did with meticulous care.[3] We are fortunate, therefore, in possessing an accurate record of his negotiations with
the Burmese authorities ; but little more than that, since he
was not concerned with giving a picture of the country he
was visiting for the first time. Everything he entered in it
was strictly relevant to the business on hand. There is not a
gleam of humour, or of anything warmer than business con-
ciseness to be found on any page of this valuable compilation.
Its opening paragraphs are typical of the bald uninspired style
that continues from start to finish :—

" October 14th, I arrived in Ship *Loyall Captain*, at
Syrian, and in three days more, we got up to the *Town*.

" 17th, I went a shoar and delivered the *Governour of
Madrass*, his *letter* to the *Princes*, and *Governours* of
Syrian, acquainted them who I was, and upon what
design come ; and craved their assistance in my speedy
despatch for Ava, which they promised.

" 19th, I landed the *Present*, which was carried to
the *Custom House ;* and the next day I went to the
Runday,[4] or *Town hall* (a *Place* where those that are of

---

[1] Muslin.   [2] Dalrymple "Oriental Repertory," II., pp. 352-4.
[3] It is given in full in *ibid.*, II., pp. 355-89, and in " Factory Records :
Miscellaneous," Vol. 18, ff. 40-74.
[4] Probably a corruption of the Burmese *Yondaw* (Yon = court, daw =
honorific affix). Probably the honorific affix was used because the Governor
of Syriam, who presided over the court, was usually a brother of the king.

the *Government*, are obliged every day to meet, as well to
hear *Complaints*, and administer *Justice*, as to despatch
all other *Publick Affairs*) and desired the *Present* might
be cleared of the *Custom-House*, that I might be forwarded with all expedition, for *Ava ;* The *Governour*[1]
answered that the next day, they would themselves go
to the *Custom-House* and see them cleared."

Then followed a wrangle between the envoys and the
Burmese authorities, who were curious to know how much of
the present was destined for the king, and how much for the
various other officials. Fleetwood refused to enlighten them
on this matter ; so they countered by threatening to report
to Ava that the whole present was for the king, a proceeding
likely to involve the envoys in some embarrassment and extra
expenditure. Fleetwood, undaunted, told them that they
might report what they liked, and the Syriam officials, seeing
that further pressing was useless, gave leave for the present
to be cleared. Fleetwood then " delivered to each their
Present, made up in *small Bundles*, as if it had been so sent
them, by the *Governour of Madrass*." The officials thus
favoured he classes as two princes, four governors, and two
" ovidores " or " persons appointed to take notice of all
passages in the Runday and advise them to Ava."[2] The
princes were members of the Burmese royal family. As we
have already seen, Syriam in the seventeenth century usually
had a governor of royal blood, sometimes a brother of the
reigning king. He would be entitled the " myowun " or
" myosa."[3] Which of these two had precedence does not

The Burmese letter " y," corresponding to the Arakanese " r," is often
transliterated into English as " r." Thus at a much later date the Burmese
town Yangon became in English, Rangoon. For a description of the
Syriam Yondaw in 1709, *vide* Appendix V.

[1] Probably the real governor's deputy. Fleetwood usually calls the
governor, " prince." It was not customary for him to be present at
meetings of the Yondaw, but he appointed a deputy to represent him
there.

[2] The word is derived from the Portuguese *Ouvidor*, meaning " auditor."
It was a translation of the Burmese name for these officials—*nakhandaw*,
" royal ear." There were similar officials at the capital, to whom Fleetwood
gives the same title.

[3] Myowun = town governor ; Myosa = eater of the town : a significant phrase.

appear. It was not customary for a Burmese city to have two myowuns, though at a later date under the Alaungpaya dynasty Ava, when still capital of Burma, had two such officials. The four officials, styled governors by Fleetwood, were probably the usual four departmental heads found in a Burmese provincial city: the " Yewun," or " Lord of the Waters," chief of the war-boats and all other shipping, and next in importance to the myowun ; the " Akunwun," or collector of land revenue, the " akaukwun," or collector of Customs, and the " sitkedaw," a combined judicial and police officer, whom we have met with earlier.[1]

After obtaining permission to depart for Ava, the embassy was delayed for some days by the necessity for washing some of the painted piece-goods, which had " quite lost their gloss " on the voyage across the Bay. Not until 9th November did they embark in the river craft they had hired for the next stage of their journey. Here, again, it was necessary to give to the master of the boat his customary present, consisting of a piece of coarse cotton stuff and a beetela coat. The official told off to accompany them on their journey had likewise to receive a gratuity—a piece of cotton goods, a coat, a pair of slippers, a china plate and thirty viss of ganza.[2]

The journey up-stream to Ava was uneventful. On 23rd December the mission arrived at the capital, one of its subordinate members, Arthur Seymour, having been sent ahead to advise the Court of its approach and prepare a house for its reception. Although promised, the house had not materialised when the envoys reached Ava, so another member of their retinue named King was despatched to the " two chiefs, Governours Nemeaseasee and Sereajeakeodang "[3] with presents, asking that the promised house should be placed at their disposal as early as possible. The two ministers assured

---

[1] In Chapter VI., p. 121.

[2] By this time the value of ganza had depreciated considerably (vide post, Chapter X., pp. 203-4).

[3] Fleetwood uses the word " governor " very loosely. Of these two, the former seems to have been a member of the supreme council of Burma, the Hluttaw, and so was probably a " Wungyi " in charge of one of the departments of State. The latter, apparently a member of the more influential, though less exalted, inner council, the " Byedaik," was probably an Atwinwun, i.e. " Minister of the Household." (Vide Hobson-Jobson, s.v. Woon.)

him that the house would be ready on the following day. When the morrow dawned, however, nothing had been done. Fleetwood therefore went in person to the two ministers, " carrying to each a ps. of Beetela for 'tis the Custom here, never to go to a great man empty-handed." Due deference having been shown to the great men, the house immediately was forthcoming. It had been ready all the time, but it was beneath the dignity of the Burmese ministers to have any commerce with underlings. This sharp lesson was not lost upon Fleetwood : in future he was scrupulous always to go in person, when dealing with these two dignitaries.

Until the house was ready for his reception, Fleetwood stayed with an Armenian named Baba, with whom was living also the unfortunate Bartholomew Rodrigues. With these two he took counsel as to the best method of approaching the Burmese Government with his proposals. Their advice was that he should conduct his business through the two ministers, with whom he had already come into contact in the matter of the house, since these two, according to Baba, possessed the greatest influence with the king. Fleetwood mentioned that in Syriam he had heard that the king could best be approached through his favourite mistress, and accordingly he had come prepared with letters of recommendation to some of her relatives. But Baba strongly dissuaded him from pursuing this course, telling him of the recent disgrace of a " prince of the country " who had resorted to it.

At this juncture the official interpreter arrived on the scene to offer his services, and gave to Fleetwood a list of Burmese officials to whom it was customary to give presents when negotiating with the king. It was a somewhat formidable one, comprising six " Governours of the Runday," two " Privy Councillors," three Ovidores,[1] six Pages " that always attend on the King," the " Mrowhon "[2] and his " lieutenant,"

---

[1] These, as we have seen above, were Nakhandaws. Fleetwood explains that at Ava they " always attend the ministers of the Runday, and are sent to the king, upon errands, as occasion obliges." It was the function of the Nakhandaw to report to the king each evening all transactions in the Hluttaw, and transmit all royal orders to that body.

[2] Myowun, i.e. Governor of the city. Fleetwood describes him as " Governour of the Military Affairs."

called the " Tomwhon." [1] Likewise he was advised to pro-
pitiate the " *Two Secretarys*, and their *assistants*, whose
business it is, to take notice, and keep account of all *Strangers*,
I mean *Forreigners*, that come to Ava, as well *Merchants* that
come to *Trade*, as those who having been cast away, or taken
in any of the *prohibited Ports*, are made *Captives :* These are
called *Colvoons*.[2] They examine all *Boats*, that go from *Ava ;*
take *lists* of their *Lading*, and dispatch them ; They are here
called *Governours* of the *Bandall*,[3] which is the Place where all
Forreiners do inhabit."

In this list of high Burmese officials it is noteworthy
that the existence of two distinct governmental bodies, the
" Runday " and the " Privy Council," is referred to. These
were respectively the " Hluttaw," the Supreme Court of the
realm, competent to deal with all causes, both executive and
judicial, and the " Byèdaik," a sort of Council of the Household, composed mainly of atwinwuns, and possessing the
special confidence of the king. Little is known of the exact
functions of these two bodies in the days before the Alaungpaya
dynasty (1752-1885).[4] It would seem that as far as prestige
and nominal power were concerned, the Hluttaw had the
higher authority, but probably the Byèdaik, composed as it
was of officials who had important financial functions and
special influence in the palace, was a more potent factor in
shaping the royal decisions. In this connexion it is interesting to note that of the two ministers described to Fleetwood
by the interpreter as possessing the chief power at Court,
Nemeaseasee was a member of the " Runday," and is called in
the diary " Principal Minister, without controul and is the

---

[1] This must be a corruption of the Burmese " Atwinwun," an official
of lower rank than a Wungyi, a minister of the highest rank with a seat
in the Hluttaw.   The word " Atwinwun " means Minister of the Court or
Household.   Often such a person possessed greater political influence than
a Wungyi.

[2] I can find no explanation of the derivation of this word in the usual
sources.   I suggest tentatively that it may be derived from the Burmese
" kala " (foreigner) and " wun " (administrative officer).

[3] Probably " pandal " (a shed), and thus signifying the temporary
bamboo erections that would be put up for the reception of foreigners.

[4] Our best information is contained in Taw Sein Ko's " Selections
from the Records of the Hluttaw," but these relate almost entirely to the
reign of the last Burmese king, Thibaw, 1876-85.

mouth of the Court," while Serejeakeodang was a member of the Byèdaik, and is styled in the diary " the King's particular favourite." Burmese administration was complex, and depended largely upon customary rules of procedure, so that although in both theory and fact the appointment and dismissal of ministers depended entirely upon the will of the king, in practice, unless the latter were able enough to assert himself vigorously in the administration, power tended to fall into the hands of such ministers as by their personality and abilities naturally took the lead. King Minrekyawdin (1673-98) was apparently little more than a figure-head, whose policy and administration were mainly controlled by his ministers.

On 25th December the " Governours " instructed Fleetwood to be in readiness to deliver the present in state to the king on the 31st, and on the 26th they gave him audience for a preliminary discussion of his business. The three ministers present at this meeting were Nemeaseasee, Serejeakeodang and another named Suctuagee, classed as a member of the Hluttaw, and described by the interpreter as " one who has the greatest title, and takes place of all the rest, but being very old, does not much concern himself in the affairs of the Government." They were presented with silk and cotton piece-goods, Patna glass bottles, and bottles of rose water, Suctuagee receiving a poorer share by far than the other two, who, in addition, were favoured with a musket apiece and Higginson's letters.[1] Fleetwood then apprised them of the main objects of his mission, keeping strictly, however, to the points enumerated by Higginson in his official letter to the king. The interview closed with vague promises of assistance on their part.

The intervening days between this interview and the 31st were taken up with what seem to us pointless discussions with various officials on questions of detail connected with the royal present. The interpreter came from the ministers to ask whether the whole present were for the king, or a part were to be reserved for the crown prince.[2] Fleetwood warily

[1] *Vide ante*, p. 167.
[2] The Burmese title for this dignity was Yuva Raja. He was Sanè, who succeeded his father peacefully in 1698.

replied that in the absence of definite instructions from his chief on this point, he left the matter to the decision of the king. This provoked the further question whether, if all went to the king, he had anything left over to the prince. To this he returned a flat " no." Having failed to draw him by means of this ruse, the ministers showed him the reason for their apparent solicitude on behalf of the crown prince. They brought to his notice the list of the present sent to Ava by the Syriam authorities, asking why many things that passed the Customs were not included in the list submitted by him at Ava. So the Syriam officials had carried out their threat. Luckily, however, Fleetwood's obvious explanation, that he had already had to deplete the original list by many presents to officials, satisfied the ministers, and they let the matter drop.

On the 31st in great state the present was delivered to the king, " carried by as many *Cooleys,* as we could get, to the No. of 160, in small Bambo *baskets.*" It consisted of all manner of piece-goods, together with three gold sashes, a gold shawl, twenty Patna glass bottles, forty bottles of rose water, four boxes of various spices, two fowling pieces, three muskets, the clockwork china woman and twenty viss of sandal-wood, the last item presented by Fleetwood on his own account. The royal reception of it shall be narrated in the words of the diary :—

> " The Letter [1] was carryed by Mr. *King* on *horseback*
> before the *Present;* and myself, attended by the

---

[1] Higginson had evidently studied how to address a Burmese monarch, since his letter opens with the following grandiloquent flourishes : " To his *Imperiall Majesty,* who blesseth noble *City* of *Ava* with his Presence, *Emperour* of *Emperours,* and excelling the *Kings* of the *East* and of the *West,* in *glory* and *honour* the *clear firmament* of *Virtue,* the *fountain* of *Justice,* the *perfection* of *Wisdom,* the *Lord* of *Charity,* and *Protector* of the *Distressed :* The *first mover* in the *Sphere* of *Greatness, President* in *Council, Victorious* in *Warr;* who *feareth none* and is *feared* by *all; Center* of the *Treasures* of the *Earth,* and of the *Sea, Lord Proprietor* of *Gold* and *Silver, Ruby's, Amber,* and all *precious Jewells, Favoured* by *Heaven,* and *honoured* by *men,* whose *Brightness* shines through the *World,* as the *light* of the *Sun,* and whose *great name* will be preserved in perpetual memory." But he made one striking omission : " Lord of many white elephants." On this point *vide* Hamilton's account of the Burmese king's titles in Appendix VII. A century later, in the days of the Company's waxing political power, its governors did not address the Burmese king with all his wealth of honorific epithet.

Linguist,[1] followed the *Present* : when we came to the *Garden Gate*, where the *King* was, we alighted ; where we were met by one of the *Ovidores*, who was there ready to conduct me in, and to direct me in the manner of approaching the *King* ; here I took the *Letter* from Mr. *King* and stayed almost a quarter of an hour, before the *Gates* were opened, When we fell down upon our *knees* and made *three Bows*, which done we entered the *Garden*, the *Present* following, and, having gone about half-way from the *Gate* to the *Place* where the *King* was seated, we made *three Bows* again as before, when we were gott within 15 yards of the King, we made *three Bows* again, as we had done before ; and were ordered to sit down ; after we were sat down, the *King* ordered the *Ovidore* to receive the *Letter*, and about half a quarter of an hour after, asked me the *three usual questions* viz. How long I had been in my passage from *Madrass* to his *Port* of *Syrian* ? How many days from *Syrian* to *Ava* ? And, at my departure from *Madrass*, If I had left my *Governour* in good health ? I told his *Majesty*, that I had been about 30 days in my passage from *Madrass* to *Syrian* ; about 42 days from *Syrian* to *Ava* ; And that at my departure from *Madrass* (thanks to GOD) I had left my *Governour* in *good health*, supplicating the *Divine power* for the continuation of his *Majesty's* health and happiness ; After this, I sat about half a quarter of an hour longer, and then was dismissed." [2]

True to Burmese custom, no mention was made at this ceremonial interview of the objects of Fleetwood's mission to Ava. The four following days were occupied by Fleetwood in doling out presents to high officials on his list, who had not yet received their due perquisites. On 6th January a present arrived from the king, " consisting of *Rice*, *Grain*, all sorts of *Green Trade*, that the *Country* afforded, Jagara,[3] Cocos,[4] etc."

---

[1] An old word for interpreter. Hobson-Jobson, s.v. Linguist.

[2] Cp. Hamilton's account of the royal reception of ambassadors at Ava in Appendix VI.

[3] Jaggery, coarse brown sugar made from the sap of palms, and still an important local product in Burma. (*Vide* Hobson-Jobson, s.v. Jaggery.)

[4] Cocoa-nuts.

But still the Burmese Government remained silent regarding the requests made in Higginson's letter. The ministers were sitting tight, partly in order to impress the embassy with the dignity of their Government, partly in order to force them to lay all their cards on the table. Any show of promptitude on the part of the Burmese would have lowered their prestige in their own eyes. So they maintained a completely inscrutable front until they had forced Fleetwood to take the initiative. Then began further haggling, in the course of which the Burmese ministers strove to find out how far Fort St. George meant to go in the matter of establishing a factory in the country. They threatened that unless Fleetwood produced the exact articles of trade, which he had been commissioned to negotiate, no reply of any kind would be vouchsafed to Higginson's letter. So on 9th January he delivered to Nemeaseasee a series of eleven articles, wherein were contained petitions for such trading privileges as, in accordance with his instructions, he deemed it wise to request.

Fleetwood's articles were a much whittled-down edition of Streynsham Master's. The first contained the usual request for general liberty of trade, with freedom of access to, and egress from, Burmese ports. By the second remission of a part of the normal Customs duties upon imported goods was requested, and the suggestion was proffered that the Company should be treated to a greater remission than private individuals, several of whom, it was represented, had obtained the abatement of one-third of the duties. The third related to cases similar to that of Bartholomew Rodrigues ; it asked that English ships, forced by storm or lack of provisions into a Burmese port, should not be seized and confiscated, but on the contrary should receive all reasonable assistance from the officers of Government. The fourth dealt with cases such as those of Thomas Samuel and Adrian Tilbury ; the estates of deceased Englishmen were to be " left to the disposall of the surviving English according to their manner and will." The fifth sought the co-operation of the Burmese Government in restoring to the Company's authorities deserters from its service. By the sixth, power to deal with debtors, similar to that requested in Streynsham Master's articles, was sought.[1]

[1] *Vide* Chapter VI., p. 112.

The seventh contained the petition that the English " may have free liberty, as always, to *repair* their *Ships*, in *Sirian ;* and if occasion be, to make *new ones ;* and that your *Majesty* would be pleased to permit them to make *Timber Docks*, which will save the great trouble, and expence, they are yearly at in cleaning the *Docks*, as they now are, to make them fit to receive *Ships*." By the eighth the Company desired freedom to export rice and timber for the supply of Madras, " they having great occasion for those things there." By the ninth, permission to continue in possession of the old house and ground at Syriam was requested, as also liberty to build further dwelling-houses and godowns, if required. The tenth drew the king's attention to " the poor *English Captive*, *Thomas Browne* who is the only *one surviving*, of *four* that were accidentally drove onto *Tauwy*[1] by *Storm* as they were going for *Atcheen*, about 10 years ago, in the *Service* of the *English Company ;* that your *Majesty* would be pleased to give him leave, to return to his *Native Country* and *Friends* after his so long Captivity." In the last Fleetwood urged that he should be vouchsafed an early answer, in order that he might return to Madras before the break of the wet monsoon, thereby rendering it possible for Fort St. George to despatch a " resident " to assume control over English trade at Syriam in the following sailing season. The request for freedom to make and export saltpetre was omitted. The officials, with whom Fleetwood consulted when these Articles were being translated into Burmese, warned him that not only would such a request be refused, but " the mentioning of it, might, probably, if the *King* should be disgusted at it, hinder his granting severall things."

From 9th January to the 22nd, although the assiduous envoy daily importuned the ministers, he could get nothing more out of them than vague promises of assistance. Not only did his visits to them cost him a good deal in presents, but during this time the various other officials, with whom he had come into contact and had not yet gratified, took the opportunity to apply personally for their " accustomary presents ; " and perforce he had to oblige. The two ministers,

---

[1] Tavoy.

Nemeaseasee and Serejeakeodang, through whom he had conducted all his business with the Government since his arrival
in Ava, took advantage of his repeated visits to ply him with
questions about conditions at Fort St. George, and Higginson's
reasons for wishing to reopen the Syriam factory.   Apparently
they were decidedly suspicious of the sincerity of Higginson's
intentions in the matter.   They asked Fleetwood whether he
thought " his designs of resettling in this *Country*, were real ; "
to which he cautiously replied that he could not think them
otherwise than real, " if his *Majesty's* favourable concession
to such *Petitions*, as had been presented to him, did any ways
answer his expectation, or give him the least encouragement."

At last the Burmese Government bestirred itself.   On
22nd January a messenger from the Hluttaw bade Fleetwood
attend that august assembly on the following day for his
answer.   " Accordingly the next day, in the morning, I went
to the *Runday*, where after I had waited about an hour,
Fearundameck came to me, out of the *Palace*, bringing with
him a *Black Book*, out of which (having together with myself
performed the *usual Ceremony* of *bowing three times* towards
the *Palace*) he read viz. :—

> " ' That the *Persons* of *Bartho. Rodriguez*, and all
> those that belonged to him, his *Majesty* had ordered to
> be restored to liberty ; and that his *Majesty* had been
> pleased to *abate* one *third* part of the *Customs ;* That to
> the rest of the *Petitions*, I should receive Answer ; and
> the *King's Present* to the *Governour*, when I did advise
> them of my being ready to depart.' "

The impatient envoy, thoroughly at a loss to understand
the cause of this further delay, went in a state bordering upon
exasperation to Nemeaseasee, protesting that he was anxious
to depart at once.   From him he learnt that the king had
referred the rest of his requests to the Hluttaw, which would
give him its answers to all points in detail on the following
day.   Accordingly, on the morrow, Fleetwood repaired once
more to the Hluttaw, and was informed of the decisions
arrived at by the ministers.   Their general tenor may be
summed up thus : If the Company would reopen its factory
in Burma, the Government would show favour to it in

individual cases of such matters as were mentioned in Fleetwood's articles.   But the Company could expect nothing unless it either reopened its factory or appointed a resident to control English activities at Syriam.   Thus, to the first article, the ministers replied that the particular privileges sought therein had never been denied to the Company ; if, therefore, it would reopen the Syriam factory, the ready assistance of the Burmese Government could be counted upon.   The second article, petitioning for remission of Customs duties, had, as we have seen, already been answered by the king.   To the third, concerning the seizure of ships, the ministers refused to give a general answer, " it being directly against the *Laws* and *Customs* of the *Country*."   If, however, the Company would reopen its factory, the ministers would, they assured Fleetwood, be always willing to " befriend " its servants in cases of this sort.   As far as the fourth article was concerned, the ministers protested that the estates of deceased Englishmen had never been seized, when there were other Englishmen in the country to take charge of them.[1]   In reply to the fifth and sixth, it was argued that as the requests were for what was long-established custom in the country, the Company had " no reason to suspect the contrary."

To the seventh article the Burmese Government replied that it would afford all assistance in its power to the Company to enable it to put the Syriam dock into fit condition for use in repairing ships, but that if shipbuilding were contemplated, the Company must appoint a resident to assume charge over its operations at Syriam.   " He (Nemeaseasee) insisted mightily upon the *Governours* first sending somebody to *reside* at *Syriam*," wrote Fleetwood in his diary.   After much pressing, however, permission was given for the two specified ships to be built " as soon as we pleased."   In the case of the eighth article, the ministers refused to allow the export of rice and timber until the Company re-opened a factory in

---

[1] This may have been true; I have seen no real evidence to the contrary.   In 1714, Captain Roger Allanson reported to the Fort St. George Council that he had prevented the Burmese Government from seizing the estate of a Mr. Francis Dalton, who " died in Pegue in the absence of the shipping intestate."   After settling up the dead man's affairs he paid proceeds, some 744 pagodas, to the Company's account.   (" Madras Public Proceedings," 3rd and 13th September, 1714.)

Burma. On the other hand, ready acceptance was given to the ninth article, and Fleetwood was informed that an order to that effect would be sent to Syriam. The tenth article caused some difficulty. The objection was raised that Thomas Browne's name was not mentioned in the Governor's letter. The ministers therefore offered to make his release conditional upon the Company reopening its factory. Fleetwood, however, refused to be put off in this way, and for some days literally pestered the ministers to withdraw this condition. " I used all the arguments, I could think of ; the poor man's pitifull complaints of the hardships he had always undergone there, and his continuall importunitys to solicit his releasement, did prompt me to stir the more in this particular." At last the ministers promised to use their good offices in behalf of Browne, and the assiduous envoy had to rest content with this rather vague assurance. He was less successful in his endeavours to secure the return of Bartholomew Rodrigues' property. To all his arguments the ministers replied that by the laws of the country such goods were confiscated, and " it was never yet known, that *any such Goods*, had been *restored*, and that they were afraid to urge the thing too much (though they had used their endeavours about it) finding the *King* so positively averse to it." Fleetwood indignantly pointed out that nowhere else in the world would such treatment be meted out to seamen, especially when they were strangers, and ignorant of the customs of the country. His latter argument merely elicited the reply that if they were ignorant of the customs of the country, it was their fault. Regarding the matter of Adrian Tilbury's estate, the ministers said that they had never heard of the man, but would make enquiries, and if anything belonging to him were found, it should be restored.

On 26th January Fleetwood was summoned to the Hluttaw to receive the royal present and letter to the Governor of Madras. The present comprised 300 viss of elephants' teeth, a number of lacquered boxes, 1500 viss of raw lac, and 2500 viss of tin, the last-named item to be delivered at Pegu. On returning to his quarters, he proceeded to work out the value of the present, and soon jumped to the uncomfortable conclusion that it came far short of what he had been led to expect. But when he brought this to the notice of Nemeaseasee, the latter and his colleagues were adamant in their refusal to procure any increase, and Fleetwood wisely refrained from further solicitation.[1]

From 26th January to 9th February the embassy was mainly engaged upon preparations to depart for Madras. Presents of ivory, tin, lac, musk, and hurtaul [2] were received from the chief ministers, while in return Fleetwood made further presents to them, and settled up accounts with other officials from whom he had received help, particularly the interpreter, Pasquall Rodrigues, about whom, curiously enough, he had been cautioned, " as one that, perhaps, for his own advantage, might play me a Knave's-trick." On the contrary, he had found him extremely helpful and obliging, and an excellent linguist. His leave-taking with Serejeakeo-dang and Nemeaseasee was most cordial. The former " gave me some *Musters* of *Jewells*, to be made in England, and earnestly recommended to me, the care of having them done and sent to him, as soon as possibly might." Both assured him of their friendship, and promised every assistance should the Company send further missions to Ava. A few days earlier they had given proof of their genuine solicitude in his behalf by securing the much-sought-after release of the unlucky Thomas Browne.

On 9th February the embassy left Ava, making all speed down stream to Prome, which was reached on the 22nd. Here they had some trouble with the Ausons, who demanded heavy bribes under threat of having the boats unladen and their cargoes examined, a proceeding that would have caused four or five days' delay. After much bickering, Fleetwood had to give way ; but he took advantage of meeting an Armenian on his way to Ava to send a report of their behaviour

---

[1] He probably under-estimated it, since in 1697, when despatching Thomas Bowyear to Syriam, Higginson wrote in his instructions : " I have received a profitt, by the returns of the *Present*, last sent to the *King*, which hath engaged me to make another attempt ; and to send another *Present*, double to the amount of the said profitt " (Dalrymple, " Oriental Repertory," II., p. 397). As the value of the second present was 600 pagodas, we may assume that his profit on the first was not less than 300 pagodas, a return of about 33 per cent. on his initial outlay.

[2] Yellow arsenic for dyeing purposes. (*Vide* Hobson-Jobson, s.v. Hurtaul.)

to the Government. " I was very much surprised at this manner of usage, from such mean inconsiderable fellows, having all the time I was at *Ava*, been very civilly treated and respected by every body ; and especially by *themselves*."

Six days later, on 28th February, he arrived at Syriam, and proceeded to lade the royal present on the *Loyal Captain*. On the 30th he was summoned to the Runday to hear the king's order read regarding the Company's privileges at Syriam. It was couched in almost identical terms with the reply vouchsafed him in the Hluttaw. But he was somewhat perturbed to find that it contained no mention of permission for the immediate construction of two ships there, as he had been promised. Nor was there specific mention of it in the royal letter to Higginson. This strange omission must have been due to oversight on the part of the scribes responsible for drafting the royal letter and order, since the royal sanction to build these two ships is definitely mentioned in Nemeaseasee's letter to the Governor of Madras,[1] with which Fleetwood was entrusted, along with others from Serejeakeodang and Monkeodang Rundameck, in reply to Higginson's letters to them.

At Syriam the Ausons again pestered Fleetwood for more bribes ; this time as a sort of thank-offering for the persons who had been released from captivity. Although the other local officials took their part by assuring the perplexed envoy that this was the custom of the country, he at first stoutly refused to gratify them. But, reflecting upon the fact that he had still to make the journey to Pegu to take delivery of the tin promised by the king, and that it was in the power of the Ausons to cause him considerable delay and inconvenience, unless he acceded to their importunities, he finally gave way, and propitiated them with two pieces of beetelas. They gave him no further trouble, and he was able to make a speedy journey to Pegu, where he took delivery of the tin.

On 12th March the whole of the present was safely stowed on board the *Loyal Captain*, and everything was in readiness for the departure of the mission. But still one more passage of arms was it necessary for Fleetwood to have with the authorities before he could leave. The " Chief Prince " at

---

[1] Dalrymple, "Oriental Repertory," II., p. 392.

Syriam informed him that he interpreted the royal grant of abatement of Customs to apply not generally to the Company's trade, but personally to Fleetwood in respect of any one ship that he might send on his own account to Syriam. The exasperated envoy therefore had to go to the trouble of writing to Ava asking that a clear order on the subject might be sent to Syriam. He also pointed out the omission of permission to build the two ships in the royal order, " which I likewise prayed them to take some care about, that upon our arrivall at *Sirian*, we might have no farther trouble about it : For if it should be otherwise, and that we should have any further disputes, either about the *abatement* of *Customs*, or the *liberty* of *building*, The *Governour* of *Madrass* would have all the reason in the World, to think himself abused, and would accordingly resent it."

On 17th March the *Loyal Captain* sailed from Syriam with the returning embassy. But for all Fleetwood's haste to finish his mission in time to cross the Bay before the break of the wet monsoon, his ship was unable to make her destination. Not until ten months later did she reach Fort St. George.[1] The cause of this is not easy to discover. Higginson, in his official letter to the Government of Burma entrusted to Bowyear in 1697, stated that the *Loyal Captain*, " coming out late from Syrian, lost that Monsoon." [2] But against that we have the fact that two ships from Syriam arrived at Fort St. George as late as the 20th and 25th of April respectively.[3] Presumably they started out later than the *Loyal Captain*. Further, it must be remembered that the wet monsoon never breaks as early as the middle of March. The probability is that she was caught in one of the early cyclones that occur in the Bay of Bengal before the break of the monsoon. As these are of short duration, this would explain why ships starting out later than the *Loyal Captain* completed their passages without difficulty. From a letter written by Fort St. George in October, 1696, to Sir John Gayer at Bombay, we learn that she was driven out of her course by contrary winds, and was forced to put into Acheen. The incident is interesting as throwing light upon one of the more important

---

[1] Dalrymple, *op. cit.*, II., p. 402. [2] *Ibid.*
[3] " Fort St. George Diary and Consultation Book, 1696," pp. 56, 60.

obstacles imposed by Nature in those days on the development of regular trade between the East India Company and Burma.

Fleetwood's diary supplies us with our first complete account of negotiations between the Company and a King of Burma. From it we catch glimpses of the inner workings of that curiously complicated and inefficient machine, which functioned as the central government of the country. The baneful system of perquisites, through which its subordinate officials were rewarded in lieu of receiving salaries—a system unfortunately common to most countries of the Far East— was one of its worst features, and strongly militated against the development of extensive commercial activities in the country. The complete ignorance of the outside world that prevailed at Ava is very striking, and serves to explain the long continuance of the more unreasonable of Burmese customs in the matter of the treatment of foreigners. The unwillingness of the Government to bind itself by a written agreement was really but one aspect of Burmese conceit, and was in no way due to any desire to keep foreign trade out of the country. Had an agreement of this sort been made, the king's successor would not have been bound by it, so that in effect it would have been of little use. The Burmese Government understood neither the need for, nor even the essential nature of, written agreements with foreign Powers. So long as foreign merchants would submit to calling themselves the " servants " of the " Lord of Water and Earth," and every now and again supplicate the golden feet to show pity on them, reasonable enough conditions might be obtained. But their continuance was precarious, subject as it was to the vagaries of a capricious sovereign will, that needed the frequent stimulus of inordinate flattery for it to adhere to a consistent attitude of benevolence.

There can be no doubt that the Burmese Government, according to its own lights, dealt not unhandsomely by Fort St. George in these negotiations. Although it obviously mistrusted the sincerity of Higginson's professed intentions of reopening the Syriam factory, it treated his envoys with true Burmese courtesy, and generously granted the chief objects of the mission. Further concessions, it announced, would be forthcoming, if the Company would definitely re-establish trade with Burma, for which development of affairs it expressed itself as extremely anxious. The Government's official letter to Higginson [1] dealt with the main features of the negotiations in the following manner :—

> " We have ordered the *Governours* of *Sirian*, that the *Shipmen* and *Merchants* that come upon *your Ships*, to *Sirian*, shall have *houses, Godowns, Docks* and all things necessary for the fitting of *Ships ;* and that they shall despatch the same, or see the same done, upon the arrivall of your *Ships* as shall be necessary. To your *Messengers*, we have given the *same place* and *houses*, that formerly belonged to the said *Company*.

> " Concerning the Goods of *Adrian Tilbury*, who died at *Mortivan*, in the *Kingdoms* of his *Imperiall Majesty*, we have no account of it by writing, nor know certainly any thing of it.

> " As for the *Petition* for the restoring of *Bartholomew Rodrigues*, his *Ship* and his *goods*, it is such as has never yett been granted, by any of his *Majestys Predecessors ;* But in consideration of its being made by the *Governour* of *Madrass*, who is his *Ancient Servant*, he has conceded to the giving *liberty* to *Bartholomew Rodrigues* and *all* his *People*.

> " Concerning the *Customs*, we [2] have likewise prevailed with his *Majesty* to abate *one third part* to all the *Ships*, that belong to the *Governour* of the *English Company*.

> " To the Company's Messenger, we gave all assistance, and gave him, the same *house* and *Godowns* that formerly belonged to the said *Company*, and by our Petitions to his *Majesty*, have caused him to be dispatched, that he may return this *Monsoon*.

> " In compliance with your *Messengers* request, for the releasement of all the *English*, that were in the *Empire* of his *Majesty*, we have assisted, and interceded with his

---

[1] Dalrymple, " Oriental Repertory," II., pp. 390-2.

[2] I.e. the ministers responsible for drafting the letter, which, although styled the " King's Letter " in Dalrymple, was probably the work of the Hluttaw.

Majesty, to release *those English,* which fell into the *Port* of *Tavay* in a *boat.*[1]

" The *mighty* and *powerfull Emperor* has done the honor to the *Governour* for the *English Company* in *Madrass,* to send him a *Present,* being 1500 Viss *Lack,* 2500 Viss *Tin,* 300 Viss *Ivory,* 6 *Earthen Dishes* and 8 *Lackered Boxes.*"

The next move lay with Nathaniel Higginson.

[1] Why the plural ? Fleetwood mentions only Thomas Browne ; the rest, according to the diary, were dead.

CHAPTER X

THE PERIOD OF INTERMITTENT RELATIONS, 1697-1723

CHAPTER X

THE PERIOD OF INTERMITTENT RELATIONS, 1697-1723

UPON Fleetwood's return to Madras early in 1697 with a full account of his transactions with the Government of Burma, the Fort St. George Council was summoned to a special consultation to consider " the settleing of a method whereby the Trade of that place may be rendered usefull to this, perticulerly for the repaireing and refiting of shipps." [1] Nothing was actually decided at the time, but soon afterwards the idea of forming a private joint stock company among the Company's servants stationed at Madras for developing the Syriam trade began to be mooted. In July definite proposals to this effect were laid before the Council, and an attempt was made to float a company. [2] Subscribers, however, were in no haste to support so risky a venture ; so for the time being the idea had to be dropped. Instead, it was decided to send a certain Thomas Bowyear to reside in Syriam in the capacity of " Chief of the English affairs in Pegu," and thus in part fulfil Higginson's promise to the Court of Ava. He was further to reopen negotiations with the Burmese authorities for the redemption of Bartholomew Rodrigues's cargo and the grant of further trading privileges which, as we have seen, had been made conditional upon the Company's appointing some responsible person to reside in Burma, and assume control over the English trade there. [3]

Thomas Bowyear, like his predecessors, Fleetwood and Lesly, was not strictly speaking a Company's servant. In the Fort St. George contemporary records he was classed as a " freeman inhabitant " of Madras. Just previous to his despatch to Burma, however, he had been employed by Higginson upon a mission to Cochin-China, his account of

[1] " Fort St. George Diary and Consultation Book, 1697," p. 15.
[2] *Ibid.*, 1697, p. 84.   [3] *Ibid.*, 1697, p. 102.

which was sent home to the Directors in June, 1697, along with Fleetwood's diary of the Burma mission.[1] He was provided with copies of all the documents relating to the Fleetwood mission, including the latter's instructions and diary.[2] In addition, Higginson—now styled Lieut.-General of India, for Affairs of the Right Honourable English East India Company—furnished him with a letter of appointment, instructions, letters to the " King of Ava," his chief minister and the Governor of Syriam, and presents to the value of 600 pagodas. His letter of appointment created him " Chief for Affairs of the Right Honourable English East India Company, and English Nation " at Syriam. He was empowered to reside in the Company's house there, and all Englishmen trading in Burma were required " to pay due respect and obedience " to him.[3]

On account of the failure of the joint stock project, Higginson again financed the cost of the present out of his own pocket. He had made a handsome profit out of the returns of the last present, and this fact alone, he explained in his instructions to Bowyear, made the matter of the redemption of Bartholomew Rodrigues's goods a point of honour. So " if the returns of the *Present*, shall stand in competition with, or hinder, the restoring of *Bartho. Rodrigues* his *Cargo*, I had rather forego, the receiving of any returns for the *Present*, than hinder the *restoration* of the *Cargo*." This, therefore, was to be one of the chief objects of Bowyear's negotiations with Ava. He was also to use his best endeavours with the Burmese Court to clear up doubtful points left unsolved by the last mission : the matter of Adrian Tilbury's estate, the exact interpretation of the royal grant of remission of one-third of the normal Customs duties, the shipbuilding

---

[1] " Fort St. George Diary and Consultation Book, 1697," p. 61. Bowyear's account of his mission to Cochin-China is in " Factory Records : Miscellaneous," Vol. 18, ff. 1-22. Coming first, it provides the title for the volume—a misleading title, seeing that most of the documents in the volume deal with the two missions to Burma of the years 1695 and 1697 respectively.

[2] Dalrymple, " Oriental Repertory," II., p. 396.

[3] *Ibid.*, II., p. 401. Higginson's instructions to Bowyear are in " Factory Records : Miscellaneous," Vol. 18, ff. 79-85, and in Dalrymple, *op. cit.*, II., pp. 396-404. For convenience of reference I have used the latter.

question, the much-desired permission to export rice and timber freely to Madras, and the matter of the confiscation of ships forced by adverse circumstances into Burmese ports.

Regarding shipbuilding, Higginson was more explicit than he had been to Fleetwood. What was required, he wrote, was " a *generall liberty* of *building small Boats* with one *Mast*, and of such a length, to serve great *Ships ;* under which notion *Brigantines*, of 40 or 50 Tons, may be built, which will be of great service to the Right Hon. Company, for the future." He stressed the importance of the proposal to obtain the right to the free export of rice and timber, " without which the Pegu Trade will signify little." If Bowyear could not obtain general permission, he might try to secure the right to export annually a small quantity of each commodity ; then by well-applied bribes to the Burmese officials it would be possible to augment this amount in practice. Higginson doubted the possibility of persuading Ava to abrogate the ancient custom of seizing ships driven into Burmese ports, so far as it affected the Company's shipping. His remarks on this subject show how clearly he perceived the real cause of the Burmese Government's reluctance to make grants of a general nature. " If you cannot obtain a generall Order," he wrote, " demand from the *Governours*, their *promise* to *assist* in *procuring* the *Kings favour*, when occasion requires ; when they will expect to be *Pishcashed*[1] and that is the true reason, why they will not suffer such *Generall Grants* to pass, that we may have a constant dependance on their assistance ; and be compelled to *pishcash* them."

The Fort St. George authorities were still anxious to avail themselves of the supplies of saltpetre, that they knew could be obtained in abundance in Burma. Bowyear was instructed to sound the Government once more on this subject, but he was warned to be extremely tactful in mentioning the matter, lest it should prejudice the rest of his business. If the king could be prevailed upon to make a contract to deliver a certain annual amount to the Company, Bowyear might bargain to supply broadcloth in exchange at the rate

[1] From the Persian *pesh-kash ;* it was used by Englishmen of this period with the meaning, " to make a present to a great man." (*Vide* Hobson-Jobson, s.v. Peshcush.)

of 1 yard for every 100 viss of saltpetre, or failing that, for every 30 viss of lac. Broadcloth had very little sale in India, because of its unsuitability for the climate. This was not the first time that attempts had been made to palm off on Burma goods that India would not buy.[1]

On 15th September, 1697, Bowyear departed for Syriam on board the *Pegu Merchant*, attended by a smaller vessel named the *Ruby*. " I do not find any *Record* of Mr. *Thomas Bowyear's Embassy*," wrote Dalrymple, in the Introduction to the second volume of the " Oriental Repertory." Apparently Bowyear kept no diary. Our sole source of information concerning his stay in Burma is a letter written by him in February, 1700, in reply to one from Fort St. George, which is no longer extant.[2] It runs thus :—

" I presume this trade may be worth the prosecuteing and that it might not be thought the R^t: Honble: $Comp^a$: rejects it, the King being desirous of a trade I have sent Capt: Hancocke to Ava where he will remaine till farther orders from yor: hon^r: $\&c^a$: Councill he being well disposed to the Service and willing to try his fortune w^{th}: a small adventure between Capt: Man^{ll}: da Silva and himselfe I sending Seaven pieces of Beetella's with him to present the Governour at his first arrivall. I am told the king[3] is consern'd that the $Comp^a$: has sent him noe present now haveing pretended to a Settlement in his Father's time, as by the Present I brought[4] and he having granted most that I requested and willing to grant more, wonders what should be the reason, and he having been told that I goe away this year and withdraw the ffactory is a reason that our business has not gone so well as it might and that I have noe answer to a Small present, sent him before the Ships arrived, requesting his order for the factory house, a Lingua,[5] and what was wanting of the returns of the ½ customes last year on Capt:

---

[1] *Vide ante*, Chapter IV., p. 76.

[2] " Letters to Fort St. George," Vol. VII., pp. 27-8.

[3] The king referred to is Sanè (1698-1714), the son of Minrekyawdin, who died in 1698.

[4] In 1697, when despatched by Higginson to reside in Burma.

[5] Interpreter.

Watt's his cargoe & since of the ½ of what M^r: Fenwick bro^t: Saying he would referr it to the next year.

" The Armenians have all grants of the half customes and Gregory (who requested it) liberty of building,[1] & by what I can understand they have good returnes of their Presents. The king is indeed ready to grant almost anything that can in reason be desired for the incourage- ment of a trade for more perticulers I beg leave to referr to my arrivall. M^r: Pearce remains here in Syriam till the next monsoon designing then for Ava I shall wait on you by y^e: Masshahee Capt: Plumbe Command^r:."

On 8th March this letter was received at Fort St. George, and three days later its writer arrived on board the *Messahia*.[2] If by reading between the lines one may hazard a guess at the condition of affairs between the Company and Burma, it seems more than possible that with the change of governors at Madras in 1698 occurred also a change of policy in relation to Burma.[3] During the next few years the records of Fort St. George contain few references to Burma save the names of ships departing for, or arriving from, Syriam. No mention is to be found of the appointment of a successor to Bowyear, and Fort St. George made no attempt even to conserve the privileges gained under Nathaniel Higginson.[4] Apparently for a time all official interest in the Burmese trade was lost, and the private trade left unregulated. The evidence on this point is conclusive. In 1708 a new Chief of the Affairs of the English was appointed in the person of a certain Robert Stokes, who had petitioned in the following manner to be allowed to settle in Burma under the Company's notice and protection :—

" I having formerly been at Syrian in the Kingdom of Pegue am desirous of returning thither to reside for some time, *and as the Honble: Company have privileges there,*

---

[1] Ships.

[2] " Fort St. George Diary and Consultation Book, 1700," pp. 23-4.

[3] In 1698 Higginson was replaced by Thomas Pitt.

[4] In 1700 the Fort St. George Council decided to transport certain " notorious and incorrigible villains " to Burma, but for what reason is not known (*ibid.*, 1700, p. 70).

which they don't enjoy at present [1] and as I am informed
are invited to resettle a Factory there, by that King, I
humbly desire of your Hon^r: &c^a: that I may have the
Liberty to remain there under the notice of a Company's
Servant,[2] That ile (*sic*) oblige myself to be no way charge-
able to the Company thereby, and to return whenever
your Hon^r: &c^a: shall think fitt to recall me further
desiring that the Honble: President will honour me with
his Letter to that King, therein mentioning upon what
account I settle there." [3]

We have further evidence regarding Fort St. George's
neglect to follow up the missions despatched by Nathaniel
Higginson. Alexander Hamilton, who, it will be remembered,
visited Syriam in 1709, states that the trade formerly carried
on by the English merchants of Fort St. George with that
port, "where many private Traders got pretty good Bread
by their Traffick and Industry," was then almost entirely
in the hands of the Muslims and Telugus of South India,
and the Armenians, who had the monopoly of the ruby trade.
The English, he writes, confined themselves to the business
of building and repairing ships.[4]

Possibly the Burmese refusal to allow the Company to
export saltpetre was one of the chief causes of Fort St. George's
lack of interest in the Syriam trade during these years.
Hamilton mentions that at the time of his visit to Burma its
export was forbidden on pain of death.[5] Evidently also Fort
St. George was able to procure indirectly more than sufficient
lac from Burma, since in January, 1706, we find the Directors
writing to the President and Council in the following terms :—

" Lacks are here so dull a Commodity, occasioned by
y^e: vast quantityes of late imported that they sell at one

---

[1] The italics are mine.

[2] Possibly Gulston Addison is referred to here, since it appears that
Stokes went to Burma on this occasion in the employment of a certain
" Pegu Joint Stock," of which Addison was chief director, and almost
proprietor.

[3] "Madras Public Proceedings," 29th March, 1708.

[4] Hamilton, "A New Account of the East Indies," I., p. 367 and II.,
p. 41.

[5] *Ibid.*, II., p. 41.

third of y^e: Price they did some years ago so that we would not have you send any Pegu sticklack till further order." [1]

Stokes's expedition to settle in Burma throws interesting light upon the private trading activities of the Company's servants at Madras. Apparently he merely requested official permission to settle there as a private merchant under the Company's protection. But the instructions given him by Thomas Pitt suggest that there was more in it than meets the eye at first glance. He was given powers and status very similar to those granted to Thomas Bowyear eleven years earlier. And as we have seen that the latter's mission was connected almost entirely with private trading matters— particularly those in which certain of the Company's servants at Fort St. George were deeply concerned—we shall naturally wonder what was behind this grant of special powers and status to Stokes. Thomas Pitt's instructions to him are of sufficient interest in this connexion to be given in full. They run thus :—

"You having by your Petition dated 29th March 1708 requested our Countenance & assistance in your designe of settling at Pegu, (which place is under the direction of this Presidency) of which having duely considered, we hereby grant and order you to act in the following manner.

"First on your arrivall at Pegu you give the Gov^rs: [2] letter with your Present to the Prince of Syrian, and acquaint him that you have letters for the King and primere Minister, as also presents, and desire his advice how they may be forwarded to Ava, which Presents must be all given in the Honble: Company's name, tho' at your own charge.

"Secondly that whereas the Comp^a: have a piece of ground at Syrian, and a small house upon it, wee hereby empower you to take possession off, & thereon build such houses as shall be most convenient for yor: accomodation, but at no manner of charge to the Company, on which

[1] " Records of Fort St. George: Despatches from England, 1701-6," p. 79.
[2] i.e. Thomas Pitt's.

house you may hoist St: Georges fflag, and hereby order you to acquaint all English that come there that they presume not to hoist any flag on the shore.

" Thirdly the Company having great priviledges in that country, of which we desire you to inform yourself, and afterwards to use your uttmost endeavours & advice, as also assist all others to preserve the same.

" Fourthly we must not omitt to advise you to avoid all manner of disputes with the Governm^t:, especially so as to bring it to a rupture between you and matters in such confusion as was lately at Acheen, for if the Governm^t: be unjust to you, or that any English do an action dishonourable to the Nation or prejudiciall to the Company's affairs, do not you proceed any further against 'em than by a fair representation of the case, and demonstration of their injustice, and to our own people give 'em due warning & friendly admonishm^t:, and if that do's not prevail lay all before us and wait our orders for your further proceedings. We wish you good success in your undertakings and again recomend to you the entire preservation of the Company's priviledges which you have promis'd shall be done without any charge to them." [1]

Four years later, when Stokes was dead, a claim made against a private company called the Gulston Addison Joint Stock, by Captain Armiger Gosling on behalf of a certain Captain Roger Allanson, gives us our necessary information regarding the real nature of Stokes's activities in Burma. In Gosling's petition to the Fort St. George Council Stokes is termed " Resident at Syrian in Pegue for affairs of Gulston Addison Esq: &c^a: joynt Stock Merchants." [2] Gulston Addison, who died at Madras in October of the year 1709, was the brother of the essayist. He entered the Company's service in 1694,[3] and six years later was appointed Under Searcher at the Sea Gate at Fort St. George on a salary of £30 per annum.[4] In 1709 he was promoted to be a member

---

[1] "Madras Public Proceedings," 10th May, 1708.

[2] *Ibid.*, 7th July, 1712. In this petition Stokes is wrongly named Thomas at the beginning, but is given his correct name of Robert later on in the document.

[3] Love, "Vestiges," II., p. 67, n. 3.   [4] *Ibid.*, II., p. 64, n. 2.

of Council, and in September of that year, just thirty days before his death, received notice from the Directors of his appointment as President and Governor of Fort St. George.[1] How long his " Pegu Joint Stock," as it is termed in some documents, had been in existence at the time of his death, the records do not tell us.   It is probable that it began its operations only in 1708, when Stokes was granted permission to settle at Syriam.   Being a private concern, it would not normally receive attention in the official proceedings of Fort St. George.

In his petition Gosling asserted that Stokes, on behalf of the Gulston Addison Joint Stock, had sent Allanson to Ava to procure elephants' teeth.   This mission, it is interesting to note, is the one referred to by Dalrymple in the following passage, taken from his " Letter concerning the Negrais Expedition " :—[2]

" In 1709 Mr. *Richard Allanson*[3] (mentioned by *Hamilton*, under the name of *Allison*) went on an *Embassy* to Ava ; with a Letter from the famous Diamond-Governor *Pitt*.   *Hamilton's* Account of his Observations, is all I have met with regarding his *Journey*, and therefore refer you to that Book ; which, though generally extremely partial, where our own Governments are concerned, in other Things, except when under the influence of superstition, is well worth attentive perusal."

Allanson, it appears, not only bought the required amount of ivory for the Gulston Addison joint stock, but in addition some on his own account, which he intended to consign to Gosling on his return from Ava early in 1710.   According to Gosling's story, Stokes refused to allow Allanson's private purchase to be despatched to Madras on board the joint stock's ship, the *Gulston Galley*, but offered to buy it of him for 366 pagodas 21 fanams,[4] payable within 21 days of the ship's arrival at Madras.   Allanson accepted, and on 9th April, 1710,

---

[1] Love, *op. cit.*, II., p. 69.   [2] " Oriental Repertory," I., pp. 104-5.

[3] In the " Madras Public Proceedings " his name is given as Roger Allanson.

[4] This amount is given as the equivalent of 36,676 viss of ganza, an indication of the depreciation in value of the Burmese currency.

Stokes executed a promissory note to the above effect in his favour. The money was never paid, and although Stokes on his death-bed promised to include the amount in his will in favour of Allanson, and one of his executors, Robert Raworth, a member of the Fort St. George Council,[1] promised to see the debt discharged, the trustees of the Gulston Addison joint stock, to whom Gosling had applied after Stokes's demise, refused to honour the note.

On the Council taking up the matter, it appeared from the evidence of one John Neville, chief mate of the *Shaalem*, another ship belonging to the Gulston Addison joint stock, that Allanson's ivory went on board that ship to Bengal, where it was sold along with a consignment belonging to the joint stock. The trustees of the joint stock, Edmund Mountague and Bernard Benyon,[2] objected to the claim on the ground that nothing was specifically paid into the joint stock's account in respect of the sale of Allanson's ivory, though they admitted that the debt was entered up in " a sort of waste book," in which Stokes kept his accounts while in Burma. In explanation of this, however, they suggested that he had probably sold the ivory privately. But the Council was of the contrary opinion, and ordered the trustees to pay up the debt.[3]

We learn more of the Gulston Addison joint stock from the record of another successful claim against it made in the same year by Edmund Bugden,[4] who had been sent over to Syriam by the trustees of Addison's estate in May, 1711, to

---

[1] Deputy-Governor of Fort St. David in 1713, where he raised an unsuccessful rebellion against Edward Harrison, Governor of Madras.

[2] Who took Raworth's place as a trustee some time between May and September, 1711.

[3] " Madras Public Proceedings," 22nd July, 1712.

[4] He entered the Company's service in November, 1692 ; in 1695 he was appointed to the staff of the Fort St. David factory as a writer. (" Fort St. George Diary and Consultation Book, 1695," p. 170.) In 1697 he was classed as Secretary and Factor at Fort St. David. (*Ibid.*, 1697, p. 103.) In 1699 he became Assistant to the Sea Customer, and in July of the following year was appointed second at Madapollam. At the end of the year, however, he was fourth in Council at Masulipatam on a salary of £30 per annum. He left the Company's service shortly afterwards, and became a free merchant at Madras, where in January, 1702, he joined with other free merchants in sending a petition to the king. (*Ibid.*, 1702, pp. 6, 7.)

wind up the affairs of the joint stock in consequence of
Addison's death.   Bugden had been allowed by the trustees to
take with him, free of freight charges, a limited amount of
goods [1] for private trading on his own account.   But, on being
refused a passage for the goods he had bought in Burma
with the proceeds, he had sold them to the joint stock at
what he asserted to be reasonable rates.   The trustees, however, had refused payment for these goods.   He claimed a
sum of slightly over 13,000 pagodas, representing a profit of
160 per cent. on his original outlay.   The Fort St. George
Council passed orders in his favour, subject to a deduction of
57 pagodas, 18 fanams in respect of wages paid to John
Beser, Bugden's personal assistant, and 150 pagodas for
" extraordinary expence in diett and Liquors." [2]

After Stokes's death, there is no further mention of the
appointment of a resident Chief of the Affairs of the English
Nation at Syriam until 1724.   As few English traders ever
resided in Burma throughout the rainy season in those days,
it was apparently the custom to appoint a Chief each year
from among the Madras private traders, who resorted to
Syriam during the " sailing season."   By such a makeshift
method did Fort St. George seek, on the one hand, to retain
some sort of control over English trade in Burma, and on
the other sufficiently to impress the Burmese authorities so as
to prevent the Company's trading privileges in Burma from
lapsing.   But, as we shall see later, the Chief's authority was
vague, and could usually be flouted by unlicensed traders with
impunity.   Apart from Gulston Addison's short-lived venture
the Company's servants at Fort St. George showed no inclination to interest themselves in the commercial possibilities of
Burma during the first two decades of the eighteenth century.
Even the permission to build ships at Syriam, which had been
so important an objective in the negotiations set on foot by
Higginson, was not utilised by Fort St. George during this
period, though the private traders availed themselves of it.
Still, during this period there are a number of isolated incidents
arising out of Fort St. George's connexion with Burma to be

---

[1] Limited to 5000 pagodas in value.
[2] "Madras Public Proceedings," 11th September and 28th November,
1712 ; 16th and 26th February and 2nd March, 1713.

recorded, though rather for their interest than for any importance that can be attached to them.

In 1706 ambassadors from the King of Burma to Aurungzeb, the Mughal Emperor, arrived in Madras with royal letters requesting the Governor to " give them his Assistance and Advice in conducting them the safest way to the King's Court." [1] The required assistance was afforded, and apparently in the following year the embassy returned to Burma once more by way of Madras. In 1707 Fort St. George reported home that some Arabs, resorting to Syriam for the purpose of shipbuilding, had there captured an English ship, the *Friendship*, and were very insolent to the English.[2] The Directors replied that the " Muscatters " were to be prevented from entering Burmese ports ; [3] whereupon Fort St. George sent back information that representations on the subject had been made to the Burmese authorities—presumably at Syriam—which they hoped would prove successful.[4] We hear no more of the incident, but there is no indication that the Arab trade with Burmese ports, which still continues to this day, was ever interrupted as a result of the Company's action. In 1708 a rather amusing occurrence was reported to the Fort St. George Council, which caused it no little trepidation. An Indian conicopoly, or accounts clerk, who went to Burma on one of the Madras ships, forged a letter to the King as from the Governor of Madras, and sent it, together with a present, to Ava, " for which he had an advantageous return in Elephants." [5] Whether the Burmese Government ever discovered the trick does not appear. The trickster, however, on his return to Madras, was put into prison by Governor Thomas Pitt, " to prevent the pernicious consequences that attend such vile practices." But, on it being discovered that he had done business in Burma on commission for several Madras merchants, " to whom he had not yet rendered any accompt," it was decided to let him off with a fine of 200

---

[1] " Madras Public Proceedings," 11th April, 1706.
[2] " Records of Fort St. George : Despatches to England, 1701-2—1710-11," p. 67.
[3] " Fort St. George : Public Despatches from Court," XIV., pp. 105-30.
[4] " Records of Fort St. George : Despatches to England, 1701-2—1710-11," p. 102.
[5] " Madras Public Proceedings," 19th August, 1708.

pagodas, and the execution of a bond never again to go to Burma. The Council feared lest the infliction of a long term of imprisonment would jeopardise his creditors' chances of securing their money.

In 1711 the Mughal Shah Alam exchanged presents with Sanè, King of Burma. Shah Alam sent to the Burmese monarch a dress of honour, and received in return a present of twelve elephants which, at the request of the Mughal ambassador, were allowed to pass through Madras Custom free. During that and the following year two Burmese embassies passed through Madras to the Mughal Court, in both cases not without incident. A servant attached to the first was accidentally shot and mortally wounded by one of the Fort St. George sentries, Sergeant Johannes Bassing, a Dutchman, who was amusing himself by taking a shot at a large bird, when the Burman suddenly emerged from behind a hedge carrying a pot of water. Bassing received a severe reprimand, and was dismissed the Company's service.[1] In the case of the second embassy, the Mughal Government wrote to Fort St. George with the request that it should be prevented from proceeding by way of Bengal. Fort St. George, however, replied refusing to take action in the matter, " forcibly detaining any Kings Embassadors, being contrary to the Laws of this and all other Nations in the World, and in this Particular case might give the King of Pegue a reasonable pretence to seize the shipping and effects belonging the Inhabitants of this place, which are very considerable in his Dominions and might be entirely lost." [2] The ambassadors were therefore allowed to depart for Bengal on board a ship, called the *Elahee*, belonging to the King of Burma.[3] Evidently Sanè possessed the nucleus of a mercantile marine. The records of this period mention two ships classed as belonging to the King of Burma, the *Elahee* and the *Salaimat*. The former had an English pilot named Richard Osborne. Unfortunately, we catch only fleeting glimpses of these ships, when their arrival or departure from Madras is entered in the Fort St. George Diary. The fact, however, is of great interest. Recent historians of Burma have been so obsessed by the idea

---

[1] "Madras Public Proceedings," 1st and 7th November, 1711.
[2] *Ibid.*, 15th July, 1712.   [3] *Ibid.*, 24th July, 1712.

that the Toungoo dynasty was played out in the eighteenth century, that scant attention has been paid to Sanè. As far as can be ascertained, he was the first King of Burma to possess sea-going vessels.

In 1711 King Sanè wrote to Fort St. George asking to be supplied with two clocks, constructed according to the description given in his letter. The translation of his letter, entered in the Fort St. George Consultation Book,[1] is of sufficient interest to be given here in full. It runs thus :—

" In the jurisdiction of Sunapranda[2] and Thamadiaha[3] the precious Kingdome of Ava and Golden Court, Raja of Ni and King of twenty and three Kingdoms and Monarchys, Lord of Silver, Gold, Amber, Rubies, Mines, and Red and Gold Pallaces 12 in number made in gold, Lord of the Elephants of great vallue, Lord of many Horses of great price, Lord of many Army's, Lord of this World, the Excellent high and mighty Lord.[4]

" His order to the Governour of Madrass being inform'd that amongst the English Nation there are many able men and that without much trouble a Clock may be had, I desire that it may be thus vizt: that it strikes the hours distinctly beginning in the morning by one and soe on till twelve having two Images to strike the hours on the bell or Clock this and another Clock of Malte (*sic*), with a Woman's Image pouring oil in a Vessell which runns all the hour, and when it is out the said image fills it againe, and soe every hour, the King having heard of these things will have much to be done to get them, and if not to be gott, to send a man here to make them, and shall return to his Country, I have sent by Capt: of the Ship Cojah Simon to the Governour of Madrass two Rubye rings if amongst the English or the Portuguese there is any Curiosity to be gott let it be sent, if my desire is accomplish'd there shall be great reward according to my Piety &c^a:."

[1] " Madras Public Proceedings," 24th February, 1711.
[2] Sonaparanta, a title of classical Indian origin used to indicate the central part of the Burmese king's dominions. It probably meant " golden frontier-land." For this and the following reference, *vide* Hobson-Jobson, s.v. Sonaparanta.
[3] Tambadipa, " copper region."
[4] Cp. Hamilton's account of Sanè's titles in Appendix VII.

Unfortunately, the records do not tell us what Fort St. George did in the matter.

In 1710 Fort St. George reported home to the Directors that the quantity of ganza then being imported from Burma was depreciating the value of lead to such an extent that the warehouse-keeper had been ordered to sell off his whole stock of lead at whatever price he could make, subject to a reserve of 6 pagodas per candy.[1]   There is much evidence in favour of the view that what Caesar Fredericke, in the sixteenth century, had described as a mixture of copper and lead, had by the beginning of the eighteenth degenerated into lead only, though still appearing in the Company's accounts under the euphemistic title of ganza.   Hamilton calls ganza plain lead,[2] and although Hobson-Jobson gives us a quotation from the Dutch writer Valentijn dated 1726, in which it is called brass mixed with lead, the metal exported from Burma at this time under the name of ganza had probably little else than lead in its composition.   Yule,[3] writing in the middle of the nineteenth century, mentions that the Burmans used lead in their bazaars for small purchases.   He does not call it ganza : apparently by his day the name had dropped out of use. This view is further strengthened by the following resolutions, passed by the Fort St. George Council at a consultation on 14th February, 1712 :—

" Order'd that for the future Pegu lead be bought for use of this Garrison and other settlements under the Presidency being allwaies cheaper than Europe lead, and every way as serviceable for Amunition.

" Order'd that the Warehouskeeper do buy Twenty five Candy to be imediately ship't off for Vizagapatam." [4]

Coincident with the progressive adulteration of ganza we notice a proportionate depreciation in its currency value. In 1712 the value of the Madras pagoda was quoted at 100 viss of ganza.[5]   When we remember that in the days of the first Syriam factory (1647-57) a viss was said to have been " nearest 16d. starling," [6] the amount of its depreciation will be at once

[1] " Fort St. George Despatches to England, 1701-2—1710-11," p. 119.
[2] " A New Account of the East Indies," II., p. 41.
[3] " Mission to Ava,", p. 259.
[4] "Madras Public Proceedings," 14th February, 1712.
[5] *Ibid.*, 22nd July, 1712.   [6] O.C. Duplicates, No. 2147.

evident. Taking the value of the pagoda in 1712 to have been
about eight shillings, we find the viss of ganza worth no more
than about one penny. This enormous shrinkage in the
commercial value of the Burmese currency resulted in the
substitution of silver for ganza as the medium for large transactions. Shipbuilding and repairs in the eighteenth century,
for instance, were paid for in bar silver, and in the records of
Fort St. George consultations regarding these matters, mention
is usually made of so many hundred ounces of silver being
despatched to Syriam to defray the expenses. European
travellers as early as the sixteenth century noted silver as one
of Burma's imports, and in the following century the East
India Company's servants who visited the country remarked
upon the strictness with which Customs duties had to be paid
in silver. The immense depreciation in the value of ganza
meant that it was quite impossible, for obvious physical
reasons, to make use of it for anything more than petty
bazaar business, and even among the Burmese themselves a
kind of silver currency had come into being probably before
the beginning of the eighteenth century. Hamilton's account
of this new form of Burmese currency is extremely interesting.
Writing of the import of silver into Burma, he says :—

" Silver of any sort is welcome to them. It pays the
King eight and an half per cent. Custom, but in lieu of
that high Duty, he indulges the Merchants to melt it
down, and put what alloy they please in it, and then to
pass it off in Payments as high as they can. Rupee Silver,
which has no Alloy in it, will bear 28 per cent. of copper-
alloy, and keep the Pegu Touch, which they call flower'd
Silver, and if it flowers, it passes current. Their way to
make flowered Silver is, when the Silver and Copper are
mixt and melted together, and while the Metal is liquid,
they put it into a shallow Mould, of what Figure or
Magnitude they please, and before the Liquidity is gone,
they blow on it through a small wooden Pipe, which makes
the Face, or Part blown upon, appear with the Figures
of Flowers or Stars, but I never saw any European or
other Foreigner at Pegu, have the Art to make those
Figures appear, and if there is too great a Mixture of

Alloy, no figures will appear.   The King generally adds ten per Cent. on all Silver that comes into his Treasury, besides what was put on at first, and tho' it be not flower'd, it must go off in all his Payments, but from any Body else it may be refused if it is not flower'd." [1]

As we have noted above, no coinage proper was introduced into Burma until the middle of the nineteenth century, except in the case of the British province of Tenasserim acquired in 1826.   So the curious and unsatisfactory practices described by Hamilton must have operated as a very serious handicap to the development of Burmese foreign trade.

Earlier in this chapter we have discussed Fort St. George's method of retaining some vestiges of control over English trade in Burma, by means of the appointment of a " Chief of the Affairs of the English Nation " at Syriam from among the Madras private merchants, who annually resorted thither in the sailing season.   This post was for a number of years in the second and third decades of the eighteenth century held by that remarkable character, Captain George Heron. In the sailing season of 1720-21 there occurred in Syriam an extraordinary incident, Heron's connexion with which, three years later, brought down upon his head a severe reprimand from the Directors which apparently resulted in his retirement from business in Burma.   The incident arose out of a private ship, the *Lusitania*, owned by Alexander Orme,[2] the father of the historian, in partnership with Francis Hugonin, chief gunner at Fort St. George, putting into Syriam for repairs, and, so far as we can judge her supercargoes, flinging Heron's authority to the winds in their relations with the Burmese authorities.   The affair is of interest as throwing light upon the conditions under which the private trade with Burma was carried on at that period.   But the account of it contained in the Fort St. George records has also an intrinsic interest which justifies the inclusion here of a somewhat lengthy extract from the original documents relating to it.

[1] Hamilton, " A New Account of the East Indies," II., pp. 42-3.
[2] Mentioned in the Fort St. George " List of Sea Faring Men not Constant Inhabitants " of 1714.   Chief at Anjengo in 1728 (Love, " Vestiges," II., p. 422, n. 2).

On 20th April, 1721, Stephen Orme,[1] one of the super-cargoes of the *Lusitania*, laid a formal complaint on behalf of her owners before the Fort St. George Council, accusing one Cojee Zechary, an Armenian shipbuilder of Syriam, of the murders of the ship's chief mate, Charles Wankford, and gunner, John Dalziel, at the Moharram festival in Syriam on the night of 28th October, 1720. He further accused George Heron of obstructing the course of justice, " by espousing the cause of Zechary," when the case came before the Yondaw of Syriam. In laying his case before the Fort St. George Council, Orme furnished them with a copy of his diary, entitled " An Account of our Voyage to Pegu and Transactions there." [2] This document, which contains a complete, though one-sided, account of the affair, runs as follows :—[3]

" Left Fort St. George June 19th 1720 in the morning and made the Island of Andemands the 29th ; from thence we steer'd for the Pegu Coast, and on July the 2nd fell in about twenty leagues to the Westward of Syrian River.[4] On the 3rd made the river in the evening. Next morning we got in, but was obliged to ship our cable, & on the 6th arr^d: at Syrian.

" The first thing we did was going to the Ronda [5] to give an Acc^t: who we were, what goods we brought, what burthen our ship, how many men and guns we carry'd, and that we had a present for the King. Then we waited on the Prince, requesting his favour, letting him know at the same time we had a particular present for himself. He seem'd pleas'd, promising us his protection, and having treated us with a Beetle [6] we took our Leave and went to Capt: Heron's, where we lodg'd.

" July the 7th we took the fittest Dock for our purpose

---

[1] His relationship to Alexander Orme does not appear in the account of this affair in the " Madras Public Proceedings ; " probably Alexander was his father.

[2] " Madras Public Proceedings," 20th April, 1721.

[3] I have modernised the punctuation, which in the original renders the task of reading very difficult. The spelling, however, is unaltered. For the full account of the case, see " Madras Public Proceedings," 20th April—11th May, 1721 (India Office) ; or " Madras Public Consultations," Vol. LII., pp. 87-126 (Madras Record Office). Love, "Vestiges," II., pp. 210-12, gives a brief reference to the affair.

[4] Now the Rangoon River.   [5] *Vide* Appendix V.

[6] Betel leaf with areca nut for chewing.

we could get, and apply'd ourselves to make it fit to receive our ship, it wanting length, breadth and depth.

"August the 12th M^r: Tornery [1] went to Prone [2] for Plank and Timbers, and met with better fortune than he expected, for the King, being mightily pleas'd with his Present, sent orders to the Government at Prone to seize all Plank and Timbers for the great ship. Likewise he order'd six thousand Baskets of rice to be deliver'd us at the Curr^t: Price, [3] which acco^ts: we are to make up with an Armenian the King owes money to.

"September the 6th got the Ship into the Dock, and by M^r: Blyth's advice pull'd to pieces her upper Works to the main Whale, taking out everything we found bad. We likewise cut two streaks fore and aft below the main whale, that we might be sure her Juttock Timbers were good, which proved so. Within her we cut the ceiling fore and aft, where the timbers joyn'd, but found every one good, except in the run of her abaft, where was 19 bad, which M^r: Blythe ordered to be cut out.

"September the 26th M^r: Tornery return'd from Prone and bro^t: some Plank, and on the 29th went to Pegu.

"October the 1st arrived the greatest part of our top timbers, which I had sent severall people different ways to procure, it being what we most wanted. And now stay for nothing but begin to make new.

"October the 8th our Lascars, with those belonging to two ships, deserted, and kept in a body with colours flying, arm'd with Bamboos &c^t:. Their Complaint was they wanted six tecull [4] per month with salt, oyl, &c^t:, and unless they might have everything demanded, they would dye before they would surrender.

---

[1] The other supercargo of the *Lusitania*.   [2] Prome.

[3] The present Burmese basket of paddy weighs 46 lbs. In 1759 the price of rice was 15 baskets to the rupee, but it was probably much cheaper in 1720, since in 1759 Burma was at war and had passed through a generation of internecine strife. (*Vide* Harvey, "History of Burma," p. 354.)

[4] A tical weight of uncoined silver, which, as we have already seen, was taking the place of ganza for payments in Burma. The Burmese name for this was *kyat*; it was probably in those days equivalent to about 1¼ rupees in value. The modern Burmese word for the Indian rupee introduced by the British administration is also *kyat*. (*Vide* Hobson-Jobson, s.v. Tical, for many references to the use of the word.)

" I immediately went to Capt: Heron and told him the story, asking if his were gone too. He told me no. I ask'd him if he would go to the Prince. He answer'd no, upon which I left him and went myself (not empty-handed). My reception was such that the Prince sent out his soldiers and brought every Lascar belonging to the three ships to me. Those belonging to us he deliver'd up, to do as I thought fit with them. The rest he let go where they would.

" One of our Lascars being cut in one or two places in the head, I wrote a note to Capt: Martin, intreating he would assist him ; but rec^d: an answer, Capt: Heron would not let him ; and from that time he gave orders to his People that none should dare come near us. If they did, they should not come into his house again. His resentment did not stop here, but hurry'd him to the Prince, where to our great diversion he proved himself a most obstinate, malicious, senseless fool by unsaying everything he had said to him before. For at his arrivall [1] he told the Government the Company would send a great ship to him, and upon her arrivall promis'd them severall things, expecting she would be consign'd to him, and so to have it in his power to make himself great at the expense of others. But now we did not belong to the Company, and, to make short the story, everything his fruitfull imagination, with a long experience in mischief, could suggest, was too good for us. The Prince himself sent for us, and told us the above story, adding that he saw that we minded our own business and troubled ourselves with nobody else ; that we not only took care ourselves to do nothing contrary to the Law of the Country, but our People also ; therefore we might depend upon his friendship. He advis'd us to take care of Capt: Heron, for he was our Inveterate Enemy.

"The occasion of Capt: Heron's anger, we conjecture, sprung from the following Acco^ts: (we never having had any word with him, neither did we know he was angry).

" At our arrivall he wanted to make Presents for us to the King, Prince and Governours, but bringing those Presents with us disappointed him.

" He likewise had promised the Prince that the King

[1] In Syriam from Madras.

should have some of our Ships guns, which, we told the Prince, we had not power to part with.

" Also we did agree with him in his advice to pay the same Customs for the Sloop as for the Ship, but thought it better to make her pass for the Ships boat, which, he said, we could not ; but we did.

" We likewise did not entertain his Cheif Mate as overseer in repairing our Ship, at twenty Pagodas per m:°, because we could not think his way. And upon our Lascars running away, altho he deny'd going [1] to the Prince with us, he was sure it could not be made up with them, but by him, as he said to sev[ll]: Persons. But when he found his Mistake, he was still more mistaken by imagining his honour could be touch'd, and resenting it, as above.

" October the 28th being the time of the Moors Feast, (Hossen Jossen) our Serang,[2] Tendell [3] and Lascars complain'd they could not pass in the street without being affronted by Cap[t]: Heron's Lascars and Seign[r]: Zechary's, but they hop'd they might have liberty to resent it ; which we positively forbid, ordering them not to mind anything they said, for if we knew they struck anybody without they were beat first, they should be made examples of. This Complaint gave us occasion to advise Cap[t]: Heron of it by a note, assuring him our Lascars had positive orders not to hurt any of his. But we rec[d]: no other answer than what he said to our servant, that carry'd the Note ; that the Ship was great, but the People had little Wit. M[r]: Tornery, who was arrived from Pegu, went to Zechary and advised him the same. In the evening, when they left off work, as usuall our People went to the Feast, some to celebrate it, others to look on.

" About eleven a Clock at night we were rais'd from our Cots with an Acco[t]: that Zechary and his People were killing our cheif Mate and Gunner ; upon which M[r]: Tornery and myself and one Englishman took arms and went towards the place, where we were told the bodys lay, some of our Lascars joining us in the way. In our march we met a large company of Zechary's and Cap[t]: Heron's People, w[th]: colours flying and Lanthorns, coming from the same place, who fled as soon as

---

[1] Refused to go.   [2] Overseer of Lascars.
[3] Petty officer of Lascars ; boatswain.

they saw us. We went on and found the report too true. We saw our Cheif Mate and Gunner lying in their Blood, barbarously murthered, being bruis'd in severall places of their bodys, and beat all over with clubs. Our third Mate we met almost dead, and return'd with him home. In the way we met a Lascar, who said he belong'd to Zećhary, which we made a Prisoner, also another who calls himself Capt Heron's Tendell, and who severall people knƌw was one that first began the Quarrell.

"October the 29th in the morning early we went to the Prince for justice, who told us we should have justice, and advis'd us to bury our dead, then get our Witnesses ready against the next day, and come to the Ronda, or place of Justice, where the whole affair should be strictly examin'd; for there never was such a piece of barbarity acted before in Pegu. We took our leave, bury'd the dead, and employ'd the rest of our time to find out such persons who were Eye Wittnesses to the murther, and not belonging to our Ship, having enô of them already.

"October the 30th the English in Generall went to Ronda, carrying the Wittnesses with us, Severall were examin'd, and some, that were impeach'd to have been accessory to the Murther, were secured. Then they deferr'd a further examination till the next sitting. Before we came to the Ronda, M^r: Tornery and myself told Capt: Heron that this was a melancholy unfit time to be angry with one another, therefore intreated him to lay aside all animosity's and unanimously joyn with us in prosecuting the Murtherers of his Countrymen; That if we had done anything, we would ask his pardon, or give any satisfaction, if he would be pleased to let us know what it was that affronted him. But his answer was he knew enough. In the Ronda while the Wittnesses were examining, and every one of us attentive to what they said, he could not keep his temper, but instead of prosecuting the Murtherers he fell a railing at us. We again told him we would satisfy him in every thing, and wait upon him at his house, as soon as we had done, begging he would think on the Blood spilt and revenge that first; then he might take what satisfaction he tho^t: fit of us. We added that the Prince and Governours must entertain a very mean opinion of the English to see us

quarrelling with each other at such a time that the reputation
of us all lay at stake ; and if we did not get justice, 'twas high
time to quit Pegu to the Armenians ; that all private Quarrells
ought to be laid aside to serve a publick cause ; especially he
had no excuse for not doing it, when we were ready to wait
upon him and ask pardon, as soon as he would let us know in
what we were faulty.   But his answer was : not to come to
his house.   Then, as we were going out of the Ronda, [he]
bid us deliver up his Tendell.   We told him we had proof of
his being one of the first that began the Fray, and had very
great reason to believe him guilty of the murder, as we were
sure his Serang was, and since he would believe nothing
against his people, we could not deliver him, but would to
justice.   Sometime after, we were going to his house, accompany'd wth: Cap^{ts}: Blyth and Cornelius, but were stopt by
Capt: Martin, who was order'd not to let us come in ; and we
went home.   A little after, News was brought that he had
seized our Tendell and Nockedesob,[1] and put them in the
stocks ; upon which all our people came in a body, desiring
leave to go and release their comrades, crying out Capt: Heron
took the Armenians part and valued not the Blood of the
English.   However, we pacified them by saying the Governour
of Madrass would do us justice on Capt: Heron, and that it
was absolutely necessary for us to be quiet, that the Government might do us justice on the Murtherers, which we could
not get if we took our own satisfaction ; therefore desir'd
them to mind their work, that the Ship might be got out of
the Dock, then we need fear nothing ; and in the meantime
we could keep a strict watch, that we might not be surpriz'd
and massacred as our poor Countrymen were; for which time we
took it by turns and watch all night, continually going the
rounds of our compound.   When all was quiet, we enquired
after more wittnesses and got severall.   We also examin'd the
two persons we had, and found he that call'd himself Zechary's
Lascar belonged to Capt: Heron ; and not having any positive
proof that he was in the Fray, we sent him with a note to
Capt: Heron, advising [2] the same he would not read the note,
but order'd the Fellow to carry it back again.

---

[1] Native pilot.   (*Vide* Hobson-Jobson, s.v. Nacoda.)
[2] " Who advised."

" November the 1st all the English in Generall went to the Ronda except Capt: Heron and his Family. Sev^ll: Wittnesses were examin'd, and the rest were deferr'd to the next day, and most of those impeach'd as accessary to the murder were seized.

" November the 3rd we went to the Ronda, but Capt: Heron did not come. The Governours told us 'twas needless to examine any more of our witnesses, but they would draw a confession from those impeached by Torture. Accordingly an Armenian was first brought out and tortur'd with some more. Upon what was drawn from them ten of Zechary's boatmen were seized, being all armed and with him at the murder. Then they said 'twas needless to examine further, so got up and went to the Prince, deferring sentence to the next day ; yet told us 'twas evident Zechary was guilty, as well as the rest accused, and that we should have justice the next day. We returned home, and in the evening the Linguists came to us from the Prince and Governours, assuring us we should have justice, for they had resolved to secure Zechary the next sitting, advising us to insist upon it with earnestness. This Message we did not like, nor their dilatory way of proceedings. We foresaw 'twas to make Zechary open his purse, and we knew Capt: Heron had private conferences with Aga Nooree, which gave us the greatest suspicion we should not get justice. However, we were resolv'd to do what we could.

" November the 4th early in the morning we waited on the Prince, but Capt: Heron being there, we took a little walk till he was gone, then return'd. We told him [1] that since the Governours in the Ronda had examin'd as many witnesses as they thought necessary, and confess'd 'twas evident Zechary and his followers were guilty of the murther, and that it was to no purpose to examine any further, we could not help wondering why he was not secured ; that we came to beg his security first, then that he would do us justice on all that had a hand in the murder. He told us to go to the Ronda, and there we should have justice, advising all the English to go together. He told us Capt: Heron had been with him, and promised to go with us ; 'twas best for all the English to meet and consult before we went to the Ronda. We told him we had no

---

[1] The Prince.

more to say than to demand justice ; therefore it was needless
to consult, but we would go all together, as he advised ; so
took our leave. This discourse increas'd our suspicions,
especially one Question he ask'd : if in England Murder could
not be made up with money. We answered him No, The
Law of God and England commanded Blood for blood. We
went immediately to Capt: Heron's, whom we expected would
treat us roughly ; and as we came in at one door, Aga Noore
went out of the other slily. But we were disappointed, being
rec^d: smiling. He told us he had been with the Prince, and
that the Prince said he would deliver Zechary to be carry'd
to Madras ; but he answer'd he wanted justice here, for that
the Armenians were very strong in Madras, and we could do
nothing there. He also told us the Prince said he could not
put Zechary in prison without the King's order, and advis'd
us not to insist upon securing Zechary. We answered, if
Zechary was not secured, we had no reason to expect justice,
but to believe the whole Government brib'd, and that the
acco^t: of the murther would not be fairly represented to the
King. Therefore we must insist upon it in publick. He
seemed to acquiesce, and we went all together to the Ronda.
But there he only demanded a fair acco^t: might be sent to the
King of what had passed, and that he might also write. But
no sooner did we hear what he said, but we desir'd to be heard ;
and every Englishman except Capt: Heron and those belonging
to him demanded justice on the murtherers, and if the Government had not power to do justice without the King's order,
that they would immediately seize Zechary and the rest that
were not yet secured, that had a hand in the murther ; that
if this was not granted, 'twas evident we could not have
justice. This made the Governours at a stand. They asked
Capt: Heron if he joyn'd with us in the same demand, which
forc'd him to answer Yes. They immediately got up and went
to the Prince, desiring us to stay in the Ronda for an answer.
A little after, Capt: Heron was sent for, and returned soon
with this answer : that the Government could not secure him,
but would be bound for his appearance, and that whatever
the King's order was should be executed. We parted, takeing
the Linguists with us, went to the Prince and told him that
since Zechary was not secured, we must expect the same

treatment our poor Countrymen received from his hands and Followers, without any colour of an affront given them. However, since we had so fair warning, we would be ready and not be butchered, as they were. He excused his not securing Zechary for want of power. We said, if he had not power to secure him, he was greater than the Prince, and before any orders might come from the King, might do any mischeif he pleased. For our part we had done all we could. He himself was convinc'd who the murtherers were, and knew who was and who was not secured, and on him alone laid the whole affair; and should any fatal Consequences ensue, 'twould be owing to Zechary's Liberty. He sent for Zechary and told him that if any harm happened to our People, and the Authors not found, it should be imputed to him. This is all we got so took our leave. The Linguists coming away with us, we ask'd them the meaning of this change; We enquir'd what Capt: Heron had said to the Prince in the morning. They told us Capt: Heron would not take them with him, but carry'd a strange Linguist, so they could not tell; but by what the Prince told him, when he was sent for from the Ronda, they had been consulting in Zechary's favour; for the Prince ask'd him why he went from what he said yesterday, and he answered he could not hinder us from speaking. But the Prince being nettled said he was like a drop of water, which a man might pour as he would. They told us they were confounded at the alteration since last night, and nothing could occasion it but bribery. They knew Aga Noore had been with Capt: Heron often during the tryall; they also knew the Prince and Government had been offered money, which they refused. But Capt: Heron being there so early with a strange Linguist, and so great an alteration in the whole Government immediately upon it, convinced them it was so.

" Reflecting on all that had passed, M^r: Tornery and myself concluded it best to wait on Capt: Heron in hopes to see a little further in this last affair; so seem'd satisfy'd, as if we believ'd the King would certainly do justice. He told us he would write about it, and we should see his Letter, how earnest he would be with the King, that we might be convinc'd how much he wanted the murtherers to be punished; and assured

us he had not been Idle, but solicited the Prince and Government when we did not know it.   We answer'd we believ'd so,
and after a little while we went home.   The next day he sent
his letter for us to read, in the Portugueeze Language ; after
which it was translated into the Language of the Country,
and deliver'd to the Government to be sent to the King, with
an Acco^t: of all that had passed in the Ronda.   All this
seem'd to us deceit.   However, we thought the freer we were
with Capt: Heron, we should know the more, therefore sent
his Tendell, and in a note told him we hoped he would secure
him, that he might be brought to justice at Madrass.   But the
next evening we repented that we had let him go, for he came
to our Compound arm'd with a knife.   Our Tendell seeing
him bid him begone, asking what he wanted ; and the Fellow,
being afraid of being seized, went away swearing he'd kill our
serang.   We immediately advis'd Capt: Heron by a note that
his Tendell had been in our compound arm'd with a knife.
'Twas unaccountable, after so much blood spilt, that there
was still danger of more.   His serang already was prov'd
guilty, w^ch: ought to be a sufficient reason to have an eye
over the rest.   He had been always advis'd, as was now,
therefore if after this any of his People were seen in our Compound after sunset, they would run a hazard of being shot.
The answer to this was that he was at home and had not been
in our Compound.

   " November the 14th Zechary was at Capt: Heron's house,
and on the 16th Capt: Heron got his serang's liberty, which is
an undeniable proof how earnest he was in prosecuting the
Murtherers.

   " At this time we got advice that a Vessell[1] Capt: Blyth
was building for Zechary, which Capt: Heron had often
wanted, but the other would not sell, was now deliver'd to
Capt: Heron, which convinc'd us he had not been Idle, but
solicited the Prince and Government when we did not know
it.   At this time Zechary, following the example of Capt:
Heron, got his two Serangs and Nockedesobs liberty, pleading
Capt: Heron had got his.

   " November the 23rd we waited on the Prince desireing

   [1] Named the *Diligence*, upon which Heron returned to Madras in
April, 1721.

he would permit us to take a copy of all that the Wittnesses had affirm'd in the Ronda. He answered we might, and told us he was advis'd that Cojee [1] Simon, Aga Nooree and Zechary had been consulting with Cap.: Heron at his house, and ask'd us if we knew it."

Here, somewhat abruptly, the diary ends, followed in the Fort St. George records by copies of the depositions of the various witnesses examined before the Yondaw. The most interesting of these was the eye-witness account of the murders given by John Underwood,[2] the third mate of the *Lusitania*, who feigned death, when knocked down in the scrimmage, and thus managed to escape. According to his evidence, Zechary not only urged on his men to commit the murders, but himself gave Wankford a mortal wound.

Heron's reply to Orme's charges was not very convincing. He explained his reluctance to support Orme as having been due to the latter's refusal to submit to his authority as Chief of the English, and his independent negotiations with the Burmese authorities in the matter of the repairs to his ship. Orme, he said, had proclaimed that Syriam was " a free port where all would be treated alike." This had annoyed the Burmese authorities, who had taxed him (Heron) with deceit, since he had reported the *Lusitania* to them as a ship under the Company's protection. Orme, when questioned on this by the Fort St. George Council, had to admit its truth. He was therefore administered a severe reprimand. But when Heron came to deal with the murders and his own part in the subsequent proceedings before the Syriam Yondaw, he was treading on thin ice. He admitted Zechary's guilt, but at the same time protested his own strenuous endeavours to bring the Armenian to justice. In support of this he laid before the Council two documents : the first a copy of his letter to the King of Burma ; the second purporting to be a translation of a contract between Zechary and himself for the sale of the *Diligence*, executed two months before the murders took place. He further asserted that in accordance with a

---

[1] A corruption of *khwāja*, a title of respect applied to rich merchants in India (cp. " Hodges Ismael," in Chap. II., p. 37).

[2] *Vide* Appendix VIII.

royal order from Ava Zechary received due punishment. This, however, was denied by Orme, who brought forward counter-evidence of a damning nature. It shall be related in his own words :—

> " The King of Avah's orders upon the news of the murther arrived at Syrian December the 7th and were as follows : That Zechary should ly in the sun three days, be bored through his cheek, and cut in the neck and back seven times, also pay 100 viss of silver, and that each of the other concerned should have 100 Blows, Providing what was related was true ; and Cap[t]: Heron, being Cheif of the Company's affairs, must know the whole story. Therefore he must be asked in the publick Ronda if the relation of the murder was true or no. If he said Yes, Zechary &c[t]: must suffer as per order. Captain Heron was asked, and his answer was, he was asleep when the murder happen'd, and knew nothing of the matter."

And Orme proceeded further to point out with unimpeachable logic that if the king had received Heron's letter, in which he unequivocably denounced Zechary as guilty of the crime, no such proviso to the royal order would have been sent. The letter, he said, was a sham ; it was never meant to reach Ava.

The Fort St. George Council decided to report the whole affair home to the Directors. This, as has been mentioned earlier, brought down upon Heron a very severe reprimand from London,[1] and there the matter ended. There seems to be no doubt that Heron, partly out of pique at the flagrant disregard of his position shown by Orme and Tornery, and partly because of long acquaintance with Zechary, did, indeed, obstruct the course of justice in this case. He may even have been well paid for his obtuseness. But the case shows clearly how weak was the Company's control over the private traders in Burma, when even its own servants carried on unlicensed trade there, and could with impunity fling in the teeth of its representative the argument that Syriam was a free port, besides successfully carrying on independent negotiations with Ava for supplies of wood.

[1] " Fort St. George : Public Despatches from England," XXV., 14th February, 1722-3.

CHAPTER XI

SHIPBUILDING AND THE LAST YEARS OF THE SYRIAM FACTORY, 1722-1744

CHAPTER XI

SHIPBUILDING AND THE LAST YEARS OF THE SYRIAM FACTORY, 1722-44

In the first half of the eighteenth century Burma did not assume great importance in the eyes of the East India Company. Between Bowyear's mission at the end of the previous century and the withdrawal of the English from Burma in 1744 as a result of the destruction of the Syriam factory by the rebellious Talaings, no important negotiations were carried on between Fort St. George and Ava. The hopes of establishing lucrative trading relations with Burma, raised again and again in the course of the seventeenth century, died a natural death in the eighteenth century. Lac had, by 1700, become a drug in the English market. Saltpetre might not be exported. The Armenians possessed a monopoly of the ruby trade, though it is true that the bulk of the trade was attracted to Madras. The metals, which Burma was known to possess in abundance, could not be exploited to any satisfactory extent owing to royal policy. Burmese wood and rice, for which there was a strong constant demand at Madras, could only be exported in driblets, and by much palm-greasing of the royal officials. No large-scale trade, worthy of the attention of the Company, could be engaged upon, because royal policy was too inconsistent, and the Government refused to be bound by concessions or agreements of a general nature. The Government at Ava preferred to deal with private traders, to whom it could make individual concessions. That sort of trade entailed plenty of service to the golden feet, and much giving of presents to royal officials. Ava loved to feel that from its majestic height it might, if it pleased, deign to notice the (" not empty-handed ") prayers of the white kalas [1] and extend its pity to them.

[1] Burmese word for " foreigner " ; when used alone signifies the Indian.

Under such conditions the Company, with other fish to fry on the mainland of India, had no energies to waste upon developing trade with Burma. The connexion with Syriam was maintained chiefly for shipbuilding purposes ; but the private trade between Madras and Syriam was by no means negligible, and served to swell the Fort St. George Customs returns. In the year 1739 no less than nineteen ships arrived at Madras from Syriam.[1] Of course, no matter how unsatisfactory its relations with Ava, the Company dared not sever its connexion with Burma. The presence of the French there, and later the activities of Dupleix's shipbuilding agents, were sufficient arguments against such a step. Not that the French, during the period under review, ever made any attempt to oust the English from Burma. Before the War of the Austrian Succession, in fact, the records contain no complaints whatever of French competition there. The Company's activities in Burma during this period bore little or no direct relation to its affairs in India. Its correspondence with its " residents " in Burma is concerned almost entirely with instructions on the one hand, and reports on the other, about shipbuilding. Not until the great Anglo-Spanish and Anglo-French struggles loom upon the horizon towards the end of the thirties, does any other subject receive much attention in the records relating to Burma. Then, as might be expected, renewed attempts were made to tap Burma's much-discussed resources of saltpetre.

After the retirement of Captain George Heron as a result of the Directors' censure for the part he played in the trial of Cojee Zechary and his accomplices, the Company's official representative in Burma received the title of " resident." The holders of the title were, like the Chiefs of the Affairs of the English Nation, chosen from among the private traders : they were free merchants or seafaring men of Madras, not in the service of the Company.[2] But their special function at Syriam was to assume control over the Company's ship-

[1] " Madras Public Proceedings," 1739, *passim*.
[2] Dalrymple, " Oriental Repertory," I., p. 105, calls the residents " mere Supervisors of the Private Trade, and not immediately in the *Service* of the *Company*." Even Smart, who for so many years represented the Company at Syriam, was classed in the Fort St. George records as a " free merchant " (Dodwell, " Calendar of the Madras Records, 1740-4," p. 70).

building operations, which in the thirties became fairly extensive. On appointment, they had to pay down a large sum of money as security to the Fort St. George Council. By the Directors' orders in 1730 the amount was fixed at 2000 pagodas.[1] This was due to the fact that large amounts of bullion and consignments of equipment were entrusted to them in respect of orders for ships placed with them. They were also empowered to draw upon the Company for additional sums of money in cases where the original outlay was insufficient.[2] Residents received no salaries. Their official position in Burma afforded them many advantages that could be turned into profit, especially in respect of the Company's shipbuilding orders.

The residents were usually undistinguished people, whose names rarely appear even in such a comprehensive work as Love's "Vestiges of Old Madras." A Captain Charles Wybergh held the post in 1724 and the following year,[3] being succeeded by Lewis Tornery, Stephen Orme's associate in the *Lusitania* affair. The latter, however, annoyed Fort St. George by failing to seize a French pirate named Alano, who went to Syriam for the purpose of building " a large ship which may be of the utmost ill consequence to the Trade of India." [4] He was therefore superseded in favour of Captain James Berriman, who held the post from 1726 to 1731.[5] Berriman's successor, Samuel Palmer, had, like Tornery, a short career. He was unable to make good the balance of money entrusted to him on the Company's behalf, and on Monday, 31st December, 1732, the Fort St. George accountant reported to the President and Council that " he had made an elopement and was not to be found." [6] The next resident was a Captain

[1] " Madras Public Proceedings," 25th July, 1730. The amount was equal to £800.

[2] *Ibid.*, 28th January and 27th March, 1732.

[3] *Ibid.*, 13th and 18th July, 1724.   [4] *Ibid.*, 22nd June, 1725.

[5] *Ibid.*, 15th August, 1726. His widow, *née* Mary Gyfford, married William Henry Southby in 1740, and his daughter Frances married in 1756 Sir Thomas Rumbold of Woodhall Park, Herts. Their second son, George Berriman Rumbold, inherited his father's baronetcy (Love, "Vestiges," II., p. 298, n. 3, and III., p. 149). In 1730, when he returned to Burma, after a stay in Madras, he sailed on board the *Elohisanee*, belonging to the King of Burma, Taninganwe (1714-33) (" Madras Public Proceedings," 3rd August, 1730).

[6] *Ibid.*, 31st December, 1732.

John Kelsall, about whom the records give us hardly any information. Possibly from the fact that in 1735 his wife, on her own petition, was granted a passage home with her two children on the *Prince of Orange* by the Fort St. George Council, we may infer that he died somewhere about that time.[1] He was succeeded by the last of the Syriam residents, Jonathan Smart, who held the post until the factory buildings were burnt to the ground by the Talaings at the end of the year 1743.

With regard to the Company's shipbuilding activities at Syriam, the Fort St. George records contain ample details. Before 1730, although the Company actually bought one or two small craft built at Syriam, no ships seem to have been constructed there to its order. Occasionally ships had been sent there for repairs, but before the regular appointment of a resident, these were executed under the supervision of the captain of the vessel, who procured supplies of timber and hired such labour as was available. As a contribution towards the expenses involved, it was usual to send across a cargo of goods under the charge of a Company's servant for disposal in Burma. With the appointment of a resident general charge of the work was entrusted to him, and in the case of each vessel despatched for this purpose a " general letter " would be directed to him, containing full instructions concerning the exact nature of the repairs to be executed. Thus, when the brigantine *George* was sent to Syriam for repairs in 1726, Captain Berriman, the then resident, was instructed to take care " that the materials be good and the work well and frugally perform'd, But . . . as we intend a thorough repair, that nothing proper and necessary be wanting, That being to be new sheathed they do first search her Bottom carefully to see where she is Iron Sick and drive spikes everywhere where wanting, That her upper works be well strengthened, and masts and yards survey'd, and if any of them faulty, that they may be chang'd for good and sound sticks, and that she be return'd to us in January with a particular account of repairs done and of stores then abroad." [2] Her master, Captain Tye, took with him 2500 ounces of silver, partly to defray the cost

---

[1] " Madras Public Proceedings," 27th September, 1735.
[2] *Ibid.*, 6th September, 1726.

of her repairs, and partly " for fitting her up with Timbers and plank of the largest dimensions she can take in, to be used here in the Company's Works which will save the profit upon what we are usually oblig'd to buy for their Account." [1] In the following year, the *Marlborough* was sent to Syriam for a similar purpose. Her master was provided with 1500 ounces of silver to defray the cost of refitting her, and of providing her with a return cargo similar to that of the *George*.[2]

Between 1730 and 1740 we have record of six ships built for the Company in the Syriam dockyard. Four of these were classed as sloops, one as a galley and one as a brigantine. Two of the sloops were built for the Bengal service ; the other two for use on the west coast of India.[3] A complete list of the stores, etc., despatched to Syriam for one of the west coast sloops of 50 tons burthen, is to be found in the " Madras Public Proceedings." [4] They included 3 anchors, 1 grapnel, 3 cables of European manufacture, 17 coils of cordage of various sizes, materials for making a " compleat Suit of Sales," 15 cwt. of junk, sail needles, twine, brass box compasses, 1 two-hour glass, 2 half-hour glasses, 2 two-minute glasses, buckets, lanterns, a " hand-trumpet," deep-sea and hand leads with their respective lines, barrels of tar, tallow, some " pump-leather," carpenter's tools, and red, white and blue materials for flags. A crew, consisting of an English master and mate, a Serang and ten Lascars, was also sent across from Madras to take her over when completed.

After several years of experiment, however, the Company came to the conclusion that Syriam was not a good place for shipbuilding. When, in 1738, Fort St. George was in need of a new ship for voyages between Madras and the west coast factories, it was decided to place the order with Bombay rather than Syriam. The causes of this change of policy are

---

[1] " Madras Public Proceedings," 6th September, 1726.

[2] *Ibid.*, 1st, 11th, 18th, 22nd, and 27th September, 1727.

[3] They were used for traffic with harbours too shallow for larger ships to enter.

[4] Entered after the Minutes of the Consultation of 27th July, 1738. This boat was the *Carolina*, which through being built larger than her original specification, was stranded in Cuddalore harbour in 1740 and never refloated.

set out in the Minutes of the consultation at which the decision was made :—

" The reasons which induce us to desire she may be built at Bombay rather than Pegue are that We are inform'd the Sloop which was built at Bombay for the Service of Bengall last year did not cost above ten thousand Rupees whereas we compute from the accounts now before us those built at Pegue cost at least twelve Thousand Rupees apiece and are Twenty tons less in Burthen, besides the work at Bombay is infinitely better and though it has formerly been reckon'd very dear Building there, yet the Impositions of the Government make it much more so in Pegue and We reckon the Profits of a Loading of Cotton or Pepper from Bombay if deducted from her Cost will reduce it to a reasonable price." [1]

In January, 1740, Fort St. George reported home to the Directors that owing to the high cost of Pegu-built sloops, all shipbuilding orders would, in future, be placed with Bombay.[2] In the same year one of the Pegu-built sloops, the *Carolina*, was stranded in Cuddalore harbour ; she had been ordered specially for the purpose of voyages to harbours too shallow for ships of greater draught to enter, but contrary to instructions, had been built too big. Her draught was $6\frac{1}{2}$ feet, whereas in the dry season there was only 4 feet of water at the Cuddalore bar ; [3] consequently she was held up there for many months, while various expedients for floating her were tried without success. Finally, after being stranded for nearly four years, when every possible effort to get her out of the harbour had been exhausted, she had to be broken up.[4] The Fort St. George Council laid the blame for this catastrophe upon the incompetence of the Syriam shipwrights. " When we order'd this sloop to be built at Pegue," they wrote home to the Directors in September, 1741, " we directed she should

---

[1] " Madras Public Proceedings," 16th January, 1738.
[2] Dodwell, " Calendar of Madras Records, 1740-4," p. 12.
[3] " Letters to Fort St. George," Vol. XXVI., pp. 1-2.
[4] Dodwell, *op. cit.*, p. 481. Her materials were sold for 919 pagodas (*ibid.*, p. 496).

not exceed forty tons burthen [1] . . . but we have had no reason from thence why she was more, except that the master that brought her over told us, namely that [it occurred] from the obstinacy and ignorance of the builder. We have in some former letter told your Honours what wretched fellows we are obliged to employ there, for which reason and several others we have resolved for the future when we want any more vessels to desire they may be built at Bombay." [2] Another complaint made against boats built at Syriam was that they were never properly finished, and hence had to be sent elsewhere for completion. [3] But the chief objection against them seems to have been their excessive cost, a disproportionately large item in which were the " exorbitant presents " which had to be made to the Burmese officials in return for permission to build. [4] Here we have but another example of the way in which the bad administrative methods and intransigence of the Burmese Government helped to frustrate the natural economic development of the country. Burmese teak was then unsurpassed for shipbuilding, especially in those days of sea-fights, because the effect of cannon shot did not cause it to splinter. Had the Government but adopted a reasonably healthy attitude towards the industry, one of the Burmese ports might have become the leading shipbuilding depôt in the East comparatively early in the eighteenth century.

The *Lusitania* affair had drawn the Directors' attention to the fact that unlicensed private traders were resorting to Syriam, and it was resolved to take measures against this abuse of the Company's rules. Early in 1727 Fort St. George received instructions from London to send home all such interlopers. Orders were accordingly passed by the Council that four unlicensed traders—Miles Barne, Thomas Pritchard,

[1] This was not strictly true ; the Minute of the Consultation at which it was decided to order this sloop gives her size as " about forty tons " (" Madras Public Proceedings," 21st September, 1737).

[2] " Fort St. George : Public Despatches to England, 1741-2," p. 6.

[3] " Letters from Fort St. George," Vol. XXV., p. 22 ; Dodwell, *op. cit.*, p. 251.

[4] On this point, see Smart's letter to Fort St. George in " Letters to Fort St. George," Vol. XXVI., p. 8.

James Lauder, and Lewis Tornery—were to return to England.[1] Barne and Pritchard, who were in Madras at the time, were allowed to proceed to Burma to wind up their businesses, under strict agreement to return to Madras and take ship for home. Tornery and Lauder were in Burma when the order against them was promulgated. Instructions were therefore sent to the resident at Syriam to see that they obeyed it. Tornery, however, managed to secure exemption from the order,[2] and continued to trade in Burma until the Talaing rebellion of 1740 placed a temporary check upon English commercial activities there. Ten years after this attempt was made to stamp out the unauthorised English trade in Burma, things had once more developed to such a pitch that George II.'s proclamation, forbidding any British subjects from residing or trading in the East contrary to the Company's privileges, was ordered to be posted up in the factory building at Syriam, and the resident instructed to arrest all such offenders, and send them to be dealt with by the Fort St. George authorities.[3] Whether this measure was effective or not, the records do not show : the chances are that it was not.

The trade in Burma rubies at Madras, stimulated by Streynsham Master's *cowle* issued in 1680, continued throughout this period, though with but moderate success. During the early years of the century a monthly statement of the amount derived from the ruby brokerage was made to the Fort St. George Council. In 1734, however, it was farmed out to three Indian merchants for five years at an annual rent of 800 pagodas.[4] As the broker was allowed to take 1 per cent. from the buyer, and 2 per cent. from the seller, of all precious stones except diamonds, it will be seen that the trade, although not great, was by no means negligible. The Talaing rebellion hit this trade so hard, that in 1741 the Fort

---

[1] " Madras Public Proceedings," 25th April, 1727. Tornery, according to Dalrymple ("Oriental Repertory," I., p. 105), wrote a " compleat Description " of the Burmese Empire, of which no trace could be found in 1759. It has not yet been discovered.

[2] " Madras Public Proceedings," 8th May, 1727.

[3] *Ibid.*, 15th June, 1737.

[4] *Ibid.*, 17th March, 1735, and s.v. Ruby Brokerage in the " List of the Honble. Company's Revenues in Fort. St. George," at the beginning of the 1735 volume.

St. George Council had to reduce the rent to 500 pagodas a year, though with the proviso that if the brokerage produced a revenue greater than that amount, the whole was to be paid to the Company, less a special allowance to the collectors for their trouble.[1]

In 1737 the question of obtaining supplies of saltpetre from Burma was once more raised, this time by the Fort William factory. In March of that year Governor Stackhouse wrote privately to the President of Fort St. George, asking him to approach the Burmese Government for permission to export this increasingly necessary commodity. It was difficult, he wrote, to procure adequate supplies in Bengal; if therefore, a sufficiently large quantity could be procured easily from another source, the Bengal Government might be forced to lower the prohibitive price, which had been placed upon it. He further suggested that from information he had received regarding the amount available in Burma, " it would be worth the Company's while to give a very considerable present to the King " in return for a grant of freedom of trade in this article. The President forthwith wrote to Jonathan Smart, the resident at Syriam, to sound Ava with regard to the proposal.[2] Smart entrusted the negotiations to an influential Armenian merchant named Coja Simon. From conversation that he himself had with the " Prince " of Syriam, Smart gathered that the omens were favourable to the success of the project. The prince, in fact, went so far as to promise his own good offices in the matter, and assured Smart that there was saltpetre enough in the country to load many ships annually.

On 18th December, 1737, Smart reported to Fort St. George that the Burmese Government had intimated to Simon that " it was not impracticable to gain the Liberty of Exporting Saltpetre," and had asked whether, in return for such a grant, the Company proposed to offer a present, or pay an annual rent. Fort St. George's reply showed that the Council suffered under no illusions regarding the precise value of grants of trading rights, made by the Government of Ava. Their experience of that Government, Smart was

---

[1] Dodwell, "Calendar of Madras Records, 1740-4," p. 214.
[2] " Madras Public Proceedings," 16th January, 1738.

informed, was sufficient to convince them that " we can have no Relyance upon their Faith so as to put any considerable value upon any of their grants ; besides, if we are rightly inform'd of the Constitution of the Government, no grant of his Present Majesty will be binding upon his successor, for which reasons we shall never advise the Company to give any considerable present nor pay anything annually for a Liberty, the enjoyment of which will be very precarious." In their opinion, they said, " the only certain and secure Termes " upon which the Company could export saltpetre would be by payment of Customs duties upon every 100 viss taken out of the country. But, before that could be decided upon, they must know whether the quality of the saltpetre was sufficiently high for the Company's use. Smart was therefore requested to send a few sample bags of it " to make Tryal of." These, when received, proved to be of a much lower quality than the Bengal variety : the refiner reported that in the process of refining Burma saltpetre lost five-eighths compared with the Bengal kind's one-fourth. This discovery somewhat damped Fort St. George's ardour. The Council decided that nothing further could be done until Smart had furnished full particulars as to the price at which the commodity could be exported.[1] But before any further development occurred, the Talaing rebellion had broken out, and the chaos to which Burma was reduced during the next decade and more, completely frustrated Fort St. George's hopes of obtaining saltpetre from that source. The negotiations petered out, though as late as July, 1742, Smart was still being pressed by the Madras Council to exert himself to persuade either Ava, or the upstart " king " of Pegu, to come to terms in the matter.[2]

Mention has been made early in this work of the grievous sufferings of the Talaing peoples of Lower Burma at the end of the sixteenth century, when their country was the main theatre of operations in the devastating wars between Burma and Siam. The terrible depopulation of the Delta region, graphically described by the European visitors of that period, had utterly exhausted the Talaings, and rendered them

---

[1] " Madras Public Proceedings," 21st July, 1738.
[2] Dodwell, " Calendar of Madras Records, 1740-4," p. 288.

powerless to continue their ancient struggle for existence against the Burmans : a struggle, which dated as far back as the middle of the eleventh century, when Anawrahta of Pagan, the creator of the first unified Burmese empire, had sacked their capital city of Thaton, and made pagoda-slaves of its royal family. With the removal of the Burmese capital from Pegu to Ava in 1635, the control of the Burmese kings over the southern districts, not immediately in the neighbourhood of the cities of Prome, Pegu and Syriam, and the main high-way of the Irrawaddy, began to slacken. In the eighteenth century, when the Toungoo dynasty had lost its early martial vigour, this process was accelerated. Military weakness in dealing with raiders and rebels brought about the final debâcle, which gave to the Talaings their great opportunity. The Manipuris, tributaries of Burma in the days of Bayinnaung (1551-81), raided Upper Burma to the very walls of Ava. The Gwe Shans of Okpo[1] rebelled, and ravaged the Shwebo district. Finally, the Burmese Governor of Pegu, taking advantage of the preoccupation of Ava with these disturbances, proclaimed his independence in 1740 and marched on Syriam. Mutiny, however, broke out among his troops, and in the resulting chaos the Talaings, goaded to desperation by ruinous taxation and the memory of past sufferings, rose as a body against their Burmese masters, and massacred every Burman they could lay hands on in the larger towns of their country, including Syriam. A " king " was soon forthcoming in the person of Smim Htaw Buddhaketi, an ex-priest, strangely enough a scion of the Ava house,[2] whom the Talaing leaders proclaimed King of Pegu in 1740. Before this new assault from the south, Burmese resistance for the time being col-lapsed, and the rebels soon held all the country as far north as Prome and Toungoo, even carrying their raids up the Irrawaddy to the outskirts of the Burmese capital.

At the end of December, 1740, came the first intimation to Fort St. George of this dramatic turn of events in Lower Burma.[3] A letter, dated the 11th of that month, was received

---

[1] *Vide* note by Harvey, " History of Burma," p. 354.

[2] But as a King of Burma often had some scores of children, it must have been no difficult task to most people to prove royal descent.

[3] This was their earliest news of the Talaing revolt ; at least three months earlier they had heard of the Governor of Pegu's rebellion (Dodwell, *op. cit.*, p. 98).

from Jonathan Smart and several other Madras traders, " advising of a Revolution in the government and a great Massacre committed by the Peguers on the Burramores in that Kingdom." [1] Some four months later there arrived another despatch from Smart, containing a detailed account of the Talaing capture of Syriam. [2] He describes it thus :—

" After the Prince of Pegue [3] was cut of which was on the 18th day of November, the government of Syrian [4] raised an army to secure the passes that were inlets into this province from which time we had nothing but continual contradictory alarms that the enemy [5] were comeing. Four days before Syrian was taken, the Prince sent me an order from the Rounda to dismount the factory guns and send them to the Alfantigo. [6] Whereupon I immidiately withdrew them. [To] mention the daily reports that were spread would be troublesome and useless to your honour &c[a]: ; wherefore I take leave to proceed to the very day the new powers made their incursion which was December the 4th about sunrise at which Cap[t]: Collings forced my chamber door informing me that the Peguers and Siamers [7] had in tumult and violence entered this city. A small time afterwards, the Prince came to the gate which leads to the factory and by two messengers sent for me to attend him there. Whereto I sent answer that I very well knew that an enemy had entered the city which made me affraid the English factory would not be fully sufficient for me to

[1] " Madras Public Proceedings," 29th December, 1740.

[2] " Letters to Fort St. George, 1741," pp. 35-7. He wrote two letters in December, 1740, but this one, written to justify his own relations with the opposing parties, gives a more comprehensive and detailed account than the previous ones.

[3] The rebellious Burmese governor.

[4] The Burmese officials.   [5] The Talaing forces.

[6] A Portuguese word meaning " custom-house." (Vide Hobson-Jobson, s.v. Alfandica.)

[7] Probably Talaings from Siamese territory, whither many had fled in earlier days away from Burmese oppression. It is noteworthy that the Siamese Government at this time made no move in support of the Talaings ; relations between Ayuthia and Ava remained cordially friendly. The King of Siam was offended at the upstart's request for a Siamese princess in marriage. (Harvey, " History of Burma," p. 214 ; Wood, " History of Siam," p. 234.)

maintain and which only was my business as being a merchant and having nothing to do with warlike disputes, at the same time desireing him to take care of his city, and that he should want no assistance in my power to give him ; which return occasioned his comeing to the factory when he advised me that the Peguers were only a body of fourty or fifty robbers and desired I wou'd go and repulse them. To which I replyed h[e] might easily see my force was not above four or five Europeans which I thought too few to defend the factory against an army that other people had informed me amounted to near ten thousand men. I also took leave to tell him that he had distressed the Company by keeping their gunpowder in the Alfantigo, whereupon he immidiately gave orders for it to be delivered and I sent people for it. He took his leave by telling me he wou'd go in search of the enemy and desired I would defend the bridge adjoining the factory, but he had not left me ten minutes till I saw him flying with the utmost speed to the waterside and by plungeing into the river got into a small boat and fled.

"A few minutes after, the General of the Pegue army [1] sent a message to me advizeing orders to be given to all strangers to keep at home and that they should not be molested either in person or estate which I thought prudent to do and to advize others to the same, since the Peguans had taken the city and the Burmar government were entirely overthrown."

The new King of Pegu—Seminto or Sementho, as he is called in the English contemporary records, the word being a corruption of his first two names, Smim Htaw [2]—wrote to Smart soon after the capture of Syriam, informing him that the " great oppressions " practised by the Burmese upon the Talaings were the cause of the massacre, and assuring him that he had given strict orders that strangers should in no way be molested. Smart replied that " as strangers we were only merchants and were to submit to the ruling power, let

[1] Binnya Dala, previously Master of the Royal Elephant Stables at Pegu.

[2] Wood, op. cit., p. 234, gives his name as Saming T'oh, but wrongly states the date of his accession as 1742.

the government be Peguer or Siamer." [1] Evidently Smim
Htaw was extremely anxious to cultivate friendly relations
with the English Company. On 21st December, 1740, he wrote
again to Smart, placing the foreign trade of Syriam under his
control, and promising better treatment to the Company than
it had received at the hands of the Burmese. The translation
of this letter, forwarded by Smart to Fort St. George, is as
follows :—

> " Pinhahusaradi, Pinhaquintao, Pinhaarintuma, [2] these
> three are the great governours and [gene]rals of the
> Kingdom of Pegu.
> " The King Sementho, notifyes the Honourable Com-
> pany, that he having advice that the Burmar Prince of
> Syrian design'd to take and imprison all the Peguers,
> Siamers, Tavays [3] and all strangers and resolv'd to burn
> them by treachery, for this reason, I Samentho was
> obliged to send my soldiers to kill all the governing
> Burmars that were in Syrian ; and as now the governing
> Burmars are destroyed, the strangers, Peguers, Siamers
> and Tavays will again be at peace ; and as I have had
> the good fortune to be acquainted with the Hon'ble
> Companys for these several years : I therefore now
> entreat you that from henceforth you would contribute
> all that is in your power for the good of the country and
> all strangers. All the custom and duties and entries of
> ships at the custom house you may fix and settle accord-
> ing to your pleasure in such a form as to please everybody,
> and not after the manner the Burmore government have
> done in laying very intollerable duties. And as I now
> rely upon you and shall hereafter have great confidence
> in you, I hope you will not fail of your good friendship
> which I have in very great remembrance. In the mean-
> time you'll do me the favours to take under your govern-
> ment all the strangers, Christians, Moors Mallabars and
> Chinese and all affairs that concern them you'll transact
> entirely at your pleasure. There is a ship at Syrian of the

---

[1] " Letters to Fort St. George, 1741," p. 8. Dalrymple, " Oriental
Repertory," I., p. 105, comments upon Smart's attitude.

[2] Talaing titles. Pinha, now transliterated Binnya, means " lord."

[3] People of Tavoy district.

Burmore King of Ava ; that ship I give to you for your service."

This was followed up by an urgent request that Smart should pay a visit to the new king at Pegu. At the same time, as a proof of their good faith, the Talaing authorities committed into his charge the clearance of a small Chinese vessel, which had arrived from Junkceylon, and had been granted a rebate of half the Customs duties formerly imposed under the Burmese régime.[1]

We have no information of the extent to which Smart assumed the new duties entrusted to him by the Talaing Government. As his letters to Fort St. George contain no hint of refusal on his part to accept them, we may infer that for a time [2] he was actually " Shabunder " of Syriam. His ready acceptance of the new régime, coupled with the fact of his previous refusal to give assistance to the Burmese Governor of Syriam against the Talaings, made him the subject of much discussion at Fort St. George, where he was represented as having definitely taken sides with the Talaings against the Burmans. Who started the tale we do not know, but the reports which reached Smart of the construction put upon his behaviour caused him, as early as December, 1740, to send Lewis Tornery to Madras by the *Speedwell* to discredit the " vile aspersions " that had been cast upon him and the other occupants of the English factory.[3] In his letter of 17th March, 1741, he made another effort to clear his character, as we have seen, by giving a detailed account of the part played by him at the time of the Talaing entry into Syriam. Moreover, he asserted that he had saved the lives of over 2000 Burmans, and that in his relations with the new Government he had used every endeavour to persuade it to adopt a policy of moderation. Unfortunately, we have no means of verifying the truth of these statements.

The accusations made against Smart caused him to tread more warily in his relations with Pegu. When he wrote to Fort St. George in December, 1740, he had fully decided to

---

[1] " Letters to Fort St. George, 1741," p. 8.
[2] He returned to Madras for a few months in 1742.
[3] " Letters to Fort St. George, 1741," p. 8.

accept the invitation to confer personally with Smim Htaw. But he was not long in perceiving that such an action on his part would lend colour to the very charges he was so concerned to refute. He therefore postponed indefinitely his intended visit, and wrote humbly to Fort St. George for instructions in the matter.[1] The Fort St. George Council, on the other hand, does not seem to have attributed much importance to these accusations. In February, 1741, at Smart's request it was decided to send him 15 cannon, 12 muskets, 4 blunderbusses, 3 pairs of pistols and a stock of ammunition, in order that the factory might be put into a more defensible condition.[2] In this connexion it is also noteworthy that when, in July, 1742, Smart was returning to Syriam, after a short stay at Madras, he was once more confirmed in his appointment as resident, and instructed to continue negotiations on behalf of the Company with whatever Government was in power.

The above evidence would seem to be sufficient to clear the resident's character of the more serious imputations against it. As officer in charge of a purely trading concern in a foreign country, Smart would have placed himself and English interests in a somewhat dangerous position, had he acceded to the Burmese governor's request for armed assistance against the Talaings, especially when it was a foregone conclusion that the latter would easily capture Syriam. This was no petty rising, without a chance of doing more than a considerable amount of damage before it petered out, but a national movement, strong enough ultimately to bring about the ruin of the Toungoo dynasty, which had ruled Burma for over two centuries. Smart undoubtedly pursued not merely the wise, but the only possible, course in immediately recognising the *de facto* Government at Pegu, in view of its overwhelming defeat of the Burmese in Lower Burma. Any aid given to the Burmese Governor of Syriam would have been equivalent to putting one's head into the lion's mouth, while hesitation on Smart's part to accept the post of controller of foreign trade and Customs at Syriam under the new Government would have tended to arouse Talaing suspicions, and thus might have rendered his position impossible. It must

---

[1] " Letters to Fort St. George, 1741," pp. 36-7.
[2] " Madras Public Proceedings," 12th February, 1741.

further be remembered that he firmly believed that the Talaing victory was likely to be permanent. In his letter of 17th March, 1741, from which we have already quoted, he wrote of the condition of affairs between the two combatants in the following terms :—

> " The new powers have extended their conquest as high as Prone[1] which city they took possession of the 21st of January last, without any kind of opposition ; the Burmars being fled towards Ava to a man as also the Europeans and other strangers, except M[r]: Golightly and a few Mores and Malabars who thought best to throw themselves upon the conquerors and by that means have got safe here under their protection, of which and their friendship I have not yet had the least occasion to doubt ; but on the contrary am obliged to wave many offers that are made to me from court. And in regard to the probability of their establishing themselves in possession of the Government, I really think it depends altogether upon their own care and fidelity to themselves, for the Birmas are actually so infected with fear that they will not attempt a recovery by arms, whatever they may try to do by other treacherous means, which I am no ways apprehensive they will be able to affect, but believe the new powers will not rest till they have compleated their conquest toward which they are preparing an army to go against Ava, and the Pegue court have appointed persons to settle and govern the towns, aldeas[2] and country already conquered."

The above defence of Smart's behaviour has been given chiefly in order to present what seems to be a juster view of it than that offered by such writers of Burmese history as have lightly accepted Dalrymple's careless insinuation against him in his " Letter concerning the Negrais Expedition," already referred to earlier, which, it will be remembered, was written less than twenty years after these events took place.[3]

[1] Prome.

[2] A Portuguese word meaning " villages." (*Vide* Hobson-Jobson, s.v. Aldea.) The Burmese local areas were the *myo*, " township," and the *ywa*, " village."

[3] In 1759.

At the end of a brief account of the episode, which bears un-
mistakable marks of his having consulted some, at least, of
the original records, he makes the following statement :—

> " Living Testimony places the Character of Mr. *Smart*,
> the Resident, in an infamous Light, and taxes him with
> having involved the *English* in the dispute, between
> these blood-thirsty Parties, in neither of whom could
> any Confidence be placed ; as the savage disposition,
> common to all Civil Wars, is in *this*, perhaps, more brutal,
> than in *any other* Country." [1]

But although obviously in a position to ascertain the true
facts of the case, he allowed this view to pass into publication
without qualification.

In his letter of March, 1741, already referred to, Smart
reported that he had joined with some others in a scheme to
buy a sloop, and make a voyage up-stream to Prome for the
purpose of rescuing certain Englishmen and others, who had
fallen into the hands of the Burmese. He assured Fort St.
George that the sloop would not be used " in any hostile
manner against either party." [2] We do not hear whether
this project was ever carried through. Similarly, we hear no
more of his intended visit to Pegu. In his letter on the subject,
as we have seen, he announced his intention to do nothing
in the matter until he received instructions. So far as can
be ascertained, between the time of his letter and his return
to Madras in 1742, he received no instructions of any kind
from Fort St. George. The cause of this is not far to seek.
At a consultation at Fort St. George on 18th January, 1742,
the decrease in the land Customs of Madras was attributed to
the fact that no ships sailed to Burma in the year 1741.[3]
This was not strictly true, since a French ship, the *Bon Voyage*,
left Madras for Syriam on 10th June, and put in again at
Madras on 28th December on her return voyage to Pondicherry.[4] But she carried no written instructions to Smart.

---

[1] " Oriental Repertory," I., p. 106.

[2] " Letters to Fort St. George, 1741," pp. 37-9.

[3] It must be borne in mind that in the English reckoning of that time
the year began on 25th March. Several ships sailed from Madras for
Syriam in the period from 1st January to 24th March, 1741, N.S.

[4] " Madras Public Consultations, 1741," pp. 92 and 164.

By the end of the year 1741, notwithstanding Smart's reports to the contrary, Fort St. George began to doubt the success of the Talaing rebellion.[1]   It is not surprising, therefore, to find that when, in July of the following year Smart, after a brief visit to Madras, returned to Syriam armed with fresh instructions for negotiating with the predominant party in Lower Burma, he was provided with two letters, couched in identical terms, one addressed to King " Sementho " of Pegu, and the other to the King of Ava.   The appropriate letter was to be delivered to whichever he found in possession of Syriam on his arrival there.   He was strictly charged to keep clear of all political engagements, and to use his utmost endeavours to obtain leave to export saltpetre.[2]   The urgency of obtaining a large stock of gunpowder was becoming daily greater, since England was at war with Spain, and on the brink of war with France.

Smart found the Talaings still in possession of their territory; but their attitude towards him had undergone a radical transformation.   He was obliged to submit to so many affronts from the Government there ; he wrote to Fort St. George that he would be unable to remain in the country, unless the factory were supplied with a military guard.[3]   The cause of this change of attitude on the part of the Talaing Government is not clear.   Probably Smart's adoption of a rôle of stricter neutrality, and his previous failure to co-operate with the new Government to the full extent desired by it, aroused its suspicions against him.   Possibly the Talaings had learnt that he had returned to Burma prepared to negotiate with either side.   On the supposition that who was not for them must be against them, they probably suspected Smart of treachery.

On receipt of Smart's request for a guard, the Fort St. George Council, " taking into consideration the great advantages which this Place has formerly received from the Pegue Trade and that the Exports thither and Imports from thence pay a duty of five per C^t: to the Company," decided to send over a sergeant, corporal, drummer, and twenty topasses for

---

[1] Dodwell, " Calendar of Madras Records, 1740-4," p. 203.
[2] " Madras Public Proceedings," 19th July, 1742 ; Dodwell, *op. cit.*, pp. 287-8.
[3] " Madras Public Proceedings," 5th February, 1743.

the defence of the factory. These were accordingly despatched on 6th February, 1743, on board the *Exeter*.[1] Some months later, however, the Fort St. George authorities, fearing they might regret this step, sent a message to Smart by the *Mermaid*, asking him to send back the soldiers on that boat, " if the Circumstances of affairs there will admit of it." [2]

The soldiers were, indeed, sent back on board the *Mermaid* ; but the circumstances which admitted of this course were not such as either Smart or the Fort St. George President and Council had envisaged. Late in 1743 a Burmese raid into the Talaing country made such headway as to result in the re-occupation of Syriam, and the temporary expulsion of the Talaings. The victorious Burmans submitted the city to a terrible three-days' sack (10th-12th November), in the course of which they plundered the French, Armenian, and Portuguese churches and the warehouses of the foreign merchants. The English factory alone escaped the general pillage, probably because of its small, though trained and well-equipped garrison. Finally, the raiders succeeded in getting gloriously drunk, and the Talaings, returning to the attack with overwhelming forces, recaptured the city with little difficulty. On their return, however, they disarmed Smart's soldiery, looted the English factory, and burned it to the ground.[3]

Thus ended the English factory at Syriam. Smart sent back his troops on board the *Mermaid* and himself followed shortly afterwards. The *Mermaid*, however, was unable to make Madras, being blown out of her course by contrary winds. Instead she put in at Vizagapatam, where she landed the troops, who made their way overland to Madras.[4] No attempt was made to reopen the factory. For one thing, the chaos in Burma rendered the prospect of settled trade hopeless.

---

[1] " Madras Public Proceedings," 5th and 6th February, 1743.

[2] *Ibid.*, 6th September, 1643.

[3] *Ibid.*, 5th March, 1744 ; Dodwell, " Calendar of Madras Records, 1740-4," p. 434. The latter gives a slightly different account from the former, which attributes the looting of the French Armenian, and Portuguese churches to the Talaings upon their return, and not to the Burmans, when they entered the city. The account in Dodwell, *op. cit.*, is a précis of Smart's own letter on the subject written on 14th January, 1744. I have preferred this to the other, which appears in the Minutes of a consultation.

[4] Dodwell, *op. cit.*, p. 441 ; " Madras Public Proceedings," 5th March, 1744.

But it must also be remembered that the development of active hostilities between the British and the French on the mainland of India and at sea paralysed Fort St. George's trading activities for some years. Not until the Treaty of Aix-la-Chapelle, in 1748, brought to an end the War of the Austrian Succession, and Fort St. George, captured by the French in 1746, was handed back to the English, could the Company redirect its attention to the possibilities of trade expansion in Burma. But in 1753, when next a foothold was sought on the opposite shores of the Bay of Bengal, the spot chosen by Fort St. George for the erection of a new factory was not Syriam but the island of Negrais, a place deemed safer from intrusion than the Burmese port.

Meanwhile, events had marched rapidly in Burma. A new national champion, Alaungpaya, had arisen in Upper Burma, and was steadily reducing the rebellious Talaing districts. When negotiations were reopened between the East India Company and the Burmese, the English envoys were received by Alaungpaya as Emperor of all Burma. ·He gave them permission to settle at Negrais and Bassein. But in 1759, the critical year of the Seven Years War, Armenian intrigues brought about the massacre of the whole factory staff at Negrais, and once more the Company ceased its operations in Burma.

When, after the Seven Years War, the English were again free to commence trading operations in Burma, neither Negrais nor Bassein found favour in their eyes. Syriam, too, was no longer attractive: Alaungpaya's new creation, Rangoon, already eclipsed it in importance. English trade, therefore, was directed chiefly to the new port.

The destruction of the English factory at Syriam in 1743 rings down the curtain upon the early relations of the East India Company with Burma. After it, an interval of ten years elapsed before any attempt was made to recommence activities in the country. Thenceforward, with the accession of a new dynasty to the throne of reunited Burma, and the contemporaneous transformation of the Company from a trading body to a political power, the relations between the two began to develop along entirely different lines, culminating in the Anglo-Burmese War of 1824-6. Rangoon supplanted Syriam as the base for British enterprise in Burma. Calcutta supplanted Madras as the directing centre of British relations with Ava. Politics supplanted commerce and shipbuilding as the main subject of those relations.

APPENDICES I–VIII

APPENDIX I

COINAGE USED BY THE EAST INDIA COMPANY IN ITS TRADE WITH BURMA

THE gold pagoda had been the standard coin of South India under the Empire of Vijayanagar. The origin of the word is obscure. (For full discussion of it see Hobson-Jobson, s.v. Pagoda, Love, " Vestiges of Old Madras," I., p. 192.) After the fall of Vijayanagar at the battle of Talikot in 1564 its pagoda and subsidiary coins, the fanam and cash, still remained the standard currency in the Golconda kingdom and on the Coromandel Coast. This coinage was used by the East India Company's merchants throughout the period covered by this book. The Masulipatam pagoda was worth seven shillings and sixpence sterling in Methwold's early days. " A Pagoda equall in weight and alloy to a Frenche Crowne, and worth there seuen shillings sixpence sterling," he writes of it in Purchas, V. (1626 ed.), p. 996. Later on in 1639, when the Company obtained the right to mint coins at Madras, its pagoda was considerably less in weight than the Masulipatam one, which henceforth was known as the " old pagoda " in contradistinction to the " new pagoda " of Madras. Love, in his " Vestiges of Old Madras " (see particularly Vol. I., pp. 192-6), gives the ratio of value between the new pagoda and the old pagoda as 1 is to 1·39. Later in the seventeenth century Bowrey (" The Countries round the Bay of Bengal," 1669-88) gives the old pagoda as worth twelve shillings and the new pagoda as worth eight shillings.

The fanam (Tamil panam, " money ") was also a gold coin, but with a considerable amount of alloy in its composition. It bore various values according to the locality in which it was minted. Love gives the following local values :—

In Golconda the fanam was equal to $^1/_{12}$ of the pagoda.
In Porto Novo ,,   ,,   ,, $^1/_{18}$,,   ,,
In Pulicat   ,,   ,,   ,, $^1/_{24}$,,   ,,
In Madras   ,,   ,,   ,, $^1/_{36}$,,   ,,
(See also Hobson-Jobson, s.v. Fanam.)

The copper cash, a name probably derived from the Tamil *kasu* through the Portuguese corruption *caixa*, was a minutely small coin of very low value, eighty of which went to the fanam.

In Methwold's day the silver rupee had not yet been coined in South India, but large quantities of silver dollars, known as " pieces of eight," " reels of eight," " pieces of 8/8," or " ryalls of eight" were imported.   There are many instances of the East India Company's factors using this coin for purposes of calculation in the seventeenth century.[1]   In 1621 Matthew Duke at Masulipatam, writing home to the Company (O.C. No. 983), mentions the pagoda as worth " about 1½ riall of eight, Spanish money."   The value of the rial at the time of Forrest and Staveley's embassy to Pegu was about four shillings and sixpence sterling (Foster, " English Factories, 1618-21, p. 158).   They therefore took with them to Pegu goods worth about £200 sterling.   The total proceeds of the venture, including what was realised of Samuel's estate, amount to barely £193 sterling.

[1] On this point, *vide* Foster, " John Company," Chapter III., wherein he gives an interesting account of the East India Company's early experiment in coining these dollars.

APPENDIX II

NOTE ON THE ALLEGED EXISTENCE OF ENGLISH FACTORIES IN BURMA BEFORE 1647

WRITERS of Burmese history, who have had occasion to deal with the matter of the earliest contact between that country and the East India Company, have one and all asserted the existence of English factories there early in the seventeenth century. Sir George Scott is of opinion that as a result of Anaukpetlun's invitation to the Company, factories were established at Syriam, Ava, and Bhamo in 1619. He proceeds further to say that " these establishments remained in the country, with occasionally a somewhat hectic life." [1] Sir Arthur Phayre [2] thinks that English factories were probably in existence at these places as early as 1612. He does not specifically connect their foundation with the episode of Thomas Samuel, though he mentions a part of the story. Messrs. J. S. Furnivall and W. S. Morrison, the compilers of the " Burma Gazetteer : Syriam District," state in one part of their volume [3] that an agency of the East India Company was founded at Syriam in 1612, while further on [4] they give the date of the foundation of the English factory there as 1639. The most recent writer on the subject, Mr. G. E. Harvey says [5] : " From about 1627 onwards both the English and Dutch East India Companies had branches in Burma under junior representatives. These branches were closed from time to time, and although profits were occasionally considerable, steady trade was impossible because of the disturbed state of the country. The English were at Syriam, Ava, and Bhamo, the Dutch at Syriam, Pegu, and Ava."

The number of conflicting details contained in these accounts, serve mainly to show in what obscurity the subject is wrapped. It would seem that the chief evidence relied on by these writers is to be found in two vaguely worded passages in Dalrymple's " Oriental Repertory." [6] The first occurs in Dalrymple's notes written in 1759

---

[1] Sir George Scott, " Burma from the Earliest Times to the Present Day," p. 133.
[2] " History of Burma," p. 273.
[3] Furnivall, J. S., and Morrison, W. S., " Burma Gazetteer : Syriam District," Vol. A (Rangoon, 1914), pp. 28-9.
[4] *Ibid.*, p. 192.
[5] " History of Burma," 1925, p. 191.
[6] Vol. I., p. 98 ; Vol. II., p. 345.

on the subject of the expedition to settle the island of Negrais in the year 1753. The passage runs thus : " It may afford you some entertainment to receive a brief Account of several attempts, made, in ancient times, towards an *Establishment* in this *Country*, so far as I have been able to meet with any Records. This Account must necessarily be obscure, from want of complete memoirs. . . . In the beginning of the seventeenth century, it appears, both the *English* and *Dutch* had considerable Commerce in the *Buraghmah Dominions ;* the *English* had *Establishments* at *Syriam*, at *Prom*, at *Ava ;* and on the *borders*, of *China ;* probably at *Prammoo*. . . . On some dispute with the *Buraghmah Government*, the *Dutch* threatened (if they did not even attempt) to bring in the *Chinese ;* this very justly gave umbrage to the *Buraghmah*, who immediately turned both *English* and *Dutch* out of his Dominions ; many years elapsed before the *English* could obtain leave to return ; and the *Dutch* never were re-admitted."

The second passage occurs in a letter of instruction given by Nathaniel Higginson, Governor of Fort St. George, to Edward Fleetwood and James Lesly on the occasion of their mission to Ava in 1695. It runs : " The Right Honourable Company had Factorys at *Syriam* and *Ava*, in former years, but withdrew them ; the *Trade* proving *unprofitable ;* the terms and priviledges of the Trade then enjoyed, does not appear in any writing, because the *King* never gave any *Phirmaund*, or *Articles* in writing."

Dalrymple gives neither dates nor references in support or explanation of these statements, but it is noteworthy that he does not mention the story of Thomas Samuel, and makes no statement that can be construed into meaning that the earliest English factories in Burma were established by invitation of the king. The records of the East India Company surviving from this period are undoubtedly defective, but had English factories existed in Burma previous to the foundation of the Syriam factory in 1647, the contemporary records must have contained some reference to them. Previous to the erection of Fort St. George into a presidency in the year 1652 the Company's stations around the Bay of Bengal and on the Coromandel Coast were subordinate to the chief factory in Java (either Jakatra or Bantam). The Java papers of the period previous to 1647, whether in the Factory Records series or in the Original Correspondence, contain no reference whatever to English factories in Burma, and, in fact, hardly a single reference to Burma. In addition to this it is significant that in the papers relating to the foundation of the factory at Syriam in 1647, no mention is made of previous, or already existing English settlements in the country.

Finally it should be borne in mind that William Methwold, who received Anaukpetlun's offer, did not advise the founding of a factory in Burma. Neither in his letters home from Masulipatam nor in his " Relations of the Kingdome of Golchonda " is there any mention of such a possible development. Samuel, when a prisoner in Pegu, was allowed to carry on trade.   Forrest and Staveley, on their mission to Pegu for the restoration of Samuel's goods, took out piece-goods with them at the Company's charge and traded with them, as has been related, during their stay in the country.   But these haphazard operations were in no way connected with the foundation of factories. Possibly it is these proceedings that have misled writers into thinking that factories existed in Burma at so early a date.   But it is difficult to understand how anyone could imagine that English factories were founded in Burma as early as the year 1612, when de Brito was still in possession of Syriam !

APPENDIX III

HAMILTON'S ACCOUNT OF THE MERGUI MASSACRE, 1687

THE next place on the continent, to the southward (of Pegu), is Merjee, a town belonging to the King of Siam, situated on the banks of the river of Tanacerin, lying within a great number of small uninhabited islands. The harbour is safe, and the country produces rice, timber for building, tin, elephants, elephants' teeth, and Agala wood.[1] In former times a good number of English free merchants were settled at Merjee, and drove a good trade, living under a mild, indulgent Government; but the old East India Company envying their happiness, by an arbitrary command, ordered them to leave their industry, and repair to Fort St. George, to serve them, and threatened the King of Siam with a sea war if he did not deliver those English up, or force them out of his country, and, in anno 1687, sent one Captain Weldon in a small ship, called the *Curtany*, to Merjee with that message. He behaved himself very insolently to the Government and killed some Siamers, without any just cause. One night when Weldon was ashore, the Siamers, thinking to do themselves justice on him, got a company together, designing to seize or kill the aggressor, but Weldon, having notice of their design, made his escape on board his ship, and the Siamers missing him, though very narrowly, vented their rage and revenge on all the English they could find. The poor victims being only guarded by their innocence, did not so much as arm themselves, to withstand the fury of the enraged mob, so that seventy-six were massacred, and hardly twenty escaped on board the *Curtany*; so there was the tragical consequence of one man's insolence.

Before that fatal time, the English were so beloved and favoured at the Court of Siam, that they had places of trust conferred upon them, both in the civil and military branches of the Government. Mr. Samuel White was made Shawbandaar or Custom-master at Merjee and Tanacerin, and Captain Williams was admiral of the King's navy; but the troublesome company, and a great revolution that happened in the state of Siam, made some repair to Fort St. George, others to Bengal, and some to Atcheen (Hamilton, *op. cit.*, in Pinkerton's "Voyages and Travels," VIII., pp. 429-30).

[1] Eagle-wood, an aromatic wood. (*Vide* Hobson-Jobson, s.v. Eagle-wood.)

APPENDIX IV

NOTE ON THE ALLEGED SETTLEMENT AT NEGRAIS IN 1687

A CURIOUS mistake, which has crept into certain English historical accounts of Burma, is a further reason for the discussion of the Negrais episode of 1686-7, which forms the subject of Chapter VII. It has been asserted that at this time Fort St. George actually established a settlement on the island. Apparently Symes,[1] in the historical memoir with which he prefaces his account of his embassy to Ava in 1795, was the first writer to perpetrate this error. The passage in question runs thus :[2] " The Island of Negrais was likewise taken possession of by the English, and a survey of it made by one Weldon, in the year 1687. On this island the Government of Fort St. George established a settlement. Little benefit, however, seems to have been derived from the acquisition : the affairs of the India Company, and indeed of the nation, were in too precarious a state in another quarter of Asia, to admit of sparing the supplies of men and money requisite for its effectual support."

This would seem to imply that the attempt to settle Negrais was made after Weltden's expedition. But against this is the indisputable fact that the Records of Fort St. George contain no reference whatever to anything of the kind. After the return of Ambrose Moody's abortive expedition made in October-November, 1686, there is no record of any further attempt to establish a settlement on the island until the year 1753.

The origin of Symes' error is not apparent. As he seems to have had access to Dalrymple's " Letter Concerning the Negrais Expedition "[3] (of 1753), in which both Moody's and Weltden's expeditions are referred to, but with no suggestion of any settlement resulting from the latter's, it is strange that he should have made the statement referred to above. Dalrymple's account of the expeditions of 1686-7 is as follows : " However there was now (1686) a Resolution taken to settle at *Negrais*, considered at this time as part of the *Arrakan Dominions*, and a Sloop was accordingly sent to make a *Survey* of it ; but losing her Passage, she returned, which prevented the Expedition. . . . In 1687, Captain *Weldon*, with whom *Dampier*

---

[1] Michael Symes, " An Account of an Embassy to the Kingdom of Ava sent by the Governor-General of India in the year 1795."
[2] *Ibid.*, p. 5.   [3] " Oriental Repertory," I., pp. 97-132.

mentions to have made a voyage to TONQUEEN, went in the *Curtana* to *Mergui*, to declare War against SIAM. In his return he touched at *Negrais*, of which he made a *Survey ;* and having destroyed some *Siamese Inscriptions*, and *Hutts*, took possession of the *Island ;* hoisted colours, and left an Inscription, on Tin, of his Proceedings." [1]

Too much reliance upon the authority of Symes has led a recent writer to perpetuate his error. Sir George Scott, in his " Burma from the Earliest Times to the Present Day," has the following passage : [2] " Attempts were made in 1680 and in 1684 to establish factories at Syriam, and in 1686 both Arakan and Burma addressed the Governor of Madras. In the following year, Captain Weldon, ' one Weldon ' as Symes calls him, was sent from Madras to Mergui, to declare war on Siam. He does not seem to have got there, but he did descend upon Haing-Gyi, which is the Burmese name for Negrais Island in the Bassein River. He ' destroyed some Siamese huts,' which were certainly not Siamese, whatever else they may have been, surveyed the island and annexed it, and the Government of Fort St. George, which should have known better, planted a settlement there. It did very little, but the memory remained." Evidently the memory of man in this instance is too unreliable to be of much use to the historian, especially when its defects cause the imagination to be drawn upon.

[1] "Oriental Repertory," I., p. 103. [2] P. 150.

APPENDIX V

HAMILTON'S DESCRIPTION OF THE " ROUNDAY " IN A BURMESE PROVINCIAL CITY

ALL cities and towns under this King's dominions are like aristocratical commonwealths. The prince or governor seldom sits in council, but appoints his deputy, and twelve councillors and judges, and they sit once in ten days at least, but oftener when business calls them. They convene in a large hall, mounted about three feet high, and double benches round the floor for people to sit or kneel on, and to hear the free debates of council. The hall being built on pillars of wood, is open on all sides, and the judges sit in the middle on mats, and sitting in a ring there is no place of precedence ; there are no advocates to plead at the bar, but every one has the privilege to plead his own cause, or send it in writing to be read publicly, and it is determined judicially within the term of three sittings of council; but if any one questions his own eloquence, or knowledge of the laws of equity, he may empower a friend to plead for him ; but there are no fees but what the town contributes for the maintenance of that court, which, in their language is called the Rounday, and those contributions are very small. There are clerks set at the back of the judges, ready to write down whatever the complainant and defendant has to say, and the case is determined by the prince and that council, very equitably; for if the least partiality is found awarded to either party, and the King is made acquainted of it by the deputies at court, the whole sentence is revoked, and the whole Board are corrected for it, so that very few have occasion to appeal to court, which they may do if they are aggrieved ; and if an appeal is made on ill grounds, the appellant is chastised, which just rigour hinders many tedious suits that arise where there are no penalties affixed to such faults.

The judges have a particular garb of their own. Their hair being permitted to grow long, is tied on the top of their heads with cotton ribbon wrapped about it, and it stands upright in the form of a sharp pyramid. Their coat is of thin betella, so that their skin is easily seen through it. About their loins they have a large lungee or scarf, as all other Peguers have, that reaches to their ancles, and against the navel a round bundle made of their lungee, as big as a child's head, but stockings and shoes are not used in Pegu (Hamilton, *op. cit.*, in Pinkerton, *op. cit.*, VIII., p. 424).

APPENDIX VI

HAMILTON'S OBSERVATIONS ON THE SUBJECT OF THE ROYAL RECEPTION OF AMBASSADORS AT AVA

THE King's palace at Ava is very large, built of stone, and has four gates for its conveniencies. Ambassadors enter at the east gate, which is called the Golden Gate, because all ambassadors make their way to him by presents. . . .

When an ambassador is admitted to audience in the palace, he is attended by a large troop of guards, with trumpets sounding, and heralds proclaiming the honour the ambassador is about to receive, in going to see the glory of the earth, His Majesty's own sweet face ; the ambassador is attended with the master of the ceremonies, who instructs him to kneel three times in his way thither, and continue so with his hands over his head, till a proclamation is read before he dare rise. Some of his elephants are instructed to fall on their belly when the King passes by them. This relation I had from one Mr. Roger Alison, who had been twice ambassador from the governor of Fort St. George, or his agents at Syrian, to the court of Ava (Hamilton, *op. cit.*, in Pinkerton, *op. cit.*, VIII., p. 423).

APPENDIX VII

HAMILTON'S OBSERVATIONS ON THE SUBJECT OF KING SANÈ'S TITLES

HIS subjects, if they may be so called, treat him with fulsome adulation. When they speak or write to him they call him their god (or in their language Kiack), and in his letters to foreign princes, he assumes the title of King of Kings, to whom all other Kings ought to be subject, as being near kinsman and friend to all the gods in heaven and on earth, and by their friendship to him all animals are fed and preserved, and the seasons of the year are regularly kept: the sun is his brother, and the moon and stars are his near relations, Lord over the floods and ebbing of the sea; and after all his lofty epithets and hyperboles, he descends to be King of the white elephant, and of twenty-four white somereroes or umbrellaes. These two last he may indeed claim with some show of justice, for I have seen elephants of a light yellow both in Pegu and Siam, but who ought to be called their lord is a question not yet decided; and as King of the twenty-four somereroes, I believe few Kings will care to dispute that glorious title with him, for those somereroes are only common China umbrellaes, covered over with thin Chormandel beteelas, and their canes lackered and gilded; and because his own subjects dare not use any such umbrellaes, he wisely lays his imperial commands on all other Kings to forbear wearing of them when they go abroad (Hamilton, *op. cit.*, in Pinkerton, *op. cit.*, VIII., pp. 422-3).

APPENDIX VIII

JOHN UNDERWOOD'S ACCOUNT OF THE SYRIAM MURDERS, 1720

("Madras Public Proceedings," 20th April, 1721)

The Certificate and Declaration of John Underwood

I, JOHN UNDERWOOD, do hereby declare that on the 28th day of October last there were five Europeans and myself went to see the Moors Feast at Syrian in Pegu and when we came into the Moors street, we saw nobody coming near us only—as usuall at their Feast—the People were dancing round a Fire. As we were going to their Church, Capt: Heron's & Zechary's Lascars came privately into the road way and stopt our Lascars from going to the Church; and one of Zechary's or Capt: Heron's Lascars, having a large Bamboo with a Torch at each end, swung it up and down so that the fire fell amongst the Lascars whereupon they fell to blows, and the Lascars of the *Lusitania* beat them and went to the Church, and when they went they danced and sung as usuall at such time, and the whole disturbance seem'd at an end. But presently after, Zechary came on horseback and whip't the people as they passed, and turn'd back again and did the same. The third time riding thro again, he and his horse fell down, and I went to assist him; but he took me by the Collar, and at the same time an Armenian broke my head. I asked Zechary what he designed to do with me. He made me no answer, but said to his Lascars—in their language—La Mar Banchut, and they knocked me down twice. And after that the third time they knocked me down again, and kept me down till they thought I was dead. Whilst they beat me, I begg'd and desired them to leave of both in the Moors & Portugueeze Languages; but it was in vain, for they abused me so long that they thought I was dead. And when they thought I was dead, one Man call'd out Basta Basta Churda, and then they began to leave me, but as they passed they struck at me. At last there was no more than two left, who stood by me; at which time Mr. Wankford happening to pass by me and ask'd, Whose that, Underwood? I told him there was all that was left of me, for I was almost dead. The two Fellows, that stood by me, cry'd out and call'd, Duserer Wollom hy, Duserer Wollom hy. They then collected themselves together & fell beating of Mr. Wankford, he all the time crying out, Mutt Mar, Mutt Mar; but they did not

256

regard his entreatys, but continued beating him. At that time Zechary cry'd out, Mar Morter, Mar Morter, and Mr. Wankford was kill'd in half a moment's time. As soon as they had despatched him, the Gunner and Mr. Orme's Steward running along, they left Mr. Wankford, and follow'd Mr. Orme's Gunner and Steward, crying out, La Mar banchute. At that time there was a man came to me & bid me get up. But I told I could not, neither was I able. So he & another carry'd me to the same place where Mr. Wankford lay, which was four or five yards from me, and then they left me. I saw the Gunner the second time come running, being pursued by the Lascars. In the mean while I roll'd myself in Mr. Wankford's blood to make my cloaths bloody. But the Lascars came and felt of my cloaths, to see if I was bloody, and went into the Moon light and looked at their fingers, so that they pass'd me, calling me names. At last Zechary's son with six or seven Lascars came to me, holding the point of his creese or dagger close to me, and look'd me in the Face ; and calling me many names, he left me. After he was gone, a Portugueeze and one of the Country People carry'd me to Mr. Orme's house. And I do hereby declare what I have here writ is true, and to the truth of which I am ready to swear, Wittness my hand this twenty second day of December Anno Domini One thousand seven hundred and twenty one.

JOHN UNDERWOOD.

Jurat, coram me
20 *Aprill* 1721,
    Francis Hastings.

BIBLIOGRAPHY

BIBLIOGRAPHY

I. OFFICIAL SOURCES, CALENDARS AND PRINTED COLLECTIONS OF DOCUMENTS

(a) India Office MS. Records

" The East India Company's Original Correspondence from India with Collateral Documents originating at any Place between England and Japan." 72 vols. Covering the period 1603-1708. (Referred to in footnotes by the abbreviation O.C., and the number of the document. *N.B.*—The documents are numbered continuously throughout the whole series.)

" Factory Records : Java," Index Nos. 1-3.

" Factory Records : Fort St. George " :—
Consultations, 1655-1704.
Letters Despatched, 1661-1704.
Letters Received, 1672-1704.

" Factory Records : Masulipatam " :—
Consultations, 1670-85.
Letters Despatched, 1640-85.
Letters Received, 1622-85.

" Factory Records : Miscellaneous," Vols. 3A, 6, 7, 7A, and 18.

" General Records : Home Miscellaneous " :—
Vols. 711, 712 (Index of O.C.).
Vol. 34 (Letters to India).

" General Records : Court Minutes." (Consulted in published series up to 1666, in original MS. volumes after that date.)

" Madras Public Proceedings, 1705-45."

(b) Calendars and Collections of Original Material

Sainsbury. " Calendar of State Papers, Colonial, East Indies, 1513-1634." (Referred to by abbreviation C.S.P.C.E.I.)

Danvers and Foster. " Letters Received by the East India Company from its Servants in the East, 1602-17."

Sainsbury and Foster. " The Court Minutes of the East India Company, 1635-66."

Birdwood and Foster. " The First Letter Book of the East India Company, 1600-19."

Sir William Foster. " The English Factories in India, 1618-67."

"Press Lists of Ancient Records in Fort St. George." Published by the Government of Madras.

H. DODWELL. "Calendar of the Madras Records, 1740-4."

H. STEVENS. "Dawn of British Trade to the East Indies." (Contains a reprint of the Court Minutes of the Company from 1599 to 1603.)

(c) PUBLISHED RECORDS OF FORT ST. GEORGE

"Notes on and Extracts from the Government's Records in Fort St. George, Madras." Madras, 1871.

A. T. PRINGLE. "Selections from the Diary and Consultation Books of the Agent Governor and Council of Fort St. George, 1681-5." Madras, 1893-5.

MADRAS RECORD OFFICE PUBLICATIONS :—
"Diary and Consultation Books, 1672-81 and 1686-1702."
"Public Consultations, 1741."
"Letters to Fort St. George, 1681-88, 1693-4, 1699-1700, 1740-1."
"Letters from Fort St. George, 1679, 1688-9, 1693-4, 1696-1702."
"Despatches from England, 1680-6, 1701-6."
"Public Despatches to England, 1694-6, 1701-2–1710-11, 1741-2."

II. PRINTED COLLECTIONS OF ORIGINAL MATERIALS AND CONTEMPORARY AUTHORITIES

A. DALRYMPLE. "Oriental Repertory," London, 1808. Reprint of portions relating to Burma. (Superintendent, Government Printing, Burma. Rangoon, 1926.)

"PURCHAS his Pilgrimes." *N.B.*—The Maclehose reprint contains all references made herein to the original four volumes of the work. Vol. V., published in 1626 under the title, "Purchas his Pilgrimage," and containing in its supplement William Methwold's valuable paper on the "Relations of the Kingdome of Golchonda," has never been reprinted.

J. STEVENS. "The Portuguese Asia : a Translation of Faria y Sousa's Asia Portuguesa," London, 1695.

ALEXANDER HAMILTON. "A New Account of the East Indies," Edinburgh, 1727. (*N.B.*—For some references to this work I have had to use the reprint of it to be found in Pinkerton, "Voyages and Travels," London, 1811.)

A. MACGREGOR. "Translation of 'A Brief Account of the Kingdom of Pegu,' by an anonymous Portuguese writer of the early seventeenth century," in *Journal of the Burma Research Society*, Vol. XVI., Part II., August, 1926.

SIR R. C. TEMPLE (Editor). "The Diaries of Streynsham Master, 1675-80," London, 1911.

"Tavernier's Voyages," extract from, in Pinkerton's "Voyages and Travels."

HAKLUYT SOCIETY'S PUBLICATIONS

J. H. VAN LINSCHOTEN. "The Voyage of John Huigghen van Linschoten to the East Indies."

T. BOWREY. "A Geographical Account of the Countries round the Bay of Bengal, 1669-79."

"The Diary of William Hedges, 1681-7" (ed. Yule).

R. H. MAJOR. "India in the Fifteenth Century."

"The Voyage of Pyrard de Laval."

"The Book of Duarte Barbosa."

JOHN FRYER. "A New Account of East India and Persia, being nine years' travels, 1672-81."

III. LATER WORKS

J. ANDERSON. "English Intercourse with Siam in the Seventeenth Century," London, 1890.

BAYFIELD. "Historical Review of the Political Relations between the British Government in India and the Empire of Ava . . . to the end of the year 1834," Calcutta, 1835. Also published as a Supplement to R. B. Pemberton's "Report on the Eastern Frontier of British India," Calcutta, 1835.

BIGANDET. "An Outline of the History of the Catholic Burmese Mission from the year 1720 to 1887," Rangoon, 1887.

G. BIRDWOOD. "Report on the Old Records of the India Office," London, 1891.

J. BRUCE. "Annals of the Honourable East India Company," 3 vols., London, 1810.

HENRI CORDIER. "Historique Abrégé des Relations de la Grande-Bretagne avec La Birmanie," Paris, 1894.

H. DODWELL. "Report on the Madras Records," Madras, 1916.

SIR WILLIAM FOSTER. "A Guide to the India Office Records, 1600-1858," London, 1919.
"John Company," London, 1926.

FURNIVALL AND MORRISON. "Burma Gazetteer : Syriam District," Rangoon, 1914.

G. E. HARVEY. "A History of Burma," London, 1925.

SIR W. W. HUNTER. "A History of British India," 2 vols., London, 1912.

LOVE. "Vestiges of Old Madras," 4 vols., London, 1913.

D. MACPHERSON. "History of the European Commerce with India," London, 1812.

J. Nisbet. " Burma under British Rule and Before," 2 vols., London, 1901.

E. H. Parker. " Burma, with special reference to her relations with China," Rangoon, 1893.

R. B. Pemberton. See Bayfield.

Sir A. P. Phayre. " History of Burma," London, 1883.

P. E. Roberts. " History of British India," Oxford, 1921.

Sir J. G. Scott. " Burma from the Earliest Times to the Present Day," London, 1924.

J. G. Scott and Hardiman. " Gazetteer of Upper Burma," Rangoon, 1900.

Vincent Smith. " Oxford History of India," Oxford, 1921.

Symes. " An Account of an Embassy to the Kingdom of Ava," London, 1800.

W. A. R. Wood. " History of Siam," London, 1926.

Yule and Burnell. " Hobson-Jobson : a Glossary of Anglo-Indian Words and Phrases," London, 1903.

" The Indian Antiquary," 1897. Article by Sir R. C. Temple, " Currency and Coinage among the Burmese."

" The Journal of the Burma Research Society," April, 1927. Article by D. G. E. Hall, " English Relations with Burma, 1587-1686, with an Appendix containing extracts from the ' Fort St. George Diary and Consultation Book, 1680,' relating to the mission of Joao Perera de Faria Junior to Ava, and including the full text of Streynsham Master's Articles of Commerce."

INDEX

ACHIN, 45.

Addison, Gulston, 10, 194 n.², 196, 199; Joint Stock venture, 10, 196 et seq.

Agra factory, 77.

Ahom kingdom, 16.

Aix-la Chapelle, Treaty of, 241.

Aka (fees), 111.

Akaukwun, Akawoon, the, 111 n.², 170.

Akbar, Emperor, 18.

Akunwun, the, 170.

Alano, French pirate, 223.

Alaungpaya dynasty, 12, 170, 172.

Alaungpaya, rise of, 12, 241; mentioned, 3, 16, 27 n.³

Allanson (or Allison), Captain Roger, 179 n.¹, 196, 197 and n.², 198, 254.

Allison, Roger, 197, 254. See Allanson.

Ambassadors, royal reception of, 175, 254.

Amboyna, 44, 45; "massacre" of, 45.

Anaukpetlun, 28 and n.¹, 32; restores order in Burma, 28; campaigns against Siam, 33, 34; seizes Thomas Samuel and Company's property, 7, 33, 41, 42; invites trading relations, 43, 247, 248.

Anawrahta, 16, 231.

Anderson, J., "English Intercourse with Siam," cited 131 et seq. passim.

Anglo-Burmese War (1824-6), 12, 242.

Anglo-Dutch Treaty of Defence, 44-5, 50.

Anglo-Dutch Wars:
First, 8, 60, 65, 69, 76; and English commerce, 69, 77; attitude of Dutch to English in Burma, 69, 70; effect on English company's activities, 8, 9, 69-70, 71; naval superiority of Dutch in Indian Ocean, 69; Treaty of Westminster, 45.

Second and third, 83.

Antheunis, Lucas, 24, 31, 32, 34; letter to Samuel, 33, 34; claims restoration of Company's goods after Samuel's death, 34, 92.

Arab trade with Burmese ports, 200.

Arakan, 15, 25, 27, 31, 130 n.²; king of, 130 and n.², 142; navy of, 37 n.², 49; piratical operations by feringi mercenaries of, 49.

Arakanese raid on Pegu, 27, 31.

Archer, Samuel, 62, 63, 64.

Armagon factory, 49, 50.

Armenian intrigues, 241.

Armenians in Pegu ruby trade, 116, 194, 221.

Assada merchants, 76.

Assam, 16.

Assayer, the, 90.

Atwinwun, the, 170 n.³, 172 n.¹

Aurungzeb, 137, 200.

Austrian Succession, War of, 12, 222, 241.

Ava, city of, 15, 54, 73, 170.
as Burmese capital, 11, 54, 72, 73-4, 94, 170, 231.
king's palace, 254.
king's storehouses at, 73, 74.
trading post at, 8, 44, 72-3, 74, 83 n.², 108, 110, 166, 247, 248.
reception of the factors in, 59.

Ayuthia, 15, 27 n.¹, 31; factory, 83, 130; French Company at, 131.

BABA (Armenian), 171.

Balasore, 59, 63, 77, 142.

Ball, George, 35 n.², 36 n.⁵

Bandas, the, 44, 45.

Bangkok, 31 n.¹

Bantam, 32, 51, 58, 77.

Barne, Miles, 227, 228.

Basra, 50.

Bassein, 19 and n.¹, 96, 241; river, 129.

Bassing, Sergeant Johannes, 201.

Batavia, Dutch East India Co. at, 105.

Batavia Presidency, 45, 50.

Bayinnaung, 16, 28, 73, 231; commercial policy of, 17, 18; and political unity, 17, 26; death, 26.

APPENDIX

The Tragedy of Negrais

THE TRAGEDY OF NEGRAIS.

BY

D. G. E. HALL

———

CONTENTS.

THE TRAGEDY OF NEGRAIS.

INTRODUCTION.

In my " Early English Intercourse with Burma, 1587-1743 ", published three years ago, I strove to set forth all that could be gleaned from existing records concerning the earliest period of English enterprise in this country, a subject previously shrouded in almost complete mystery. The present work deals with the next phase in the history of the English connexion with Burma. · It traces the history of the tragic settlement on the island of Negrais and of the relations of the East India Company with the rival Courts of Pegu and Ava, during the period 1752-61. And the story I have to tell constitutes a not unimportant episode in Anglo-French relations, hitherto neglected by the historian.

Previous accounts of English enterprise in Burma during this period, notably those of Symes and Harvey, have been based almost entirely upon the information found in the papers on the subject collected in Dalrymple's Oriental Repertory. Now Dalrymple had no access to the records relating to the origin and early history of the Negrais settlement; they were of a secret nature, and I have recently discovered them in the Military Consultation Books of Fort St. George. Apparently they have never till now been used by any writer who has had occasion to deal with my subject. The complete story therefore has never been told; and it will be seen that the previously missing portion includes what to the general student of history is its most important phase ; and one indeed without which the remainder lacks point and meaning.

For some years the main body of material for filling in this inconvenient gap in our knowledge has been available in printed form, *i. e.* in the Records of Fort St. George, Diaries and Consultation Books, Military Department, 1752-4, published by the Government Press, Madras, in 1910-11. Other previously unexplored sources, which have yielded valuable material are the Madras Public Proceedings, the Home Miscellaneous Series of India Office Documents, that Office's collections of Coast and Bay Abstracts and of Despatches to Madras, and Professor Dodwell's Calendar of Madras Despatches, 1744-55 For French activities in Burma and elsewhere in the East I have made much use of Henri Martineau's recently completed monumental work, *Dupleix et L'Inde Française* (4 vols., Paris 1920-28), which gives long verbatim extracts from original sources. With the aid of this material, supplementing that previously known, though imperfectly studied,I am here attempting to tell the complete story of the Negrais episode; not, however, a patched up edition of the old story, but a new one, for, like the picture in a jig-saw puzzle, the fitting in of the key parts previously missing gives an entirely new character to the whole.

Some objection may be raised to my application of the now frowned-on name Talaing to the people of Lower Burma. I should therefore explain that this was the name consistently applied by the Burmese, at the time of which I am writing, to the people known to Europeans as " Peguers " or " Peguans ", *i. e.* supporters or subjects of the Kingdom of Pegu, which was conquered and absorbed by Alaungpaya. It is therefore in this sense rather than any strictly racial one that I have used the word. I have felt that the use of the word Mon, which today has a racial connotation, might lead to a certain amount of confusion. Actually in the eighteenth century both words were used somewhat loosely by Europeans. As an example of this I may quote the following passage in the journal of the geographer, Dr. Buchannan, who came with Symes to Burma in 1795: "The Burmas call themselves Myamma, by the people of Pegue they are called Pumma. These latter, called by the Burmas Talain, call themselves Moan." (Home Miscellaneous, Vol. 687, 11.)

My grateful acknowledgments are due to the staffs of the India Office Library and Record Department for the great help afforded me in the search for the materials upon which this monograph is based.

D. G. E. HALL

CHAPTER I

THE ORIGIN OF THE SETTLEMENT.

"In the year 1753," writes Alexander Dalrymple, "an Expedition to settle at Negrais was undertaken ; As the particular Motives, for this Scheme, were communicated only to a Secret Committee, of these, or of the Plan laid down, if there was any, I can therefore say nothing,"[1] He does, however, offer one useful clue to the origin of the settlement in the shape of a paper of anonymous authorship entitled "The Consequence of Settling an European Colony on the Island Negrais."[2] This was apparently written in, or slightly before, the year 1750, and was furnished to him by " my deceased friend Governor Saunders", who had been responsible for despatching the expedition under David Hunter, which seized the island in April 1753. In this paper all the general conditions favouring the selection of Negrais as a site for an English factory are adumbrated. Main stress is laid upon the value of the island for the foundation of a " Capacious Harbour for Shipping, being secured against all sorts of winds". Herein shipbuilding and repairs could be carried on more safely than at Syriam, where, it was alleged, the silting of the river threatened to make it before many years impracticable for ships of large burthen. Moreover, it was far removed from the neighbourhood of the savage and confused struggle, which had raged in Burma since the establishment of the rebel kingdom of Pegu in 1740. In its neighbourhood were to be obtained inexhaustible supplies of teakwood and abundance of food. Further, it could easily be occupied and held by a European power. But the climax of the argument appears to be reached in the following brief and pregnant sentence : "In case of a War with any European Nation, of what consequence would it be, to have a safe and capacious Harbour for Ships, at such a small distance from Madras and Bengal."

In 1750 war with a European nation in the East was a far from remote contingency. The War of the Austrian Succession, which had been formally terminated two years earlier by the Treaty of Aix-la-Chapelle, had witnessed the first serious Anglo-French conflict in India ; and although the contest on land had been limited to the Carnatic, the events of the struggle had clearly demonstrated the importance of sea-power as a determining factor. For the French maritime forces, organised at Mauritius under the brilliant direction of Labourdonnais, had in 1746 suddenly and unexpectedly won the command of the sea from their

---

1 Oriental Repertory, I, 97.

2 *Ibid.*, I, 129-132. The island herein referred to is the one known to the Burmese as Haing gyi, not Diamond Island. For a discussion of this point see Hall, Early English Intercourse with Burma, 1587-1743, 129.

rivals and captured Madras. And although the French supremacy at sea was not maintained, a sharp lesson had been read to the East India Company. When therefore with the peace Madras passed once more into British hands, its Governor, Thomas Saunders, began to devote attention to the matter of strengthening English naval control over the Bay of Bengal.

The matter was indeed urgent, since it soon became obvious that, so far as the South Indian arena was concerned, the Treaty of 1748 had brought little respite to the harassed English. There the French under Dupleix were feverishly developing their power in new directions, ever seeking new vantage points, and threatening to encircle Madras with a ring of territory under their control. Thus, although trade still remained the chief pursuit of the English Company, Governor Saunders was drawn more and more into the task of circumventing the designs of Dupleix. And the vortex of the struggle rapidly expanded until it touched the opposite shores of the Bay. The causes of the English settlement at Negrais therefore must be sought in French activities in the much distracted land of pagodas. And the political motive will be found to predominate.

Since the closing years of the 17th century the French had carried on intermittent trade with the Burmese ports. They had gone there solely for the timber and crude oil required in shipbuilding. For many years no attempt had been made to develop settled trading relations with the country : the risks were considered too great. Dupleix's arrival in India soon altered this state of affairs. He saw the vast potentialities of the Burmese ports to a sea power. In his " *Mémoire sur la situation de nos établissements en 1727* " he emphasized the importance of planting a French shipyard at Syriam. " *Les bois y sont pour rien; les ouvriers seuls causent toute la dépense*," he wrote.[1] His efforts resulted in the despatch of a French agent, named Dalvarez, to the Court of Ava. This man returned to Pondicherry in 1729 with royal letters conceding certain commercial privileges, including the grant of a piece of ground at Prome and permission to maintain a "bancassal", or godown, at Syriam. In the first flush of enthusiasm for the new enterprise Dupleix himself was badly stung. Early in 1732 he bought a small ship, *Le Fidéle*, which he consigned with a cargo valued at between sixteen and seventeen thousand rupees to Lewis Tornery,[2] a shipbuilder at Syriam, who was to supply a return cargo of naval stores. But in some way or other his supercargoes and a French resident named Dubois contrived to cheat him of the greater part of the returns of the venture.[3]

---

1 Alfred Martineau, *Dupleix et L'Inde Française*,, I, 44,

2 For further information concerning this man see Hall, *op. cit.*, 207, etc.

3 Martineau, *op. cit.*, I, 516-7.

The French " factory ", which was opened at Syriam as the result of the royal sanction accorded in 1729, was a shipyard presided over by a professional shipwright, a private contractor working on a commission basis, like his English counterpart of that period. The home authorities would have preferred one of their covenanted servants for the post, but no one with the requisite technical knowledge was available. The first "Chief" La Noë built four ships for Pondicherry during his term of office. Two of them, the *Fulvy* and the *Fleury*, were large ships, the former of which distinguished herself later on in operations against the English. The others, the *Marie Gertrude* and the *Diana*, were of the brigantine class. In 1737, when La Noë left Syriam, he was succeeded by Puel, a sea-captain famous in Eastern waters, who obtained a further grant of land at Syriam for the erection of necessary buildings. The outbreak of the Talaing rebellion, however, soon put a stop to this projected expansion. The hostility of the rebels caused Puel to abandon the factory in January 1742. He returned to Pondicherry with such naval stores as he could carry with·him. The remainder he entrusted to the care of a French missionary, Père Wittony. [1]

In the meantime the War of the Austrian Succession had begun ; and soon the Anglo-French struggle in the Carnatic fully absorbed the attention of both sides, to the exclusion of schemes of expansion in Burma. That country too remained absorbed with its own internal strife. Year after year the fluctuating struggle continued between the rebel Talaing kingdom of Pegu and the Burmese of the north. There was little serious campaigning : each side carried on a series of raids into the other's territory, carrying devastation far and wide and depopulating the country. The original monk-king Smim Htaw Buddhaketi set up in 1740, proved utterly incompetent as a leader. In 1747 therefore a new king, Binnya Dala, was installed with great pomp at Pegu. He and his brother, the Uporaza or Heir Apparent, adopted a more vigorous policy, and by the time that the Treaty of Aix-la-Chapelle brought the Anglo-French war in India nominally to an end, the power of the Talaings extended north-wards as far as Prome and Toungoo, and the Southerners were raiding up to the walls of Ava itself. At this juncture the Burmese, no longer able to make a stand in the open against their rivals, began making overtures to Yunnan. The Talaings on the other hand, conscious that their position would never be secure until Upper Burma were completely subjugated, sent an embassy to Pondicherry in 1750 soliciting military assistance from Dupleix.

The opportunity was too good to let slip. Without hesitation Dupleix promised men and munitions. But before implementing his promise he decided to take stock of the situation in this land of white elephants. So in July 1751 there arrived at the Court of Pegu the Sieur Bruno[2]

1 *Ibid.*, II, 163-4.
2 Misspelt Bourno by most English writers from Dalrymple to Harvey.

Dupleix's agent, sent by him to spy out the land and suggest a line of action. Bruno was publicly received by Binnya Dala on July 28th, in the royal palace at Pegu. There he repeated Dupleix's promise of military aid, and pledged his sincerity by drinking from a golden goblet a beverage composed of water and the ashes of a small piece of yellow paper, upon which, before it was burnt, the customary formula used for oaths had been inscribed. He returned to his master to report that with five or six hundred well-equipped French troops it would be a simple matter to gain control over Syriam and its river. And Dupleix, seeing in the astounding enterprise the chance of building a new French empire on the banks of the Irrawaddy, wrote home to the Directors of the Compagnie Francaise strongly pressing the venture.

It was not long before the ever-watchful Thomas Saunders at Madras heard of the diplomatic activity between Pegu and Pondicherry. The English factory at Syriam had come to an end not long after the withdrawal of the French Resident, Puel. It had been burnt to the ground by the Talaings late in the year 1743. Thereafter official relations between the East India Company and Burma had lapsed. Out of this arose an extraordinary and tragic incident, the effects of which will have to be noted later. The Ostend Company's Bankibazar factory, regardless of a clause in the Anglo-Austrian treaty of 1731 stipulating the suppression of its parent company, had continued to trade under the protection of the Austrian flag. In 1744, probably owing to English and Dutch intrigues, it was besieged by the faujdar of Hugli. Unable to hold out, its Chief, Francois de Schonamille, with about a hundred of the garrison took ship for Burma, intending to transfer trading operations to a sphere definitely vacated by his English rivals. Soon after his arrival, however, he and the majority of his followers were treacherously massacred by the Talaings.[1]

Meanwhile, although there was neither English resident nor factory at Syriam, English private traders and shippers still frequented the port. To what extent we have no record. Probably one of them, Captain Thomas Taylor, was the author of the anonymous paper on "The Consequence of settling an European Colony on the Island Negrais", printed by Dalrymple. [2] Another, Robert Westgarth by name, was a shipwright at Syriam at the time of Bruno's mission to Pegu, and apparently possessed some degree of influence at Court. Presumably through him the Madras Council was informed of Binnya Dala's negotiations with Dupleix.

Thomas Saunders's first move, on hearing of the Pegu-Pondicherry *rapprochement*, was to write home to the Directors suggesting that in view of a rumour that the French intended to obtain from the Court of Pegu

---

1 Cambridge Hist. of India, V, 115, 142. Madras Public Proceedinge, s. v. s Jan. and 29 July 1745. Dodwell, Calendar of Madras Despatches, 1744-1755, xix.
2 Dalrymple suggests his name and that of a Captain Barton as the possible authors.

the cession of the Island of Negrais, the Company should forestall them by planting a settlement there. From the correspondence it does not appear whether he knew anything of the East India Company's previous connexion with the island, in 1686, when its settlement had been projected as a counterpoise to the development of French influence in Siam [1]. On that occasion the company had been wise enough to abandon the scheme before it burnt its fingers. Long before it was possible for Saunders to receive a reply to his letter, came the news of Bruno's mission to Pegu. The effect of this may be seen in an entry in the Fort St. George Military Consultations under the date February 10th, 1752[2]. It records a decision made by the Council to send the *Porto Bello* sloop to Syriam for repairs, and to appoint Robert Westgarth the Company's Resident there, entrusting him with the task " of resettling our affairs at that place upon the best footing we can to prevent as much as we are able the French from encroaching on our trade." In explanation of this decision it was stated that the French had lately secured permission to establish a factory and hoist their colours at Syriam, and that they were rumoured to have designs upon the island of Negrais. Westgarth, therefore, was especially urged to forestall them by obtaining, if possible, a grant of the island to the East India Company.

But before the *Porto Bello* set sail for Syriam, a letter arrived from the Court of Directors in London instructing the " Private Committee " of the Madras Council " to endeavour making a Settlement on the Negrais." So, at a consultation on June 15th, the original arrangement made for the *Porto Bello* was altered. Instead she was to go to Negrais in company with a smaller vessel, the *Fortune.* She was to convey thither Thomas Taylor, who was placed in command of the expedition, together with " a Sergeant, a Corporal, six private Men, thirteen Coffrees, some Lascars and all things necessary for establishing a settlement." Then, having landed them, she was to proceed on to Syriam for her repairs, and also to convey to Westgarth his belated instructions. During her absence Taylor was to use the *Fortune* to make a thorough survey of the island and its neighbourhood, and especially to look out for a good site suitable for a harbour and capable of fortification.

Thomas Taylor's expedition arrived at Diamond Island on June 29th, 1752,[3] and established its base there. It was not long before its leader became aware that he had put his head into a hornet's nest. The local officials were thoroughly alarmed by this unwarranted intrusion. All attempts at conciliation proved fruitless. A force of several

---

1 This episode is recounted in Hall, *op. cit.*, 129-138.

2 Records of Fort St. George: Diary and Consultation Book, Military Department, 1752. (Government Press, Madras, 1910.) The Military Consultation Books of this period contain the records of "secret" consultations, and are similar in nature to the series, which at a later date is termed " Secret and Political." Hence, therefore, Dalrymple's ignorance of the origin of the settlement.

3 Fort St. George Diary and Consultation Book, Military Department, 1752, 61.

hundred men soon collected and threatened to cut to pieces Taylor's inconsiderable escort. In great alarm he threw up some defensive works on his island, and retained the *Porto Bello* at hand, so that he might cut and run, should the situation become intolerable. But his worst embarrassment came from a different quarter. The heavy rains of the south-west monsoon ruined his encampment on shore. Inevitable disease decimated his numbers and paralysed his activities. In these desperate straits he held on for some weeks, until he had made a rough map of the neigbourhood and formulated suggestions for the guidance of Fort St. George in the matter of the permanent occupation of Negrais Then, when the increasing hostility of the people and the ravages of fever rendered his position untenable, he evacuated it and sailed off with his two ships for Syriam, resolved to obtain some form of royal saction before proceeding any further with the business.[1]

News travelled with surprising rapidity in old Burma. Very shortly after Taylor began his operations in the Negrais vicinity, Robert Westgarth at Syriam got wind of what was afoot from the Talaing officials. A little later, by a private vessel from Madras, he received a duplicate copy of the instructions despatched to him by the *Porto Bello*. With all speed he sent a message by way of the creeks to Taylor telling him that the Talaings had recently captured the city of Ava, and warning him against adopting a high-handed attitude towards the people. Then he hastened off to the capital to make the best of a situation, which, he rightly guessed, had caused no little commotion there.

He found the King, Binnya Dala, extremely suspicious of the Company's designs. No one ever settled on the island, and it was no place for trade, he told Westgarth. What, he asked, could be the Company's intention in settling at so remote a place? Westgarth did his utmost to assure the disgruntled monarch that the expedition was a peaceful one, and hinted that aid from the Company against the Burmese might be the reward for compliance with its requests. But the King would commit himself to nothing until such time as the official letters and presents from the Governor of Madras, entrusted to *Porto Bello*, should arrive. Later Westgarth had a more encouraging interview with the King's brother, the Uporaza, or Heir Apparent, the dominant personality at this ramshackle court. The latter assured him that the French proposals would not be entertained. The English had a long-standing connexion with the country, he said. They should therefore be given freedom of trade, notwithstanding French intrigues to the contrary. Westgarth returned to Syriam not ill-pleased with the impression he created. "I have strove much, ever since the French came here, to frustrate their schemes," he wrote off to the Fort St. George Council, "and I hope ere long (though I must work with caution) to have them quite rooted out of this place."[2]

---

1 *Ibid.*, 61-2.
2 *Ibid.*, 60.

On September 15th, much to Westgarth's relief, Thomas Taylor arrived at Syriam. With as little delay as possible the two Englishmen repaired to the Court of Pegu bearing the official letter and presents from the Governor of Madras. Earlier on, when news of Taylor's occupation of Diamond Island had first reached Pegu, a royal order had been issued commanding his presence at the capital to explain his intentions. His prompt arrival, before actually receiving this fiat, served to lull the government's worst suspicions. It added strength to Westgarth's previous assertions regarding the peaceable nature of the expedition. Also, at the latter's suggestion, Taylor wisely supplemented the official present with a gift of some guns, small arms and ammunition. His reception by the King therefore was not lacking in cordiality. He was promised the immediate restoration of the old factory site at Syriam together with all the trading privileges previously enjoyed there; and it was arranged that the Uporaza should go in person to make formal delivery of the land to Westgarth.

On the subject of Negrais, however, the king and his brother were adamant. The Company's official letter to the king was written in Persian, a language rarely met with by Burmese rulers in their diplomatic intercourse. There was some delay in the proceedings while a translation was being made. In the interval the Uporasa exerted every possible effort to dissuade Taylor from further pursuance of the project. The island was, he said, "a very sickly place," and a mere harbourage of rogues. Its grant to the English would cause them and the French to quarrel. Bassein was infinitely preferable for a settlement : the Dutch, he urged, had formerly carried on a prosperous trade there. On their return to the royal presence to hear the formal reading of the letter, Binnya Dala confronted the envoys with the same arguments. The letter itself clinched matters ; it was on translation found to be couched in general terms only. There was no specific reference to Negrais in it. Here was a providential loophole for the King. Until the Company made formal request for the island, he said, nothing could be done. And from this position all further arguments failed to move either him or his brother. In a subsequent private interview the Uporaza told the discomfitted envoys that the French had never asked for the place. He had allowed the baseless rumour to became current in order to keep the English, as he said, " in suspense."[1]

So Taylor and Westgarth returned to Syriam, the former to superintend the repair of the *Porto Bello*, the latter to take over the factory site and assume the duties of Resident. Both wrote to Madras for further instructions. On September 29, the Uporasa arrived at Syriam to hand over the factory site.[2] This he did with due ceremonial on Sunday October 1st. At the same time he gave some sort of assent to a list of

1 *Ibid.*, 81.
2 *Ibid.*, 79.

trading privileges apparently drafted, and presented to him, by Westgarth. A copy of these was shortly afterwards submitted by the latter to the Madras Council, so that they might be embodied in a formal agreement to be negotiated with the Court of Pegu.[1]

Although Westgarth wrote saying that he " was at a loss to know " what exactly had been the former trading privileges of the Company in Burma, the draft articles to which he said he had secured the Uporaza's assent were largely a restatement, in slightly more favourable terms, of those upon the basis of which Sir Streynsham Master had in 1680 attempted to re-establish English trade with the country[2]. There was the same most-favoured-nation clause granting to Company's ships the right to pay no more than half the import duties levied on those of other nations[3]. Company's servants and British subjects trading under its protection were to enjoy freedom from interference on the part of the local officials. Disputes among the English were to be settled in accordance with English law by the Resident, who was to enjoy all the privileges exercised by former holders of the post. Country merchants, who broke their contracts, might be imprisoned or otherwise punished by the English according to Burmese custom[4]. The country government was to abstain from confiscating the estates of English subjects lying within its boundaries. The English were to be free to build and repair ships at Syriam without let or hindrance, especially in regard to such matters as the procurement of timber, etc., and the management of their lascars. Ships might leave Syriam freely, subject to the king being duly notified in each case. There was also a vague promise of free trade to all parts of the kingdoms of Pegu and Ava, and of free export of all the commodities produced therein.

How seriously the Uporaza's assent to these articles was to be taken the subsequent history of the negotiations with the Court of Pegu will show. His main object was to obtain a plentiful supply of military stores. The French had made great promises. But Bruno was away at Pondicherry, and nothing had yet materialised. The offer of generous terms to the English would serve as a useful hint to the French, and could easily be withdrawn if the latter fulfilled their promises. Meanwhile the Talaing government greatly embarrassed Thomas Taylor by its insatiable demands for arms and ammunition.[5]

The factory site handed over to Westgarth by the Uporaza was a mere heap of ruins. Pending instructions from Madras, he did nothing beyond enclosing it with a bamboo fence. He suggested the erection of a

---

1 " Preliminary Articles agreed to by Upper Raja on Sunday the 1st October 1752, " Fort St. George Diary and Consultation Book, Military Department, 1753, 17-18.
2 Hall, *op. cit.*, 109-113.
3 Clause 2. Clause 4 of Streynsham Master's Articles.
4 Hall, *op. cit* , 113.
5 Fort St. George Diary and Consultation Book, Military Department, 1753, 18.

brick house and godown surounded by a plank fence, similar to the former factory, if the Fort St. George Council would be willing to incur so great an expense.[1] In all his letters Westgarth strove to impress upon the Madras Council the necessity for heavy expenditure if English influence in Burma were to be firmly re-established. The rebuilding of of the factory at Syriam would itself be a very costly undertaking. The struggle with the French in his eyes mainly resolved itself into a contest in bribery. To secure the upper hand the English, he insisted, must make more valuable presents than the French to the Court of Pegu. So pressing were his demands for money that his employers, in sending him a first draft of Rs. 10,000, thought fit to let drop a gentle hint that there was no intention to sink a great deal of money in the concern. The Residency at Syriam, he was reminded, had never previously put the Company to any expense. Hence he must be " as frugal as possible " in the matter of presents. He was advised to imitate the methods employed by such former Residents as Kelsal and Smart in carrying out his duties, and he was pointedly warned that he must submit his accounts with regularity.[2] Large commitments at Syriam or Pegu had no place in Thomas Saunders's schemes.

Taylor also received from the Madras Council at the same time a consignment of the same amount. When the money arrived, he and Westgarth, upon notifying the Court of Pegu, were gratified by its complete exemption from payment of customs duty. The King, in issuing the order, remarked that when the Company sent a great quantity of goods, he would take his customs. There followed a catastrophe, common enough in this land of bamboo houses, but decidedly suspicious when all the circumstances are taken into account. On December 28th, while the two men were away at Pegu, Westgarth's house at Syriam was burnt out. Most of the money stored there, including the consignments recently received by Taylor and himself from Madras, was saved, though a trifling portion was melted. But his books and papers were destroyed, together with some of the personal belongings of Taylor and Captain Grierson of the *Porto Bello* and much of the material purchased for the repair of that vessel.[3] Westgarth, in reporting the matter to the Madras Council, could offer no satisfactory explanation of the fire. " There are many people here," he wrote," when they want to plunder will go in the night and throw fire on straw houses on purpose to accomplish their wicked designs and I know not but this may have been my case."[4] But apparently nothing was plundered, nor did he allege any definite attempt. Subsequent events, as we shall see, serve to strengthen the suspicion that he was anxious for a plausible excuse for cooking his accounts.

---

1 *Ibid.*, 1753, 17.
2 *Ibid.*, 1752, 62.
3 *Ibid.*, 1753, 28.
4 *Ibid.*, 1753, 28.

While the agents of the East India Company were thus engaged in re-establishing its influence in Burma, Bruno had been absent at Pondicherry. Early in November 1752 he returned to Syriam in a small sloop. He was the bearer of a letter from Dupleix to the King of Pegu. Of this soon after its delivery, Westgarth was able to procure a copy, the following rough translation of which he forwarded to Madras :

" I sent my people into your country last year to desire you to deliver them the ground the King of Ava formerly gave to the French Company, which you have done and gave my people many promises of your friendship and that you would send your ships to my port but I have seen none yet, and am surpriz'd you don't keep your word with me, for I have never seen anything that ever belong'd to you but a letter which nobody in my country could read so have sent Mr. Bruno again to you to know what you intend to do, and if you chuse to keep my friendship I desire you will help Mons Bruno to get the new ship done with the utmost despatch and the eight guns he lent you last year, you must deliver back to him for the use of the ship, and on his departure I have order'd him to deliver the factory to the Revd. Padree Paulo Nirini till such time as I send my orders to him.[1]

Not a reference of any sort to the pledged military aid. Nor did Bruno bring with him the valuable present of warlike stores, including 500 stand of arms, that he was said to have promised on the occasion of his previous visit. Dupleix, it would appear, was playing for time. He had as yet received no reply from Paris to his letters on the subject of intervention in Burma. And he was already too deeply involved in India to embark upon an enterprise of such magnitude, so far from his base, without the active help of the home authorities. Binnya Dala was greatly annoyed by the letter. He refused to honour Bruno with an audience. The latter was informed that his business could be conducted only through the Uporaza. At the same time the insignia of a minister of state was pointedly conferred upon Westgarth. It consisted of a gold betel box, a goldmounted sword, and what the Englishman described as a " gurgelet with a gold cover "[2]

But the Sieur Bruno knew how to play his cards. There were at the time in Syriam two influential men, who viewed with alarm the revival of English influence in the country. One was an Armenian shipbuilder, Coja Nicous by name, who belonged to a community desperately hostile to the rise of English power in the East. The other was the Italian priest and schoolmaster, Father Nerini, who was devoted to the French interest. Together with these two men Bruno went privately to the Uporaza with a pretty story. The English, he said, intended to fortify Negrais. Then would the Queen of Hungary send four ships to join the English there,

1 *Ibid.*, 1753, 29·
2 *Ibid.*, 1753, 30.

and vengeance would be wreaked upon the Court of Pegu tor the massacre of de Schonamille and his Ostenders in 1745. This information, said Bruno, he had been commissioned by Dupleix to convey to the King; and he was authorised to say that if the King would allow the French to establish a fort on the China Bakir river, they would engage to keep the Ostenders away. The manoeuvre succeeded in its immediate object. For although the Uporaza scouted the idea of allowing the French to fortify the China Bakir, his suspicions regarding English designs at Negrais were once more aroused. Bruno's influence indeed was soon in the ascendant, so much so that he boasted to Westgarth that he had warned the Uporaza of the possibility of a surprise attack by the English with the object of seizing the guns claimed by the French. When therefore Taylor and Westgarth complained to the King that the factory site granted by him to the French at Syriam belonged to Lewis Tornery, who, they claimed, was an English subject, they could get no redress. The Court of Pegu, they soon found, was resolved to take full advantage of its position of *tertius gaudens* as between the rival companies. "He [the King] and the Upper Rajah," wrote Taylor to the Madras Council, "seems to me to be politick men, and will wave a discourse very dexterously when they don't like it and never want an excuse to evade any promises they make and when they give an order to any Europeans for the Government here, they obey or disobey just as they please and to complain is no more than to make presents again and the same order is given and serv'd as before without any notice taken."[1]

This episode was speedily followed by incidents at Syriam instigated by Bruno for the purpose of discrediting the English. Coja Nicous, the Armenian, seized an English officer of a ship, bound him and had him thrashed unmercifully in one of his godowns. When Westgarth, in his capacity of English Resident, laid formal complaint before the Yon at Syriam, Nicous sent a message to the Court of Pegu accusing the English of having gone armed to the Yon, and of having threatened the officers of government there. The King, who was building a new palace at Pegu, sent orders for Taylor and Westgarth to come to his assistance. When they arrived with lascars, ropes and blocks for hauling the gigantic wooden columns into position, and with the customary presents on such an auspicious occasion, they were met by ·the Uporaza, who soundly rated them for the alleged insult to the royal officials at Syriam. They rounded on him, and a stormy scene ensued. In such outspoken terms, in fact, did they defend themselves, that the official interpreter fearing for his own life dared not translate what they said. In the end peace was restored : the help they brought was welcome. And the King was sufficiently gratified to present Westgarth with an elephant and to commiserate with him on the loss of his house. (2) When, however, they returned to Syriam, they found that in their absence Nicous had committed

---

1 *Ibid.*, 1753, 30.
2 *Ibid.*, 1753, 34, 36.

a further outrage on an English sea-captain and had publicly announced that he would have the English colours pulled down and the English themselves hounded out of the country.[1] Protest to the Court of Pegu proved to be useless. It involved presents, false promises and further presents in an endless succession. Moreover, the King and Uporaza adopted an attitude of increasing coolness. Coja Nicous had become a *persona grata* at Court, and through his instrumentality Bruno's cause went ahead. So Taylor and Westgarth reported to Madras in March 1753.

This news had a decisive effect upon the mind of Thomas Saunders, Governor of Madras. From the moment when the rumour of French designs upon Burma was first whispered at Madras, he had been the moving spirit in the effort to checkmate them. But the early reports of Taylor and Westgarth had caused him to hesitate regarding the advisability of going on with the Negrais scheme; especially when he heard of the Uporaza's assertion that there never had been any intention of ceding the island to the French. In the meantime, however, the Directors of the East India Company at home had committed themselves to the new enterprise. In December 1751 instructions had been despatched to Madras detailing the procedure to be adopted in settling Negrais, and announcing the appointment of David Hunter, late Deputy Governor of St. Helena, to take charge of it, and of Thomas Coombes of the Fort Marlborough Council as second in command.[2] Indeed, the hope was expressed that arrangements for the settlement of the island had already been put in hand. This despatch found Saunders more anxious to throw his whole weight into furthering Stringer Lawrence's operations against the French in the Carnatic, than spare much-needed troops and ships upon a venture, which he had come to regard as of very doubtful value. He made no haste, therefore, to act upon his instructions. When, however, late in 1753 he received information from Taylor and Westgarth that on account of the strong francophile tendency of the Court of Pegu all hopes of negotiating the cession of Negrais were at an end, his doubts were resolved. Further delay, he felt, would be dangerous, and might " give time to our competitours to render the scheme abortive."[3] So, early in April, David Hunter in the *Colchester*, accompanied by the sloops *Porto Bello*, *Cuddalore* and *Fortune* and the snow *Arcot*, left Madras with a considerable company of troops and workpeople bound for Negrais. His instructions were "to take possession of the island in his Brittannick Majesty's name for the Company."[4] On April 26th, the expedition anchored at its destination.

Thus opened the first act of the tragedy of Negrais. But the full irony of the situation remains to be shown. For on January 2nd, 1753

1 *Ibid.*, 1753, 35.
2 Dodwell, Calendar of Madras Despatches, 1744-1755, 161-2.
3 Saunders's instructions to David Hunter in Fort St George Diary and Consulation Book, Military Department, 1753, 48.
4 *Ibid.*, 1753, 48.

the Council of the *Compagnie Générale des Indes Orientales* despatched a letter to Dupleix summarily rejecting his grand scheme for French expansion in Burma. The factory concessions already made to the French by the Court of Pegu, they wrote, were sufficient for ordinary proposes of shipbuilding, and would involve no more than a guard of twenty or thirty soldiers. Beyond that he was straitly forbidden to go. His more ambitious scheme, they warned him, would be certain to provoke a further contest with the English ; whereas the various nations should live at amity in Asia. And Dupleix, powerless in this case to disregard his orders cursed the commercial mind and abandoned the project.[1]

CHAPTER II

THE EARLY HISTORY OF THE SETTLEMENT.

David Hunter's official instructions as head of the expedition to take possession of the island of Negrais display clearly the predominance of he political over the commercial motive in the enterprise.[1] He was first of all to seize the place. Then he was to offer the Court of Pegu a treaty of alliance whereby, in return for the Company engaging to support the King with troops "against his enemies foreign and domestick, by sea or land", the latter was to cede the island, grant permission for the erection of a fortified factory at Syriam, and confirm the articles of trade that Robert Westgarth had already negotiated with the Uporaza. Hunter was also instructed to demand "suitable satisfaction" for the outrages perpetrated by the Armenian Coja Nicous against British subjects. For the purpose of these negotiations he was furnished with an official letter and present from the President and Council of Fort St. George to the King of Pegu. Along with these he was also to forward to that King a letter from Muhammad Ali, the candidate supported by the Company for the nawabship of the Carnatic against Dupleix's tool, Chanda Sahib, wherein the writer assured the King that he might safely rely on the fidelity and friendship of the English by whom alone he (Muhammad Ali) had been preserved from the wicked attempts of his enemies.[2]

While preparations were in progress for the despatch of the Negrais expedition, Captain Dugald McEacharn arrived at Madras from Tavoy bringing a proposal from the "King" of that place for an alliance with the Company in return for which he promised a monopoly of the trade of his port. A Dutch threat to seize Tavoy by force in order to exploit its not inconsiderable tin trade was the alleged cause of this move. At this time Tavoy was, nominally at least, subject to Siam. Its ruler, however, like most petty princes in Indo-China, enjoyed a large measure

---

1 Fort St. George Diary and Consultation Book, Military Department, 1753, 48-9.
2 *Ibid.*, 1753, 42 The contents of the letter were drawn up by Thomas Saunders.

T

of practical independence so long as he paid his tribute. His entire object in negotiating with the Company was apparently to procure as extensive supplies of arms and ammunition as possible. These the Madras Council was in no position to provide to a prince likely to be of no use to it in the struggle with the French. Also the "king" of Tavoy was reported to be a supporter of the Burmese cause against the Talaings. The Madras Council therefore contented itself with a non-committal statement of friendship, and at the same time regretted that its embarrassments in the Carnatic struggle prevented it from having any warlike stores to spare.[1] A letter couched in these terms and addressed to the "king" was entrusted to David Hunter with private instructions that if he had an opportunity to transmit it to its destination, he should give the Court of Pegu to understand that nothing prejudicial to its interests was intended.[2]

The recruitment of men for the expedition to Negrais was particularly difficult. Taylor's experiences in that neighbourhood had given it a bad name. Thomas Coombes, who had been named by the Directors as second in command, excused himself on the plea of ill-health. In his place a young 'writer' in the Company's service at Madras, Henry Brooke, was selected by Hunter to proceed with him upon the unwelcome task.[3] The requisite artificers and labourers for building the new station had to be impressed, a "very despotick act", as Thomas Saunders expressed it in his instructions to Hunter, but one which was forced upon him by the exceptional circumstances. Hence they must be especially well treated, he warned Hunter, and, if country labour could be substituted, should be returned to Madras without delay. On account of the Carnatic struggle Madras could not furnish the expedition with adequate stores of rice and gunpowder. An urgent request was therefore despatched to the "gentlemen at Bengal" asking them to purvey direct to the new settlement supplementary supplies of those necessaries.[4] Similarly troops for the garrison could ill be spared, and reinforcements, urgently needed by Stringer Lawrence for the defence of Tiruviti against

---

1 *Ibid.*, 1753, 37-8. Dodwell, *op. cit.*, 210.

2 Captain Dugald McEacharn, the moving spirit in this overture, had brought over a draft treaty and had even gone so far as to hoist the British colours over his house at Tavoy in anticipation of being made Resident there. The affair has all the appearance of a 'stunt' out of which McEacharn hoped to do a good thing for himself. Nothing came of the proposal. In June 1753 he returned to Tavoy with a present of a brass field piece and guncarriage to its ruler from the Madras Council, and with a letter to that potentate stating that the Company accepted his offer of exclusive trade "with great chearfulness" but regretted its inability to supply him with either men or munitions on account of the "troubles" in "these parts". Fort St. George Diary and Consultation Book, Military Department, 1753, 95, 99.

3 *Ibid.*, 1753, 39. Brooke was 25 years of age at the time. He had served at Madras since August 1751.

1 *Ibid.*, 1753, 39.

Dupleix's lieutenant Maissin, had to be depleted in order that a guard of 34 Europeans and 72 "coffreys"[1] might sail with the expedition.[2]

On April 26th, 1753 Hunter's expedition arrived at the island and anchored off the spot previously indicated by Thomas Taylor as the best site for a settlement. It soon became evident that Taylor's very cursory survey of the locality was of little value. The chosen spot for the erection of a fortified post was entirely without a water supply. After two days' search one was discovered near the north-east point of the island. But the locality was covered with dense jungle, and it took a week of clearing operations before a camp could be pitched and the soldiery disembarked. Even then water had to be carried a quarter of a mile to the camp. There followed a dreary succession of disasters. The expedition, as we have seen, started out from Madras with inadequate supplies of rice. It had been hoped that food could be procured in the Negrais neighbourhood. So, after the work of pitching the camp and disembarking the troops had been completed, Hunter resorted to the mad expedient of cutting down the food supplies of the coffreys and ordering them to fend for themselves by hunting.[3] A serious mutiny ensued. The infuriated coffreys seized firearms and ammunition and attacked the Europeans, who were for a time forced to take refuge on the ships. But the mutineers were unable to make effective use of their arms, and a successful counter-attack by the Europeans cleared the camp. The rebels, however, got away into the jungle with a good deal of plunder, and although most of the latter was ultimately recovered, only ten of the mutineers were captured. The remainder either fled to the mainland or were drowned in attempting to swim the channel.

The loss of so many labourers seriously hindered the work of building the accomodation urgently needed on shore. To make matters worse the wet monsoon broke with great violence soon after the arrival of the expedition. The settlement was regularly flooded at high tide, and a decimating sickness broke out, almost completely suspending operations Provisions ran so short that when at the end of September Hunter despatched his first report to Madras, he represented that his small company was only kept alive by the turtle, which could be caught in abundance on Diamond Island.[4] The ' multitude of tigers", he said, rendered it practically impossible to hunt with success the deer and buffaloes, with which Haing gyi was well stocked. As for trading prospects, these, he

---

1 Arabic *Kāfir*—an infidel, unbeliever in Islam. Name applied by English to black Hindu peoples of South India.

2 For these operations see Camb. Hist. of India, V, 130-31.

3 I have accepted Dalrymple's version of the affair in *op. cit*, I, 126, Hunter's own report of the affair is specious: "Our people had work'd so well that I thought proper that evening to give orders for a party of them to go a hunting the next day or otherwise to divert themselves as they lik'd." (Fort St. George Diary and Consultation Book, Military Department, 1753, 173.)

4 *Ibid.*, 1753, 175-176.

thought, were hopeless, since the proximity of the sea rendered it dangerous for country craft, built only for riverine use, to traffic with the island.

It was a melancholy report written by a sick man, who begged to be allowed to return to Madras before the beginning of the next wet monsoon, as he feared he might not survive a further spell of it in so unhealthy a locality. He had sent Henry Brooke to conduct the negotiations with the Court of Pegu. What were the chances of success in that direction, he could not say. Brooke was detained at Syriam by sickness. There was, however, one hopeful sign : on September 9th Thomas Taylor had arrived from Pegu with a royal order to the Governor of Bassein granting permission for the Company to establish a factory there and Hunter had accordingly despatched Taylor thither with all speed "to reside there in the best manner he could for the present".

The Madras Council on receipt of this despatch hastened to send across a small supply of provisions, and such reinforcements as they could spare —a meagre thirty men. At the same time they wrote off urgently to Calcutta to forward a cargo of salted meat, rice and other cereals to the harassed settlement. But to Hunter's request to be allowed to return to the Coast to recuperate his health they returned a courteous but firm refusal. He was reminded that the Board of Directors had specially appointed him to command the expedition. This had been done over the heads of the Madras Council which had been given no further powers in the matter than those of affording him " all the assistance we are able". Having provided him with a second-in-command in the person of Henry Brooke, they had, they opined, discharged their full responsibility in respect of the management of the expedition. As the success of the new venture was "of the utmost consequence", his absence at so early a stage might gravely prejudice it. Instead, they offered him the helpful suggestion that he might take up his residence at Syriam during the monsoon period, and direct operations from that more salubrious spot.[1] The next letter they received from Negrais came from Henry Brooke. He announced that on December 24th " David Hunter Esq., departed this life of a fever which continued eight days."[2]

The attitude of the Madras Council towards Hunter in this business is somewhat intriguing. A mere superficial glance at conditions in South India at the time will be sufficient to show that Madras could spare little help for what it had come to regard as an undertaking of doubtful value. It is possible, also, that Governor Thomas Saunders was piqued at having been granted by the Directors so little discretion in the matter of the Negrais expedition. But the true explanation probably lies in the personality of Hunter himself. Of overweening ambition, he was cold,

---

1 *Ibid.*, 1753, 177, 185-187.
2 *Ibid.*, 1754, 14.

haughty and difficult to work with. According to Dalrymple he had no real interest in the Negrais scheme, but regarded his appointment there as a stepping stone to the presidential chair at Madras. Moreover he had influential connexions at home : he was related by marriage to Alderman Baker of the City of London, who had been Chairman of the East India Company in 1752. Such a man, able to pull strings at home, would not be welcomed back to Madras from the malarial swamp to which for the time being he had been relegated.[1]

Hunter's death brought a most unwelcome problem before the Madras Council. A successor had to be appointed. Members of the Council, in deadly fear of being called upon to take up the unpopular post, waxed eloquent in their efforts to prove that a man of council rank was not required. All except Thomas Saunders were of opinion that the appointment should be given to a man ''skilled in fortification and maritime affairs''.[2] Thomas Saunders alone plumped for a man of council rank : and on the score of the precarious condition of affairs at Negrais he overruled the objections of the rest of the Council. It is interesting in passing to note that what is reported of this discussion shows clearly that commercial considerations were entirely in the background.

But it was one thing to appoint a man, and another thing to persuade him to accept the post. After much difficulty Charles Hopkins, Chief at Devecotah was selected.[3] He put forward the plea of ill-health, and escaped. Two others, Percival and Smith, similarly evaded the much-dreaded task. Finally the Council decided that its only possible course was to leave Henry Brooke in chief command of the station, and appoint Thomas Taylor to the position of second-in-command.[4] The latter was at the time titular Resident at Syriam. Westgarth, having disregarded repeated warnings regarding his extravagance and exorbitant charges for repairs to ships, had early in 1754 been ordered to Madras to explain his conduct. A committee appointed to scrutinize his accounts had pronounced them "irregular, perplex'd and contradictory, which must proceed from ignorance or something worse".[5]

In Taylor's place at Syriam it was decided to appoint a shipwright named Henry Stringfellow, who was already in business there privately. But it was laid down that he was to receive no allowances, ''as the station is only nominal and merely to keep up our pretensions to a factory

---

1 Dalrymple, op cit., I, 12.. According to this authority the Alderman "disquali-fied" at about the time when Hunter was proceeding to Negrais, and thus put an end to the latter's hopes.
2 Fort St George Diary and Consultation Book, Military Department, 1754, 19-20
3 Ibid., 1754, 34-39.
4 Ibid., 1754, 56-7.
5 Madras Public Proceedings (India Office copy), 1754, 166-7, 172-3. He was dismissed the Company's service. (Dodwell, op. cit., 218)

there".[1] This last point is interesting. Since Westgarth had formally taken possession of the old factory site and enclosed it with a bamboo fence, nothing had been done towards reopening the factory There is, in fact, ample evidence to show that the Madras Council never intended to reopen it. Thus although Hunter, on setting out upon his ill-starred venture, received official instructions to ask for "a factory and fortification at Syriam", he was also told to explain to the Court of Pegu that he was establishing a settlement at Negrais as "a place of more safety", and because "the risque of Pegu river renders it hazardous for ships of large burthen." [2] And in a personal letter accompanying the instructions Thomas Saunders wrote for his guidance: "If you succeed in this affair, I imagine there will not be a necessity of a fortification at Syrian, as all trade and business can, I am informed, be much better carried on from the Negrais."[3] The factory was never reopened Stringfellow carried on in his capacity of Resident without allowance until Alaungpaya's capture and destruction of Syriam in 1756. That is to say, he was a private shipwright recognised by the Company as its agent for the execution of repairs to its ships at Syriam.

Notwithstanding Thomas Taylor's early description of Negrais as a place "as valuable as any the King of Pegu has", and one which produced wax, ivory, wood oil, resin, teak and some iron,[4] it was not long before the Madras Council came to realise that not only could no commercial advantages be expected from the new settlement, but its upkeep was an almost intolerable burden. Its toll upon health and ever life was nothing short of disastrous. In spite of all efforts to check their devastations, malaria and "bloody flux" so decimated the working numbers of Europeans and Indians alike as to render the task of carrying on the ordinary work of the settlement practically hopeless. Thus although David Hunter reached the island on April 26th, 1753, he was still living on board ship on September 20th, when he despatched his first report to Madras. "We have begun to build some houses for our accomodation," he wrote, "and I hope soon to take up my quarters ashore.............This month past we have not been able to do anything all our artificers and lascars being sick." And at the end of the same letter; "Mr. Maul, our surgeon, being very much indispos'd, I have permitted him to return to the Coast for the benefit of his health. This happens extremely unfortunate, as I have scarcely a man about me either officer or private, but what are sick."[5]

At first it was hoped that the thorough clearance of the factory site would render it healthier. But this proved illusory. In January 1754

1 Madras Public Proceedings, 1754, 677. Fort St. George Diary and Consultation Book, Military Department, 1754, 73, 74-5.

2 *Ibid.*, 1753, 48.

3 *Ibid.*, 1753 49.

4 *Ibid.*, 1752, 61.

5 *Ibid.*, 1753, 175-6.

Henry Brooke wrote despondently to the Madras Council: "We have also had such an universal sickness for some months past raging amongst us, that of the [military] not half have been able to do duty, of 40 lascars [not] 20 in the best days could be muster'd to the works. The 40 Bengal lascars and coolies also, tho' they arriv'd here in November last have fallen sick in proportion, and the Mallabars to a man have been render'd useless."[1] In the same month Charles Knapton, the engineer sent to supervise the construction of fortifications, wrote that the works designed by Hunter would require 500 men working full time for at least six or seven months, but that was impossible, since during the monsoon months there were not five "well men" on the island.[2]

By that time it was generally agreed that the main cause of the trouble lay in the fact that at every spring tide the whole site was flooded, and with the ebb the shore was "covered with ooze and small fry, which putrifying must viciate the air."[3] Such a spot could never develop into a centre of commerce. Worse still, it was overlooked by a hill at the back and was therefore not easily defensible. There was, Brooke reported, a better site at the north-east point of the island, "wholesome" and with what he was assured by the seamen was a safe and convenient harbour. It could be well defended by placing a battery on the north-west point. He recommend therefore that this new site should be tried. The Madras Council accepted the recommendation, and in October 1754 authorised the removal of the settlement to the proposed site. Brooke, however, was warned not to construct any "expensive or capital" works; but to put up merely what was necessary for immediate defence against a "country enemy".[4] Until further experience should indicate how the new site was likely to turn out, as little money as possible was to be spent upon it. Meanwhile the whole question was referred home to the Board of Directors.[5]

But the removal of the settlement to a better site afforded no solution to the commercial problem. And although political rather than commercial considerations had been the main cause of the establishment of the settlement, it had been hoped that enough trade would develop there to cover at least the cost of maintenance. This hope also proved illusory. David Hunter was not long on the island before he realized that if trade was to develop, it could only be through the establishment of a factory at Bassein. Hence, when the Court of Pegu urged this step as a means of drawing the English away from Negrais, he sent Thomas Taylor to open up trading operations at Bassein. Shortly afterwards he wrote to Madras: "If ever we shall be so fortunate as to have

1 *Ibid.*, 1754, 16.
2 *Ibid.*, 1754, 30.
3 Madras Public Proceedings, (MS) 1754, 676-7.
4 *Ibid.*, 1754, 677.
5 Coast and Bay Abstracts, Vol. 6, 28.

our affairs settled with the Pegu Government, I think that place Persaim must be the head settlement. It lies in the centre of trade and is able to subject any number of men, whereas the Negrais has neither of these advantages."[1]

On Hunter's death Henry Brooke pressed the same view upon the Madras Council. In January 1754 he wrote of the Negrais settlement : "I cannot think it will be for many years, if ever, a place of profit to the Hon'ble Company. The country for 80 or 100 miles about is compos'd of islands almost entirely destitute of inhabitants, and cover'd with woods. A fine harbour, plenty of wood and good water, but scarce in the dry season, are the only advantages it can boast of. It is in itself incapable of maintaining a number of inhabitants, and must therefore be dependant on other places for the necessaries of life. And the great river leading to Persaim and Ava, from whence all provisions and merchandise must come, lies open to the sea above us, and is at most times, but particularly in the south-west monsoons, extremely dangerous for the country boats to approach us. These inconveniences will ever make provisions scarce. Persaim, which lies about 80 miles from hence, has none of these inconveniencies. It has, by all accounts, the advantage of a fine air, a good rice country about it, a river safe and navigable for the largest ships, and is capable of maintaining any number of inhabitants. I am therefore of opinion, if ever the Hon'ble Company may reap a profit from the trade of this country, they must make Persaim the head settlement."[2]

The Madras Council was not at first in a hurry to act upon these proposals. To Hunter they returned an inconclusive answer, though at the same time suggesting that he might enquire whether Bassein was a suitable place to which trade might be transferred from Syriam.[3] But, as time went on, and prospects at Negrais failed to improve, the idea began to chrystalise of opening up a big trading centre at Bassein, while still retaining Negrais as a guard post, from which the entrance to the river might be commanded. When therefore in March 1754 the Council heard that it was about to be favoured with a mission from the Court of Pegu soliciting military aid against the Burmese leader, Alaungpaya, it was decided for the time being to suspend construction of the extensive fortifications, originally planned for Negrais, and Henry Brooke was instructed to press for the cession of Bassein together with the surrounding country to a radius of some five or six miles.[4] But he was warned to erect no buildings at the new station until a treaty had been concluded: for the time being a "slight banksall" would suffice.

---

1 Fort St. George Diary and Consulation Book, Military Department, 1753, 175.
2 *Ibid.*, 1754, 15.
3 *Ibid.*, 1753, 186.
4 *Ibid.*, 1754, 73-4.

The story of the abortive negotiations for this proposed treaty is told in the next chapter. Whether Thomas Saunders seriously expected to obtain so extensive a cession of territory at Bassein is doubtful. But the situation which dictated the proposal is clear. The Negrais settlement had become a very costly white elephant, and it imposed upon the Madras Council's resources a greater strain than they could continue to bear.[1] For strategical reasons it was deemed necessary to hang on to the island; since, although the French could apparently do nothing on a big scale in Burma, the presence of Bruno at the Court of Pegu constituted a threat to the English naval position in the Bay of Bengal. If, however, the island was to be retained, trade with the country must be developed in order to render the settlement as nearly self-supporting as possible. Syriam, for reasons already explained, was not favoured as a trading centre. And Bassein possessed the obvious advantage of direct and easy communication with Negrais.

But the prospects of successful trade there were by no means rosy. Thomas Taylor, the Company's first Resident, obtained some sort of recognition from the Uporaza, and started a timber trade on a small scale. But apparently the Talaing officials made his task as trying and difficult as possible. And when the treaty negotiations lapsed in the autumn of 1754, he warned the Madras Council that so long as the Court of Pegu held Bassein there was slight hope of the Company developing successful trade there. " Persaim by all accounts is a wholesome country," he wrote. " At least I found it so from the beginning of of September till March, at which time our people were sickly at Negrais. It is a ruined city that formerly belonged to the Portugueze, and at present round the ruins is a fence made of thick plank about twelve or fourteen feet high. It is about 1400 yards in length and about 900 yards in breadth. It has likewise a ruined citadel of about 350 yards in length and 250 yards in breadth, and round the outside of the walls for about two mile is the ruins of many brick houses, Mallabar and Pegu pagodas. It seems as if it had been a place of great consequence. The Tallapoys have informed me that by their manuscripts a great number of Chinamen inhabited this place, and they not only traded to the east part of China, but to the west part overland ; and at the time the Portugueze governed the city, it had a very extensive trade, and that the N. E. point of the Little Negrais was then inhabited. We have discovered there a founda tion of a brick house and a large Malabar tank.

Persaim River has a communication with the grand river to Ava and joins it a little below Prone. And I have been informed by Burmur merchants and Armenians, who have lived in Ava many years; that great

---

1 By October 1755 it was estimated that the expenses of maintaining the settlement since its foundation totalled 59, 528 pagodas, and that the shipping and workmen employed in connexion with it cost between five and six thousand rupees a month. On this outlay there had been hardly any return. (Coast and Bay Abstracts, Vol. 6, 72.)

quantities of saltpetre has been produced in the country beween Prome and Ava, and before the revolution it might be bought at the rate of eight pagodas per candy for the first sort. The country likewise produces silk and cotton, and I think in all probability a cloth manufactory might be carried on, as I have never seen a house without a loom and spinning wheel, and that we may dispose of great quantities of woollen cloths. The people in general seen to be fond of it, and what is now sold goes through the Malabar hands, so that by the time the Peguers or Burmurs gets it, [it] amounts to near one hundred per cent. on the Madras price.

The present Government of Pegue is excessively arbitrary, so that the King, when he pleases, can demand everything in the world that any of his subjects has. And if there is any such thing as slavery in the world, I think the Peguers wear that yoke. And they think that all Europeans, that come into their country, is as much their slaves, and that they have as much right to their properties as to their own subjects'. And it is from this principle that they are jealous of having a European power independant of them in their country. "[1]

So, at the end of the year 1754 two things had become clear : firstly that without a sucessful trading station at Bassein the Negrais settlement would become a dead weight upon the Company's finances ; and secondly that while the Court of Pegu held sway over lower Burma there was little hope for the development of English trade in that region.

CHAPTER III.

NEGOTIATIONS WITH PEGU AND AVA.

The grant of trading privileges reported by Robert Westgarth as the result of his early negotations with the Uporaza had been viewed by Madras with entire scepticism. Almost immediately after Hunter's expedition left Madras, however, concrete evidence of a favourable turn to English fortunes in Pegu was forthcoming. A vessel belonging to the King entered the port with a cargo for disposal there. It brought a letter from Westgarth containing the interesting information that the King had refused Bruno's application that it should be sent to Pondicherry. Hoping therefore that by a show of generosity on its part this auspicious breeze might be encouraged to blow with constancy, the Madras Council decreed that the goods belonging to the King should be landed free of customs duties, and further that two gilt palanquins should be sent by the ship on her return voyage as presents to the King and Uporaza.[2]

But constancy was quite the last virtue to be expected of the Court of Pegu, especially in view of the circumstances in which it was placed,

1 Madras Public Proceedings, 1754, 702.
2 *Ibid*, 1753, 52-3.

Hunter in his first letter from Negrais warned the Madras Council to place no confidence whatever in the rebel government. "The reputation of our forces," he wrote, "seem'd at first to fling them into some consternation, and their fears, I believe, induc'd them to flatter Mr. Westgarth with fair promises. But notwithstanding all we have done, and the concessions they have made, I am yet far from depending on their sincerity. The trouble they are at present involv'd in with the former lords of the country about Ava takes up most of their attention, and not without reason, if I am rightly informed. The family, who lately possess'd the government, have a strong party and gain ground daily ; and I think it is very probable they may in a short time recover their kingdom again. The present King of Pegu was formerly a silversmith at Syriam, and his brother, the Upparajah, was a writer in the Alfantiga.[1] I am told the people in general talk contemptuously of them, so far as they dare under the yoke of an absolute tyrant. It seems a mob rais'd him to the dignity, and it is not unlikely the same fluctuating spirit may soon pull him down again. If this should happen, our presents and our sollicitation has [sic] hitherto been to very little purpose. "[2]

As soon as possible after the founding of the Negrais settlement Hunter deputed Henry Brooke to Syriam with the royal present and the official letters from the Madras Council to the King of Pegu. Brooke took with him a signed and ratified copy of the articles of trade previously negotiated by Robert Westgarth with the Uporaza. He was instructed to carry out his business in concert with Westgarth.[3] The Court of Pegu, however, refused to have anything to do with Brooke. It would not negotiate with a subordinate Instead, Westgarth was despatched to Negrais with a royal order for Hunter himself to appear at Court. When this invitation was politely refused, the Pegu authorities began a campaign of systematic obstruction to English shipbuilding and repairing operations at Syriam. When Westgarth appealed to the Government, publicly it granted all his requests for workmen and supplies ; privately it instructed its local officials to refuse them. Native labour was terrorised into boycotting the English, and the Company's own lascars even were enticed away.[4]

On January 11th, 1754, with affairs at this pass, and Hunter dead, Henry Brooke wrote despondently from Negrais : "The King and Rajah,[5] as well as Peguers in general, [?are] extreamly jealous of foreigners, since the time of the Portuguese, who defended their fort at Syriam for many years against their whole nation.[6] It will not therefore be an easy matter to prevail on them to ratify the Articles agreeable

---

1 Customs House.
2 *Ibid*, 1753, 174-5.
3 *Ibid*, 1755, 175.
4 *Ibid*, 1754, 18.
5 *i.e.* the Uporaza, called in much of the correspondence the Upper Raja.
6 A reference to Felipe de Brito's occupation of Syriam, 1599-1613.

to Mr. Hunter's plan."[1] "The King of [Pegu is] only trifling and drawing us," wrote Westgarth at the same time from Syriam, "for I plainly perceive they have no inclination to com[ply] with our demands any further than what fear induces them to." [2] A little later he reported that the chief objections raised by the Court of Pegu to the Articles were to the clauses granting to the Company most-favoured-nation treatment and the right to import goods duty free. [3] Brooke therefore was authorized to reply—in writing, not in person—that these privileges constituted "no more than what is granted to us on this Coast by the Mogull, who is sensible that by this indulgence we have been induced to carry on a very extensive trade."[4] He was also to emphasize the fact that the Company offered the King reciprocal trading advantages in all its settlements. This, we may remark, was far from being a *quid pro quo*, since the amount of trade carried on by natives of Burma at the Company's stations in India was negligible.

Meanwhile developments were in progress which caused another temporary relaxation on the part of the Court of Pegu of its intransigent attitude towards the English. In December 1753 the Burmese patriot-hero, Alaungpaya, had recaptured the ancient capital city of Ava, and early in the following month the Pegu forces had been cleared headlong out of Upper Burma. And Dupleix, dissatisfied with the shilly-shallying conduct of the Court of Pegu in the negotiations with Bruno, had despatched some boatloads of military stores to the Burmese.[5] To deal with this new danger the Uporaza hurried northwards with all his available forces. Before his departure he intimated to Westgarth that if the Company would come to his assistance, it might trade at Bassein on its own terms. And a Talaing Mission, headed by no other than the Armenian, Coja Nicous, was deputed to Madras urgently beseeching the Council to send over men and arms.[6]

Early in April 1754 Nicous and his subordinate Toppelo, who according to the custom of his country was charged with the task of spying upon his chief's actions, had an audience of Thomas Saunders at Madras. They represented that in return for an annual present the King would allow the company to hold the Island of Negrais, and would grant free trade at the towns of Syriam, Bassein, Martaban, Prome, Pegu, "Tangoore", and "Don Bassey", and certain other privileges. To Saunders's query whether, on account of the proved unsuitability of Negrais as a trading station, Bassein might be occupied for this purpose, Nicous replied that although the Court of Pegu hesitated to raise up a

1 *Ibid*, 1754, 15,
2 *Ibid*, 1754, 17.
3 *Ibid*, 1754, 64, 72.
4 *Ibid*, 1754, 72.
5 *Ibid*, 1753, 196.
6 *Ibid*, 1754, 64, 74.

rival port to the detriment of Syriam, he had no doubt that all objections to this would vanish, if the much-needed troops and warlike stores were forthcoming. Saunders thereupon stated "that he would very readily assist the King, if the Company's affairs would admit of it." And he added that in proof of his friendly intentions he would send over a detachment of troops for the King's service, if the ships arriving from England that season brought the expected reinforcements [1] And he followed up the discussion by ordering that a treaty should be at once drafted, embodying all the points upon which agreement had been reached.

When the draft was presented to the ambassadors, it turned out, as had all along been anticipated, that they were invested with no "conclusive power". Saunders, however, would commit himself to nothing until such time as the Talaing promises should be confirmed by a written document under the royal seal of Pegu. Accordingly late in July a copy of the proposed treaty was despatched to Henry Brooke at Negrais, with instructions to do his best to secure the Court of Pegu's official ratification.[2] And the ambassadors were dismissed with the injunction that they were to return by way of Negrais, where they would pick up Thomas Taylor, who would accompany them to Pegu for the purpose of completing the negotiations. Military aid, however, Saunders told them rather disingenuously, could not immediately be sent, as the ship, on which they were to return, carried French colours, and no other was then available.[3] They were furnished with a present of "Europe Curiositys" for the King and Uporaza ; a musical clock, a silver-mounted gun, a pair of silver-mounted pistols and "a curious agate cabinet set in gold" for the former ; for the latter a brass-mounted gun, pistols and a "gold repeating watch curiously ornamented with Mocha stone" The total cost of these amounted to a little over 635 pagodas.[4] It was hoped that they would be an "introduction" to the treaty.[5]

The draft treaty[6] purported to be one of friendship and alliance between "the Honourable the United Company of Merchants of England trading to the East Indies" and "the great King of Pegue, Son of the Sun and Brother of the Moon and Stars." By the first two clauses the King was to cede to the Company "freely and absolutely" the island of Negrais and the town of Bassein. The third conferred upon the Company and its servants "full and unlimited" trading privileges at the towns named by the ambassadors. By the fourth the Company was to have "free liberty" to employ the people of the country at the "usual and

---

1 *Ibid*, 1754, 86.
2 *Ibid*, 1754, 168-9
3 *Ibid*, 1754, 166.
4 *Ibid*, 1754, 169.
5 *Ibid*, 1754, 169.
6 *Ibid*., 1754, 166-8.

accustomed wages." The fifth assured the Company of royal support in the maintenance of its privileges.

In return for these concessions the Company, by clause six, was to present the King annually with " some European or other curiosity " in respect of its tenure of Negrais and Bassein. By clause seven reciprocity of treatment in commerce was to be given to the King and his subjects at all the Company's ports in India. Clause eight contained the kernel of the proposed alliance. By it the Company pledged itself "to aid, assist and defend the King of Pegue and his successors against all their enemys by sea and land, and for that purpose to furnish such a number of troops with proper warlike stores, as the occasion may necessarily require, and the said Company can conveniently spare from the defence and protection of their own territories," upon condition, however, that the King defrayed the whole cost both of the troops and of the warlike stores. Finally in clause nine the Company promised to give no aid to the " King " of Tavoy, were he to attack Pegu, but to protect and defend the latter against the former, should the occasion arise.

Regarding this document one question immediately arises: did Governor Saunders seriously contemplate armed intervention in Burma ? Both in form and in intention this draft treaty is an early example of a type of agreement that the East India Company was coming to make with Indian princes in order to strengthen its position, mainly, of course, as against the French.[1] The obvious aim of this one was the elimination of French influence from Burma. In sending to Henry Brooke the copy of the draft treaty Saunders urged him " to bring affairs to a speedy and successful conclusion," and Thomas Taylor was instructed to "press the immediate entering on the affairs."[2] But this haste had as its objective rather the queering of Bruno's pitch than actual military intervention on behalf of Pegu. If the former could only be accomplished by means of the latter, then Thomas Saunders must first have a treaty before committing himself. What the Court of Pegu offered in the hour of crisis, it would, he well knew, retract in the moment of victory. His proposals, therefore committed the Company to nothing. If the Talaings wanted military assistance—and the urgency of this was not lost upon Saunders—the price at which the Company would afford it was the cession of Negrais and Bassein together with most-favoured-nation treatment in commerce. But the wording of clause eight of the proposed treaty left ample loop-holes by which, if necessary, the Company might escape from its obligations. We know also that the English entered upon these negotiations with one eye upon the Burmese. During the rainy season of 1754 Alaungpaya was consolidating his power in Upper Burma preparatory to undertaking a great onslaught upon Pegu during the ensuing dry

---

1 Cp. in particular the Treaty with the Nizam negotiated by Brigadier John Calliaud in 1766. (Aitchison, "Treaties, Engagements and Sanads," VIII, 280-283.)

2 Fort St. George Diary and Consultation Book, Military Department, 1754, 169.

season. No one could say in what direction the fortunes of war would turn when the campaigning season recommenced in November.

But to the Court of Pegu Dupleix's present of arms and ammunition to Alaungpaya was a more powerful argument than paper promises of conditional assistance, without the backing of even an instalment of real aid. Taylor's visit to Pegu therefore achieved nothing. Even a present of two magnificent palanquins from Madras to the King and his brother failed to move that " perfideous court."[1] When on delivering this present Taylor pressed them to come to terms, they flatly refused to entertain any notion of ceding territory at Bassein, and revived their old objections to the Negrais settlement. But in order that the negotiations should not drop, they hinted at the possibility of allowing the Company to occupy a spot on the Syriam river in return for a considerable annual present.[2] Taylor, however, left Pegu in disgust and the treaty was shelved indefinitely. Meanwhile the French were supplying the Talaings with military stores, and the influence of Bruno was predominant at Pegu.

At the beginning of the dry season of 1754-5 a great Talaing counterthrust at Ava failed ignominiously. At about the same time, in November, Thomas Taylor returned to Madras ill and worn out.[3] From the account, which he gave, of conditions in Burma, Thomas Saunders made up his mind finally that the Burmese were the winning side. He accordingly wrote off to Henry Brooke instructing him to cultivate friendly relations with Alaungpaya.[4] Shortly afterwards he handed over the reins of power at Madras to his successor, the more cautious and conciliatory Pigot.

In February 1755 Alaungpaya took Prome. Early in March the Talaings, under the pressure of the Burmese victorious advance into Lower Burma, evacuated Bassein. The Burmese, upon reaching the town, burnt it to the ground, though studiously avoiding injury to the Company's godowns there. A few days later a Burmese embassy appeared before the Company's house at Bassein announcing to Captain George Baker, who was in charge of the station, that they were the bearers of a letter from the Burmese King to the Company's Chief at Negrais desiring friendship and alliance[5]. Baker accompanied the envoys to Negrais, where they were accorded a friendly reception. For the time being, however, Henry Brooke could do no more than return a non-committal answer: he was without definite instructions for dealing with so unexpected a development. Moreover, he had neither men nor military stores to spare. But he felt that the situation should at once be taken in hand, and he despatched the following penetrating survey of it to George Pigot;—

1 Dodwell, *op. cit.*, 257.
2 Coast and Bay Abstracts, Vol. 6, 48.
3 He died in March 1755. (*Ibid.*, Vol. 6, 76.)
4 Dodwill, *op. cit.*, 257.
5 Dalrymple, *op. cit.*, I, 137.

"To conclude with the King of Pegu on advantageous terms I now despair of. How can we expect it, when even now, though he wants our assistance, yet he will not assure us that he will maintain our soldiers, though they should fight and lose their lives in the defence of his country? Has he not used us ill on all occasions? Has he not, as much as in him lay, underhand endeavoured to ruin us, by preventing the people to work for us and to bring us rice, etc, victuals, though his country might have supplied us? There is much difference between soliciting and being solicited. We are pursuing the man who is unwilling to assist us, yet, if he had it in his power, would not; and are courted by the King of Ava, who is ready and able to favour us. To turn the deaf ear to his address and tender of his friendship would in my opinion be an act of imprudence. But you cannot listen to him without offending the other. What then is the medium? Had we a force here sufficient to carry weight, we could easily turn the balance of power in favour of the Buraghmahns. To accomplish this would require brisk force. And a vessel to lye at Dagon, in Syrian river, would be absolutely necessary, and would not only prevent supplies of arms, etc., from passing through Syrian river, but prevent all the King (of Pegu's) war boats from going up the rivers towards Prome. Then the Buraghmahns could come even to Syrian unmolested, which together with a junction of our troops by these rivers, would probably carry everything before them, and settle the affairs of this place in one campaign. But should we not concern ourselves in this affair, the French, who have openly espoused the Peguers' cause at Syrian, may turn the scale against the Buraghmahns, which now seems to incline to their side. What should we then expect from his Majesty of Pegu? Or yet, in case the Burghmahns should meet with success in the next campaign without our assistance, we cannot then hope for those favourable conditions we may at this juncture reasonably expect. I have thus candidly given you my opinion of our affairs here, that you may be acquainted with the most minute circumstances; and though troops are expensive, yet they are necessary. If you will think proper to spare any, October is the best month for their arrival here. In the interim I shall, with the utmost circumspection, give no just cause of offence to either party, though our being on this island, I believe, is sufficient to the King of Pegu."[1]

But the Madras Council would make no move. It was felt that with the French menace in South India becoming ever more acute, neither troops nor munitions of war ought to be spared for an enterprise, the advantages of which would be, as George Pigot wrote home, "precarious."[2]

His policy therefore was to concentrate upon the struggle in India. For this reason strict neutrality in the Burma civil war was, he decided, a prime essential. Moreover, there was nothing to be derived from

1 Dalrymple, *op. cit.*, 196-7. The letter is dated 13th April 1755.
2 Coast and Bay Abstracts, Vol. 6, 73.

trade with Burma—save expense. Shortly after this decision was reached, a further application from Captain Dugald MacEacharn at Tavoy on behalf of its "King" for warlike stores was refused. MacEacharn was informed that while it was the Council's desire "to maintain a good correspondence" with that ruler, "our occasions here for men and warlike stores are so large, that it is not in our power to send him any." And in the minutes of the consultation, at which this resolution was passed, the fact that the "King" of Tavoy was a likely participant in the Burma civil war was noted, and the significant statement recorded: "It was never our decision to engage in it on either side."[1]

The return journey of the Burmese ambassadors, deputed to negotiate with Henry Brooke at Negrais was not without incident. On their outward journey they had left their escort of twenty war boats at Bassein, and had performed the remainder of the journey in company with George Baker upon a Company's schooner. On returning to Bassein they discovered that during their absence a force of 1800 Talaings in 60 war boats had captured the escort and seized the town. An attempt was made by the victors to persuade Baker to hand over the envoys. Instead, however, he turned his ship about and sailed back to Negrais, where he landed his charges and left them for safety. He then returned once more to Bassein, which he reached on April 10th, to find that it was held by only 500 Talaings, who shortly afterwards, on learning of Alaungpaya's victory over their main army at Danubyu, left hurriedly for Syriam. On May 2nd, a Burmese force re-occupied Bassein. They informed Baker that their king had routed the Talaings and was encamped at Dagon. It was now safe for the Burmese envoys to leave their place of refuge at Negrais; and early in June they passed through Bassein *en route* for Alaungpaya's headquarters bearing with them Henry Brooke's reply to the new conqueror.[2]

So far Alaungpaya's victorious march to the south had proceeded almost without a hitch. Its culmination at the great Buddhist shrine at Dagon, where in great state he made public offerings and prayers, had, as indeed it was meant to have, a decisive moral effect throughout the country. A previous success at Lunhse had led the King to rename the town Myanaung—"speedy victory." At Dagon he made a far greater claim—as yet unrealised—by renaming the place Yangon—"the end of strife." Actually the strife was by no means ended. Pegu, the capital of the Talaing country, and its busy port Syriam, still held out, and their reduction would involve siege operations for which the Burmese army was ill-equipped. Up in the north too there was serious trouble. The Manipuris were raiding. The Shans were rebellious. And a son of

---

1 MS. Madras Military Consultations, (India Office copy) 1755, 90, s. v. Cons. of June 4th.
2 For the above details, and for the whole story of English negotiations with Alaungpaya, save where otherwise stated, the authority is Dalrymple, *op. cit.*, I, 133-226.

Mahadammayaza Dipati, the last Burmese king of the old dynasty, was threatening invasion from Siamese territory. Before the key position of Syriam could be attacked, therefore, the affairs of the north had to be attended to. Under such circumstances the arrival of strong French reinforcements, earnestly solicited by Bruno, might easily turn the scale once more in favour of the Talaings. Bruno who had been placed by the Uporaza in charge of the defence of Syriam, was no mean antagonist, and the situation bristled with possibilities for the French.

Guns and ammunition constituted Alaungpaya's most pressing need. He had drawn a blank in his first attempt to secure assistance from the Company. Before leaving for the north he decided to make a further effort. So, in the middle of June, when the beginning of the wet monsoon imposed a halt upon operations on a big scale in the delta region, he despatched a second embassy to Henry Brooke, bearing a present of two horses, 100 viss of lac, 100 viss of ivory and a ring. At about the same time he set out for his capital of Shwebo, leaving a strong force at Dagon to mask Syriam. On June 24th the Burmese embassy escorted by 20 war boats and 690 men, arrived at Bassein, and a few days later Captain George Baker once more accompanied Burmese envoys to Negrais.

The situation had altered considerably since the arrival of the first Burmese mission in March. The Burmese successes at Danubyu and Dagon now rendered the maintenance of strict neutrality practically impossible. Henry Brooke therefore deputed Captain Baker and Lieutenant John North to return with the ambassadors to their master with a present of a twelve-pounder, three nine-pounders, 80 cannon balls, four chests of powder and a quantity of smaller presents including a mirror. They were empowered to conclude " a treaty of friendship and alliance between that Prince and our Honourable Masters."[1]

After a long and tedious journey, in the course of which North died of dysentery at Pagan, the mission reached Shwebo on September 16th, and was given public audience of the King on the following day. After the usual ceremonious questions had been put and answered, the King began to upraid the unsuspecting Baker for the scandalous way in which a number of English ships had taken part with the French and Talaings in an attack upon the Burmese forces at Dagon, in spite of the strongest assurances of friendship given him by a Company's servant there, before he had left for the capital. He showed plainly that he suspected Henry Brooke of having had a hand in the business. And although Baker in reply expressed in the most emphatic terms his opinion that so far from being complicated in the affair, Henry Brooke would be every bit as angry about it as Alaungpaya himself, it soon become obvious that the King had lost whatever trust he had previously had in the sincerity of the

---

1 *Ibid.*, I, 143.

Company's attitude towards him. What had occurred at Dagon had made a deep impression upon his mind, ·so much so that he was determined, when the opportunity should present itself, to exact vengeance to the uttermost. At this point therefore it will be necessary to turn from the Shwebo conversations to examine the occurrence in the neighbourhood of what may henceforth be referred to by its modern name of Rangoon, to see what exactly it was that had so inconveniently introduced a complicating factor into Anglo-Burmese relations.

CHAPTER IV.

THE AFFAIR OF THE ARCOT·

On April 4th, 1755, the snow *Arcot* under the command of Captain Robert Jackson put out from Madras bound for the island of Negrais with official letters and a large consignment of money for Henry Brooke,[1] and a new ' assistant " for the station, one John Whitehill, a Company's servant, a young man in his twenty-first year, who had recently joined the Madras establishment as a " writer " on the princely salary of £5 a year, and was destined many years later to retire from the Governorship of Fort St. George with a very unsavoury reputation.[2] In her passage across the Bay the *Arcot*, not a good ship at the best of times, ran into severe monsoon weather, and was unable to make Negrais. And her condition became so leaky that her commander directed his course to Syriam, where he hoped to repair his vessel, and in the meantime convey the bullion and letters through the creeks by native craft to the Negrais factory.

After a passage of nearly two months he arrived on June 1st in the river off Syriam. There to his surprise he learnt that the Company's Resident, the shipwright Henry Stringfellow, had upon Alaungpaya's occupation of Dagon transferred business to that place, whither he had gone in the Company's schooner *Hunter* together with three English private trading vessels. A message from Stringfellow to Jackson advised him likewise to proceed to the new port, where under the patronage of the King of Burma, who had established friendly relations with Henry Brooke, he might obtain all the necessary assistance for the repair of the *Arcot*, and boats to despatch to Negrais.

Accordingly the *Arcot* went on to Rangoon, where she anchored on June 6th, and Captain Jackson deputed Whitehill to the King, bearing a small present of a fowling piece and two bottles of rose water and with

1 Madras Pub ic Proceedings, 1755, 75, 141, 171.

2 In the official records his name in invariably given as Whitehill. But it was clearly pronounced Whittle. William Hickey spells it Whittle (Memoirs, I, 182) and Whittall (*Ibid*, II, 140). In a letter signed by Whitehill, given in full in Dalrymple's Oriental Repertory, I, 195, the name appears as Whithal. Nevertheless Dalrymple, a contemporary of Whitehill's at Madras, always refers to him as Whitehill.

a request for assistance in the repair of the ship and boats for transport to Negrais. All this was readily promised ; but on the next day, when at the King's request all the English at Rangoon, headed by Whitehill and Stringfellow, went to pay their respects at Court, they were detained there the whole day, and during their absence from their ships Burmese troops were sent on board with a peremptory demand for all their guns, small arms and ammunition. On the *Elizabeth*, a private ship from Bengal commanded by Captain Swaine, the demand was complied with. Captain Jackson, however, was on board his own ship ill with dysentery. He flatly refused to hand over anything, and threatened that if the demand were persisted in, he would go over to the Talaings at Syriam. A second attempt to seize the *Arcot's* guns on June 8th was met by an equally firm refusal by Jackson, who on this occasion made a show of preparing to leave the port by force. At this Alaungpaya sent him a reassuring message to the effect that no further attempt to seize the guns of the English ships should be made, and Jackson was promised all the assistance he might require, including boats to send to Negrais.

Jackson and Stringfellow therefore settled down to the business of repairing the *Arcot*. But apparently a further cause of dispute with the King soon developed. According to Jackson's story—unfortunately the only actual narrative of these events that we possess—Alaungpaya sent boats and letters to Henry Brooke at Negrais a few days after the arrival of the *Arcot*. After an absence of a fortnight the royal boats returned with a message from Brooke to Alaungpaya to the effect that the Negrais factory was about to depute Captain George Baker and Lieutenant North as ambassadors to the King. Brooke's letter was shown by the King to Whitehill, who, on reading it, complained that he had not been allowed to communicate with Negrais, when the royal boats had gone thither. This the King stoutly denied, asserting that before the boats set out, the men had been ordered to go on board the *Arcot* and collect letters for Negrais. Such is Jackson's story ; and it is interesting to note that Dalrymple dismisses as groundless the accusation that Alaungpaya prevented the English from sending letters to Negrais on this occasion.[1]

Jackson's narrative is vague and confused, especially in the matter of dates ; and it does not square with the known facts of Brooke's intercourse with Alaungpaya as set forth in the previous chapter. For we have no record of any correspondence between the two between the March embassy and the one which left Rangoon in the middle of June and resulted in the despatch of Baker and North from Negrais on July 17th. And it must be borne in mind that Henry Brooke's reply to the March embassy did not reach Bassein until June 3rd., and therefore could not have arrived in Rangoon until a week or ten days later. Further, almost immediately after the despatch of the June embassy—and long before an answer could have been received at Rangoon—Alaungpaya set out on his

1 *Op. cit.* I, 179.

journey northwards to Shwebo. Jackson's facts therefore must have been badly muddled. Throughout this whole period he was suffering from acute dysentery, and, by his own account, was often lightheaded, and was not expected to recover.

Nevertheless, with all due deference to Dalrymple's judgment, it is more than probable that the root point, upon which the story is based, was correct, namely that the *Arcot's* people were prevented from sending letters to Negrais when Alaungpaya's embassy set out from Rangoon in the middle of June. Burmese kings in their dealings with foreigners had a habit of issuing orders to which their officials were covertly instructed to give an antithetical interpretation. And we may justly infer from Jackson's story, in spite of all its obvious imperfections, that by the time that Alaungpaya left Rangoon for the north Jackson, Whitehill and their fellow English had good cause to regret their abandonment of Syriam in order to seek the patronage of the Company's new potential ally. Thus was the way made easy for an intrigue between the discontented English at Rangoon and the Talaing Uporaza, And as the trusty ally of the Talaings, the Sieur Bruno, was also secretly corresponding with the Burmese King, the situation was not without its humour. In fact, Bruno's messenger to Alaungpaya also carried some of the correspondence that passed between the Uporaza and the English.

At the moment when Alaungpaya's victorious advance had culminated at Dagon, Bruno had gone with three ships ostensibly to congratulate the conqueror ; in reality, of course, to gain some impression of the relative strength of the Burmese forces. While he was on shore, his second-in-command, for some apparently unaccountable reason, sailed off back to Syriam. So thoroughly were Burmese suspicions aroused by this act, that Bruno was only allowed to return to his ship on solemnly undertaking to bring back the truant vessel and on leaving behind as hostage a young French Eurasian named Lavine. He never redeemed his promise, though he continued to correspond with Alaungpaya until the latter's departure for Shwebo. Presumably while on shore he saw enough to convince him that for the time being the Burmese effort was spent. The Burmese indeed had no siege equipment capable of making the slightest impression against the stout defences of Syriam. Meanwhile the hostage Lavine was taken into Alaungpaya's service. We shall meet him later.

Shortly before Alaungpaya's departure up country, a messenger of Bruno's, bearing a letter to the King, managed to smuggle into Jackson's hands one from the Uporaza dated June 16th and addressed to all the English at Rangoon,[1] The letter announced that the writer was about to lead a great attack upon the Burmese position at Rangoon, and the English were asked to refrain from firing upon the Talaing fleet. They

---

1 Dalrymple gives the full translation of it, I, 192-3.

were reminded that the Court of Pegu had granted the Company trading concessions at Syriam, Negrais and Bassein, and on the strength of these they were invited to return to Syriam, where, the Uporaza assured them, they should be received, as formerly, with sincere friendship.

To such an overture, coming at such a time, the disgruntled English were in the right mood to lend a favourable ear. Moreover, the "usurper", as Jackson refers to Alaungpaya in his journal,[1] was forced to return to Upper Burma by very serious disaffection, which might conceivably rob him of the fruits of his victorious march to Dagon. After his departure the Talaings with their French allies were likely to experience little difficulty in disposing of the small Burmese force that would be left to hold Rangoon. Jackson therefore replied that the English were the Uporaza's friends; they would not molest his forces, and would be glad to seize the first opportunity of escaping from the Burmese. But he sent the message verbally. A letter might have committed him too far, besides which it could be easily intercepted.

Shortly after this Alaungpaya with the main Burmese army set out towards Prome on the first stage of his journey to Shwebo, leaving a garrison of some 15,000 men at Rangoon. As soon as he was clear of the neighbourhood, the projected Talaing attack was launched. It proved an utterly farcical affair. The Talaing flotilla stole up the river by night, directed a futile bombardment against the Burmese position and returned to Syriam without even attempting a landing. The English ships in Rangoon harbour maintained strict neutrality throughout; but when the Talaings retreated to their base, the English made no attempt to join them, although Jackson's message had hinted that they hoped to do so.

Their inaction was equally annoying to both sides. The Talaings had hoped for active support. The Burmese read into it a treacherous understanding with the enemy. A week later Jackson received a second letter from the Uporaza upraiding him for not having replied to the first. The messenger announced another impending Talaing attack upon Rangoon. After some delay the English sent a joint reply signed by Jackson, Whitehill, Stringfellow and two captains of private vessels, Swaine and Savage, and addressed to both the Uporaza and Bruno.[2] They promised that if aided to escape from Rangoon, they would assist the Talaings " to the last drop of their blood ". The letter was conveyed to Syriam by a boat belonging to Swaine.

But the cat was out of the bag. Before the Uporaza's letter had been delivered to the English, Bruno's two lascars, who had brought it, had fallen into the hands of the Burmese, who had sent them on to Alaungpaya at Prome together with a copy of the letter. The English,

---

1 *Ibid.*, I, 178-9.
2 The full text is given in Dalrymple, *op. cit.*, I, 194-5.

therefore, were summoned on shore, confronted with the facts and required to give a definite assurance of help against the Talaings. Jackson was still—according to his own story—too ill to leave his ship. So Whitehill acted as spokesman. They could do nothing, he said, without consulting Jackson. Also, without orders from the Company, they were bound to play the part of neutrals. Only if actually attacked by the Talaings would they join in on the Burmese side. The Burmese allowed them to return to their ships, but a strict watch was kept upon them.

A few days afterwards the expected Talaing attack was made. As the flotilla, headed by two large French ships came up the river, the Burmese made a frantic appeal to Jackson for help. This was disregarded, and when the bombardment began, the English joined in with the French and Talaings. Again, however, the attack was fruitless. The Burmese were driven from their boats ; but the Talaings could not be prevailed upon to follow up this initial success by a land attack. Alaungpaya's victories had thoroughly demoralised them. So a farcical bombardment was kept up for seven days, until the Talaing ammunition was exhausted. Little damage was done on either side. When it was over, the English ships sailed away with the rest to Syriam. There they were " very handsomely" received by the Uporaza, and Jackson, at Bruno's suggestion, went under the care of a French doctor.

The Uporaza had now come to realise how serious were the consequences of his rejection of Thomas Saunders's treaty proposals. He had thrown the English into the arms of Alaungpaya. In an interview with Whitehill and his companions he showed them the correspondence he had had with Saunders and Hunter, and lamely tried to explain away the breakdown of the negotiations. It was not his fault, he protested. The Company had sent envoys with inadequate powers for concluding a treaty. If, however, Henry Brooke would either come in person or depute Whitehill, matters could be settled " according to the Company's desire". So letters to this effect were despatched to Negrais in boats furnished by the Uporaza.

But Henry Brooke had had too much experience of the methods of the Court of Pegu to pay serious attention to this new move. He knew the motives which inspired it, and the man with whom he was dealing. To the Uporaza he replied that he would be unable to leave Negrais until Whitehill arrived there. Then either the latter or he himself would come to Syriam to talk matters over. He requested that in the meantime all the Company's vessels then at Syriam should be sent to Negrais. One sentence in his letter must have been written with no little malicious pleasure : he announced that he had sent an embassy with a present of cannon to Alaungpaya. To Jackson he wrote that the *Arcot* was required at Negrais by September 19th ; Jackson was to settle an outstanding account for repairs executed upon the schooner *Hunter* and get away from Syriam with all speed.

As the ships were not in a condition to sail at once for Negrais, Whitehill decided to go on ahead of them. His request for boats was willingly granted by the Uporaza, who supplied him with twenty war boats and entrusted to him further letters for Henry Brooke. In these the prince protested his sincere friendship for the English, begged for all the warlike stores that the Negrais factory could spare, and asked that such Talaings as had taken refuge at Negrais, when the Burmese captured Bassein, should be sent to swell his forces at Syriam. Whitehill, who arrived at Negrais on August 26th,[1] found that his chief had no intention whatever of allowing himself to be drawn into any further relations with the Court of Pegu. So the Uporaza's boats were returned to him with no warlike stores, no Talaing refugees and no commissioner for concluding an alliance. Instead, Brooke sent a peremtory demand for the restoration of the guns, which had been seized by the Talaings from the old Syriam factory in 1743, when they had destroyed it.

The Uporaza's annoyance was intense. He called up the English and told them that Brooke wanted the guns in order to make a present of them to the Burmese, "that he might get some more rubies from Dagon Pagoda."[2]   Nevertheless he sanctioned the departure of the English ships for Negrais, at the same time entrusting to Jackson a letter remonstrating with Brooke for his conduct. Only the schooner *Hunter* actually sailed—on September 26th. The *Arcot* sprang so bad a leak that she had to be beached for repairs. These entailed a month's delay. But when she was at last ready to put to sea, the Uporaza refused to let her go until he should hear further from Henry Brooke. The English allowed him a few days in which to repent of this outrageous decision. But the prohibition was maintained. So headed by Jackson and Westgarth they waited upon the prince. An angry scene ensued. They would all be detained until the affair had been reported to the Governor of Madras, the prince told them. Jackson in reply threatened to leave without waiting for permission ; Bruno, he said, was at the bottom of the whole business. At this the Uporaza's anger flared up. The English were his prisoners, he shouted. Had he not redeemed them all from Dagon ? They should not leave until the King of Pegu thought proper. And from this decision no arguments availed to move him. A strong body of soldiers mounted guard over the ships of the English, sentries were placed over their houses and every form of restraint imposed upon them.

But this severity was soon relaxed. A Bengal ship under Captain Douglas was permitted to depart on leaving behind her guns. Incidentally the Uporaza was in debt to her captain to the extent of 26 viss of silver.[3]

1 Dalrymple, *op. cit.*, I, 185, note. Madras Public Proceedings, 1755, 551.
2 Dalrymple, *op. cit.*, I, 186.
3 The Burmese silver tickal (100 to the viss) was then worth about 2 shillings in English money.

Later another Bengal ship, the *London*, under Captain Henry Karr, was allowed to leave, and upon her Jackson was able to smuggle through to Negrais the stores and bullion he had brought from Fort St. George for delivery there. But the embargo on the *Arcot* was maintained, and Jackson was personally treated with great indignity, if we are to believe his own story. When helpless in bed with dysentery, he wrote, he was struck by a Talaing officer, and could obtain no redress. Also, fabulous accounts of Talaing victories, and even of their recapture of the city of Ava, were poured into his ears, so that he was led to believe that the Burmese cause was doomed.

At length, apparently in December 1755, a great combined land and water attack upon Rangoon was planned, and the English were promised that in return for participation they would have liberty to depart. So three English ships—presumably those of Jackson, Westgarth and Swaine— accompanied the Uporaza's and Bruno's flotilla upon a third abortive enterprise. The defences around the Shwe Dagon Pagoda could not be carried, and a raft of burning boats, launched by the Burmese, broke up the attack by water. Then at last was Jackson allowed to leave, on January 5th 1756, but only after he had handed over five of the *Arcot's* guns. His unseaworthy ship, in attempting to make Negrais, was caught in a gale which blew her far out of her course, and she ultimately put into Vizagapatam.[1]

This extraordinary episode had important results upon Anglo-Burmese relations. It made an ineradicable impression upon the mind of Alaungpaya, breeding in him a secret mistrust of the English, which was one of the main causes of the horrible massacre that put an end to the Negrais factory in 1759. It is probable that Jackson's story, although one suspects him of liberally bestowing whitewash upon his own part in the affair, does not contain any serious distortion of the facts. His excuse of having acted under compulsion on the occasion of the third attack upon Rangoon was accepted by the Fort St. George Council, and in such terms was the matter reported home.[2] It is interesting, however, to find Henry Brooke at a later date adopting a much less charitable view of the episode. When in 1760 he was asked by the Fort St. George Council to give his opinion on the causes of the Negrais massacre, he unhesitatingly attributed the catastrophe to the reprehensible conduct of the English at Rangoon in 1755. " I never heard that these gentlemen had any authority either from the Coast or Bengal for such unwarrantable proceenings; they had none from Negrais," he wrote. " It was then, and is still, my opinion that had not this act of open violence been committed by those gentlemen at Dagon, we should have obtained much better terms for the Company than those we have done................The captains of country vessels in general gave great cause of complaint to the natives by their violent and ungovernable behaviour." [3]

---

1 Dalrymple, *op. cit.*, I, 199-200. Madras Public Proceedings, 1756, 67.
2 Coast and Bay Abstracts, VI, 97.
3 Madras Public Proceedings, 1760, 199-201.

CHAPTER V.

THE TREATY WITH ALAUNGPAYA.

Captain George Baker's interview with Alaungpaya, which, for reasons narrated in the previous chapter, began so inauspiciously, ended more pleasantly than might have been expected. Indeed, a somewhat piquant note was introduced by the King's vast amusement at the tone of Henry Brooke's letter. He and his whole court broke into a hearty laugh when the following passage was read out and duly translated into Burmese : " As you will by this means obtain an alliance and friendship with so great a power as the Honourable East India Company, who can send you such assistance as will support your Majesty's throne against all future rebellions, domestic feuds and foreign enemies."[1]. In three years, said Alaungpaya, he had extended his conquests a three months' journey in each direction. He was now about to take Pegu. What madman could dream that after such successes he needed help to capture the last town of all? Had he so much as asked for it? He had beaten the Talaings with bludgeons only, so great had been his superiority. He had now but to complete his conquest of the country. And then, he added significantly, would he go " in quest of Bourno".

When the reading of the letter was finished, the King drew his sword. "Captain, " he said to Baker, " See this sword. It is now three years it has been constantly exercised in chastising my enemies. It is indeed almost blunt with use; but it shall be continued to the same till they are utterly dispersed. Don't talk of assistance. The Peguers I can wipe away as thus." And he drew the palm of one hand over the other. Then, when Baker begged him not to take the Company's offer in bad part, the King cut him short. " See these arms and this thigh, " he said pulling his sleeves over his shoulders, and tucking up his pasoe to his crutch. "Amongst a thousand you won't see my match. I myself can crush a hundred such as the King of Pegu." And he proudly pointed out in the crowded audience chamber the hostages of the princes who now owned his sway, making them pass before the English ambassador. "To all which," wrote Baker in his journal, "I gave the most suitable, or what I conceived would be the most agreeable, answer; for I thought that was the avenue to his heart." Indeed, the diplomatic captain not only expressed his admiration of all that he was expected to admire, but he concluded his remarks with the pious hope that his Majesty's royal progeny would " to the end of all time perpetuate the memory of their unparalleled predecessor. " Distinctly mollified, the King ended the audience by ordering the draft articles of the treaty to be translated into Burmese for consideration on the following day.

Baker soon discovered that a rather difficult cross-current had to be negotiated. As was to be expected, it arose from Armenian intrigues.

---

1. Dalrymple, *op, cit.*, I, 150.

An Armenian, Gregory, one of the ambassadors of Alaungpaya, who had accompenied Baker from Negrais, was the intermediary in all his dealings with the King and Court, carrying messages and accompanying the Englishman as interpreter at audiences. Baker had early cause to suspect his integrity in the matter of the wording of royal messages. He was also obviously hand in glove with a compatriot of his named Zachary, [1] whom he had induced to desert the Talaing cause. This worthy, presumably in Bruno's pay, was doing his utmost to persuade the King to throw over the English in favour of the French. His intense hatred of the English was, of course, a trait common to most Armenians throughout Asia in the eighteenth century—due probably to the apprehension that their own influence at native courts was endangered more by the English than by any other European nation. By emphasizing the treacherous part played by the English ships in the recent Talaing attacks upon Rangoon, and by impressing upon the King that Bruno's action there was a " mad trick," for which he would be punished on his return to Pondicherry, Zachary almost prevailed upon Alaungpaya to depute him upon an embassy to the president of the French settlements on the Coromandel Coast.

For some time the King toyed with the idea. Baker, however, was aware of what was on foot. So, when the King in going through the English proposals sent a message to Baker asking whether the Company, in return for trading privileges, would be willing, in lieu of the suggested payment of some European curiosities, to supply him with an outright payment of a thousand muskets and twenty pieces of cannon for operations against Pegu, the Englishman promptly guaranteed that immediately upon his return to Negrais seventy-five muskets and six pieces of cannon should be despatched to him, and a ship sent to the Coromandel Coast to bring over as soon as possible fourteen pieces of cannon and 525 muskets for delivery. He further promised that, if possible, the number of muskets should be made up to the stipulated one thousand. This was all *ultra vires,* but Baker believed that his promises could be implemented. And they served their purpose, for they cooked Zachary's goose. The King threw over his suggestion.

Other difficulties, however, cropped up. The King would not allow the Company to settle at Syriam, he said; he intended utterly to destroy the town. Instead, the English might establish their trade at the new port, Rangoon, that was about to be built at Dagon. At a later interview Alaungpaya said he would permit the Company to open factories at Bassein and Rangoon, and straightway dictated an order to that effect. When Baker drew his attention to the omission of Negrais, he went off into a long tirade against the behaviour of the English ships at Rangoon, and before the Envoy could bring him back to the point, summarily

---

1. Possibly the son of the Zechary responsible for the Syriam murders in 1720. *Vide* Hall, Early English Intercourse with Burma, 209-210.

ended the audiences, telling Baker to return on the following day. But there were no further audiences. Alaungpaya's " favourite concubine " was suddenly taken ill and died, and the King's great grief at this calamity furnished him with a handy excuse for sending Baker back to Negrais with his mission unaccomplished. Instead of a treaty, the Envoy was entrusted with a royal order granting the Company permission to settle on a spot 2800 yards square on the river bank opposite to the town of Bassein and conferring a number of vague trading privileges.[1] And the King sent Baker a message asking him to meet him again at Rangoon. Baker left Shwebo on September 28th after a stay of less than a fortnight. On October 30th he was back in Negrais.

By January 1756, Alaungpaya had settled the affairs of the north sufficiently to admit of his return to Rangoon. There he arrived with considerable reinforcements at the end of February, and immediately siege operations were set on foot against Syriam.[2] Robert Westgarth and a few English private traders still remained in the beleaguered town, probably in the belief that its stout defences would be adequate against an enemy possessing no siege artillery. The Uporaza himself proceeded to Pegu leaving the defence of Syriam in the hands of his chief Wungyi assisted by Bruno. Early in the siege the Frenchman suffered a serious loss; a ship of his grounded and was disabled by Burmese gunfire. His only other available one had been sent to Pondicherry for assistance.

At first Alaungpaya contented himself with blockading tactics, gradually tightening the meshes of his net around the doomed city. In July, however, after elaborate preparations, he launched a surprize night attack, which was completely successful. The garrison fled almost without striking a blow. The greater part of it escaped, but all the Europeans in the town fell into Alaungpaya's hands. Most of the English were—rather significantly—released. Westgarth, however, seriously wounded in the struggle, was forbidden by the King to receive medical attention, and died of his wounds.[3] Upon the French and their confederates the full weight of the King's vengeance descended. Bruno was roasted alive.[4] Father Nerini, the head of the Catholic Mission to Burma, was beheaded. The rank and file escaped immediate death for a worse fate—forcible service with the Burmese armies.

There was a tragic irony about Bruno's fate. During the siege he had attempted to negotiate with Alaungpaya; but the Talaings had discovered the intrigue and put him under restraint. Two days after the fall of Syriam, while Bruno was still alive, two French vessels, the *Galatee* and the *Fleury*, laden with military stores and troops, sent from

1. Madras Public Proceedings, 1760, 209.
2. Useful accounts of this episode are to be found in Cordier's Historique Abrégé, 8, and Symes's Embassy to Ava, 29-32.
3. Madras Public Proceedings, 1760, 200.
4. *Ibid., loc. cit.*

Pondicherry for the assistance of the Talaings, put into the Rangoon river and sent up a boat for pilot. Their boat fell into the hands of the Burmese, who sent down the required pilot in a country boat bearing a letter, which the King forced Bruno to write, decoying the ships up the river. The trick was successful. On the way up the pilot purposely ran the French ships aground, so that they fell an easy prey to the Burmese war boats. Their cargoes of artillery, muskets and every kind of military requisite, were extremely welcome to Alaungpaya, and he spared the lives of some 200 of their crews in order to impress them into his armies.[1] The officers, however, were beheaded.

A companion ship of the two captured ones, which had parted company with them during the voyage, was delayed six weeks by bad weather. On entering the Rangoon river she was fortunate enough to be warned of what had taken place, and so made good her escape to Pondicherry. Luckily for Alaungpaya the French could make no reprisals: Dupleix had gone back to France, and the Seven Years' War had begun. He, of course, was sublimely ignorant of the fact that in massacring Europeans he was sowing the wind from which his successors were one day to reap the whirlwind His object was to teach foreigners that they should give no help to rebel Talaings. In this his logic was at fault, since his own self-constituted authority was of more recent origin than that of the Court of Pegu. And Bruno was no worse than the men he was dealing with. His misfortune lay in failing to "spot the winner."

Captured Syriam, stripped of everything of value, was utterly destroyed as a city. In its stead as chief port of lower Burma, Alaungpaya's new creation, Rangoon, close to the renowned Buddhist shrine of Dagon, was sedulously developed. And it must not be thought that motives of either revenge or sentiment were the main cause of this. It had long been realised that Syriam harbour was becoming dangerous to ships of larger burthen on account of silting. Alaungpaya was bent upon establishing a port worthy of the new kingdom he had carved out with his sword. His choice of Rangoon for this purpose shows that he possessed the true instincts of the nation builder.

Captain George Baker was unable to fulfil his engagement to meet Alaungpaya again at Rangoon. The heavy death roll at Negrais led to his appointment to command the Company's sloop *Cuddalore* [2]. In that capacity he arrived at Madras early in February 1756, bringing with him John Whitehill, whose health had broken down at Negrais, and letters from Henry Brooke asking to be permitted to return for the same reason[3]. His request was granted, and on March 15th the *Cuddalore* returned.

---

1. On this point Harvey, History of Burma, 231-233 is illuminating.
2. Her captain, Nathaniel Hammond, had died there.
3. Madras Public Proceedings, 1756, 60, 63-4.

to Negrais with a new Chief, Captain John Howes [1] and a cargo of rice, salt and building materials. She was instructed to return immediately with Henry Brooke and a cargo of timber. [2]

In Baker's stead as ambassadors to the King of Burma Henry Brooke early in the year 1756 deputed Ensign John Dyer and Doctor William Anderson to proceed to Rangoon and secure, if possible, a ratification of the proposed treaty. On April 12th, while they were still absent, Captain Howes arrived at Negrais to take over charge of the settlement from Brooke. He found a sick and dispirited man, who, beyond sending this mission, had done nothing to follow up Baker's previous one. In particular the piece of land near Bassein, that Alaungpaya had granted to the Company had not yet been occupied. It was not the site chosen by the English, Brooke explained to Howes. He had asked for a piece of rising ground, easily defensible, called Pagoda Point, at Old Bassein. This the King had refused on the ground that a very ancient pagoda crowned the eminence, which was hence regarded as sacred. He could not afford, he said, to alienate the priesthood, when he was as yet not very firmly established on the throne. [3] Howes was all for insisting upon a grant of Pagoda Hill; but Brooke was equally insistent that to do so would be useless.

Soon after Brooke's departure for Madras, the two envoys returned from the Burmese camp. They had not succeeded in persuading the King to ratify the treaty; but they brought with them a letter from Alaungpaya to the King of Great Britain inscribed on gold leaf, and another for delivery to the Company, couched in almost identical terms, but written on gilt-bordered paper. These documents were the nearest approach to a treaty that a King of Burma could permit himself to condescend to. And it is interesting to note that many years later Colonel Burney, when Resident at Ava, discovered copies of them among a collection of Alaungpaya's " orders, "[4] They were dated April 1756, and were forwarded to London along with Fort St. George's general letter of June 6th, 1757. [5] They were received by the Board of Directors early in the following year, and the gold-leaf letter appears to have been presented to George II through " Mr. Secretary Pitt." [6]

1. He was a soldier, and the Fort St. George Council received a sharp rap over the knuckles from the Board of Directors for appointing him instead of a civil servant. (Despatches to Madras, 1753-9, I, 934.) Actually the only available civilian, Andrew Newton, Chief at Devecotah, had refused to go on the plea of ill-health.

2. Madras Public Proceedings, 1756, 66, 121.

3. Madras Public Proceedings, 1760, 200-201.

4. Vide Burney's edition of Bayfield's Historical Review of the Political Relations between the British Government in India and the Empire of Ava, (Calcutta, 1835)

5. Coast and Bay Abstracts, Vol. 6, 65. Whether Howes or his successor, Newton forwarded them to Madras I have been unable to discover. Probably the latter, otherwise the delay in despatching them home is inexplicable.

6 Vide Appendix I.

A peculiar interest attaches to it as the earliest direct communication between a King of Burma and a King of England. The translation of it preserved at the India Office [1] runs thus:

" The King, Despotick, of great Merit, of great Power, Lord of the Countries Thonahprondah, Tomp Devah and Camboja, Sovereign of the Kingdom of Burmars, the Kingdom of Siam and Hughen and the Kingdom of Cassay, Lord of the Mines of Rubies, Gold, Silver, Copper, Iron and Amber, Lord of the White Elephant, Red Elephant and Spotted Elephant, Lord of the Vital Golden Lance, of many Golden Palaces and of all these Kingdoms, Grandours and Wealth whose royal person is descended of the Nation of the Sun, Salutes the King of England, of Madras, of Bengal, of Fort St. David and of Deve Cotah, And let our Compliments be presented to His Majesty and acquaint him that from the time of Our Ancestors to Our time, there has been a great Commerce and Trade carry'd on by the English and Burmars, with all possible Liberties, Affection, Advantage and Success, till the time of the Revolution in Pegue, when an entire Stop was put to them and to Our Correspondence, tho' Our inclination and desire of Corresponding with His Majesty and his Subjects remain'd always lively and Constant with Us.

" At the time of the Revolution in Pegue, his Majesty our friend, was pleased to send Mr Brooke to settle at Negrais the one End of our Kingdom, of which we were apprised after his arrival there, and tho' Jealousy naturally Reigns in Kings, yet We were greatly pleased and Rejoiced at the News, and to give proof of our sincere Amity with His Majesty and his Subjects, We have, on Mr. Brooke's applying to Us in his Majesty's Esteemed Name, given and granted the Place he Wanted at Passaim, and have caused a Deed with Our Seal affixed to it, to be sent to Mr. Brooke, and have Commanded Our Governor at Passaim personally to attend to Measure and deliver up the said desir'd Place, which has accordingly been Done.

" If one King be in Union and Amity with another they may be of Utility to the Interest of each other.

"We and our Generation are inclin'd to preserve a Constant Union and Amity with his Majesty and his Royal Family and Subjects.

''Given the 10th of the Moon of the Month of Cawchong year 1118 Burman Stile (being April 1756 English Stile). Let this Letter be engraved upon a Golden Plate, and forwarded to the King of England·''

Unfortunately neither the British Government nor the Directors had any idea of the signal act of condescension to which the descendant of

---

1. Home Miscellaneous, Vol. 95, 27-8. Part of the first paragraph containing the King of Burma's titles is quoted by Dalrymple (I, 106-7), who was a "writer" at Fort St. George when the letter arrived there in 1757.

the Nation of the Sun had committed himself in thus addressing the earth-born ruler of a foreign land. On July 5th, 1758, the Directors replied to Madras: "We have presented the King of the Burmur's Letter to his Majesty. If his Majesty should think fit to make a Reply, it shall be transmitted to you to be delivered together with a Letter from the Company in answer to That from the King of the Burmurs. In the meantime, if you think it necessary, you may make an Apology for our not transmitting them"[1] Neither answer nor apology were ever sent and the King of Burma nursed his wounded pride until the occasion came for taking a fearful revenge.

The explanation of the English apathy is not far to seek. Long before the Directors received Alaungpaya's letters they had sent out orders for the abandonment of trading operations in Burma, leaving it to the Madras Council's discretion whether actually to destroy the Negrais factory buildings and evacuate the place. England was in the throes of her great struggle with France. The tide had not yet turned in her favour. She was too much absorbed with other matters to be bothered with matters of Burmese policy. Especially so since the elimination of French influence through the fall of Syriam. For the time being Burma was of trifling importance to the Company. And Madras was too busily engaged in its terrific duel with Pondicherry to make the "apology" suggested in the Directors' letter.

We must now turn back to affairs in Burma from the time of the return of Dyer and Anderson to Negrais. The passage in the royal letters relating to the grant of land at Bassein is vaguely worded. It would appear to warrant the belief that the King had been prevailed upon —in spite of his previous refusal—to permit the Company to establish its factory on Pagoda Hill. Such, indeed, was the interpretation given to it by Captain John Howes, who in July 1756 went personally to Bassein where on the disputed eminence he began to build a fortified station officially dubbed Fort Augustus. And for this undertaking he had apparently received the permission of the Governor of Bassein[2]. The English flag was formally hoisted over the new fort on August 5th in the presence of the Governor and other local dignitaries. Howes then returned to Negrais, leaving his second-in-command, Lieutenant Thomas Newton, in charge of building operations, which were pressed forward with all speed.

Burmese religious sentiment, however, had been outraged. And when, soon after the opening of Fort Augustus, the Governor of Bassein left for Rangoon, the opposition grew intense. Adequate supplies of fresh food could not be obtained for the garrison, and inevitable sickness broke out. Howes therefore instructed Newton to quit the place, leaving

---

1. Despatches to Madras, I, 934.
2. Madras Public Proceedings, 1756, 599-600.

only a corporal and two or three men to mount guard over the buildings. On September 9th, before this order had been carried out, news came of the death of Howes at Negrais. Pending the appointment of a successor Newton was now the officiating Chief of the Negrais Settlement. His first exercise of his new authority was to carry out of the complete evacuation and abandonment of Fort Augustus, withdrawing its garrison, guns and stores to the parent settlement.

The foregoing account of the abortive attempt to plant a fortified trading post on Pagoda Hill at Bassein is taken from the official report submitted by Newton to the Madras Council after the death of Captain Howes. We possess also a brief reference to the affair from the pen of Henry Brooke some four years later. In this document, after mentioning that before his departure from Negrais he had warned Howes not to attempt a settlement on the spot in defiance of Alaungpaya's wishes, he wrote : "And after my arrival on the Coast I heard that Captain Howes had applied for it and was denied; that he afterwards possessed himself of it by force, and having erected some works was compelled to abandon them by the King, who expressed great displeasure thereupon."[1] Which is the true account? The available records give us no clue. No reference was made to the incident when in the following year Ensign Lester was negotiating with Alaungpaya. The King and his advisers were insistent that the Company should "settle" at Bassein "on the bank of the Persaim River, opposite to the Pagoda Hill, and the old Town of Persaim."[2] But " Fort Augustus " was not so much as mentioned.

During the rainy season of 1756 Burmese operations against the Talaings were suspended. Only the city of Pegu itself remained unsubdued. Here, behind countless stockades and with no lack of artillery—of a sort, was concentrated the remnant of the Talaing forces together with the King and his Court. In October, with the arrival of the dry season, the Burmese forces began to close round the city, systematically devastating the countryside and deporting the population. Once more urgent need of warlike stores led Alaungpaya to send a mission to Negrais. Thomas Newton managed to spare twelve chests of gunpowder from his inadequately stocked magazine, and the Burmese paid cash down.[3]

As the siege proceeded, however, the Burmese demands for this most desirable commodity became insatiable, and the inability of the English to satisfy them annoyed the King so much that he was reported to have " let drop some expressions intimating that when he had reduced Pegu, he would dislodge the English from Negrais." [4] Thomas Newton became alarmed. War conditions in India beween the English and

---

1. *Ibid*, 1760, 201
2. Dalrymple, *op. cit.*, I, 223.
3. Madras Public Proceedings, 1757, 21.
4. *Ibid,* 1757, 380.

French had resulted in the almost entire neglect of the unpopular settlement. Not only was his stock of powder too low for him to cater for the needs of the Burmese, but, in his own words, it was fit for nothing but salutes.[1] At the end of March 1757 he warned the Madras Council that he would not answer for the consequences of a further refusal of the Burmese demands.[2] So desperate indeed did he consider the plight of the settlement, that he went to the length of detaining as a guardship a Bengal private vessel, the *Fort William*, which mounted sixteen guns and carried a well-armed crew of nearly sixty hands.

The situation, however did not develop so badly as Thomas Newton had anticipated. In May the Burmese carried Pegu by storm.[3] Its capture was the signal for an appalling holocaust, in which almost all that was distinctive of the ancient city, save its religious shrines, perished. Soon afterwards, with the conquered King, royal family and Court of Pegu in his train, Alaungpaya began slowly to make his triumphant return to the capital. Before starting he despatched a letter to Thomas Newton informing him of what had taken place, and requesting him to join him on the way up stream to Prome. The letter intimated that the King had " some matters of consequencé" to communicate to Newton,[4].

Newton decided that the opportunity was ripe for reopening the treaty question. But he thought it imprudent personally to leave his post. He therefore deputed Ensign Robert Lester [5] as " ambassador extraordinary" to the King and sent along with him the best present the settlement could afford. Its chief item was a four-pounder and guncarriage " compleat".[6] It was arranged that the mission was to be sent upon the Company's schooner *Mary* to Bassein. There it was to be met by Antonio, an interpreter of Portuguese extraction, who possessed some degree of influence at the Burmese Court. He was to provide transport from Bassein to the royal presence.

Lester on board the *Mary* left Negrais on June 26th, 1757, and arrived at Bassein late in the evening of the following day. Not until July 3rd did Antonio put in an appearance, and he then informed the already

---

1. *Ibid.*, 1757, 381.

2. *Ibid.*, *loc. cit.*

3. Picturesque accounts of the siege are given by several writers, notably Harvey, *op. cit.*, 232—236, and Symes, *op. cit.*, 33—39, the former being largely based upon the official Burmese version given in the Konbaungset Yazawin, the official Burmese chronicle of this period.

4. Dalrymple, *op. cit.*, I, 201.

5. Symes gives his name as Lyster. As his account of the mission is based upon Dalrymple's, who was at Madras at the time, and spells the name Lester, the reason for the discrepancy does not appear. But there are many inaccuracies in Symes's first chapter.

6. For the full list see Dalrymple, I, 203.

impatient envoy that the boats for transport to the royal flotilla would not be ready for another six days. In the meantime he appeared to be mainly employed in extorting money from the Talaings of the district, often by means of torture. Ostensibly the proceeds of his exactions were for the royal exchequer, and he was so busy, he told Lester, that he had no time even to have a translation of Newton's official letter to the King prepared.

On July 13th the mission left Bassein. It was the height of the rainy season. The boats were very inadequately protected against the weather, and Lester suffered great personal discomfort. His protest merely provoked an unpleasant display of insolence from Antonio and an English renegade, who was acting as the latter's assistant, one William Pladwell. ' I meet with many things amongst these people, that would try the most patient man ever existed," he wrote in his journal, " but as I hope it is for the good of the gentlemen I serve, I shall put up with them and proceed."[1]

On July 22nd they fell in with the royal flotilla, and on the following day, minus his sword and shoes, much to his disgust as a British officer, Lester was presented to the King on board the royal barge. A lengthy conversation took place, in the middle of which, to the immense amusement of the King, the envoy found the effort to remain in the *shihko* position for a prolongued period so uncomfortable, that he tried surreptitiously to draw up a low stool to ease his cramped limbs. Whereat with gracious condescension the King allowed him to sit upon a spar of the barge.

Throughout the interview Alaungpaya plied Lester with questions. Why was a treaty required ? Was not the gold plate, which he had given to Ensign Dyer for tiansmission to the King of England, enough? And why did the English not leave Negrais and settle at Bassein ? To the last question Lester replied that Negrais was the key to the river. The English remained there in order to prevent the French from seizing the island. If a treaty were concluded, they would make Bassein their head-quarters, leaving only a small garrison to hold Negrais. A treaty, he strove to explain, was of more importance than a letter : "it would be a means of uniting the two nations together for ages to come." Alaungpaya, apparently impressed by this reasoning, dismissed the envoy promising that his royal seal should be affixed to the treaty at a place a little higher up stream, where he intended staying on shore for a few days.

During the conversation the King interspersed his questions on the matters at issue with others of a more personal nature. He asked if the envoy could point a gun and kill a man at a great distance, whether he understood the use of cannon, whether there was as much rain in England

1. Dalrymple, *op. cit*., I, 207.

as in Burma, why he wore a shoulder knot, how much was his monthly salary, and why Englishmen did not tattoo their bodies and thighs like Burmans ; and his Majesty stood up and exposed his own tattooed thigh to the amused envoy. He then felt Lester's hand and said the English were like women because they did not tattoo. When in reply to another question Lester told him that he had personally seen the Thames frozen over and an ox roasted whole upon it, the King and all present laughed heartily. Were the English afraid of the French? the King enquired with a gleam of mischief; to which it is not very difficult to picture Lester replying that "there never was that Englishman born, that was afraid of a Frenchman." The King also was moved to indulge in a little bombast. If all the powers of the world were to come, he said, he could drive them out of his country. Thus everything passed off most amicably, and Lester retired from the barge, having been careful to make the necessary presents to the various ministers, "hoping it may be a means of getting my business done, on the Company's account, the sooner."

Alaungpaya's promise to perform so unparalleled an act of condescension as to affix his seal to a treaty with the "Tsinapatan thimbaw zeit sa" provided his servants with an equally unparalleled opportunity for graft. Three days before the royal interview Antonio had approached Lester with the suggestion that if the King were prevailed upon to conclude a treaty a "good present" should be forthcoming for himself and the Governor of Bassein. Captain Howes and former Chiefs of Negrais had made similar promises, he averred. It was useless to prevaricate or refuse; so, with much misgiving, Lester gave his word that if the treaty materialised, the two officials should have a "genteel present".

On July 26th, at noon, as Lester was proceeding up the river in the royal train awaiting intimation of the ratification of the treaty, Antonio suddenly appeared with the information that the King wished to see him. With all possible haste Lester put on his dress uniform and hurried off to the appointed rendezvous. On arrival he learnt that the King had already departed and that he was too late for an interview. It soon turned out that his late arrival had been purposely stagemanaged by Antonio, who took the opportunity of letting him know that a present of 30 viss of silver for the Governor of Bassein and one of 20 viss for himself were the price of ratification. The unhappy envoy, well aware that Antonio held all the trumps, resorted to haggling. His first offer of 20 viss, later increased to 25, to be divided between the two officials, was rejected, and he was left to think things over. On the following day, after a long discussion with the two interested parties, Lester came to terms with them and he dejectedly chronicled in his journal: "As I am positive nothing can be done but through these men, neither can I get audience to the King but through Antonio, who is my interpreter, I have taken upon me to offer them Thirty Viss, which they accepted, and promised that they would get the King's Chop affixed to our treaty, and be firmly allied to our interest."

Accordingly on July 29th, when, after some suspicious delays on the river, the envoy arrived at Myanaung, Antonio met him with the news that the treaty had been ratified, and that the King, who had arrived much earlier, and was about to leave the place, would grant him a farewell interview. So, hurrying off to the royal barge, Lester had a few minutes conversation with the King before receiving his formal dismissal. Again the King was insistent upon the Company settling at Bassein Apparently it was this point that was uppermost in his mind in sanctioning the treaty. As to that document, he said, the final details would be settled by Antonio, but the royal seal was already affixed. As on the previous occasion he was moved to indulge in a little bombast: if a nine-pound shot fired from a gun were to hit his body, he told Lester, it could not enter it. But he also struck a minatory note. He had heard, he said, that the Negrais settlement had supplied food to Talaing refugees, thus rendering more difficult his task of reducing the country. Lester must inform his chief that in future nothing of this sort must be done. As the envoy took his leave, he was on the King's behalf solemnly presented with 18 oranges, 24 heads of Indian corn and 5 cucumbers.

Lester's return journey had to be undertaken in an even smaller and more inconvenient boat than that in which he had made the outward journey. " I agreed, as I could not help myself ;" he wrote in his journal, " but I advise any gentlemen that should come on these occasions, before they leave Negrais to get a good conveyance, for of all mankind, which I have seen, the Buraghmah promises the most and performs the the least."[1]   Torrential rains laid out Antonio, Lester and nearly all their following with severe attacks of fever. Not until August 6th, could they attend to the business of settling the final details of the treaty. Then—but not until Lester had placed in Antonio's hands a written guarantee that the stipulated 30 viss of silver would be paid by the Chief of Negrais—duly ratified copies were exchanged.

Thus after countless labours and weary journeyings the agents of the East India Company had at last obtained what purported to be a treaty with the King of Burma. It was indeed a document drawn up in the form of a treaty and bearing Alaungpaya's royal seal. *Mutatis mutandis* its form and contents were almost exactly those of the draft treaty that Thomas Saunders had offered to the Court of Pegu in 1754. But it was a worthless instrument. And the haphazard manner of its ratification was undoubtedly designed by Alaungpaya to show his utter contempt of treaties. Burmese kings would do nothing that could in any way be considered compromising to their sovereign powers. A treaty

---

1 Dalrymple, *op. cit.*, I, 218.

bound them by conditions that they could not revoke at pleasure. In any case, even if Alaungpaya were willing to respect the terms of the treaty during his own lifetime, it was by Burmese custom bound to lapse at his death. Then, if the Company wished the terms to stand, the humiliating—and expensive—supplication of the Golden Feet would have to be begun afresh and renewed *ad nausiam*. It is therefore interesting to note that while Dalrymple prints a copy of this document, it is pointedly omitted from Aitchison's monumental collection.[1] There is also the further point that we stressed in connexion with the treatment of Alaungpaya's goldleaf letter by the Directors and the Madras Council. The conditions, which had produced the original impulse for such a treaty, had passed away. Dupleix was no longer in the East. Bruno was dead. Burma was united. And both English and French were too much occupied elsewhere to devote any attention to Burmese policy. At the moment when Ensign Lester was so assiduously pursuing this phantom treaty, the Company's sole concern in Burma was with the question of withdrawal.

Clause two of the treaty apportioned to the East India Company " a spot, or tract, of ground situate on the Bank of Persaim River, opposite to the Pagoda Hill, and the Old Town of Persaim, of the following extent, viz. two hundred bamboos square, each bamboo containing 7 cubits." On August 22nd, 1757, while waiting at Bassein for conveyance to Negrais, Ensign Lester measured out the ground granted by this clause, and to the accompaniment of three volleys of small arms took formal possession of it in the Company's name. Four days later he reached Negrais and handed over his various diplomatic documents to Lieutenant Thomas Newton.[2]

CHAPTER VI.

THE MASSACRE.

When in January 1755 George Pigot took over the governorship of Fort St George from Thomas Saunders, two things were obvious regarding the Company's position in Burma: firstly that the Court of Pegu would never sign a treaty, and secondly that the Negrais station would never be of any use commercially, save indirectly as subsidiary to a main station at Bassein. Pigot, who had not the same cause for interest in the settlement as his predecessor, did not mince matters in reporting home the situation as he saw it.[3] As a result the Directors' faith in the enterprise was rudely shaken. " From the accounts in your advices

---

1. Dalrymple, *op. cit.*, 1, 223-6. See also Aitchison's comment on the subject in Treaties, Sanads and Engagements, " I, 325.

2. Dalrymple, *op. cit.*, I, 222.

3. Dodwell, Calendar of Madras Despatches, 1744-1755, 257. Coast and Bay Abstracts, Vol. 6, 48.

before us of the settlement upon the Negrais and your transactions with the Government of Pegu," they wrote on December 19th, 1755, " wee have less encouragement than ever to think it will be proper for the Company to be at any further expence upon it " Pigot therefore was requested to send as explicit an account of the relative advantages and disadvantages of continuing the settlement as would enable the Court to come to some decision on the subject.

But before a reply could be received to this request, Pigot's letters of October 27th, 1755 [1] and March 2nd, 1756 [2] furnished the Directors with all the information they wanted. " You have given us by the *Hardwick* and *Eastcourt* a very clear state of the settlement at the Negrais," they wrote to Pigot in their despatch of March 25th, 1757, [3] " and it is so far satisfactory as to convince us that even supposing that settlement is not entirely to be withdrawn, it will not be for the interest of the Company to be at any further expense upon it, than merely to prevent giving the French a pretext for taking possession by our totally deserting it. These being our sentiments, we shall leave it to you to determine upon withdrawing entirely, or barely to keep possession at the least possible expense. If you judge the first to be, considering all circumstances, the best measure, you are to cause all the buildings, erections and works to be demolished and destroyed, and all the people to be brought away. But if very good reasons appear to induce you to think it really for the interest of the Company to keep the bare possession of it, the people to be employed for this service must never exceed twenty or thirty in the whole, in which there are, to save expences, to be as few Europeans as possible; and for the same reason there is to be no more money laid out in buildings and works of any kind, than will merely serve for the habitation and the necessary defence of the said people. As the utmost frugality is to be observed, Captain Howes must be recalled, and the person you shall think fit to appoint to preside over and command these people must be one of an inferior rank, and consequently at a moderate allowance. You must take care to supply them at proper times with the necessaries of life ; but none of our European ships or any of our own vessels are to be detained or continue there any longer than absolutely necessary for this service, the expences and disappointments already incurred on this occasion having been excessive and great."

A year later the receipt of Alaungpaya's gold-leaf letter in no way shook the Directors' resolution. Indeed, fearful lest the more favourable turn of events in Burma might lead the Madras Council to disregard their previous instructions, they wrote (in their despatch of July 5th, 1758): " We gave you our sentiments and directions with respect to the

---

1. Coast and Bay Abstracts, Vol 6, 72-3.
2. *Ibid.*, Vol. 6, 97.
3. Despatches to Madras, I (1753-1759), 697-8.

Negrais very fully in our letter of the 25th, March 1757, and not seeing any reason for being of a different opinion, they are to be complied with. We have been at so large an expense on account of the settlement at that place, and the unsettled condition of the Pegu country promises so very little advantage, especially in the present situation of the Company's affairs, that we cannot think of making any new settlements. Schemes of this kind must be deferred for more tranquil times. You are therefore not to be induced by flattering prospects to run us into expences, by making any new settlements." [1]   A few months later, when news of the conclusion of the treaty with Alaungpaya reached them, the Directors reiterated their decision. Everything was to be withdrawn from both Negrais and Bassein, they ordered. If absolutely necessary, " three or four black people " might be retained at each place " to hoist a flag, merely to keep up our right." [2]

The paragraph relating to Negrais in the Directors' letter of March 25th, 1757, came up for consideration by the Madras Council on April 25th, of the following year. [3]   Two months earlier, when Lieutenant Thomas Newton's report of the completion of the treaty with Alaungpaya, and of the formal occupation of the new site at Bassein, had been received, the Council, preoccupied with other more important matters, had passed a minute deferring indefinitely consideration of any further steps to be taken in Burma. [4]   When therefore it became apparent that the Directors themselves had lost all enthusiasm for a settlement in the country, the Council was only too willing to obey its instructions; and the resolution was recorded that " in the present circumstances of affairs the most adviseable measure will be barely to keep possession in the manner the Company direct." [5]

But no measures were taken by the Madras Council towards carrying this resolution into effect. In fact, Fort St. George took no further notice of the settlements in Burma until news came, in 1760, of the destruction of Negrais at the hands of the Burmese. [6]   So when in April 1759, in accordance with the Directors' instructions, Thomas Newton and the main Negrais garrison, consisting of 35 European and 70 native troops, were withdrawn, the operation was directed and carried out by the Calcutta Council. [7]

---

1. *Ibid*, I, 934.
2. *Ibid.*, I, 1017-18, Despatch of Jan. 23rd, 1759.
3. Madras Public Proceedings, 1758, 105.
4. *Ibid.*, 1758, 54-5.
5. *Ibid.*, 1758, 105.
6. Between the consultations of April 25th, 1758 and April 1st. 1760 the Madras Consultation Books contain no important references to Negrais. Receipt of Newton's letters until his departure in April 1759, is recorded either without comment or with the remark, " the consideration whereof is deferr'd to another opportunity."
7. Coast and Bay Abstracts, Vol 6, 307. Newton arrived in Calcutta on May 14th, and proceeded on to Madras shortly afterwards.

The cause of this is not far to seek. The great position in Bengal won for the Company by Clive's brilliant victory at Plassey had raised the power and prestige of Calcutta to an unprecedented level. Under Clive's first governorship (June 1758-February 1760) its pre-eminence in what we may call British India was placed upon unassailable foundations. From this time onwards Calcutta supplanted Madras as the directing centre of English relations with Burma. And in this connection it must be borne in mind that the Seven Years' War, which had opened in 1756, was being fought out mainly in the Carnatic, so far as India was concerned. There it resolved itself into a gigantic duel between Madras and Pondicherry.

During the early part of the struggle the brilliant Lally so successfully revived French power that by 1758 it had grown as strong as in the halcyon days of Dupleix. At the end of that year, when Lally laid siege to Madras, one of the critical moments of British power in India arrived. Had he succeeded, the favourable situation in Bengal would have been seriously threatened. But in February 1759 an English naval squadron raised the siege and Clive from Bengal created a diversion by sending an expedition to the Northern Circars which inflicted a crushing defeat upon a French army at Kondur, and ultimately captured Masulipatam. After this the fortunes of war turned decisively against the French. The British victory at Wandewash and the capture of Pondicherry sealed their doom, but not before they had unsuccessfully attempted to enlist against the British a rising new leader in the south, Hyder Ali.

Small wonder therefore that Madras during these critical years could do nothing for the Company's stations in Burma. And it is important to recollect that the events of those critical years 1758-60 were but the culmination of the unofficial contest for supremacy in the Carnatic that had engrossed the attention of the Madras Council unceasingly from the outbreak of the War of the Austrian Succession. Fort St. George never had its hands free to attempt seriously in Burma the role which it had so lightly assumed in planting a settlement on the island of Negrais. Thus, when a policy of withdrawal was forced upon the Company, Madras was unable even to rescue its own chestnuts from the fire. Calcutta had to take up that ungrateful task, and burnt its fingers in the process.

Before we come to deal with the last tragic scene at Negrais, two episodes, which throw some light upon it, must be briefly narrated. When Thomas Newton and the main garrison of Negrais evacuated the place in April 1759, the Company's teak timbers and other shipbuilding materials collected there had been left under the charge of Lieutenant Hope and a small guard, pending such time as the Calcutta Council could conveniently arrange for their removal. During the cold weather of 1758-9 Alaungpaya was busy leading a great raid into Manipur with the ostensible object of setting his own candidate upon its throne. His absence was the signal for a desperate attempt on the part of the Talaings to reunite on a big scale and regain their independence. The suddenness of their uprising took the government by surprise. There were massacres of Burmese in several districts of Lower Burma. The Burmese viceroy of Pegu was defeated and driven to Henzada. Alaungpaya therefore was forced to abandon his northern expedition in order to hasten down the Irrawaddy to the disaffected area. Before he arrived, however, the rebellion had been crushed by the viceroy, who, aided by reinforcements from the north, captured Rangoon, the main centre of the revolt, and with characteristic ruthlessness stamped out all resistance.

In June 1759, while Alaungpaya was on his southward journey, an English vessel, the *Lively*, commanded by Richard Dawson, and with John Whitehill as her supercargo, arrived at Rangoon on a private trading venture. [1] Our last glimpse of Whitehill was when he returned sick to Madras from Negrais early in 1756. A year later he had resigned the Company's service, presumably in order to develop certain private trading schemes of his own. [2] In 1758, however, he had "repented so unadvised a step," and petitioned for reinstatement. [3] His petition had had to be referred home for sanction. While awaiting this, he had been stationed at Sadras "to get intelligence." [4] But before the Directors' orders restoring him to the service arrived at Madras, he had—most unwisely, as it turned out—fitted out this trading expedition to Rangoon, hoping, by a method much used by traders to Burma in those days, to make a safe profit. [5] This method consisted in loading up with a cargo of coconuts at the Nicobars and disposing of them in Rangoon.

Everything went without a hitch until Whitehill, apparently ignorant of the resentment cherished against him by Alaungpaya ever since the affair of the *Arcot* in 1755, ventured late in July to visit the King at Prome. On arrival there he was immediately seized by royal order, beaten and put in irons. At the same time all his goods were confiscated. A few days later his ship, the *Lively* and another English vessel, the *Princess Carolina*, were seized by the Rangoon authorities, their cargoes confiscated and their crews made prisoners. [6] Captain Dawson of the *Lively* and his chief officer, Sprake, were sent up in irons to Prome,

---

1. Madras Public Proceedings, 1760, 180.
2. Coast and Bay Abstracts, Vol. 6, 175.
3. *Ibid.*, 264.
4. *Ibid.*. 295.
5. *Ibid.*, 357. Madras Public Proceedings, 1760, 180.
6 Madras Public Proceedings 1760, 180-1. The previously accepted version of this story, based upon Symes, *op. cit.*, 43, gives the arrest of Whitehill as having taken place at Rangoon, whence he is said to have been "sent up in close confinement to Prome." Whitehill's own report of the affair is entirely vague on this point. (Madras Public Proceedings, 1760, 243-4). The above account is based upon the report of Thomas Hobbes, second officer of the *Lively*, who inspires confidence by giving a definite date to every fact mentioned.

but were soon afterwards released and allowed to return to Rangoon. They were officially informed that they and the crews of the two captured vessels were detained as royal slaves, and would be allowed one basket of paddy a month each. The royal anger against Whitehill and Dawson, however, soon abated. They were permitted to ransom themselves for the sum of 83 viss of silver each. Whitehill was destitute of all means: his ransom, equal to 2760 pagodas of Madras currency, was advanced by an obliging Dutch captain[1]. He was lucky to have escaped with his life. The remainder of the ships' companies, having no means of raising any ransom money, and deserted by their employers, continued under restraint at Rangoon in a most miserable plight.

Not long afterwards the number of English prisoners at Rangoon was augmented from another source. On September 1st, 1759 Captain William Henry Southby in the snow *Victoria* left Calcutta to take charge of the abandoned Negrais factory. The Bengal Council felt that it was expedient to retain some more effective possession of the place, but, on account of the French war, could not make up its mind as to its future policy in Burma. Pending some decision in this matter therefore Southby was instructed to assume charge of the timber and shipping materials collected at Negrais, but to commit the Company to no further trading operations whatever[2].

In the Bay of Bengal the *Victoria* ran into a heavy storm. She arrived at Negrais on October 4th, in a badly shattered condition, having lost both main mast and maintop mast. In the harbour she found an East Indiaman, the *Shaftesbury*, which had called in for provisions and water. That evening Captain Southby went ashore to take over from Lieutenant Hope, the officiating head of the station. Almost at the same time three Burmese war-boats, carrying about 50 men all told, drew up at the settlement, and a Burmese official with his suite stepped on to the landing stage. It proved to be the Portuguese Antonio, who announced that he was now governor of Bassein, and as such was the bearer of a letter to the head of the English settlement from King Alaungpaya. This, he said, he would deliver with due ceremonial on the following day. On the next morning therefore Antonio delivered the royal missive. After the ceremony he was entertained to dinner by Southby and Hope. It was agreed that he should return on the following morning for the official reply, which was to be forwarded to the King together with a present of ten muskets, six blunderbusses, a pair of looking glasses and

---

1. Madras Public Proceedings, 1760, 174-5. On Whitehill's return to Madras the Council advanced him his ransom money on a bond payable in six months at 8 per cent. " for making good to the Dutch Captain......as otherwise it might appear a reflection on the English nation to suffer a stranger to sustain a loss in performing so humane and generous an act towards an English subject. " (*Ibid.*, 1760, 175)
2. Coast and Bay Abstracts, Vol. 6, 324, 336. Dalrymple, *op. cit.*, I, 343, Home Miscellaneous, Vol. 95, 547.

twelve decanters. Meanwhile the disembarkation of baggage and stores from the *Victoria* was proceeding, and the *Shaftesbury* was standing by in order to lend the assistance of its boats.

On the morning of the 6th, Antonio arrived early at Fort House, the temporary logwood structure which served as the settlement's headquarters. As the Burmese translation of the official reply to the King was not yet completed, he was invited to remain for dinner, which was to be taken at noon. Shortly before the meal was to commence, Southby, Hope and one of the assistants, Robertson by name, together with Antonio and the Burmese officers of his suite, were gathered in the large upper room, that served as a combined dining hall and reception room, supervising the final arrangements regarding handing over the letter and presents. Just as the servants were bringing up the meal, Southby sent Robertson to the godowns below to bring up the decanters, which formed the last item of the present. A few moments later at a signal from Antonio the Burmese suddenly shut all the doors of the hall, fell upon Southby and Hope and brutally butchered them. At the same moment on the ground floor the soldiers of Antonio's escort, who had surrounded the European guard under the pretence of trading with them, murdered them all. A midshipman from the *Shaftesbury*, who was about to enter the building, when the slaughter began, managed to break away from his attackers, and though wounded in the ribs by a spear, that was thrown at him, ran to the water's edge, where he and the *Shaftesbury's* carpenter and a number of Indians were rescued by the East Indiaman's pinnace. A few others also escaped on the *Shaftesbury's* longboat, which had just landed some of Southby's baggage from the *Victoria*.

Robertson and three soldiers in the godown beneath the hall, hearing the commotion and shrieks above, ran to the window and saw Antonio running for all he was worth towards the jungle. Just then another European assistant, named Briggs, badly wounded from several stab wounds, staggered into the godown. Realising what was afoot, they managed to close all the doors and windows before they could be attacked. Then climbing up through a trap-door they got into a room adjoining that in which Southby and Hope had been murdered. Peering through a keyhole they saw the murderers sitting on the couches with their feet upon the bodies of the slain.

Meanwhile down below and in the settlement the ghastly business went on. The Burmese of Antonio's escort were reinforced by a large party, previously concealed in the jungle, under the French half-cast, Lavine, whom Bruno had left as a hostage with Alaungpaya at Rangoon in 1755. Every man, woman and child they could lay their hands on—there was a large number of Indian labourers and servants attached to the fort—was killed. Then under Lavine's directions they turned the nine guns of the fort upon the *Shaftesbury*, which lay much nearer in than the *Victoria*. There was no lack of ammunition, as 25 chests of powder, brought by Southby for the defence of the settlement, had been landed from the *Victoria*, only that morning. The Burmese firing too was well directed. The *Shaftesbury's* second mate, Burroughs, and a seaman were killed, and her gunner badly wounded. She also sustained a good deal of damage to her rigging and hull. But she returned the fire gamely, and apparently prevented the Burmese from attacking in their war-boats either herself or the much disabled *Victoria*. The firing continued all through the night and well into the next morning, while the two ships stood to in order to pick up refugees. [1]

We left Robertson, Briggs and their three companions hiding in an upper room of the fort. Late in the afternoon the Burmese in the course of plundering the building discovered them and demanded admittance. They were promised their lives if they would surrender without resistance. It was their only hope. Accordingly they opened the door. Their captors tightly pinioned them and ordered them to go down the ladder which led from the hall to the godowns beneath. Briggs, however, in his desperately wounded condition could not negotiate the ladder. Thereupon one of his guards coldbloodedly knocked him from the top to the ground below, a drop of 14 feet, and as he struggled to rise another ran him through with a lance. Robertson and the rest were hurried off in the dusk to the war-boats, where Antonio took charge of them, unloosened their bonds and treated them with unexpected clemency. A start was at once made for Rangoon, and there they found themselves in the same sort of captivity as the ships' crews seized in the previous August.

On the morning after the massacre the captains of the *Shaftesbury* and the *Victoria*, believing that all the Europeans in the settlement had been murdered and that no more refugees could be saved, left the harbour with the ebb tide and took their vessels six miles out to sea. There the *Shaftesbury* stood by for three days to assist her disabled companion from her own stores with the task of remasting and rerigging. On the 10th of October she sailed away to bear news of the disaster to Madras. [2] The *Victoria*, in urgent need of water and ballast, made for Diamond Island, where she anchored on October 14th.

Two days later Captain Alves, seeing an English vessel about to enter Negrais harbour, sent a canoe to warn her of what had taken place. It turned out to be the *Helen*, bound from Calcutta to the Straits of Malacca, which had put in for a supply of fresh water. That night a great blaze was observed on shore, and it became evident that the Burmese were burning the settlement preparatory to evacuating it. The

---

1. The *Shaftesbury* collected 47 men and 2 women, the *Victoria* 13 men, 2 women and a child. (Dalrymple, *op. cit.*, I, 347.)
2. Coast and Bay Abstracts, Vol. 6, 356.

next morning the Burmese forces were seen to leave the place and proceed with all haste up stream in their war-borts. After they had disappeared, Alves and Miller, the *Helen's* captain, went together to the abandoned factory. There a dreadful spectacle met their gaze, " one of the most shocking sights I ever beheld, " wrote Alves in his description of it.[1] The bodies of the slain lay scattered about in an advanced state of putrifaction and recognisable only by their clothing. Everything of any value capable of being carried away had been looted. Then everything that would burn had been destroyed, buildings, gun carriages, timber and a schooner and long boat belonging to the Company, which were under repair. The sudden appearance of 15 to 20 large Burmese war-boats caused the searchers to beat a hasty retreat to Diamond Island. Soon afterwards Alves set sail on his return journey to Calcutta, whither he arrived on November 10th, 1759.[2]

To what causes may we attribute this utterly unexpected act of treachery? Robertson, writing from his captivity at Rangoon to urge the Bengal Council to take steps towards the release of himself and his fellow prisoners, stated that when he was brought before Alaungpaya, " his Majesty observed to me, that he had wrote a Letter to the King of England, on a Plate of Solid Gold, the Seal and Address of which was ornamented with precious stones to a Considerable Value, some of them as big as a Beetle nut (one he values here, as I am told, at 2 or 3 Vize of Silver, which is about 3000 Rupees) as also other letters and presents for Governour Clive and Governour Pigot, all which was delivered to the Chief of Negrais to be delivered by him ; and that he his Majesty was to this day without any Answer, notwithstanding some of these Letters had been gone three years. Therefore his Majesty could put no other Construction on it than the English and the Company looked on him and his People as Fools. These are the Reasons he gives for taking the Negrais, as also two Vessells that I hope yours [*sic*] Honours have heard of are detained here by his order; only his Majesty adds that Mr. Whitehill, who is supra cargo of one of them, fought against him at Pegu, and that he has a Right to lay hold of his Enemys wherever he finds

---

1 Dalrymple, *op. cit.*, I, 349.
2 Coast and Bay Abstracts, Vol. 6, 347. Dalrymple, *op. cit.*, I, 350. The sources of the story of the massacre given above are (*a*) Alves's " Account of the Settlement of Negrais being cut out off " in Dalrymple, *op. cit.*, I, 343-350, (*b*) the stories told by Antonio himself and Robertson to Alves during his mission to Ava in 1760 and recorded by him in his Journal, *Ibid.*, I, 356-9, (*c*) Alves's letter of October 9th, 1759 conveyed to Madras by the *Shaftesbury*, a copy of which is now to be found at the India Office in Home Miscellaneous, Vol. 95, 547-9, and (*d*) a letter from James Robertson to the Council of Fort William, Bengal, dated Dagon, 23rd November 1759, in Madras Public Proceedings, 1760, 178-180. The above account differs in certain details from the previously accepted version in Symes's Embassy to Ava, 45-8. This is due to the light thrown upon the episode by (*d*) to which Symes did not have access.

them ; His Majesty is so Enraged at him that he demands no less than fifteen hundred Musketts for his Ransom." [1]

A copy of this letter was sent by the Bengal Council to Madras, whither it arrived on March 28th, 1760, shortly after John Whitehill's return. [2] The Madras Council at once instituted an enquiry into the allegations contained in it, and also in a letter of similar tenor, recently received from the Armenian Gregory at Rangoon, wherein it was further stated that the Negrais chiefs had aided Talaing rebels against Alaung-paya. [3] Copies of these letters were accordingly forwarded to Henry Brooke at Wandewash, and to Thomas Newton, then in Madras, with a request for their explanations. Newton replied denying in forcible language all knowledge of the facts alleged, and ascribing the massacre to the " vile dispositions " of the Burmese. [4] Henry Brooke on the other hand submitted in exculpation of himself a detailed exposition of Anglo-Burmese relations during his term of office at Negrais.[5] He expressed his strong opinion that the behaviour of the *Arcot* and the other English ships at Rangoon in 1755 constituted the chief cause of Alaungpaya's resentment against the Company, and he pertinently drew the Council's attention to the fact that " Mr. Whitehill " was " one of those gentlemen who acted against the Burmahs at Dagoon."

Presumably as a result of the blame imputed to Whitehill in this letter we find the Madras Council on May 13th, 1760, considering a long screed from him and a petition from Captain Dawson of the *Lively* asking for steps to be instituted towards securing redress for the injuries, which they had received by Alaungpaya's seizure of their ship.[6] Whitehill admitted that the conduct of the English ships at Rangoon was a cause of the " King's disgusts, " but contended that the fact that he was only a passenger on the *Arcot* might be taken to be " a sufficient exculpation of me for any measures, however unjustifiable, which might have been taken by the master of her. " The real cause of all the trouble, he averred, was that the late chief of Negrais had supplied the Talaings with arms and ammunition. He also cleverly drew a red herring across the trail by a reference to the unacknowleged letter from Alaungpaya to the King of England, which Robertson had mentioned as a factor in the case. But he embellished the story in the process. In his version it was not a letter on gold leaf decorated with rubies, but a stone valued at 300 viss of silver, that Alaungpaya had sent to the " late Chief" of Negrais together with a letter for transmission to George II.

---

1. Referred to in the preceding note under (*d*.)
2. Madras Public Proceedings, 1760, 173-4.
3. *Ibid.*, 174-5.
4. *Ibid.*, 203-4.
5. *Ibid.*, 199-203.
6. *Ibid.*, 238-244.

His references to the " late Chief " were probably purposely vague. He avoided mentioning any names. Presumably the former reference was to Hope, and the latter to Newton. But as Whitehill had served at Negrais under neither of these men, and was desperately making allegations either entirely fabricated by himself or at best founded upon mere hearsay, he was obliged to take refuge in vague hints. His ruby story, however, served its purpose. It created the necessary diversion. Thomas Newton was well known to possess a large Burma ruby. He was therefore summoned before the Council to answer the imputation. 1 He admitted that he had received the royal letter in question, but without any such jewel as was alleged to have accompanied it. He produced his own ruby, which he said he had bought from a Burman. The Council on examining the stone decided that it was not " of a quality fit for a present to the King of England."2 And as Whitehill, who was also present at the examination, could bring forward no proof in support of his statement, Newton was entirely exonerated, and beyond reporting the matter home, the Madras Council did nothing further. The Directors, however, were not so easily satisfied, and suggested that the question of the origin of Newton's ruby together with that of the part played by Whitehill in the affair of the *Arcot* should receive further investigation.3

It is very doubtful if the ruby story had any basis in fact. There were, it is true, long and suspicious delays between the date when the royal letter was entrusted by Alaungpaya to Dyer and Anderson (April 1756) and the date of its despatch to England from Madras (June 1757). 4 But against that has to be set the all-important fact that the royal order directing the engraving of the letter does not mention rubies either by way of decoration or as a present to accompany it. The strong probability is that Alaungpaya invented the rubies in order all the better to impress Robertson and the other English prisoners at Rangoon with the righteousness of his indignation against the Company. Little did he realise how insignificant he appeared in the eyes of the gentlemen of Leadenhall Street, whose attention was focussed upon the Indian arena. Nevertheless the lack of imagination displayed by those gentlemen in handling the matter obviously contributed its share to the accumulation of annoyances which brought about the massacre.

---

1. *Ibid.*, 238.
2. *Ibid.*, 254.
3. See Appendix II.

4. In this connection the following facts are interesting. The Royal letter, dated April 1756, was probably received at Negrais not later than June or July of that year. Captain Howes was then Chief, with Newton as his second-in-command. Howes died at the beginning of September 1756 while Newton was at Bassein. Presumably at the time of Howes's death the letter had not been forwarded to Madras, since (a) Newton admitted receiving it and (b) Howes's last letter to Madras is dated May 10th. The letter was not forwarded from Madras to England until June 6th. 1757. I can find no reference to the date of the receipt of the letter by Madras from Negrais.

The most valuable light upon the causes of this tragedy, however, is shed by Captain Alves in his journal of his embassy to the Burmese Court in 1760, which forms the subject of our last chapter.[1] During the course of his journey to the capital Alves had an interview with Antonio, who appeared extremely anxious to whitewash the part that he had played in the affair. His story was that Hope on the occasion of the last Talaing rising had given away four or five muskets with some powder, shot and provisions to rebels. Gregory, the Armenian, coming to hear of this, had reported it to the King, taking care to multiply the number of muskets by no less a figure than one hundred. He had further warned the King that " the English were a very dangerous people, and if not, prevented in time, he (the King) would find, would act in the same manner as they had in Bengal and on the Coast ; where the first settlements were made in the same manner as at Negraise, but that, by degrees they had fortified themselves, and brought men, and all manner of military stores, in, and under various pretences, till they thought they were strong enough, then they pulled off the mask, and made kings whom they pleased, and levied all the revenues of the country at discretion."[2] And the Armenian had gone so far as to represent that the Chiefs of Negrais made a practice of preventing merchant vessels from going up to Bassein, thereby defrauding the King of customs.

Influenced by these arguments—according to Antonio's story—the King ordered the destruction of the settlement, and had sent the French Eurasian, Lavine, to carry out the design. Lavine had been instructed to take Antonio with him as interpreter, and in order to hoax the English, a royal letter had been entrusted to Antonio for delivery at Negrais. Under cover of this bogus mission the settlement was to be surprised and captured ; but Lavine was ordered to save alive as many as possible of his prisoners, in order that they might be held to ransom. Only such as resisted were to be killed.

The story rings true. It was confirmed—independently—by Mingyi Nawrahta, the Viceroy of Pegu, whom Alves met at Rangoon. There is also strong circumstantial evidence against Gregory. We have already seen him on an earlier occasion doing his utmost to wreck the negotiations between Alaungpaya and Captain George Baker. He had great opportunities for influencing the King's mind. He combined the office of " sea-customer " [3] at Rangoon with a somewhat vague one, which attached him fairly closely to the royal person. And he was admittedly the King's chief adviser in all dealings with foreigners. [4]

The causes of the massacre may therefore be briefly summed up. The conduct of Jackson and Whitehill at Dagon in 1755 had implanted

1. Dalrymple, op. cit., I, 351-398.
2. Ibid , I, 358-9.
3. Called by foreigners 'Shabander', by the Burmese 'Akawun.'
4. Dalrymple, op. cit., I, 352.

in Alaungpaya's mind an ineradicable distrust of the British. To this must be added his resentment at not receiving a reply to his magnificent gesture to the King of England. The Talaing revolt, which caused his hasty return from Manipur, made him intensely angry, and when Gregory poured into his cars the greatly exaggerated story of Hope furnishing arms and supplies to a few rebels, he resolved upon drastic measures.

But also the news of the British successes against the French in Bengal and on the Carnatic Coast had no small effect upon this decision. He feared lest a fortified post at Negrais might be used for the extension of English power in Burma in the same way as Gregory assured him Fort St. George and Fort William had been in India. He had failed by diplomatic means to persuade the English to transfer their factory to Bassein, where they could be more closely supervised. Hence the danger spot must be wiped out.

But it would appear that the actual massacre, which took place, was not intended by the King. The vitriolic hatred of the English cherished by Lavine caused the real plan to go astray in the operation.

CHAPTER VII.

THE MISSION OF CAPTAIN ALVES AND THE SEVERANCE OF RELATIONS.

Upon receiving from Captain Alves the story of the Negrais massacre the Bengal Council had to decide upon some line of action to be taken regarding the affair. The motives influencing its decision have been well summed up by Symes. [1] Revenge was out of the question. The British position in India was too weak to admit of any such measures. Equally also an irreconcilable breach with the court of Ava must be avoided as likely to open the door for a renewal of French influence in Burma. However uninviting the prospects of a settled trade might be, these was no overlooking the fact that Burmese ports offered peculiar advantages to the French for attacks upon British trade and communications in the Bay of Bengal. Further there were British prisoners at Rangoon for whose liberation some effort must be made. But it must be made with as little compromise to the Company's prestige as possible—especially in view of the fact that the Company's complete withdrawal from Burma had long been ordered, and no change of policy in this connection was, or could be, contemplated. It was therefore decided to send Captain Alves upon a mission to Alaungpaya seeking the restoration of confiscated British property and the release of all British prisoners in Burma. But for the reasons already specified and also because there was suspicion that the behaviour of the British in Burma

---

1. *Op. cit.*, 56-7.

had been partly responsible for the severity of their treatment, John Zephaniah Holwell, Clive's successor at Calcutta, addressed the King in terms of studied moderation.

Alves was despatched from Bengal late in February 1760 with instructions to proceed first to Madras in order to secure the joint action of the Fort St. George Council in his mission. There, as we have seen, the letters he brought from Robertson and Gregory caused so strong a suspicion of misconduct in Burma on the part of its own servants, that the Council detained Alves until replies had been received from Brooke and Newton to the charges specified in those missives. On May 10th he sailed for Burma, with a letter from George Pigot, which, in addition to reiterating Holwell's requests, asked for the punishment of the Negrais murderers. The Madras Council had decided that the extent of its servants' culpability in regard to the affair was negligible.

Uncertain as to the kind of reception he might meet with by proceeding direct to Burma, Alves took elaborate precautions against a renewal of his previous experiences at Negrais. Directing his course to the Nicobars, where he knew he would meet with a Dutch ship from Negapatam loading up with the usual cargo of coconuts for Rangoon, he forwarded by her a letter and present to the Amenian Gregory at Rangoon. He was, of course, ignorant as yet of the part played by this man in bringing about the massacre; and Whitehill and Dawson had advised him to deal with Gregory as one possessing considerable influence with the King.

In his letter he announced the nature of his mission, requested that the necessary boats should be sent to Negrais for the reception of the royal present, and intimated that he would anchor off Diamond island until be received a signal from Negrais announcing the arrival of the boats. On June 5th, he reached Diamond Island. The south-west monsoon was blowing so dangerously, however, that he soon had to take shelter behind Cape Negrais, about three miles from the harbour of the ruined settlement on the island. Thence he was able get in touch with a chokey[1] a short way up the river, and through the good offices of its headman sent his first officer up to Bassein with a message to Antonio. That worthy lost no time in coming down to the chokey to meet Alves. In an interview he strove to impress upon the latter his own cordiality towards the British, and explained his own part in the massacre as that of an unwilling tool. As we have already seen above he attributed the main causes of the tragedy to the machinations of Gregory and the enmity of Lavine against the British. He insisted that in order to allay suspicion Alves must bring his ship up to Bassein, and there await royal orders.

The advice seemed good. The ship was leaky and needed beaching for repairs. So to Bassein went the *Victoria*, arriving on June 28th, to

1. Burmese guard house or police post.

find that Antonio had just received a letter from Mingyi Nawrahta, the Viceroy of Pegu, notifying him of the expected arrival of the ship at Negrais, and strictly enjoining upon him the duty of securing the mission from molestation. Not a word from Gregory : but Alves learnt that immediately on receipt of his letter the Armenian had left Rangoon in haste to be the first to bear to the King the news of the mission's approach to his shores. In the meantime therefore, while awaiting orders from the Golden Feet, Alves got on with the work of beaching and caulking his vessel.

On July 7th came orders from Mingyi Nawrahta for Antonio and the Envoy to repair to Rangoon to hand over the official letters and presents so that they might be forwarded to the King. Owing to some little scheme of Antonio's—who apparently was not anxious to leave his post, rumours of Alaungpaya's death having filtered through—the necessary transport could not be obtained. Three weeks went by. Then on July 28th, came another despatch boat from the Mingyi ordering the Envoy to proceed to Rangoon immediately, and the Burmese officials, who had come up with the message, boarded the *Victoria* and in the name of the King of Burma forcibly took possession of her arms. Antonio at once produced a boat, but he passed on to Alves the disquieting news that Alaungpaya had died some weeks before,[1] and that Upper Burma was in the throes of civil war. Naungdawgyi, the late monarch's eldest son, it appeared, had been proclaimed king by the army, just returned from its inglorious expedition to Siam, but had fallen foul of one of the most popular commanders, who with 12,000 of the best troops had turned *minlaung*[2] and was in possession of the city of Ava. In utter perplexity as to what course to adopt, Alves accepted Antonio's advice to deliver up the present to the Mingyi. Whatever happened, he could plead that it had been taken from him by force, and his compliance, Anthony suggested, might cause the immediate liberation of such English prisoners as were at Rangoon. He accordingly set out for Rangoon and on August 5th handed over the royal present to the Viceroy.

He acted wisely. The Mingyi, himself a member of the royal family, was loyal to Naungdawgyi, and gave Alves a more reassuring account of the situation. The rebel general, he said, had been defeated by the royal forces, and was now closely besieged in Ava. He promised to send the present up stream to await Alves at the junction of the Irrawaddy with the Bassein river.[1] Meanwhile the Envoy, who, he insisted, must personally present the official letters to the King, was to return to Bassein, make arrangements for his absence up country, and then proceed to the spot where the boat containing the present would await him. He held out sanguine hopes of the release of all the prisoners, and acceded to Alves's

---

1, He died on May 15th, 1760.
2, Pretender to the throne.

request that Robertson, the sole European prisoner then at Rangoon, should be provisionally released. The rest, with Whitehill's ship, had been impressed into Alaungpaya's expedition against Siam, and had not yet returned. The Mingyi corroborated Antonio's statements regarding the responsibility of Gregory and Lavine for the Negrais massacre. He also informed Alves that he himself had at first been entrusted with the unpleasant task of destroying the settlement.

He had failed to carry it out, he said, because he was too much abashed by the friendly reception he met with at the hands of Hope, when he visited the island for that purpose. As the price of his disobedience he had been put in irons and pegged out in the sun with three logs of timber across his body, one at the throat, one across his stomach and the other over his thighs ; and he had not yet recovered from the shock.

A few days later, having provided himself with an interpreter in preparation for his journey to Naungdawgyi's camp, Alves together with the liberated Negrais writer, Robertson, returned to Bassein. Thither, shortly afterwards, came Gregory announcing that he brought the English translation of a letter from the King, the bearer of the Burmese version of which would arrive in a day or two. A Burmese officer, however, warned Alves to have an independent translation made of the original, when it arrived. This he did. It proved to be a royal order, crouched in friendly terms, directing Alves to proceed to the august presence. On comparing it with Gregory's version, he found that the Armenian had interpolated a number of passages, purporting to give himself special authority for dealing with matters affecting the Company's interest in Burma, and alleging that he had been soliciting Robertson's release. He discovered later that Gregory had informed the King that the mission had come with the object of resettling at Negrais and had brought with it three ships and great quantities of stores for that purpose.

On August 22nd, accompanied by Antonio and Gregory, Alves set out for the royal camp. The journey was an unpleasant one. At every chokey the boats were searched ostensibly for contraband, and although Antonio obviously did his best to save the envoy trouble, his progress up stream cost him heavily in douceurs. The royal present, he found, had been hurried on ahead of him, on account of the disturbed state of the country ; and the officers, who had brought the royal order to Bassein, even seized his private merchandise, and conveyed it with all haste to Court. One interesting item of news he gleaned on his way up stream : Lavine had been killed in an assault upon Ava.

On September 22nd Alves arrived at Sagaing to find Naungdawgyi's headquarters there. On the following morning he was admitted to the royal presence and made formal delivery of his letters. When these had been translated, he was summoned to discuss personally with the King the various points raised. His Majesty opened the conference with the statement that "he was surprised to think how the Governor of Madras, as he said in his letter, could have the face to demand any satisfaction, which he would not give; for that he looked upon all that were killed at Negraise, whether guilty or innocent, as born to die there, and in that manner; and that he could never give himself any trouble to enquire farther about the affair; his soldiers were not obliged to know who were guilty, or who were not, neither did he expect they would enquire, but, in such cases, generally killed men, women, or child as they pleased; for instance says he, as soon as ever they get into Ava, I have given them orders to spare nothing, that has life; and to burn, kill and destroy everything in it; though I know that Nittoon (meaning the general) and the soldiers are to blame; as for these People, that were not killed, you may take them with you to the Coast; the timbers, you may also have, but as your Governors at Negraise, and the masters of ships, that were seized, were the offenders, they must stand to the loss; for restitution I will make none." [1]

In answer to Alves's question regarding the cause of the massacre the King repeated the old charge that Hope had supplied the rebellious Talaings with arms, ammunition and provisions. He also added an obviously improvised one to the effect that Hope had been in league with the Talaings to the extent of receiving one half of the plunder of all Burmese boats captured by them. As to the murder of Southby and the new comers, against whom no charges of any kind could be made, his Majesty laughingly assured the envoy that they were fated to die thus, "for", said he, "I suppose you have seen, that, in this country, in the wet season, there grows so much long useless grass and weeds, in the fields, that in the dry season we are forced to burn them, to clear the ground; sometimes it happens, there is some useful herbs among these weeds and grass, which as they cannot be distinguished easily, are burned along with them; so it happened to be the new Governor's lot."

But although scouting all ideas of reparation, the King was evidently extremely anxious for the Company to maintain a station in his country. He was puzzled and rather piqued to find no reference to the subject in the letters from the Governors of Bengal and Madras. If they did not intend to re-establish a settlement in Burma, he said, then their expressions of good will must be regarded as a blind, under cover of which the mission was sent with some ulterior object. He would give the Company as much land as it wanted at Bassein, he affirmed, but there must be no settlement at Negrais. So insistent was he in the matter that Alves, foreseeing the complete rupture of the negotiations, unless the point were yielded, promised that although he himself must obey his instructions to return to India, nevertheless, if the King would

---

1. Dalrymple, *Op. cit.*, I, 373-4.

release all the Englishmen in Burma, two of them should be left at Bassein to look after the Company's property there, until "the Honourable the Governors of Bengal and Madras signified their pleasure." While on this subject the King stressed his great need of warlike stores : this apparently was his main reason for desiring the re-establishment of the Company in his dominions. When Alves explained that owing to the war with the French the English in India had no arms and ammunition to spare, the King refused to be put off. He would give the Company "as much ground, or anything else they wanted, in his dominions," he airily promised, in return for supplies of these much-desired commodities ; and he pressed Alves personally to engage on behalf of the Company to furnish him with them. The embarrassed envoy explained that he had no power to make such an engagement, but that the King might make what representations he pleased on the subject to the Governors of Bengal and Madras.

Throughout the interview the King and his Counsellors were decidedly ill at ease at finding in the official letters no mention of any plan for re-establishment in Burma. Two days later Alves was asked to go in person and show them his original instructions, so that they might be compared with the letters. There followed a pretty scene. The instructions, of course, tallied in every point with the letters. When this was made clear to the King, in angry tones he asked Gregory, who was interpreting, where were the three ships laden with stores and provisions, the arrival of which for the resettlement of Negrais he had announced. No reply came from the crouching Armenian. Then the King asked Alves for the letter Gregory had delivered to him at Bassein, passing it off as a translation of the royal summons to Court. Thereupon the envoy handed over a Burmese translation of the damning missive that he had taken the precaution of having had made during his journey up. The truth of the translation was warranted by both Antonio and the Burmese officer, who had warned Alves regarding Gregory at Bassein. At this the full storm of the royal anger broke forth. Gregory was so expert in making himself a prince that he would shortly be assuming the title of King, said the outraged monarch. Why did he not go to his comrade across the river? the King jeered, referring to the rebel general in Ava. He was forbidden the Court in future and, as he hesitated to leave the audience chamber, was seized upon by the royal attendants and dragged ignominiously out of the palace.

The envoy's difficulties, however were by no means ended with the discomfiture of this clumsy intriguer. By all manner of frivolous pretences the ministers continued to keep him waiting day after day for the royal reply to his official letters and the order for the release of the English prisoners. The reason for this, he found, was twofold. On account of the fact that the company made no proposal to re-establish a station in Burma, he was suspected of being a spy. Warned of this in the nick of time he managed to destoy his diary just before the royal officials pounced down upon his belongings, searched them, and carried off his papers to the palace. He discovered also that until he made a considerable present to each of the eight chief Ministers, the royal letters and orders would not materialize. During this period of enforced waiting he made what enquiries he could regarding the English prisoners. He could trace only five of them : Robertson and Lewis from Negrais, Helass and Lee of a seized vessel, the *Fame*, and Richard Battle of Whitehill's ship. The rest had all perished in Alaungpaya's Siam expedition.

On September 27th, shortly before the Burmese festival of Thadingyut, all the chief officers of state assembled at the palace, as was customary, to pay their respects to the golden feet. Alves deemed it wise to join the throng. The King on seeing him was so gratified that he offered to make him a present of whatever he might ask. Remembering to have seen at Rangoon three Dutch prisoners—a surgeon and two soldiers—belonging to a Dutch settlement in Siam that had been destroyed by the recent Burmese expedition, Alves asked to be allowed to take them back to Bengal with him. His request was at once granted and orders for their release made out. Unfortunately his humane intentions were thwarted. On returning to Rangoon he found that two of the Dutchmen were dead and the third had been sent on a Burmese ship to the Nicobars. In the meantime also, behind the envoy's back, a renegade Duchman at Sagaing had caused the revocation of the order for release by representing that the three prisoners were experts in the manufacture of gunpowder.

At last on October 9th, Alves carried out the necessary palm-greasing, visiting personally all the officials for whom he had to provide perquisites. On the following day therefore all his official documents were presented to him, and together with Antonio he started on his return journey to Bassein. It had been arranged that Robertson and Helass should take charge of the Company's effects at Bassein until the Governors of Bengal and Madras decided otherwise. Royal orders to this effect were entrusted to the envoy along with those for the release of the five English prisoners. He carried also letters to the Governors of Bengal and Madras from the King and from the four Wungyis of the Hlutdaw collectively, all couched in exactly the same magniloquent terms.

The journey down stream was not without incident. Three days after setting out from Sagaing Alves met Lewis and Lee being taken under Escort to assist in the siege of Ava. The officer in charge of them refused to take any notice of the order for their release, because it was addressed to the Viceroy of Pegu " *who had not seen it*" ! So Alves had to despatch his interpreter back to Sagaing with urgent appeals to three of the most influencial men about the King, and, of course, the usual presents. Meanwhile he himself proceeded slowly on towards Prome intending to wait there for the interpreter, and, as he hoped, the liberated men. From Prome he had decided to proceed first to Rangoon, so as to make sure that the remaining prisoners were not spirited away before he could claim them. On October 20th, Prome was reached. After a three days' wait the anxious envoy was cheered by the sight of his interpreter returning along with Lewis and Lee. He had out-distanced the boat carrying them to Sagaing, and there had procured an order, on the strength of which he had met them in the river and had transferred them to his own boat.

At Prome Antonio fell sick. This caused a further delay of three days, since his name was included with that of Alves on the same chokey passport, which the wily Portuguese took the precaution of keeping in his own hands. On the morning of October 26th, the impatient envoy prevailed upon Antonio to make a start. In the evening, as they were nearing Myanaung, the town was seen to be in flames. From villagers nearby they learnt that its Governor with three others, one of whom had the rank of General, had fled the court, and given the signal for revolt by burning his town and betaking himself to the jungle. It was rumoured also that one of the King's brothers had rebelled at Sagaing itself. The sudden development of a situation fraught with such unpredictable potentialities led Alves to abandon his plan of going first to Rangoon and to push on towards Bassein with all haste. By offering a special reward to his boatmen he managed to complete his journey by the 28th, and at once began to have the ship made ready for departure. A trip up to Kyaukchaungyi in quest of rice and provisions for the return voyage to Bengal furnished him with the welcome information that the revolt was not spreading. He decided therefore to hire a boat and bring away the remaining two Englishmen, Helass and Battle, from Rangoon, while the *Victoria* was being loaded with provisions, and as much of the Company's timber as she could carry.

On his arrival at Rangoon on November 4th, the Viceroy straightway handed over the two Englishmen, but requested Alves to remain there a few days until he had had letters prepared for transmission from himself to the Governors of Bengal and Madras. While waiting there Alves, was asked by the Viceroy to interrogate a certain Portuguese prisoner captured by the Burmese at Mergui, which port he had entered in a Malay prow without papers, alleging that they had all been burnt in an attack by Malays as he was on his way into the straits of Malacca from Padang on the western coast of Sumatra. He had with him on board when captured "a very handsome sett of silver handled knives and forks, with table and tea spoons, marked with a crest of a hart's head, about 4000 dollars in specie, also some gold, several suits of laced cloaths, with linnen etc. in proportion, several English musquets and other things, the shirts were marked TC. and some PS. There was also several English books, on some of which was wrote the names Ricksby, and on others Charles Mears, 1759, none of which he could read, nor anybody else he had on boards, he had also a Hadley's Quadrant, and a set of French charts, the uses of which he knew not" [1] To Alves he confessed that his name was Joseph de Cruz, but that he went by the name of Jansy. He had been gunner on an English sloop scouting for French ships off the coast of Sumatra. Off Pulo Nias the crew under his leadership had murdered their officers. Then after the booty had been divided between himself, the serang and tindal, each had stored his portion on Malay prows captured among the islands off Acheen Head, the sloop had been sunk, and he in his prow had made off for Junkceylon. It was useless for Alves to demand that Jansy should be handed over to him for trial at Calcutta. The Viceroy was adamant that nothing could be done until the matter had been reported to the King. But he promised to keep Jansy in custody until he heard from the Governor of either Bengal or Madras, and in his official letters entrusted to Alves he wrote a brief account of the man. Nothing came of Alves's attempt to bring the murderer to justice. Soon afterwards he was taken into the royal service, and thirty-five years later, when Captain Michael Symes arrived in Rangoon on his well-known mission from Sir John Shore to King Bodawpaya, Jansy held the office of collector of customs there. [2] He figures prominently in the reports of the English missions of this later period.

One other incident of note marked Alves's stay in Rangoon. On November 7th, Gregory turned up with a royal letter appointing him "sea-customer" at Bassein and authorising him to recruit a hundred families at Rangoon for the work of rebuilding the former place, which had been almost destroyed during the Talaing wars. The Viceroy, however, refused to take any notice of the royal mandate—at least while Alves was in Rangoon. One is tempted to wonder whether Gregory's precipitate exit from the audience chamber at Sagaing was stage-managed.

On November 9th, Alves with Helass and Battle left Rangoon for Bassein. Thirteen days later the *Victoria* began her return voyage to Bengal leaving behind James Robertson and John Helass in change of such property of the Company as was stored at Bassein. Late in December Alves reached Calcutta whence he at once forwarded to Governor George Pigot at Madras the letters addressed to him from King Naungdawgyi and the various Burmese officials together with a copy of his journal. These were " read " at the Madras Council's consultation of 27th January 1761 and were ordered to be circulated "for the perusal of the several members."[3] The letter from "the most high and mighty King of all Kings,"[4] after a reference to Hope's alleged conduct as the cause of the Negrais massacre, announced that Alaungpaya, his father, " sometime since, being wearied of this world, went to govern a better, '' and that he himself, on

1 Dalrymple, *op. cit.*, I, 388-9.
2. Symes, Embassy to Ava, 160—161.
3. Madras Public Proceedings, 1761, p. 40.
4. Dalrymple, *op cit.*, I, 394.

succeeding to the throne, was far from believing that the Governors of Bengal and Madras had approved of the treacherous actions of their servants at Negrais. He was willing therefore to grant to the Company the release of the Negrais prisoners, a price of ground for a settlement at Bassein and liberty to trade on payment of the usual customs duties. He particularly requested the Company to send him 1000 sieves of gunpowder, 10,000 muskets, 500,000 flints, 1000 viss of steel, 1000 viss of iron and a man able to cast iron shot. He further asked for a horse and mare, each four cubits high, and a male and female camel, for breeding purposes; " and for all these things I will give what you desire," the letter concluded. But in his covering letter to George Pigot Alves significantly stated that when he left Rangoon a Dutch ship was there belonging to the Governor of Negapatam, which had despatched to the King the principal part of her cargo, and had been unable to get any payment whatever, while the Rangoon authorities had seized a new cable by force for use in a Burmese vessel. [1]

There the matter ended—save for the withdrawal of Robertson and Helass from Bassein in 1761. Both Madras and Calcutta considered it worse than useless to make any further attempt to obtain redress for injuries. Chastisement was out of the question. So from 1760 until the mission of Symes in 1795 official relations ceased between the East India Company and the "Master of all Good Fortune." With the victory of Wandewash in 1760 the French power in India was ruined. By the Treaty of Paris three years later such stations as were restored to them were to be held as trading posts only. Hence for many years their relations with Burma were likely to cause the Company no worries. Calcutta and Madras moreover might reasonably hope to secure adequate supplies of Burma teak through the normal operations of licensed private traders, without the expense and infinite trouble of maintaining a factory in the country itself.

It is worthy of note that French interest in Burma was soon revived after the English withdrawal. In 1766 a French mission from Pondicherry, headed by one Lefèvre, appeared at the Court of Ava seeking the restoration of such French prisoners as still survived from the capture of the ill-fated Galetée and Fulvy off Syriam ten years earlier, and the renewal of privileges of trade granted in the days of Dupleix.[2] Two years later the mission returned with its object fulfilled, and shortly afterwards a small French establishment for building and repairing ships was opened at Rangoon. This had to be abandoned when the English captured the French stations in India during the war of American Independence. It never had any political significance. At the end of that war, however,

---

1. *Ibid.*, I, 398.
2. Henri Cordier: Historique Abrégé des Relations de la Grande Bretagne avec la Birmanie, 8-10.

we find Bussy and Suffren revolving in their minds a plan for making a site on the coast of Burma the headquarters of French enterprise in the east. The scheme came to nothing,[1] but later on when Great Britain entered into war with Revolutionary France, French designs upon Burma were a main cause of the revival of British relations with the "Lord of Many White Elephants". Never again, however, did any European power so much as contemplate a settlement on the inhospitable island of Negrais.

---

1. Gaudart: Catalogue des Manuscrits des Anciennes Archives de l' Inde Française I, 159.

APPENDIX I.

Letter from John Payne to Mr. [Robert] Wood 4th March 1758, enclosing a copy translation of a letter from the King of Burma to the King of England. [1]

LOTHBURY, 4th MARCH 1758.

Sir,

When I did myself the honour of waiting on Mr. Secretary Pitt and afterwards on yourself it was in order to have acquainted him or you with what probably gave rise to the letter I had to deliver, addressed to his Majesty, from the King of the Burmars a people who have a large district of land upon the Continent on the side of the Bay of Bengal, opposite to the Coast of Coromandel, and who having been long at war with their neighbours of Pegue, have at length got the better of the latter, and have been some time courting the friendship of the East India Company, who having for object their trade only, and having a few years since made a small settlement at the Negrais, at the extremity of their Country, were desirous of keeping fair with both, but not disposed to engage with either people. Mr. Brooke a Covenant Servant of the Company was ordered to succeed Mr. Hunter, who first settled there, in order to keep possession with as little expence as possible, to prevent the french, who upon our quitting, would probably have taken possession thereof, and had received from the Burman King a Perwannah, or grant, for settling in another part of his Dominions esteemed more healthy, and made some further offers of Amity, which are to be referred to the consideration of our President and Council at Fort St. George. The Company have also received a letter very much to the purport of that addressed to his Majesty, but wrote on paper instead of Plate Gold.

I am &c.
John Payne.

APPENDIX II.

The Newton—Whitehill controversy. The whole enquiry together with the correspondence from Robertson, Hobbs, etc., and the account of the examination of Brooke and Newton, was reported home in the Madras Council's Letter of 31st July 1760. (I. O. Abstracts of Letters Received from Madras, I, 3-6.) This evoked from the Directors the following reply: " It can hardly be imagined that the King of the Burmars should proceed to such a Cruel Extremity as Massacring our People at the Negrais without some Provocation and indeed upon perusal of the Enquirys You made into this affair our Conjecture is not without some foundation however We shall defer giving our final Sentiments thereon until you have agreeable to your assurance sent us the result of the further enquiry into

---

1 Home Miscellaneous (India Office) Vol. 95, pp. 23-5.

the cause of the said King's Indignation for which and the release of the Captives the *Victoria Snow* was purposely sent, you likewise assured us that the affair of the large Ruby said to have been intended as a Present to his Britannick Majesty from the King of the Burmahs but detained by Captain Newton late Chief of the Negrais should at the same time be cleared up, and indeed in Our Opinion it very much wants it, for it appears upon your Examination of Captain Newton that althô he denies having received a Ruby on that Account yet he was in possession of a large One which he alledges to have bought at the Negrais which may be true for ought We know at present but We cannot help saying there is room for suspicion, under such a circumstance, therefore you ought not to have suffered Capt. Newton to come to England until the Enquiry had been finished upon the return of the said Vessel.

Among other allegations which appear in the course of your Enquiry with respect to the cause of the Resentment of the Burmur King it is said that the People belonging to some of the Country ships had taken part with the Peguers and behaved in a hostile and violent manner towards him, and that Mr. Whitehill a Supra Cargo of one of them was one of those Persons who had acted against the Burmurs. These Allegations We hope have by this time been seriously enquired into and if made out censured as they deserve, for We will never with impunity suffer our Affairs to be embroiled by the Indiscretion and bad Conduct of Private Persons residing in India under Our Protection." (I. O. Despatches to Madras Vol. II, pp. 389-390.)

But by the time this despatch reached Madras nothing further could be done. In February 1760 Newton had resigned the Company's service on account of ill-health (Coast and Bay Abstracts, Vol. 6, 357) and not long afterwards, unable to get a direct passage home, left Madras on a ship homeward bound *via* China, threatening to launch a claim of £20,000 damages against the Company for "unjust and unlawful detention." (Abstracts of Letters Received from Madras, Vol. I, p 6.) Whitehill, notwithstanding Brooke's imputations against him, was reinstated in the Company's service, and re-elected as Alderman and Judge of the Mayor's Court at Madras. (Madras Public Consultations, 1760, 237, 264). In August 1760· he was appointed " Sea Customer in the management of the Boats. " (*Ibid.*, 1760, 373). His later career is interesting. William Hickey tells us that when "high in the Company's Civil Service at Madras" he was " much engaged in commercial concerns with the French, " and relates the story of how during the war with France (1778-1783) a British merchant vessel, the *Osterley*, was captured off Mauritius by a French privateer of which Whitehill was part owner. (Memoirs, II, 140). He is also said to have had a share in the pickings arising out of the corruption in the revenue collections in the Northern Sarkars, which Shah 'Alam ceded to the Company during Clive's second Governorship of Bengal. (Cambridge History of India, V, 283). In 1780 he succeeded Sir Thomas Rumbold as Governor of Madras, in which position his mismanagement in face of the danger from Hyder Ali led to the introduction into Parliament of a bill of pains and penalties against him in 1782. The bill, however, was dropped in the following year for want of a quorum to discuss it. (*Ibid.*, V, 193). Professor Dodwell describes him as a man "who in many ways recalls the character of Foote's *Nabob*, Sir Matthew Mite. To mediocre talent he joined a passionate acquisitive temperament, impatient of opposition, incapable of cool judgment." (*Ibid.*, V, 283). What impresses us most is his extraordinary good luck in getting out of tight corners into which his own cupidity and rashness had brought him.